Mosaic Modernism

New Studies in American Intellectual

and Cultural History

Dorothy Ross, Series Editor

❖ DAVID KADLEC

MOSAIC
MODERNISM

ANARCHISM,

PRAGMATISM,

CULTURE

THE JOHNS HOPKINS UNIVERSITY PRESS
BALTIMORE AND LONDON

9 8 7 6 5 4 3 2 1

The Johns Hopkins University Press
2715 North Charles Street
Baltimore, Maryland 21218-4363
www.press.jhu.edu

A catalog record for this book is available from
the British Library.

Library of Congress Cataloging-in-Publication Data

Kadlec, David.
Mosaic modernism : anarchism, pragmatism, culture / David Kadlec.
    p. cm. — (New studies in American intellectual and cultural
history)
Includes bibliographical references and index.
ISBN 0-8018-6438-0 (alk. paper)
1. American literature—20th century—History and criticism. 2. Modernism
(Literature)—United States. 3. United States—Intellectual life—20th century. 4. United
States—Civilization—20th century. 5. American literature—English influences.
6. Pragmatism in literature. 7. Anarchism in literature. I. Title. II. Series.
PS228.M63 K34 2000
810.9′112—dc21

                                        00-008135

In memory of Janet W. Kadlec

❖ CONTENTS

Mosaic Modernism

Introduction

This study of the modernist resistance to "beginnings, origins, and principles" begins in London, in 1912–14, with the anarchist writings that informed not only Ezra Pound's poetry but also James Joyce's experimental novel *Ulysses*. Shifting from British to American milieus, and from the teens to the early twenties, it follows the historical channels through which anarchist premises were incorporated into liberal American pragmatist philosophy and into the poetry of William Carlos Williams and Marianne Moore. As the project bridges anarchism and pragmatism with emergent notions of "cultural pluralism," it turns to the writings of Zora Neale Hurston, reading her narrative innovations of the 1930s amid a widespread American embrace of "culture." As a later African American "modernist," Hurston was positioned to recognize not the inviolability of "culture" as a counter to outworn notions of "race," but rather the growing orthodoxy of this measure of unfounded identity. In reorienting the historical political bearings of early-twentieth-century literature, this account of the antifoundationalist genesis of literary modernism not only changes our reception of a profoundly influential body of literary texts; it also offers us a new look at the mosaic, improvisational habits of association that have characterized recent movements in philosophy and in literary and cultural criticism. Speaking to scholars of early-twentieth-century literature, and to readers concerned with recent tendencies in literary and cultural criticism, it tells us much about the modern conceptions of "culture"—as both a "pluralistic" and an "indeterminate" medium—that have shaped the way that many of us think about identity at the outset of the twenty-first century.

The poets and novelists gathered into these pages—Pound, Joyce, Williams, Moore, and Hurston—scatter widely in places and points of practice. In their overlapping historical situations, however, they converge as writers who struggled against reference in language. At various moments and in various ways, each of them sought to overcome the stasis of representation, looking for ways that language might be made to embody dynamic experience. Local instances of the modernist resistance to representation can be found in the disjunctive collage methods that swirl beneath Pound's "rose in the steel dust" and in Williams's weighting of his "Babbitt metal" vernacular poems against the empty standard of English literary "gold" (C, 463).[1] This resistance is further modulated in Hurston's appraisal of "bartered" "Negro" "picture words," a medium whose transactions are more vibrant than the abstract "cheque words" of white Americans ("NE," 24–25). The modernist urge toward dynamic embodiment, in its turn, can be traced to sources including not only anarchist calls for "direct action" but also face-to-face barter exchanges. These calls reached modern writers through radical political and economic movements; but they traveled too in the more abstract guise of pragmatist writings on processes and relations—writings that were channeled into American literature through "pluralist" efforts to imagine America as a living "mosaic of peoples."[2] In its generalized form, this pervasive desire for embodiment over static forms of representation—turning as it does on a distinction between mediation and immediacy—bears a conceptual kinship to divisions ascertained by a range of modernist critics. In its specific historical lineaments, however, it provides an altogether new look at a familiar body of material.

❖   Since the late 1960s, a range of poststructuralist critics—Marxists, feminists, postcolonialists, and even some "pure" deconstructionists—have shared a tacit belief that radicalism must be progressive. Supported by Marxist premises that have traditionally merged anarchistic with bourgeois "individualism," progressivist assumptions have kept us from according anarchism its historical role in the formation of modernist aesthetics. For writers like Pound in London before World War I, the liberal state was a "mechanism" of "chicane" and "catch-words" that destroyed forms of resistance by adapting their theoretical premises and objectives to its own ("S," 255).

Contrasted with an anarchistic ethic of untheorized action, radical socialist principles were thought to be easily uprootable because they were abstractly derived. Empowering an abstractly conceived "class" of "producers," the socialist collective embodied different principles from those of the bourgeois state; but this collective was corruptible because even its material body was rationally conceived. As the Edwardian Liberals in power co-opted the Fabian-born Labour Party, many radical intellectuals came to view the Marxist tendency toward abstraction as a greater social evil than the lopsided capitalist allotment of property. More than the perpetuation of fixed structures of domination, it was the process of collective articulation, the fixing of abstract identities and objectives, that was to be resisted as counterrevolutionary. Vitalists and empirically minded radicals alike looked to anarchism as an antidote to the co-optation of radical struggle: syndicalist politics of "deeds not words" grounded the anarchist trade movement in tactical experience, emphasizing sabotage and strikes as forms of economically specific individual or trade enterprise over abstract collective initiative. These localizing and anticollectivist tendencies kept anarchism from developing a progressive bent; and the anarchists' refusal of progress has led many poststructuralist critics to discredit them as a viable force in left radical politics.

With left radical anarchism so erased from the historical horizon, early modern artists and intellectuals are portrayed as facing a falsely conceived choice. Positioned by scholars within an ideological schema that merges anarchist with bourgeois "individualist" stances, they are seen to either react against or tacitly support early-twentieth-century stagings of a progressive struggle between "dominant" and "emergent" ideologies.[3] The artist's reluctance to follow a well-marked path of subversion is here construed as a vote for the status quo. For the anarchist, however, the status quo is the very lighting of the radical way. Radicalism and reaction are finely shaded at this juncture; and they are easily confused when they are identified in terms of "progress." Raymond Williams's injunction that ideology is locally constructed indeed seems lost on critics who project their own radical premises back across the legacy of fascism and World War II to make default assessments of the politics of modernism.[4] What is radical for intellectuals in England and America today is not the same as it was for Paris in 1968. And it is certainly nothing close to the intellectual radicalism that mattered in Britain and America before World War I. By sorting out the confusion between socialistic and anarchistic varieties of radicalism, then, we discover new historical sources for the politics of modernism. Among these sources are the anarchist and pragmatist antifoundationalist premises that came together in forming modern "pluralist" conceptions of identity.

❖   A limited view of radicalism has long kept scholars from recognizing the importance of anarchism and related strains of philosophical pragmatism to the development of modern literature. Recently, however, anarchist and pragmatist movements have begun to receive their due as sources for early-twentieth-century writers. As a handful of scholars have shown, direct exchanges between anarchists and London-based writers on the one hand and between pragmatists and Boston-schooled American writers on the other were instrumental to modernism's antifoundationalist genesis.[5] But direct channels were not the only avenues of exchange between modern artists and anarchist and pragmatist thinkers. The early-twentieth-century assault on "first principles" was also forcefully applied to language and genre by writers who were engaged with contemporary social issues and who found within these issues living applications of the broadly modern antifoundationalist premises set forth by anarchist political theorists and pragmatist philosophers.

Ezra Pound, for example, found anarchist and pragmatist calls to "action" to be socially and aesthetically significant only when he came to ally such calls with radical "volitionist" programs of currency and credit reform (*GK,* 31). James Joyce, for his part, had been familiar with nineteenth-century German anarchist ideas regarding individual initiative and identity before he began work on his experimental novel *Ulysses.* But it was only the application of these premises to a set of "revolutionary" contemporary issues—including modern feminist struggles for sexual and economic freedom—that prompted Joyce to seek a formal narrative expression of individualist anarchist premises regarding the nature of identity (*CJJ,* 35). In America, William Carlos Williams, Marianne Moore, and the folklorist and novelist Zora Neale Hurston did not study directly under Harvard-based pragmatists, as did associates of theirs including T. S. Eliot, Gertrude Stein, Alain Locke, and W. E. B. Du Bois. Nevertheless, these writers shared a keen interest in contemporary social issues such as immigration, eugenics, and the recovery of an ostensibly authentic "folk culture"; this interest prompted them to draw from the conjoined lexicons of American philosophy and social theory and to variously consider pragmatism's adequacy to changing forms of identity and literary expression.

Following the lead of modern writers who turned their attention first to nineteenth-century European anarchist theorists and then to twentieth-century American philosophers and social critics, this study in literary and intellectual history reconstructs a series of interrelated "anarchist" and "pragmatist" social moments. Calls for currency reform and for a "new morality" in England, followed by the changing conceptions of identity that surrounded the eugenics movement in America, provided modern writers with vivid grounds for new inquiries into first principles and foundations. For writers ranging from Ezra Pound to Zora Neale Hurston, it was not anarchism or pragmatism per se, but rather related modern efforts to re-imagine the nature of economic, sexual, and even genetic and cultural trans-actions, that provided the most powerful touchstones for a reconsideration of genre and language. The ongoing critical recovery of new social historical contexts for modern literature enables us to see how and why antifounda-tionalist movements in politics and in philosophy shaped a series of new inquiries into the measure of modern identity, inquiries that were con-tingent on the formal literary innovations that attended them.

❖ In its focus on a handful of canonical writers, this study is necessarily specialized. But in its synthesis of a range of new historical sources for key modernist and postmodernist moments, it speaks broadly to both contem-porary critics and scholars of modernism. To begin with, it challenges con-temporary conceptions of modernism as an intrinsically reactionary move-ment. Without diminishing the fascist and anti-Semitic involvement of a number of leading modern artists, it suggests that many poststructuralist critics have been looking for the politics of modernism in the wrong places. In fashioning bad modernists as authoritarian and good modernists as champions of "difference," these critics have relied on a schematic distinc-tion between "dominant" and "emergent" ideologies, a distinction that pro-vides critics with an easy means of navigating a particularly thorny moment in literary and cultural history. By the dictates of that dichotomy, those writers who embrace "emergent" ideologies are progressive and authentic. Those who resist them are reactionary. Although postcolonialist critics such as Gayatri Spivak have, thankfully, complicated our sense of what it means to "embrace" ideologies, they have reflected too little upon the nature of the distinction itself.[6]

As a political tactic, the distinction between "dominant" and "emergent" ideologies has lent shape and force to many of the most vital social movements of the last hundred years. But it has been less productive as a tool for reading and evaluating modern art and culture. As modern writers and painters well knew, anarchists resisted above all the very formulation of an ideology as "emergent." Rightly or wrongly, they critiqued this formulation along lines that are still traversed by critics who question the humanistic notion of identity as an entitlement. In *Gender Trouble*, for example, Judith Butler sounds a resonant call for an "antifoundationalist approach to coalitional politics," one that "assumes neither that 'identity' is a premise nor that the shape or meaning of a coalitional assemblage can be known prior to its achievement." Butler's vision of a political course that articulates its aims through its actions rather than through received notions of "progress" that forestall radical action derives from a wide range of sources; but it owes something to poststructuralist readings of nineteenth-century theorists like Nietzsche. Allied to historical anarchist conceptions of identity, however, these same nineteenth-century ideas were channeled into a body of twentieth-century writings that bear both a conceptual and a historical kinship to Butler's contemporary belief that "the foundationalist tactic cannot take the transformation or expansion of existing identity concepts as a normative goal" because "the articulation of an identity within available cultural terms . . . forecloses in advance the emergence of new identity concepts in and through political actions" (*GT*, 15).

By linking Butler and other leading "antifoundationalist" theorists and critics—including neopragmatists and those "new historicists" who fashion mosaics from period discourses—to modern thinkers who appealed to untheorized action, I do not mean to say that poststructuralism is witnessing anything so grand as a renaissance of anarchist or pragmatist thought.[7] Nor do I wish to suggest that such a rebirth would be a cause for celebration. What I do hope to show is that the history of our own turn-of-the-century critical tempers is only partially written and that, as a body of literature that has been hastily fastened to what Pound called a "fascist second decennio," canonical modern writings may be able to tell early-twenty-first-century readers more than they realize about who they are now (*JM*, 12). For those readers who do not need to be convinced of the immediate significance of modernism and modern thought, moreover, the anarchist and pragmatist graftings of literary modernism help us to redefine a characteristic that is central to modernism itself: the refusal of "beginnings, origins, and principles."[8] Modernism's lasting formal legacy encompasses, in poetry, vibrant collage methods of composition and a set of revolutionary new approaches to prosody. It also features, in fiction, a complete rewriting of the laws of idiomatic expression and a reinvention of the very medium of the narrative itself. By restoring these and other formal hallmarks to a new set of social and intellectual contexts, we gain a richer understanding of the premises that were shared, and also contested, by writers that spanned not only the Atlantic, but also such deeper divides as the one that W. E. B. Du Bois called "the color-line."

ONE

Mosaic Modernism

Anarchists and pragmatists disagreed in their politics, but they shared a distaste for "first principles" or "foundations." And despite the difficulty of having to occupy a common ground of groundlessness, they formed between them an antifoundationalist union, one that cast its influence across British and American literature and culture. During the first decades of the twentieth century, British anarchists and the more liberal American philosophers and social theorists who came to ally their own writings with "*Anarchy* in the good sense" helped to trigger a chain of innovations in poetry and fiction (*ML,* 310–11). Anarchist and pragmatist assaults against "beginnings, origins, and principles" found their way to the literary page through a variety of channels. In some cases these premises reached modern innovators directly, through a firsthand exposure to the writings of leading anarchist and pragmatist theorists. Indirect influences often were even subtler and more powerful. Among the indirect conduits of anarchist and pragmatist thought were a series of largely forgotten modern political and economic movements, as well as the writings of scientists—new geneticists and even modern physicists—whose revolutionary tenets were adapted by philosophers and social theorists to a larger modernist resistance to foundations. Through these channels a range of historical antifoundationalist impulses contributed not only to modernist history collages like Pound's *Cantos* but also to the sort of story-bound narrative that characterizes Joyce's

Ulysses. In the process anarchists and pragmatists contributed to an evolving twentieth-century conceptual matrix that fostered some of the very improvisatory interpretive lenses through which modernism is now being considered anew.

Literary modernism is marked by a desire to conceive of language not as a system of signs but as a plastic medium through which meaning can be sculpted and shaped. The historical anarchist roots of this desire for a literature of embodiment offer us a new genesis for the work of "London-based" modernists like Pound and Joyce. Pound's poetic efforts to map the spontaneous relational contours of an ethical society and Joyce's narrative attempts to construct fluid forms of identity stemmed not only from modern social movements like syndicalism and currency reform but also from the strains of the anarchist theory—one individualistic, the other communitarian—that circulated among British intellectuals during the period around World War I. The writings of stay-at-home American poets such as Williams and Moore—both of whom were greatly influenced by pragmatists—are marked by later, more highly modulated varieties of antifoundationalist thought. In 1920s America, the radical affiliations of earlier modern formal innovations had been co-opted by intellectuals who were committed not to radical social change but to archaic "exceptionalist" visions of American experience.[1] These visions were expressed in spuriously "anarchic" conceptions of an improvisational democracy and in pluralistic models of national cultural identity.[2] Insofar as these American measures supported the interests of a liberal white status quo, they can be said to have domesticated and institutionalized modernist assaults on all forms of political and philosophical absolutism. Through them America's absorption of anarchist tenets came to foster a new kind of orthodoxy; it was this orthodoxy that led later American writers like Hurston to use modern narrative techniques to challenge the "foundations" that anarchist assaults on "first principles" had gradually come to cement.

1. Anarchism

Writing as the editor of the American socialist journal the *Masses,* Max Eastman described "*Anarchy*" as a "negation," or "a privative word" that "merely denies." "When you grasp it," he claimed, "there is nothing in your hand." Eastman's was a "scientific" radical's aversion to an overly "'literary'" brand of politics. In his view anarchists cultivated a dilettantish fascination with the "flavor . . . of revolt" that prevented them from developing "working hypotheses for [the] achievement" of "an end."[3] For many opponents of and adherents to anarchist politics, anarchist theory was distinguished by a refusal to use reason "to get there."[4] "Kill the Editor" was the playful headline of more than one editorial in early-twentieth-century anarchist journals. In staging the surrender of even their own credentials as public enemies, modern anarchist writers acknowledged a dilemma that their descendants later resolved at the expense of an evolving commercial marketplace. As the canny author of a best-seller entitled *Steal This Book* (1971), the 1960s anarchist Abbie Hoffman offered as a sacrificial weapon against "the system" not his own authority as a writer, but rather the livelihoods of the merchants that would both make and destroy it.

Modern writers in Britain and America absorbed anarchism as much through social movements as through intellectual channels. And although in this study of antifoundationalist sources for modern literature I do consider anarchism's role in such popular movements as currency reform and campaigns for suffrage and sexual freedom, I do not unreflectively take the history of anarchism to be uniquely a history of "action" rather than of "theory." Anarchism was a revolutionary political temper with roots in nineteenth-century French and German writings. It came to encompass a range of beliefs and practices, and it spawned an extensive and varied body of literature as well. Even among those anarchists who mouthed the theoretical slogan "deeds not words," the notion that revolutionary action should be folded into its call was the subject of lengthy, and sometimes eloquent, verbal speculation.

With respect to the role that it played in modern literary formal innovations, anarchism can be best defined as a movement that turns not just on a "negation" of theory but also on the positive belief that revolutionary change can be effected by a merging of theory with practice. The idea that meaningful political changes hinged on the attainment of epistemological immediacy is contained in a definition of the term *anarchism* put forth by Benjamin Tucker, one of the most prolific anarchist authors of the early modern era. From 1881 to 1908 Tucker worked as a publisher and as the editor of the journal *Liberty,* the single most influential English-language forum for anarchist thought. As a leader of the Boston-based "individualist" anarchist circle—a group derided by activists as "philosophical anarchists"— Tucker synthesized two of the main branches of modern anarchist thought. In the pages of *Liberty,* he worked to ally French "mutualist" traditions with more "egoistic" German ones. It was through Tucker's efforts that the doctrines surrounding each of these mid-nineteenth-century traditions—those of the mutualism of the anarchist Pierre Proudhon and those of the egoism of Max Stirner—gained an international circulation during the modern period. And though Tucker was not directly responsible for the influx of anarchist thought into modernist writing, he played a role in reviving the political appeals to epistemological immediacy that dramatically altered the shape and scope of modern literature.

In editorials written for *Liberty*, and again in the book that he published, *Instead of a Book, by a Man Too Busy to Write One* (1893), Tucker called for resistance toward the idea of governance from above. Drawing from the writings of both Proudhon and Stirner, he insisted that such a conception of governance was characteristic not only of monarchy but of democracy and socialism as well.[5] In Tucker's mind, the idea that government was a top-down matter depended on the idea that knowledge itself was anchored by an antecedent or founding principle. Somewhat paradoxically, Tucker performed an etymological recovery of the founding principle of anarchism itself, tracing it to the Greek roots of the word *anarchy:* "Anarchy does not simply mean opposed to *archos,* or political leader. It means opposed to *arche.* Now *arche,* in the first instance, means *beginning, origin.* From this it comes to mean *a first principle,* an *element,* then *first place, supreme power, sovereignty, dominion, command, authority,* and finally *a sovereignty, an empire, a realm, a magistracy, a governmental office*" (*IB,* 112). Like Proudhon, Tucker insisted that anarchism was, "at bottom," a political and not a philosophical movement. In his construction of an etymological sequence running from "*beginning*" to "*first principle*" to "*a governmental office,*" however, he suggested that philosophical premises were fundamental to political programs and that the struggle for societal change would be waged on fronts that were at once epistemological and political. And although the modern writers who came to absorb the premises of anarchism drew as much from local social movements as from anarchist "theorists," it was theoretical assumptions like this one that helped them to imagine that their own remotely formal struggles, many of which involved a reconstruction of generic and semiotic "first principles," might stand in an immediate relation to the millennial political struggles that avant-gardists variously styled as a generative artistic apocalypse, one that signaled "THE END OF THE CHRISTIAN ERA."[6]

❖ Tucker's greatest contribution to the development of literary modernism may be an indirect one. By publicizing to a range of intellectuals the powerful appeals to "immediacy" contained in Proudhon's vision of what amounted to a barter economy, he contributed to the development of the modern collage poem. As the publisher and promoter of the first English translation of *The Ego and His Own* (1907), moreover, Tucker spurred a revival of interest among English-speaking intellectuals in the "egoistic" philosophy of the mid-nineteenth-century German anarchist Max Stirner. Circulating among radical intellectuals in England, Ireland, and America, Stirner's writings greatly influenced British anarchists, including the former suffragette turned editor and essayist Dora Marsden. With assistance from Harriet Shaw Weaver, Rebecca West, Ezra Pound, Richard Aldington, and others, Marsden edited the *Freewoman,* the *New Freewoman,* and the *Egoist,* a series of London-based literary and political journals published during the years surrounding World War I. Marsden played a direct role in bringing to light an impressive selection of influential modernist texts, but she played a greater, indirect role in publicizing anarchist tenets that determined the shape of literary experiments by writers including Pound, Joyce, and Williams. Because she was an insular figure who eventually alienated even her own small coterie of well-placed readers, Marsden has waited long to receive her due recognition as a key figure in the development of modern literature. Recently, however, a number of studies have shown that during her early years as an anarchist editor, Marsden worked through both her published writings and her private letters to inculcate radical individualist thought in modern writers.[7] Those touched by Marsden's broad application of individualist anarchist tenets included the American-born expatriate poet Pound and also William Carlos Williams, a homebound writer who declined Pound's suggestion that he come join him in London. Another was the Irish-born novelist James Joyce. Joyce was living in Trieste, Italy, during the time of his initial contact with Marsden, but he kept abreast of her work through the radical London circles that supported and published his own writing.

Stirner's "egoism" provides the founding doctrine of the strictest and most recondite branch of "individualist" anarchism; many nineteenth- and twentieth-century radicals, Dora Marsden among them, differed from Tucker in believing that the atomistic philosophy of "egoism" was incompatible with Proudhon's exchange-based variety of "ethical" anarchism.[8] Stirner's book, *The Ego and His Own,* sets forth not so much a program for a new society as a philosophical critique of liberalism and of pre-Marxist varieties of "socialism." Taking individual initiative as the touchstone of meaningful political action, Stirner argued that revolutionary change would only stem from an exposure of the emptiness of abstract, generalizing forms of language. For Stirner, the chlorotic "principle" was to be distinguished from the sharp and vigorous "particular" that it smothered (*EO*, 76–80). The latter was the province of the unique and unfettered individual; as such it carried within it the seeds of revolutionary vitality. Stirner believed that because they were constructed on the scaffolding of humanist principles, liberal and early socialistic political systems supplanted the vibrant foundation of the individual in preference for the phantom antecedent—or the "first principle"—of "humanist Man." Abjuring even abstract speculation as to the society that would result from a reclamation of particular individual vitality, Stirner called only for the isolate individual to refuse the linguistic premises of the liberal state.

Stirner arose from the same left-Hegelian German intellectual circles that produced Karl Marx and Ludwig Feuerbach. Together with Friedrich Engels, Marx felt sufficiently threatened by Stirner to devote several hundred pages of *The German Ideology* to a denunciation of "Saint Max's" naive notion that the category of the "individual" might itself be something other than an ideological "phantom" of capitalism.[9] But Marx and Engels's suspicions were not shared by a growing number of early-twentieth-century radical intellectuals. Disillusioned with labor, suffrage, and Irish nationalist causes as reform-based movements that fainted quickly into complicitous unions with the state, radical intellectuals in Britain and America came to welcome the annihilating force that Stirner garnered through his denial of all but the "self" and its "property."[10]

Channeled to a number of modern writers through Marsden, Stirner's nominalistic resistance to the soul-draining and collectivizing tendencies of abstract language added force to aesthetic efforts to displace representation with embodiment through words. Stirner's nominalism was certainly not the first source of Pound's imagist call for "direct treatment of the 'thing' " (*LE*, 3), nor was it the primary impulse behind Williams's insistence that "the word" was "a part," and not "a symbol[,] of nature" (*I*, 102). Nonetheless, it lent an authority to both of these imagists' calls for a "monster project" (90) of apocalypse through a violent rupturing or a truing of the lettered substance of poetry. Stirner's appeal to the authority of the individual ego led through Pound and Williams to modern conceptions of the poem as a vehicle that spoke straight to readers—sometimes opaquely, sometimes plainly, but in all cases with a seeming immunity to the mediating influence of socially determined systems of representation. And it prompted Joyce's related notion of a literary narrative as a theater for the enactment of revolutionary conceptions of identity, conceptions prohibited by realist conventions of representation.

Marsden's nominalistic analyses of contemporary issues like suffrage and morality contributed to Joyce's belief that the autonomous individual was more vibrant, and more potent as an instigator of revolutionary social change, than was a "joiner" whose identity was conditioned by antecedent principles. As a reader of Marsden's Stirnerian discussion of the relationship between disease and identity, Joyce came to see that nominal forms of identity favored by progressive socialists, feminists, and Irish nationalists—forms that subordinated the individual to static collectivities of "worker" and "woman" and "Irish"—were in fact sickly and "paralyzing" vehicles (RW, 160–61). They stifled initiative by absorbing the individual into an abstract and antecedent collectivity. For the nominalistic novelist, it was not just words and sentences that severed individuals from the sources of their vitality. The very narrative structure of the realistic novel was apportioned according to the same abstracting and ultimately enervating imperatives.

For Joyce, the realistic novel was a stultifying medium. Insofar as it hinged on what Joyce called an "unreal" distinction between narrative voices that were removed from "the action of a novel" and characters' voices that were immediate to it, the narrative of the conventional realistic novel cast the "authorial" presence that was linked to narrative voices as a remote and fundamentally "extrinsic" presence.[11] In the spirit of modern poets like Pound and Williams, who proposed that vitality could be restored to poetry once mediating words were replaced with immediate things, Joyce sought to construct a literary narrative that would enact or embody the very vital processes of identity that were stifled by the nominalizing syntax of literary realism. He overturned one of the axiomatic conventions of narrative representation by fashioning the authorial narrator's voice as not a general presence that floats over the text but a particular one that is immersed in, and is even shaped by, the very characters and events that it relates. Joyce had half-mockingly spoken of such a live authorial presence through Stephen Dedalus, his young protagonist in A Portrait of the Artist as a Young Man. The modern author, Joyce's character waxed, would function not as an extrinsic nominal agent but rather as "a vital sea" that "flow[s] round and round the characters and the action in a novel" (PAFM, 1047). Prior to Joyce's construction of a narrative vehicle through which to embody it, the theoretical annunciation of such a presence could only ring hollow as a fanciful aesthetic pronouncement. Modernist "irony," it might be said, was an orchid cultivated in the rift that anarchism sought to overcome: the gap between theory and practice, or between representation and embodiment through language.

In fashioning his novel *Ulysses* as a vehicle for such distinguishing modern narrative techniques as "interior monologue" and "stream of consciousness," Joyce was driven by something other than perversely recondite aesthetic preferences. Taken together with the thematic concerns of an epic story about the identitarian "wanderings" of a set of outsiders or "aliens" in Dublin, these techniques represent an attempt to make the form of the novel exhibit the very sort of radical conceptions of identity that generic and grammatical conventions forbade. In conceiving the modern narrative as a medium that could show, as well as tell of, a more immediate form of identity, Joyce not only borrowed from and modulated Stirnerian nominalist premises, but he also sought to put into practice an anarchistic merging of "theory" and "practice." Through Marsden's influence, and through Joyce's own firsthand readings of Stirner (and of Nietzsche, who was at that time viewed by radical individualists as Stirner's more "poetic" complement [*E,* 352]), Joyce's signal narrative innovations in *Ulysses* emerged not only as an outgrowth of the individualist anarchistic resistance to the abstract and nominalizing tendencies of language, but also as a set of anarchistic "deeds," ones that collapsed the distinction between saying and doing and between being an artist and being an agent of cultural and political regeneration.

At a glance, the call for precision in poetry seems unrelated to the call for fluidity in narrative structure. But these techniques are linked insofar as they both work toward recovering an immediacy between the world and the text. The former harbors a faith in the possibility of representation, suggesting that a disciplined use of conventional modes of language can engender a fidelity, or even an immediacy, between word and thing. In the latter, the concern for the adequacy of poetic language is matched by a more sophisticated concern for the adequacy of genre: Joyce endeavored to render through a new kind of narrative the dynamic conceptions of identity that had been formulated by philosophers like Nietzsche and Bergson and by anarchist theorists like Stirner. Invoking "the natural object" as "the *adequate* symbol" (*LE,* 5), the imagist Pound sought a kind of clarity that amounted to a transparency between world and word, one that rendered the word so utterly true that the medium of language began to vanish. In the poems of Pound, Williams, and Moore, imagist aesthetics were soon wedded to dadaist appeals to the materiality of language and to the object status of the artwork. The call for transparency, in many cases, was part and parcel of an appeal to opacity that turned on a belief that, as Williams put it, a poem was not a representation of nature but a *part* of it (*I*, 102). And Joyce's desire to immerse his narrator into the material of his novel was an outgrowth of just this imperative. By denying the distinction between exterior and interior positions and voices in *Ulysses*, he rendered the modern novel a medium that was continuous with, and hence a *part* of, the "exterior" world that it no longer contained. In this way the narrator who passes like water through the characters and the action of *Ulysses* does not merely represent a subject in a modern world where "theory" is submerged in "activity." Rather, this narrator embodies a kind of subject that cannot be represented by the grammar of a literary medium premised on the idea of a divide between the word and the world.[12] Joyce's suspension of realism, then, facilitates a "truer" representation of the world than realism allows.

Stirner did play a role in the fashioning of both of these modern poetic and narrative appeals to immediacy, but his philosophy of the dynamic, unfettered individual "soul" served better as a negative critique of liberal political and linguistic conventions than it did as a positive model of individual identity. Modern writers were ultimately forced to look elsewhere for vibrant models that would account for the vitality that Stirner's "ego" was said to merely contain. Stirner's egoism could not sustain the imagist appeal to fidelity; for these reasons, imagism was a short-lived and rather unproductive movement in literary history. Pound eventually declared it to have been overly static, and Williams complained of its insufficient attention to dynamic "structure."[13] And despite her own insistence on precision in language, Marianne Moore was never comfortable being designated an "imagist." For these and other poets who were touched in theory by the call for directness in poetry, Stirner's anarchist appeal to the "particular" over the "principle" required supplementation from other sources. Among those sources were Proudhonian anarchist appeals to more dynamic, relational forms of immediacy, as well as the pragmatist, and cultural pluralist, models of an American universe that were not historically unrelated to this latter branch of anarchist thought. Conveyed to a number of leading modern poets, Pound and Williams chief among them, through a variety of social and intellectual channels, these more relational appeals to immediacy directed the technical innovations of a range of modernist poets. (For reasons that I discuss shortly, these appeals to immediacy had less effect on the poet Moore.) The novelist Joyce shunned such "structuralist" appeals to the immediacy of relations between things, choosing instead to supplement Stirner's rather narrow critique of abstraction with a richer account of the linguistic recovery of vitality, one that was drawn from the "egoistic" writings of Nietzsche. As a later American modernist who brought "Joycean" narrative techniques to a different philosophical and cultural climate, however, Zora Neale Hurston eventually came to encompass these more dynamic appeals to immediacy, writing them through, and finally out of, the modern literary narrative.

❖   Informed by Stirner's critique of the language of liberalism, the writings of Dora Marsden prompted modern writers to resist grammatical and narrative forms of abstraction. Through Marsden's influence, Pound's call for precision in poetry and Joyce's appeal for the fluidity of new narrative structures became aesthetic expressions of the egoistic complaint against the collectivizing tendencies of liberalism and state socialism. Under Marsden's Stirnerian tutelage, artistic invention provided evidence of the revolutionary vitality of individual initiative and enterprise. For modern poets like Pound and Williams, however, the teachings of the French "mutualist" Proudhon served to modulate Stirner's overly static and renunciative variety of nominalism, shifting it from a noun-oriented appeal to the immediacy of the "thing" to a more verb-oriented appeal to the immediacy of relations between things. Proudhon's belief that an ethical "economic organism" would come to dissolve the pernicious "political mechanism" that was common to monarchic, democratic, and socialist forms of government circulated through Benjamin Tucker's writings to a range of modern intellectuals, including radical economists.[14] The British inventor and economist Arthur Kitson, a contributor to Tucker's and Marsden's journals in the 1890s and for several years following 1910, respectively, was among the many turn-of-the-century advocates of currency reform who gained his "underconsumptionist" bearings through Proudhon rather than through Marx.[15] And it was the British anarchist Marsden who, in calling for the young aesthete Pound "to define the relation of the arts to economics," helped to nudge Pound's early imagist aesthetics in the more dynamic direction of Kitson's conception of "real" money as a relational medium.[16] Although it was only later in his career that Pound openly acknowledged Proudhon's importance to the "Social Credit" and "Volitionist" economic platforms that he embraced in the

1920s and 1930s, he suggested that Marsden's and Kitson's writings of 1912–13 might have served as the " 'unconspicuous' or apparently unimportant *seed*" of his early understanding of the importance of free channels of economic and syntactic exchange.[17]

Proudhon was the founder of the "ethical" branch of anarchist thought that many rigorous individualists, Dora Marsden among them, came to criticize as overly theoretical and utopian. In her early writings on such subjects as the gold standard, Marsden had aligned herself with Proudhon's critiques of "property" and "interest" as corrosive political instruments; but she had also recoiled from the dreamlike refuge of his "Social Contract" society, likening it to a "block of flats" built of "lily-stalks."[18] As an ethical anarchist, Proudhon called for the dissolution of political forms of government through an "economic organism" based on direct, unfettered exchanges between producers and consumers. According to Proudhon, pure economic transactions were truer and more "natural" than those politically mediated ones that were driven by the institutions of "rent and interest, the last remnants of the old slavery" (*GI*, 287).[19] As Marsden had pointed out to readers of the *New Freewoman,* Stirner was a purer anarchist than Proudhon because he laid no phantom claims to "naturalness" and because he did not theorize or speculate as to the sort of community that would emerge from a recovery of individual initiative.[20] Nonetheless, for many leading anarchists, Proudhon and Stirner remained allied as champions of an antistatist society. In Tucker's mind, for example, Stirner served as a necessary complement to Proudhon: the individual liberty that the egoist so forcefully defended was the only reliable index for the recovery of immediate pathways of exchange between producers and consumers.[21]

Pound and Williams shared Stirner's resistance toward the collectivizing tendencies of liberalism, socialism, and language; but they both came to ground their later efforts at poetic collage—the *Cantos* for Pound and *Paterson* for Williams—in Proudhon's conception of a society founded on direct transactions between producers and consumers. In the 1930s Pound openly acknowledged that his own economic leanings were fundamentally Proudhonian. Writing in "In the Wounds," his 1935 memorial for the former *New Age* editor A. R. Orage, the confused "left-wing fascist" poet declared, "Proudhon will be found somewhere in the foundations of all contemporary economic thought that has life in it."[22] Pound's capacity to reconcile Proudhon's conception of an "organic" society with the tighter imperative of Stirner's "self," moreover, was fundamental to his embrace of Mussolini. For the fascist Pound, as for the libertarian Tucker, the imperatives of the true individual were immediate to the imperatives of the "voluntary association."

In Pound's hands, Proudhonian anarchist tenets came to map an innately dynamic local community order over the sort of natural order that Ralph Waldo Emerson had esteemed when he suggested that the poet "shall use Nature as his hieroglyphic"; and, in conjunction with what we now think of as "structuralist" linguistic premises, these anarchist tenets graphed an ethic of local relations between producers and consumers onto the transcendentalist's relations between things in nature.[23] Again and again in *The Cantos,* Pound came to unearth from opaque sources evidence of the organic relationship between natural economic and cultural transactions. As a synthetic thinker who drew covertly from both Emerson and the Victorian art critic and would-be economist John Ruskin, the poet blurred the distinctions between the production and distribution of food on the one hand and the production and distribution of language and art on the other.[24] In his developing condemnation of modern economic corrosion, the line between political and aesthetic struggle was gradually erased. "With usura," or the iniquitous practice of usury, Pound would write in 1937,

> no picture is made to endure nor to live with
> but it is made to sell and sell quickly
> with usura, sin against nature,
> is thy bread ever more of stale rags
> is thy bread dry as paper,
> with no mountain wheat, no strong flour
> with usura the line grows thick
> with usura is no clear demarcation
> and no man can find site for his dwelling.
> (C, 229)

For the poet-prophet Pound, language was a medium that could not only diagnose but also remedy an economically based corruption that infiltrated social and even sexual transactions, withering the vitality that once coupled "the young bride and her bridegroom" (C, 230).[25] In the later cantos, Pound spliced Chinese ideograms into his epic tirade against abstract forms of verbal and economic exchange; and he gleaned from their visual traces an aesthetic that equated the truing of terms and of curricula with the just production and distribution of food. Pound valued these shorthand pictures of natural transactions as vivid instances of words and deeds "woven in order,/as on cords in the loom" (*C,* 709). And as a poet who felt himself to have been isolated from modern commercial literary markets, he imagined this righteous found language as the font of a new millennial order based on the lost imperatives of village agrarian production. The just order for society, Pound suggested, radiated from ancient ideogrammic characters, compounds that traced the "swan's flight" of political vision to foundational social pathways, a network rooted in the cultivation and distribution of grain.

> To trace out and to bind together
>
> .   .   .   .
>
>   out of the field, from the trees,
> Food is the root.
>   Feed the people.
> (*C,* 709)

By placing the generative order of nature at the root of both individual and communal activity, Pound came to believe a true democracy and a true fascist state were one and the same. He said in his book *Jefferson and/or Mussolini* in 1935, "The heritage of Jefferson" is "not in Massachusetts" but "HERE, NOW *in the Italian peninsula* at the beginning of fascist second decennio" (*JM,* 12). And Pound revealed the organic nature of this heritage in "A Visiting Card" in 1942: "A thousand candles together blaze with intense brightness. No one candle's light damages another's. So is the liberty of the individual in the ideal and fascist state" (*SP,* 306).

Williams was ultimately more of a liberal democrat than an anarchist or a fascist; but like a growing number of liberal intellectuals in early-twentieth-century America, he harbored sympathies toward Proudhon's conception of a society based on immanent relations. By the 1940s Williams even went so far as to follow Pound in advocating "living" varieties of contemporary economic thought in the form of the American Social Credit Movement and the "volitionist" currency theory of Silvio Gesell.[26] His understanding of the relationship between economic and poetic forms of relational immediacy is most evident in those passages of *Paterson* where he echoes the *Cantos*'s portrayal of sexual and artistic "blockage" as outgrowths of usury and other state-sanctioned impediments to economic exchange.[27] In fairness to Williams, who was eventually investigated for alleged Communist *and* fascist sympathies, he did chide Pound for his swaggering portrayal, in the *Cantos,* of the poet as the knowing restorer of this network of pathways. Williams mocked the epochal tone and scale of Pound's Usura Canto, for example, in a more modest and lilting tribute to "invention" in book 2 of *Paterson.*

> Without invention nothing is well spaced,
> unless the mind change, unless
> the stars are new measured, according
> to their relative positions, the
> line will not change . . .
>
> .   .   .   .
> . . . without invention
>
> .   .   .   .
> the small foot-prints
> of the mice under the overhanging
> tufts of the bunch-grass will not
> appear: without invention the line
> will never again take on its ancient
> divisions when the word, a supple word,
> lived in it, crumbled now to chalk.
> (*P,* 50)

Although Williams had followed Pound's suggestion that in the modern world the debasement of language had contributed to the blockage of channels of vitality, his absorption of the more processual premises of pragmatism helped him to temper Pound's suggestion that by truing such language a poet might be able to coax a utopia from even an American soil.

Among the modern writers treated in this study, Williams is a transitional figure whose writing was shaped by both European and American assaults on "*first principles.*" (Although Pound too eventually endeavored to adapt American philosophy to his aesthetic and economic theories, he did not construct his writerly aesthetics, as Williams and Moore and Hurston each variously tried to do, upon the scaffolding of pragmatist tenets.) Amid his lifelong forays into avant-garde artistic and radical political movements, Williams finally remained committed to the possibility of a vibrant liberal democratic society. Clinging to a belief in the uniqueness of America's destiny, he maintained an American "exceptionalist's" confidence in the procedures of democratic reform. For this reason it was not so much anarchism as the American pragmatists' more progressive renderings of a "mosaic" conception of the universe, or of the "*graft*-theory" that William James had likened to anarchistic conceptions of an "economic organism," that funded his conception of a poetic based on the American idiom ("WPE," 1180–81; *ML*, 310–11). As a poetic effort to measure the American idiom, Williams's "nativist modernism" reflected a forward-looking, democratic strain of American thought—one that, during the "dry decade" of the 1920s, would criticize renunciative prohibitions by posing immigration quotas themselves as a greater threat to America's integrity than foreign contamination.[28] Drawing as they do from pragmatist and related pluralist conceptions of a mosaic American identity, Williams's writings partook of a larger American "domestication" of anarchist assaults on "first principles" or foundations.

2. Pragmatism

Little has been written of the historical relationship between political anarchism and American pragmatism. American pragmatist philosophers, including the Emersonian "individualist" William James and his more socially disposed successor, John Dewey, remained committed to voluntaristic, Jeffersonian visions of American democracy. And although the deeply liberal commitments of both of these philosophers should discourage any suggestion of a serious ideological correspondence between anarchism and the improvisational philosophies that they espoused, a handful of recent historians have begun to take seriously James's intellectual involvement with nineteenth- and early-twentieth-century anarchists and anarchist traditions.[29] In his effort to conceptualize a kind of "*reality*" that was "*still in the making*," James did come to orient some of his defining ideas—including his "radical empiricism" and his "pluralism"—around "anarchistic" philosophies of "mobilit[ies] and fluxions."[30] Dewey, by contrast, was never quite as taken with anarchist philosophies or social theories.[31] As a critic of immigrant assimilation programs during the late teens and early twenties, however, he entered into a brief but fruitful dialogue with other thinkers who proposed to replace the American "melting pot" with a pluralistic "mosaic of peoples." In the process he found a local social application for the "radical empiricist" and "pluralist" premises that had been shaped by James's exposure to European anarchist thought. Insofar as James was the leading American popularizer of modern antifoundationalist philosophy, however, and insofar as his self-described "anarchist" writings came to foster deeply influential theories of American "culture," he played a primary role in laying the conceptual groundwork for the "domestication" of anarchism, or the gradual adaptation of European antistatist premises to American "exceptionalist" aims.

As a notorious labor activist who was an intellectual and a geographical neighbor of James's, the American anarchist Morrison Swift provides a touchstone for a discussion of the historical relationship between anarchism and pragmatism. In his 1906–7 lectures titled "Pragmatism," James quoted at length from one of Swift's political pamphlets. Citing passages from Swift's *Human Submission* (1905), James praised particularly the "valiant anarchist['s]" appeal to philosophers to abandon the "First Principles" upon which their "theor[ies] of the universe" rested.[32] In *Human Submission* Swift had suggested that such "cloudy" fundaments as "Being" and "Essence" should be replaced by a material that was more "present" and "actual" (*HS*, 8–9). And he invoked this material by quoting a series of newspaper stories about the struggles of the urban unemployed. One of Swift's new "First Principles" was an out-of-work Cleveland laborer, a recent widower, who led his infant children "into the basement of his boarding house" and killed them, and then "fired a shot into his [own] head." Another was a pair of elderly brothers, former shoemakers, who perished together, "victims of starvation," in their Brooklyn tenement. There was a Philadelphia tailor who, fearing blindness, "took poison"; a despondent sculptor who "committed suicide"; an out-of-work man who "smashed a window and stole in order to go to jail"; a suicidal man who "robbed a woman and then shot two men who interfered" (4–7).

Swift had a special background among the turn-of-the-century "anarchists" with whom he was sometimes reluctantly classed: he had a "pragmatist" pedigree that he renounced and tried to shield from public view.[33] As a doctoral student in philosophy in the 1880s, Swift had gained admittance to an elite circle of philosophers and "experimental psychologists" at Johns Hopkins University. Together with a fellow protégé, John Dewey, he served as a governing member of a small society of professors and graduate students who met to discuss recent writings by William James and Josiah Royce, as well as leading philosophical issues, such as the epistemological consequences of evolutionary theory.[34] The "half-ironic[ally]" named "Metaphysical Club" in Baltimore in the 1880s was led by a trio of Johns Hopkins professors.[35] Among them were G. Stanley Hall, who had taken America's first Ph.D. in Psychology (under William James at Harvard), and a neo-Hegelian philosopher, George Sylvester Morris. The society had been founded by a physicist and chemist turned philosopher, Charles Peirce. Peirce had conceived the club as an extension of the Boston circle that, during the decade before, had begun to formulate the tenets of the movement that later came to be known as "pragmatism."

The Boston Metaphysical Club had consisted of a handful of scientists, philosophers, and lawyers, along with Peirce and the new Harvard physiology professor, William James.[36] It was more than a decade after the disbanding of the Boston and Baltimore groups when James, as a recent convert to the cause against American imperialism in the Philippines, came into possession of several books and pamphlets by the anti-imperialist Swift. In his own writings and talks, James praised Swift, whom he knew as a onetime student and teacher of philosophy, as a "valiant anarchist"; and, as Deborah Coon notes, the established philosopher identified his aims with Swift's at a time when American public support for anarchism ran low. For many bourgeois Americans, the anarchistic taste for "the flavor of revolt" had run too far with the bloody Haymarket riots of 1886 and with the assassination, by an "anarchist," of President William McKinley in 1901 ("CA," 3–4).[37]

Anarchism and pragmatism share a nominalistic desire to bridge the gap between theory and practice. It was this link that led James to open his lectures on pragmatism with Swift's condemnation of the "cloudy" "Essences," or abstract principles that masked truths like the "Cleveland workingman" who, in "killing his children and himself" becomes "one of the elemental" "atoms or subatoms" "of this modern world" (*P*, 500). In James's view and, less consistently, in Dewey's as well, pragmatism shares Swift's complaint against abstract philosophical foundations. "Disdain[ing]" "verbal solutions . . . and metaphysical abstractions," it "agrees with nominalism" in its concern for "particulars" (510).[38] But the individualist proclivities displayed in James's appeal to particulars are not the sole point of agreement between pragmatism and the set of beliefs and practices that marked what James called "*Anarchy* in the good sense."[39] In his later years James did express an appreciative familiarity with the writings of individualists like Max Stirner.[40] But the political rhetoric that surrounded James's initial articulation of pragmatism as a decentralized, relation-bound method of inquiry echoes rather the Proudhonian call for a community based on unfettered relations between producers and consumers. When James claimed in 1899 that "*Every* great institution is perforce a means of corruption" and that "only in the free personal relation is full ideality to be found," he revealed his familiarity with a variety of anarchist thought that had been more formative to his development than Stirner's egoism.[41]

James encountered Proudhon's notion of a natural "economic organism" indirectly in 1870 and then again directly in the middle to late 1890s. More than twenty-five years before his own reading of Proudhon's *La guerre et la paix*, the young student of metaphysics was introduced to an abstract rendering of Proudhon's relational, barter-driven society through the writings of the nineteenth-century French philosopher Charles Renouvier. By James's description, Renouvier was a "radical pluralist" for whom "reality" was not derived abstractly from overarching principles but rather "begged piecemeal" from autonomous yet "overlap[ping]" "fact[s]." Renouvier's "masterly advocacy" of pluralism made a lasting impression on James: by the pragmatist's own account, it was Renouvier's *Essais de critique générale* that first freed him "from the monistic superstition under which [he] had grown up."[42] It was through Renouvier, moreover, that Proudhon's relation-based critique of political governance came to figure in James's intellectual development. As the French intellectual historian Jean Wahl noted in 1920, Proudhon had been prominent among Renouvier's intellectual sources: the founding anarchist had helped the French philosopher to see how and why a decentralized society based on "free-will," and on the "co-operation" that naturally followed from it, should triumph over political and epistemological "absolutism."[43]

In deriving an early species of philosophical "pluralism" from Proudhon, Renouvier toned down the radical political and economic implications of the anarchist's critique of absolutism. The early pluralist philosopher in fact appears to have admired Proudhon not as an anarchist but as an advocate of "free democracy" (*PPEA*, 62–63). But James was later driven to undertake his own reading of Proudhon's political writings. Whether or not James fully grasped "the great Renouvier's" own debt to French anarchist traditions, the ambient presence of anarchist thought in turn-of-the-century Boston prompted the philosopher's own investigation of the advocate of immediate relations between producers and consumers.[44] James's own appreciation for Proudhon's work is evident in the personal materials that his survivors bequeathed to Harvard's Houghton Library. Among the artifacts initially cataloged with the James papers were a photograph of the anarchist—part of James's collection of portraits of "great individuals" of the nineteenth century—and his own copy of Proudhon's book *La guerre et la paix*. Proudhon published his appeal to "workers [to put] an end to war by creating economic equilibrium" in 1861; but James acquired the book in the middle to late 1890s, when he began his own study of imperialism and the causes of war.[45] (Sadly, James's copy of *La guerre et la paix*, together with any marginalia that it may have contained, has been lost.)

❖ James began to feel the pull toward anarchism in general and anti-imperialist causes in particular just before the turn of the century; and it was shortly thereafter, in 1901, that he began to distinguish "radical empiricism" and "pluralism" as the two distinct flanks of a relational effort to "destroy" what he called "the notion of a[n] . . . Absolute of any sort."[46] In both its "radical empiricist" and its "pluralist" phases, James's assault on the "Absolute" was premised on the ethical authority of the decentralized "small systems" that he associated with both something that he called "*graft-theory*" and "*Anarchy* in the good sense" (*ML*, 311). As a kind of "radical empiricism," James's pragmatism had been pitched not only against abstraction and reason but also against the misdirected nominalism of traditional empiricists. Trained as a scientist, and indebted as a philosopher to British empiricist traditions, James was favorably disposed toward the inductive, up-from-the-ground procedures of materialistic thinkers; and he was suspicious of the top-down, deductive procedures of idealistic rationalists.[47] He believed that traditional empiricists were vulnerable, however, in that they failed to account for "the confluence of every passing moment of concretely felt experience with its neighbors." Rationalists capitalized on this weakness by cultivating abstract theoretical systems to account for the fissures that were left untended by empiricists. As a form of " 'radical' " "empiricism," James wrote, pragmatism would be "distinguish[ed]" "from the bugaboo empiricism" that, according to its "rationalist critics," was guilty of "chopping up experience into atomistic sensations, incapable of union with one another until a purely intellectual principle has swooped down upon them from on high and folded them in its own conjunctive categories" (*PU*, 778). The distinctly American method that he envisioned would fortify empiricism against such predatory incursions by "tak[ing] conjunctive relations at their face-value, holding them to be as real as the terms united by them" (789). Aligned with Proudhon's conception of an innately ethical "economic organism," James's later pragmatism became a means of recovering the foundational unity that had been occluded by political and rationalistic mechanisms.

James's conception of pragmatism as a "pluralistic" assault on the Absolute was bound to his conception of "radical empiricism." And though his evolving philosophy was certainly indebted to French pluralist and British empiricist traditions, these debts were ultimately entangled with James's distinctive efforts to reconcile "*Anarchy*" with Darwinian theory.[48] For James, as for Peirce, "*pragmatism*" had been a method of reorienting empiricism, one that would enable it to account for a "*reality*" that was not "*ready-made*," but rather "*still in the making*" (*P*, 599). Because this "*making*" took place not in any given thing but only in the junctures between moments in "the stream of experience," the "radical empiricist" procedures of James's assault on the Absolute entailed a "pluralistic" collapse of the distinction between "the one" and "the many." "Everything you can think of," James wrote, "however vast or inclusive, has on the pluralistic view a genuinely 'external' environment of some sort." "Things are 'with' one another in many ways, but nothing includes everything, or dominates over everything. The word 'and' trails along after every sentence. Something always escapes. 'Ever not quite' has to be said of the best attempts made anywhere in the universe at attaining all-inclusiveness. The pluralistic world is thus more like a federal republic than like an empire or a kingdom" (*PU*, 776). In this passage James's likening of the "pluralistic world" to a "federal republic" affirms the enduring liberalism of the philosopher who counted himself as "too ill" and "too old" to join the communitarian "anarchist" movements, which in his wavering estimation would come to hold the best hope for "betterment and salvation."[49] As James began to merge his politics and philosophy around the turn of the century, his insistence that "individual-ism" was not an entitlement but rather an exercise of "free personal rela-tion[s]" suggests that his developing conception of pragmatism as a rela-tional philosophy, one that located its American future in the conjunctions between the moments of experience, was in fact poised between a liberal "exceptionalist" vision of an "organic democracy" and a less nationalistic anarchist vision of a society free from the very political impediments that blocked free transactions between producers and consumers.[50]

In fashioning pragmatism as a corrective to philosophical methods that failed to account adequately for relations, James was influenced not only by Proudhon's vision of the innately ethical pathways of barter but also by Charles Darwin's idea that mutation plays an essential role in the evolution of species. In James's later writings, Darwin's theory of variation enters into dialogue with Proudhon's notion of social reciprocity: James used the model of contingent generational succession to make a temporal matter of the immediate bartered transactions that mapped out the more spatial reaches of Proudhon's utopian community. In James's hands, the very axis of Prou-dhon's notion of a field of immediate exchanges between producers and consumers was abstracted and rendered as a means of accounting for the ungoverned conjunctions between isolated moments in the individual con-tinuum, or "the stream," of experience. Describing "pragmatism" as a "ge-netic theory of what is meant by truth," he preserved the Proudhonian anarchistic emphasis on relations, adapting the imperative of free exchange between producers and consumers to the spirit of randomness and variability that pervaded modern theories of heredity (*P,* 515). Drawing from newly publicized models of indeterminate genetic succession—models that supported Darwin's theoretical "assault" on the deterministic notion of an antecedent *species*—he used the anarchists' banishment of *specie,* or gold currency, to recover the foundations of a fundamentally "individualistic" form of American democracy.[51] And he posed this self-bound foundation as a processual link between a European past and an American future.

❖   In James's study of Darwin, it was not the winnowing mechanism of natural selection, but rather the more generative, "*additive*" one of variation, that became the point of contact between "pluralism" and "*Anarchy* in the good sense."[52] As a scientist-turned-philosopher, James had from early in his career made a careful study of Darwin's and others' writings on plant and animal hybrids. In ongoing readings of books ranging from Darwin's *Variation of Animals and Plants under Domestication* (1868) to Archdall Reid's post-Mendelian study *The Principles of Heredity* (1905), he had noted theories of "sports," or spontaneous reversions to ancestral types, in the offspring of hybridized or grafted plants.[53] In a 1903–4 lecture on pluralism, James echoed Darwin by challenging the "determinist[ic]" belief that "acts of choice" must be continuous with antecedent " 'ideas' " and " 'laws of association.' " Here he left what may be his fullest account of the post-Darwinian significance of "*graft*-theory" and "*Anarchy*" to his emerging pragmatist philosophy.[54] "*What* comes," James suggested, "is really decided *when* it comes." "In these experienced cases, since what comes continues something else & is preceded by an ideal, it may be likened to a *graft.* A graft is an *additive* to a tree. No body [*sic*] can contend that it is essential. Yet it combines harmoniously, replaces another branch that would have come, or another scion that might equally well have been grafted, and redefines the 'whole tree.' It is strictly among the tree's possibilities" (*ML,* 310–11).

Through its emphasis on process, Darwin's theory of generational contingency enabled James to adapt "*Anarchy* in the good sense" to American exceptionalist conceptions of an "ongoing democratic process." In conceiving of genetic "variation" as an infinitesimal or ungoverned transaction, and in locating this transaction in the temporal field of generational succession rather than in the static one of an edenic community, James's description of the pluralistic world as a kind of grafted tree worked to modernize and also "domesticate" the utopian foundation at the root of ethical anarchist thought. Proudhonian anarchists and American pragmatists both sought to destroy "first principles," or antecedents, at the vibrant interstices of unfettered exchange. For the mutualist Proudhon, however, these exchanges were simultaneous: they traced a map of the agrarian village economy that lingered beneath anarchistic conceptions of an "economic organism." Based on the idea of barter, or a self-renewing "reciprocity" that displaced the coinage of the sovereign, they constructed from lines of unfettered commerce a society based not on remotely political directives but on a perpetually generated immediacy between the individual and the surrounding community.

James's post-Darwinian "*graft*-theory" differs from Proudhon's notion of an "economic organism" in that it does not propose to recover a "natural" unity between autonomy and voluntary association. Rather, it creates this unity in the moment opened by the very suspension of the search for a utopian foundation. As an "*additive*," the graft is vital only because it can*not* be said to be in any way "essential." Were it essential, the branch that "combines harmoniously" with the whole would be less of a branch. It would be less of a vibrant agent defined through the act of its blending and more of a static extension of the tree that precedes it. Similarly, an "event" in the stream of experience would be less an event and more an outgrowth of the antecedent that "causes" it (*PP*, 239). "Unity," as James put it in his discussion of the pluralistic graft, "is in process of achievement. What is already 'one' and 'whole' is already static. What is dynamic lives only in the parts—the line of fire. *The moment of experience*" (*ML*, 311).

Circulating among American intellectuals over the early decades of the twentieth century, the "pluralistic" phase of pragmatism that James derived from British and French philosophy, and from anarchism and Darwinism as well, laid a groundwork for new social theories and new literary practices. Modern American literary experimentalism can be said to branch off in two directions, each of which emphasized a different aspect of James's "anarchistic" attention to the conjunctions between static terms. In their ambitious collage poems, ascetic modernists like Pound and Williams—and to a lesser extent, T. S. Eliot in *The Waste Land*—aspired to recover pathways of immediacy by cutting conjunctions out of their work. For Pound in particular, the Chinese ideogram came to stand as a model of poetic economy, one that placed streamlined pictures in immediate juxtaposition, tracing an innately intelligent circuitry of transactions among them. Likening such a circuitry to the agrarian pathways through which nourishing goods circulated in a healthy society, Pound fashioned his "ideogrammic method" as a vehicle that preserved the utopian foundations of the anarchist belief in immediate relations between producers and consumers.

Another group of modernists adhered more closely to the Darwinian contours of James's more "metonymic," processual rendering of the "good" anarchists' efforts to recover true, immediate relations.[55] Gertrude Stein and Marianne Moore were among those who took literally James's injunction that empiricists should account for not only terms but also the relations that joined the isolated substantive moments from which terms were drawn. James suggested that grammar itself had served to empty experience of the conjunctions that marked the points of transition between the "larger objects of our thought." Grammar had relegated their "reality" to the dependent and functional status of particle words, or syntactic markers. Bearing no immediate relation to anything outside of the sentences that contained them, these particle words served only to govern and to subordinate. They made hierarchies of the clauses within sentences, forming pyramids of meaning and value out of the phrases and words held therein. Throughout his writings on both psychology and metaphysics, James appealed to the expressive value of syntactic markers, or connecting words. Calling for an unforced reconciliation between the "substantive" and "transitive" components of experience in *The Principles of Psychology* (1890), he had suggested that "there is not a conjunction or a preposition, and hardly an adverbial phrase . . . that does not express some shading or other of relation which we at some moment actually feel to exist between the larger objects of our thought" (*PP*, 245). We "ought to say a feeling of *and,*" he concluded, "a feeling of *if,* a feeling of *but,* and a feeling of *by,* quite as readily as we say a feeling of *blue* or a feeling of *cold*" (240, 245–46). Admonishing in *A Pluralistic Universe* (1909) that "the word 'or' names a genuine reality," James suggested that conjunctions signify more than "some moment" that we "actually feel" (*PU,* 777–78). Here, he extended his appeal to the primacy of syntactic conjunctions from psychology to the broader realm of metaphysics.

The early experimental writings of James's former student Gertrude Stein turn on what James eventually came to fashion as an anti-imperialist's assault on the distinction between expressive and functional parts of speech.[56] The opening lines of *Tender Buttons* (1914), for example, stand poised between the conjugated "nonsense" that James had championed as a map of the dynamic continuum of individual experience in "The Stream of

Thought" and the very accretive sort of writing that, according to James's later writings, says " 'ever not quite' " to not only syntactic and epistemological roundedness but also to the dominion "of an empire or a kingdom" (*PU*, 776). Stein introduced *Tender Buttons* with a section headed "A CARAFE, THAT IS A BLIND GLASS": "A kind in glass and a cousin, a spectacle and nothing strange a single hurt color and an arrangement in a system to pointing. All this and not ordinary, not unordered in not resembling. The difference is spreading."[57] In its roundabout way, Stein's writing acknowledges its own lack of transparency. It is "not ordinary," this passage feigns to admit, not to know what kind of "kind" is "in glass." Yet the nonmimetic "arrangement" that engenders such blindness is really "nothing strange." As impenetrable as it seems, writing of this sort is simply "not ordered in not resembling." And it is through a foregrounding of particle words that Stein spreads "the difference" of nonmimetic, or "not resembling," kinds of writing. The first of the three sentences that make up this passage contains an abundance of particle words—three "and's" and twice as many "a's"—that should mark syntactic functions. But these particle words cannot function as markers because the nominal phrases that they serve are incomplete. By freeing them of their service to syntax, Stein hopes to raise functional words to the expressive level of nouns and verbs. Insofar as Stein's resistance to mimetic "resembling" can be traced to both James and Picasso, it hinges indirectly on an anarchistic decentralization of linguistic and visual "syntax."[58] Throughout her remarkably diverse oeuvre, it was an effort to decentralize that drove her desire to "rid" poetry of "nouns" ("rose is a rose is a rose," she intoned) and to fashion the modern "paragraph" as not a representational unit but rather as a "space that is filled with moving."[59]

Though the "imagist" poet Marianne Moore allied herself with modernist aesthetics of austerity, she recognized an affinity between imagism and the "not resembling" aesthetic of Stein's *Tender Buttons*. Like Stein, Moore was a careful "reader" of James and modern visual artists; and it was through these readings that she came to fashion a unique poetic means of bridging the gulf between expressive and functional varieties of language. In Moore's billowy free-verse collage poems of the early 1920s, signification was decentralized not by a withholding of the complements to syntactic particle words but rather by a dizzying proliferation of syntactic offerings. Styling the overblown formulations of seventeenth-century English prose masters, she teased her poems into tangles too prolific to decipher. In poems like "Novices" (1923), she left her readers to abandon sense in favor of the associative interstices between quoted phrases and the mass of syntax into which quotations were folded. It is in the "voluntary associations" that emerge through these interstices, where images of glass, water, and language call across disembodied phrases, that the poem speaks its tribute to the power of expression.[60]

> "split like a glass against a wall"
> in this "precipitate of dazzling impressions,
> the spontaneous unforced passion of the Hebrew language—
> an abyss of verbs full of reverberations and tempestuous energy"
> in which action perpetuates action and angle is at variance with angle
> till submerged by the general action;
> obscured by "fathomless suggestions of color,"
> by incessantly panting lines of green, white with concussion,
> in this drama of water against rocks—this "ocean of hurrying consonants"
> with its "great livid stains like long slabs of green marble,"
> its "flashing lances of perpendicular lightning" and "molten fires swallowed
>   up,"
> "with foam on its barriers,"
> "crashing itself out in one long hiss of spray."
> (*MM,* 61)

A visually oriented writer, Moore crafted poems as graphic entities that signified through spatial as well as through syntactic relations. That she derived the spatial logic of her poetry both from James and from modern movements in the visual arts is suggested by a second metaphor that James used to describe his method of "radical empiricism."[61] Fashioned as it was several years before Picasso and Braque began to draw new visual collage techniques out of the edge-driven compositional directives of cubist painting, James's conception of a modern "mosaic" philosophy testifies not only to the relationship between pragmatist thought and guiding modernist aesthetic tenets but also to the vexed bearing of historical anarchism on both of these modern phenomena. As a variety of "radical empiricism" that rested on a recovery of immediate relations between terms, James's pragmatism shared something fundamental with the anarchist resistance to monarchist, socialist, and democratic forms of government. But as a fundamentally metonymic philosophy that thwarted the metaphorical imperative of even such a hidden foundation as Proudhon's agrarian village, it also differed in important ways from anarchist theory. Like James's image of the grafted tree,

which temporalized Proudhon's exchanges, invoking a processual imperative of vitality that finally appealed to an edenic notion of the individual self,
the pragmatist's notion of a pluralistic "mosaic philosophy" turned on the
tension between the appeal to, and the rejection of, a foundation, which was
articulated here as a negative framework or "bedding." "In actual mosaics,"
James wrote in 1904,

> the pieces are held together by their bedding, for which bedding the . . .
> Absolutes of other philosophies may be taken to stand. In radical empiricism
> there is no bedding; it is as if the pieces clung together by their edges, the
> transitions experienced between them forming their cement. Of course such
> a metaphor is misleading, for in actual experience the more substantive and
> the more transitive parts run into each other continuously, there is in general
> no separateness needing to be overcome by an external cement; and whatever
> separateness is actually experienced is not overcome, it stays and counts as
> separateness to the end. But the metaphor serves to symbolize the fact that
> Experience itself, taken at large, can grow by its edges. That one moment of it
> proliferates into the next by transitions which, whether conjunctive or dis-
> junctive, continue the experiential tissue, can not, I contend, be denied. Life
> is in the transitions as much as in the terms connected; often, indeed, it
> seems to be there more emphatically, as if our spurts and sallies forward were
> the real firing-line of the battle, were like the thin line of flame advancing
> across the dry autumnal field which the farmer proceeds to burn. ("WPE"
> 1180–81)

Linked by their shared appeals to the possibility of biological quilting
("mosaic" also means "chimera," or a kind of grafted animal) and by their
echoing evocation of "life in the firing line," James's graft and mosaic are at
once sympathetic toward and resistant to the anarchistic belief that a just
society can emerge from a recovery of innately "reciprocal" pathways between individual producers and consumers (*GI*, 171, 173). In James's hands,
however, the authority of the fundamental ethical community was complicated by the post-Darwinian notion that life consisted as much in the
"spurts and sallies" between terms as it did in a particular configuration
among them. In this sense it turned on a precariously "modern" distinction
between the graft and the mosaic as products on the one hand and pure
processes on the other. As these pragmatist models became mainstreamed
and incorporated into newly emerging conceptions of "culture" as a measure of authentic identity, they began to lose their processual qualities and

harden into products. The graft became the parent of the very vigorous kind of offspring that "race" was failing to produce in an age of degeneration; and the mosaic became less and less an instance of cultural making and more and more an example of the kind of thing that a culture makes.[62] In this way the mechanisms for displacing antecedents came to illustrate "*first principles*" themselves.

Pound's appeal to a millennial fascist order in the 1930s is a particularly dramatic instance of the hardening of the anarchistic avant-garde impulse.[63] But even those American modernists whose loose conceptions of democracy helped them to evade such appeals to immediacy surrendered to an aesthetic alchemy that turned processes into products. In Williams's conception of a poetry committed to a process-oriented vision of American culture, and even in Moore's less nationalistic conception of poetic language as bound to the contingencies of that which was the opposite of "race," the modernist emphasis on embodiment over representation reached new heights of imaginative expression. But the very processes championed by these experimental modernists had been mainstreamed through the American absorption of the idea of "culture." As an African American folklorist and novelist who was positioned to see the limits of modern American appeals to culture, the later modernist Zora Neale Hurston used the technique of "free indirect discourse" not to dissolve categories of "gender" and "race," as Joyce had used it in *Ulysses*, but to neutralize even the foundation of "culture" that had become the American invention of the antifoundationalist impulse. In *Their Eyes Were Watching God*, Hurston lifted "culture" from its newly sanctified bedding, using it as a piece in a mosaic that became a medium for yet a new kind of voice.

3. "Culture"

Both anarchist societies of "free personal relation[s]" and Darwinian chains of indeterminate succession contributed to William James's vision of "our actual experience" of the world. For the turn-of-the-century philosopher who sought to overhaul outmoded empiricist traditions, this "experience" was not only an "individual" matter; it also belonged to an individual who was implicitly American. James's confidence in America as a young nation whose future lay before it hinged on the belief that America could unburden itself of its European legacy. In this sense America was a kind of graft that obtained its vitality in the act of displacing the parent stock that overshadowed its identity and growth. At the same time James clung to a nascent

Emersonian belief that an American language, art, and politics might be based on dynamic signs that were mystically indigenous to the more or less literal wilderness that distinguished America from Europe. As Emerson had written, the American poet-prophet was a seer who took "Nature as his hieroglyphic." James preserved something of this idea in his suggestion that a processual and accretive American "republic" would be birthed in the unbridled "stream" of an individual's "experience"—a stream that was restored to wholeness through the removal of the European conceptual structures that had torn it asunder. The tension between these respective immediate and processual conceptions of American identity is a defining feature of American modernism, one that is exhibited in William Carlos Williams's portrayal of the grafted tree as a kind of paradisal American growth. In Williams's chapter on Columbus's voyage in *In the American Grain,* the generative life-forms that grace the shores of the New World are emblematized by an indigenous tree whose branches are variously leafed. "One branch has leaves like those of a cane," Columbus marvels at the end of Williams's essay, "and the other like those of a mastic tree; and on a single tree there are five different kinds" (*IAG,* 26).

In American literature of the 1920s and 1930s, these two competing strains—one metaphorical and "necessary," the other more metonymic and "contingent"—were adapted in various ways to newly emerging conceptions of racial and cultural identity.[64] Coupled with such historical events as modern breakthroughs in genetics and the dramatic rise of American immigration, the pragmatists' revival of deep-rooted "exceptionalist" beliefs helped to neutralize class conflict. As Vincent Sherry has shown, modernists in Britain, Pound and Wyndham Lewis especially, derived their aesthetic programs from continental European intellectuals—Gustav LeBon, Julien Benda, Rémy de Gourmont—who distinguished the aural perceptual modes of the modern masses from the more discriminating visual modes of an aristocratic elite (*RM,* 9–42). Pound's and Joyce's early writings display the tendency among European-based modernists to fashion themselves as a radical sort of "aristocracy." Adapting the cant of radical politics to their aesthetics, they identified their own enterprises with those of marginalized workers, imagining that they shared with starving coal miners an opposition not to an aristocratic elite but to the provincial middle-class rabble that undervalued their productions.[65] Pound and Dora Marsden also held these undiscriminating middle classes responsible for the numbing jingoist sentiment that culminated in the catastrophic violence of World War I.[66]

Among American artists and intellectuals of the 1920s, however, class was less of a defining divide than it had been for their European "anarchist" forebears.[67] This muting of class consciousness is due in part to the long-standing "exceptionalist" perception of America as a country defined in opposition to European cultural standards. Insofar as this rather chilly dismissal of class differences infiltrated various strata of American society, questions of identity in early-twentieth-century America came to revolve more around new ways of thinking about "racial" and "cultural" differences and affiliations. During the decade of American isolationism that followed World War I, two distinct conceptions of "culture" came to the fore. And in many ways these competing notions of culture—one promulgated by "cultural pluralists," the other by "cultural anthropologists"—reflected those conflicting philosophical premises that Jamesian pragmatists derived from anarchist and Darwinist thought, respectively. Although these divergent senses of culture often overlapped one another, they provided a conceptual axis for the tempers of American writers who struggled to redefine notions of individual and collective identity.

One group of modernists entertained a notion of America as a cultural "mosaic."[68] Displaying an affinity for the sort of pluralistic social models set forth by pragmatist social theorists like Horace Kallen, these writers devised a set of generic and linguistic practices that were based on the idea of an immediate recovery of an originary identity between individual ethnic groups and a national whole. In this they were rooted in the "metaphorical" anarchist strains of American pragmatist thought. Williams was one of a large number of American modernists to have been touched by postwar pluralistic models.[69] The idea of a cultural mosaic keyed his gradually evolving understanding of a new kind of poetic measure, one that was metaphorically grounded in not the "gold" standard of "English" but the industrial "Babbitt metal" of vernacular American speech (*W*, 9). At the same time, however, Williams suggested that this idiom gained its vitality through the dynamic "processes" by which, as James had put it, "idiom grafts itself on previous idiom" (*P*, 592). In so doing he leaned in the direction of the more metonymic conceptions of culture that Marianne Moore incorporated into her "eccentric[ally]" branching forms of poetry ("MM," 54). Here, culture was defined more abstractly as a contingent antidote to the outmoded and brittle forms of determinism that were associated with traditional scientific conceptions of race.

During the teens, twenties, and thirties, Franz Boas became a leading advocate of this latter, more "metonymic" conception of culture. As a founder

of the discipline of cultural anthropology, and as an activist who campaigned against racialist legislation, Boas insisted that contingent "environmental influences" "overshadow" "organic differences" between groups of
people (*AML,* 49). Thus, he posed "culture" as a fluidly processual alternative to more static and essentializing conceptions of group identity. From
Boas's point of view, essentialism marred not only conventional hierarchical
conceptions of race but also cultural pluralist assumptions regarding nonhierarchical racial and ethnic foundations.[70] In his commitment to dismantling deterministic conceptions of identity, however, Boas was not content to
merely posit "culture" as a substitute for "race." As a hidden factor that
conditioned the sacred "truths" of both "primitive" and "civilized" people,
culture was both an antidote to determinism and a sweeping instrument of
antifoundationalist critique (*MPM,* 203–6). Here, the anthropologist also
played a role in perpetuating and refining an antifoundationalist tradition in
American philosophy. As a critic of the very methods and processes that
undergirded scientific racialism, he helped to sharpen the active and participatory forms of social "intelligence" championed by the later pragmatist
and sometime cultural pluralist John Dewey. In formulating "culture" as a
measure of shifting, indeterminate identity, however, Boas finally provided a
touchstone for a variety of American writers. Some, like Marianne Moore,
derived new varieties of poetry from the anthropologist's notion of environmentally conditioned cultural forms. Others, like Zora Neale Hurston—who
was both a student and an associate of Boas—wrote a different sort of
measure into the American modernist canon. For Hurston, "culture" was an
abstract exceptionalist category designed to serve the white Americans who
propounded it.

❖   Boas's notions of cultural and even scientific indeterminacy were not
drawn directly from the philosophy that James associated with "*Anarchy* in
the good sense." The more essentializing conceptions of "culture" championed by modern American pluralists, however, were derived from certain
facets of James's pluralistic writings; in this sense they served to modify or
"domesticate" the very anarchist conceptual criteria that guided the modern-
istic experiments of poets like Pound and Williams. Beginning with Charles
Renouvier's and William James's own quiet debts to Proudhon, American
modernism can be shown to have stemmed from a complex "pluralist"
lineage that runs from turn-of-the-century American philosophy to Kallen's
and also Dewey's postwar writings on American culture. American modern-

ists were by no means as deeply engaged with anarchist politics as were their European predecessors. But insofar as "*Anarchy*" contributed to James's "mosaic philosophy," and insofar as modified anarchist tenets were channeled into later pluralistic conceptions of an American "mosaic of peoples," anarchism can be said to have indirectly contributed to early-twentieth-century American literary efforts to reimagine language and identity.

A small but influential group of modern American poets—T. S. Eliot, Gertrude Stein, Robert Frost, Wallace Stevens—studied with James and his pragmatist colleagues, including Josiah Royce and George Santayana, at Harvard University. As Frank Lentricchia has suggested, the "American philosophical modernism" of the Boston pragmatists provided a better foundation for many modern American writers than did the well-embalmed "Fireside" legacies of Longfellow, Whittier, and Lowell (*MQ*, 1–4). As Lentricchia and other critics have begun to tally the white modernist debt to American philosophy, however, a second group has begun to uncover a more deeply buried lineage. Cornel West, George Hutchinson, and Ross Posnock are among those who have begun to treat African American intellectual writings, and the modern literary texts that surrounded them, as variant forms of American antifoundationalist thought—forms promulgated by Harvard-trained intellectuals including W. E. B. Du Bois and Alain Locke.[71] The new historical genealogies that have sprung from such studies of American philosophy and literature have deepened our understanding of American literary and cultural history; and they have encouraged us to explore further repercussions of "American philosophical modernism." James's "radical empiricism" and "pluralism," for example, may have rubbed off on some of his own turn-of-the-century students; but it was a later group of pragmatists that, in adapting James's pluralism to the American scene, transferred his graft and mosaic models to less pedigreed poets including William Carlos Williams.

As entities that embodied the idea that "experience . . . can grow by its edges," James's graft and mosaic tell us something about Williams's efforts to fashion an improvisational poetic measure, one that the poet claimed to have stolen from "the mouths of Polish mothers." Seeking to invigorate the "crude symbolism" that sapped traditional poetic idioms, Williams had turned in the early 1920s to cubism and to a new type of heavily enjambed short-lined poem. Modeling his prosody on the Juan Gris painting that he took for his subject, Williams observed in *Spring and All* (1923) that, as a whole, the conventional "poem" was exhausted.

The rose is obsolete
but each petal ends in
an edge, the double facet
cementing the grooved
columns of air—The edge
cuts without cutting
meets—nothing—renews
itself in metal or porcelain—
(*I*, 107)

In the opening lines of this poem from his 1923 collection, Williams used a technique that would become central to his conception of an intrinsically American form of measure. Dividing his second and third lines across an integral phrase, he recreated the metonymic visual directives of an aesthetic wherein each petal "ends in/an edge." Further on in the poem, in a pair of isolated couplets, he used enjambment yet again to draw a crucial distinction from the double sense given to the words "weight" and "end." As an entity that was burdened by romantic conventions, Williams suggested,

The rose carried weight of love
but love is at an end—of roses

Now, by the avant-garde dictates of an American apocalypse,

It is at the edge of the
petal that love waits
(108)

In Williams's emerging aesthetic, the idiom that says "To hell with you and your poetry—" is only partly a matter of cadence and diction (146). More fundamentally, it is an iconoclastic visual temper that discovers "love" not within, but across, lines of poetry that no longer hold it intact. Displaced into the improvised bedding that holds its fragments apart, meaning no longer "weights" in the whole of the American flower. Rather, it "waits" at the pendant edges of the idiom that Williams engenders through his short-lined units of measure.

In fashioning an idiomatic variety of poetry that is measured by the mosaic imperatives of enjambment, Williams drew from visual artists affiliated with political anarchism; and despite his professed aversion to philosophy and to philosophers per se, he drew from pragmatist traditions as well.[72]

More than James, it was John Dewey who helped Williams to see how a poem so measured might be an intrinsically American "thing." In a 1921 issue of his avant-garde journal *Contact,* and later in his autobiography, Williams memorialized his own "discovery" of Dewey's writings on the significance to poetry of America's unassimilated immigrant populations. In his 1920 *Dial* essay "Americanism and Localism," Dewey had suggested that a vibrant American poetic would arise not from what Williams referred to as the "horrid unity" of the melting pot (*I*, 91), but rather through a national mosaic of distinctive immigrant cultures. As Dewey saw it, American immigrants were inventing the American language by submerging it in local experience. As a people who were "chiefly concerned with what goes on in their tenement house, their alley, their factory, their street," they were "too busy making the American language to devote much time to studying the English." In this way "the absorbed denizens of the locality" were forming a new kind of idiomatic nation, one that did not derive its identity from the abstract bedding of "English" or "Anglosaxondom" but rather from the ongoing directives of local experience.[73] As a "cultural pluralist" who alerted Williams to the "nativist" imperatives of pragmatism, then, Dewey channeled James's conception of the mosaic to Williams, who wove it into his conception of a heavily enjambed, "waiting" kind of measure, one whose pendant visual displays embodied the relational "weight" of the American idiom.

Williams has been widely praised as a poet who adapted free verse to American speech. Despite Williams's intermittent representation of various regional and ethnic dialects, however, his admirers have had a hard time pinpointing what it is that is idiomatic about his poetry.[74] The diction and phrasing of poems like "The rose is obsolete" from *Spring and All* display little evidence of the "up from the gutter" aesthetic that Williams later professed to have embraced in his writing (*W*, 9). And they cannot really be said to be American as "free verse" poems that displace the antecedent "counts" that govern conventional poetic meters. As a proponent of even a uniquely evasive variety of "free verse," Williams joined a range of international modernists who have followed the nineteenth-century French symbolists in taking an uncounted measure as one of their staple forms. After 1923, however, as he began to shorten his lines and drop end-line punctuation, Williams leavened his free-verse poems with instances of radically severe enjambment. In this way he alerted his modern readers to the constantly changing relations between syntax and lineation. In these poems it was the vividly illustrated changes in the degrees of alignment and nonalignment between syntax and lineation that came to form a new kind of fluxional "standard." It was this localized standard that formed the universal measure of his poetry. That Williams spoke repeatedly of this measure as "American," and that he linked it to Dewey's declaration that the American immigrant's "locality is the only universal," suggests that the improvisational unit that he came to call the "variable foot" was rooted, through both Dewey *and* James, in the anarchistically derived "mosaic" conceptions of national identity that gained prominence in America during the 1920s.

Dewey's pluralistic vision of an American social mosaic should be distinguished from James's more abstract pluralistic models of "actual experience." Throughout his career, Dewey retained a Hegelian belief that, as Richard Rorty put it, "the starting point of philosophic thought is . . . the dialectical situation in which one finds oneself caught in one's own historical period" (*CP*, 81).[75] Consequently, Dewey harbored a greater interest than James in the socially mediated character of experience; and he worked harder to bridge philosophy with social theory. Despite these differences, however, many of Dewey's ideas—ranging from his philosophical treatises to his more topical essays on American democracy and culture—were rooted in James's pluralist inquiries into the nature of "causes" and "consequences." Dewey's 1925 book, *Experience and Nature,* for example, contains what many consider to be his best effort to destroy "the spectator conception of knowledge" and to thereby transform metaphysics into an active social instrument (*CP*, 72–74, 87).[76] In this book Dewey elaborated upon the distinctive critique of a unifying causality that had animated James's conception of the graft or mosaic; and he extended James's guiding metaphors by grafting the perceiver herself into the very model of "actual experience" that the graft and mosaic were said to display. In his Hegelian rendering of James's pluralistic models, Dewey suggested that static conceptions of reality, as well as of the historically constructed subject-object distinctions that condition our experience of reality, stem from the common "philosophical error" of mistaking consequences for causes. "The idea that matter, life and mind represent separate kinds of Being," Dewey wrote, "springs" from a "fallacy" that "converts consequences of interaction of events [*sic*] into causes of the occurrence of these consequences—a reduplication which . . . confuses [our] understanding of them."[77] During his "cultural pluralist" phase of the late teens and early twenties, Dewey attempted to apply this pluralistic inquiry into "causes" and "consequences" to the living question of what it meant to be an American. In his view unassimilated immigrants embodied a more active form of intelligence, and hence a more "consequential" variety of Americanness, because they were indifferent to the antecedent "causal" measures of "Anglosaxondom."[78]

By 1915 Dewey was among a small handful of "cultural pluralists" who spoke out against programs designed to Americanize recent immigrants from eastern and southern Europe. Calling for "genuine assimilation *to one another*—not to Anglosaxondom," he joined Horace Kallen in suggesting that the national "metaphor" of the "melting pot" should be replaced by an image of America as a composite nation of "juxtapos[ed]" "cultural section[s]."[79] Kallen, who had worked as a teaching assistant at Harvard, claims to have coined the term *cultural pluralism* in conversation with one of his students, the African American philosopher Alain Locke; and Kallen traced the impetus of his new brand of national identity to the philosophical pluralism of his own teacher, William James.[80] By Kallen's account, it was James's "refusal to accept . . . that the many are appearance and only the one is reality" that had encouraged his belief that the "oneness" of American identity was "composed" of "manyness, variety, differentiation."[81] "Cultural growth," Kallen wrote, "is founded on cultural pluralism." And pluralism is possible "only in a democratic society . . . whose program liberates . . . individualities and guides them into a fellowship of freedom and cooperation" (*CD*, 43). The powerful structural affinity between Kallen's merging of "oneness" with "manyness" and Proudhon's utopian "equal[ization]" of the individual "citizen's" will with that of the community at large is probably not a direct outgrowth of Kallen's firsthand familiarity with anarchist tenets (*GI*, 268–69). (Despite his well-known commitments to liberal democracy, Kallen did indeed express a long-standing admiration for nonviolent anarchists such as Peter Kropotkin.)[82] More likely, the affinity between Kallen's and Proudhon's "immediate" societies stemmed from a series of intellectual transactions that Kallen knew little about. The period during which Kallen absorbed James's "pluralism" (1905–8) was in fact the very period during which James had marshaled anarchism to his efforts to reconcile metaphysical systems with "our actual experience of the way [the] world develops."[83] Through the writings of Charles Renouvier, and then through the writings of James himself in his anti-imperialist phase, Proudhonian anarchist premises came to temper the pluralist philosophy from which Kallen drew his "mosaic of peoples."

Unlike his successors, James did not try to fashion "pluralism" into a literal blueprint for social reform; but he did apply the related notion of grafting to the topical question of standard versus vernacular forms of English. Elaborating upon his notion of pragmatism as a "mosaic philosophy" and on the "*graft*-theory" that he likened to "*Anarchy* in the good sense," James suggested that the very "process" through which "idiom grafts itself on previous idiom" would supplant the restrictive idea of " 'the' mother-tongue" (*P*, 592). In his 1915 essay, Kallen toned down James's emphasis on an edge-driven "process," suggesting rather that in a "voluntary" *and* "autonomous" "democracy of nationalities," the hierarchical difference between an idiom and a mother tongue would simply vanish. The "language" of the "great" "tradition" "of the commonwealth" would be "English," Kallen asserted, "but each nationality expresses its own emotional and voluntary life in its own language, in its own inevitable aesthetic and intellectual forms."[84] In suggesting that America's grafted branches would somehow infiltrate the roots of the parent stock, Kallen did adhere to one facet of James's anarchistic graft. But in ignoring James's emphasis on the ongoing process rather than the outcome of grafting, he rooted his "mosaic" "commonwealth" of distinct "nationalities" in a metaphorical democratic foundation. If Kallen's "commonwealth" rested more on essentializing racialist assumptions than on an attempt to account for social mediation, it was because it was too thoroughly bound to a utopian vision of a society in which autonomy and mutuality were already joined.

Dewey's more cautious conception of a mosaic identity and idiom reached Williams in 1920, just as the American poet was beginning to gather the "small, sweet forget-me-not" aesthetics of European cubist and dadaist visual artists.[85] In his 1920 essay on the invention of the American language, Dewey certainly emphasized the "*process*" by which the grafted idiom replaced " 'the' mother-tongue" in James's formulation (*P*, 592). By locating this process in the activities of America's newly arrived immigrants, he tried to edge James's "*graft*-theory" away from its utopian anarchist proclivities, making a social and historical matter of a procedure that had remained mystical in both Proudhon's and Kallen's formulations. As a liberal intellectual who abjured the "anarchistic" notion that "the one" was immediately joined to "the many," Dewey held rather that an "individual [was brought] to a consciousness of the whole" through "a complex and continual" "social mediation."[86] Linking the contingencies of such a mediation to the Darwinian processes implicit in the pragmatists' "genetic" theory of truth, he fashioned the notion of an ongoing "experimental" method, one that was associated with both science and the immigrant experience, as the foundation of the American identity. In so doing he sought to supplant the anarchist's utopian relational village with a vision founded on the contingent processes of an "ongoing democratic experience" (*SS*, 168). Insofar as this process remained ever rooted in a national identity, however, it finally culminated, in Williams's poetry, in a metaphorical appeal to intrinsic American foundations. For Williams, as for Columbus, the miraculously variegated tree was a distinctly American spectacle.

Through Dora Marsden and Ezra Pound, Williams drew from anarchist premises to conceive of a kind of poetry that was wrought not from exogamous literary "gold" but from such "intrinsic" materials as the industrial "Babbitt metal" of vernacular "speech" (*W*, 9). Through Pound in particular, he eventually came to tap the Proudhonian sources of "Social Credit" and "volitionist" currency theories, declaring the modern "wedge" that cleaved "intimacies" to be "money [that was] articulated to government" (45–46). But it was finally Williams's absorption, through Dewey, of James's pluralistic mosaic philosophy that enabled him to situate the poem, as a formal "machine made of words" (8), in a metaphorical relation to a "character" that was both essentially modern and essentially American. Among other things, this absorption marks a survival in American poetry of the anarchistic drive toward the attainment of a "structural" immediacy between representation and reality.

❖ Cultural pluralists like Williams believed that American identity was a relational affair, drawing its authority from the dynamic lineaments of "experience." This belief was supported by the pluralistic phases of pragmatism that James identified with "*Anarchy* in the good sense." Like the pragmatists themselves, however, many champions of "culture" tempered the desire to recover the metaphoric "weight" of a lost community with less utopian efforts to reconstruct the metonymic processes, or the contingent "waits," upon which individual and, in Dewey's case, collective national identities might be founded. Stein and Moore were not altogether unswerving in their advocacy of the metonymic imperatives of James's graft and mosaic. In her lecture "The Gradual Making of the Making of Americans," for example, Stein fancied that the spatial paragraph was a uniquely American unit.[87] And Moore, despite her suggestion that the American wilderness was as much woven of words as of trees ("Sea Unicorns and Land Unicorns"), figured the "plain American" vernacular as a homely corrective to the queen's brittle

"English" ("England") (*MM*, 78, 46–47). Nonetheless, these modernists were stricter than Pound and Williams in resisting the organicism that attends metaphoric claims for poetic identity. Insofar as American pragmatists like James and Dewey succeeded in extracting anarchist premises from their antiliberal origins and wedding them first to American "exceptionalist" conceptions of dynamic "individual" consciousness and then to conceptions of an "ongoing democratic process," they are responsible for a vastly different set of appeals to "embodiment" on the part of modern American artists, appeals that channeled antifoundationalist poetic and narrative premises toward fundamentally centrist and complicitous ends.

Pragmatically schooled cultural pluralists hoped to reconstruct democracy by adapting Jamesian philosophical premises to the American national body. In this they can be said to have indirectly domesticated the utopian premises of the nineteenth-century anarchist social systems that supported James's assaults on philosophical, religious, and political absolutism. But the modern notion of America as a democratic "mosaic of peoples" was also supported by conceptions of "culture" that bore no relation to Proudhon's immanently ethical barter society. The emerging discipline of cultural anthropology, for example, aided the cause of pluralism, at least insofar as it discredited the idea of racial hierarchy. And although Boas did not openly seek to recover anything so fixed as an essential American identity, his efforts to vanquish racial differences resembled the pluralists' exceptionalist efforts in that they served mainstream white liberal causes. Like the mosaic models promulgated by Kallen and others, Boas's models of contingent culture were ultimately conditioned by his interests as a white American of European ancestry.

Exceptionalist desires to restore millennial forms of democracy provided a common ground for Boas and his pragmatist contemporary, John Dewey. As a colleague of Dewey's at Columbia University, the anthropologist contributed to the pragmatist's assault on the passifying "spectator conception of knowledge" (*RP*, 112). For Dewey, Boas's "culture" provided a vibrant contemporary means of accounting for the local contingencies of a democratic citizen's experience of the world. And though Dewey soon abandoned his attempt to graft a participatory form of knowledge onto disfranchised immigrants in particular, he retained Boas's notion of "culture" generally, using it as a substitute for "experience" in his later writings (*JD*, 345–46; *CP*, 72–73). As a careful reader of Boas, Dewey understood that "culture" provided more than a processual countermeasure to "race." It was also an abstract conceptual instrument that challenged scientific notions of "truth." In an unpublished appraisal of Boas's *Mind of Primitive Man* (1911), Dewey cited a portion of the anthropologist's book that articulated exactly this latter critique. In a long passage that Dewey quoted in full, Boas suggested that people's stocks of knowledge are increased only by an "amalgamation" of new facts "with other previously known facts." With antecedent facts present in every new amalgamation, advances always "depend upon the character of the traditional material." In primitive circles, the inherited material is often mythic in nature. But even in our modern "scientific inquiries" "we . . . embody . . . [old] hypotheses and theories in our explanations." Failing to see this, we are "apt . . . to forget entirely the general, and for most of us the purely traditional, theoretical basis which is the foundation of our reasoning, and to assume that the result of our reasoning is absolute truth" ("CSP," 404–5).[88]

For the pragmatist Dewey of 1912, if not for the later cultural pluralist, who briefly championed American immigrant populations, Boas's "culture" provided a vividly antifoundationalist challenge to the "axiom" that "knowledge is intrinsically a mere beholding or viewing of reality" (*RP*, 112). In folding the knowing subject back into the object of knowledge, it awakened the "intelligence" that drove vibrant democratic processes. Dewey interpreted Boas's critique of science as a "testimony" to pragmatism—one that was "all the more valuable" because it was "not made with any philosophic issue in view" ("CSP," 404). Boas himself had laid the groundwork for Dewey's gesture at an alliance between pragmatism and cultural anthropology. Elsewhere in *The Mind of Primitive Man,* he suggested that scientists might reckon with their residual "traditional materials" by orienting their own work around "the pragmatic method" (*MPM*, 237). Boas's own gestures toward an alliance with Dewey and James do not place him in direct genealogical proximity to modern anarchists and pragmatists, but they do reveal those lines of affinity that made "culture" a particularly vibrant form of measure for writers who pursued more metonymic avenues of identity and literary expression.

❖ Marianne Moore developed a unique set of formal practices and thematic concerns through which she devised a poetry based on metonymic associations—a poetry in which meaning was not "natural" to words but rather improvised through them by artificial means. In combination, Moore's interests in linguistic and biological detours and puns reflected a sympathy for Darwinian and related Boasian models of identity.[89] As a scientifically inclined reader of American philosophers, she followed James's and Dewey's appeals to the life sciences more closely than did most of her modernist peers. In the process she displaced the edenic exceptionalist grounds of the American mosaic, writing Darwin's theory of variation into the genesis of language itself. Despite the achievement of her free-verse collage poetry of the early 1920s, Moore is best known for the tightly crafted syllabic poems that she wrote during the decades before and after. In her 1916 poem "The Fish," for example, she laced her stanzas with a patterned syllable count—1, 3, 9, 6, 8—that did a kind of generative violence to her subject.

> All
> external
>> marks of abuse are present on this
>> defiant edifice—
>>> all the physical features of
>
> ac-
> cident—lack
>> of cornice, dynamite grooves, burns, and
>> hatchet strokes, these things stand
>>> out on it; the chasm-side is
>
> dead.
> Repeated
>> evidence has proved that it can live
>> on what can not revive
>>> its youth. The sea grows old in it.
>> (*MM*, 32–33)

In Moore's poem about the ocean's coastal containment, the syllabic "hatchet strokes" that halve "axe" from "ac-/cident" clutter the pathways between content and form. In a poetry that gathers itself through such wayward and arbitrary processes, language is displaced from shared occasions and grounds. Moore's early "high modernist" work refuses to rest on antecedent social foundations—whether racial, national, or even gendered—in favor of an eccentrically generative form of poetic expression.

Moore was a great admirer of the early individualist James; she had been introduced to his writings by Theodore de Laguna, a Bryn Mawr philosophy and government professor who wrote on the connections between pragmatism and evolutionary theory. Through her own evolving grasp of the modern science of genetics, however, the poet eventually mined from James's individualism a far less provincial set of "political" implications.[90] In her writings of the 1920s and 1930s particularly, she came to extend James's commitment to individual experience to a poetic sounding of the racial implications of the conceptual conflict between representation and embodiment. Recognizing that both language and life-forms were driven by forces too small to see, Moore likened such generative accidents to the tangle of "sports," or the genetic throwbacks that were produced by the infinitesimal cross-hybridization of domestic fruit trees. As Moore noted in "Nine Nectarines," a 1935 poem about the origins of language, valiant nineteenth-century botanists had been stymied in their efforts to trace the origins of nectarine trees. Because of centuries of mixing, the evidence of genetic ancestry offered by "sports" pointed both ways. There were cases of ancestral peach clusters sprouting from nectarine trees, Moore suggested, but also instances of nine nectarines on a peach (*MM*, 29). Through the metonymic logic that governed these vivid instances of natural collage, antecedents, or first principles, were erased.

Combining her interest in modern visual arts with her knowledge of genetic theory, Moore could "naturalize" James's image of the artificial "graft." She gathered the sports that had fascinated James in his readings of Darwin and other evolutionists into a vivid condemnation of the modern eugenics movement. Suggesting that truths were found in stories rather than in scientific studies of origins, she fashioned a culture-bound inquiry into the foundational claims of American race scientists who sought to master the genetic material of national identity. As a modern poet who wrote ceaselessly about plants and animals in generation, Moore undertook a more socially resonant exploration of contingency than any of her European American pragmatist forebears. But like those of Boas, Moore's writings on collective identity were ultimately conditioned by her status as a liberal white European American. "Culture" was a salve for a white nation that, in Moore's view, had begun to "attack its own identity," devouring itself with the divisive measures of intra-European racial hierarchy (*MM*, 35). The African American modernist Zora Neale Hurston, by contrast, claimed an awareness of the racialist uses to which modern "culture" was put. Through this awareness she engaged in a more rigorous exploration of the social dimensions of modern assaults against foundations. Hurston's exploration was unique, and finally vexing for many contemporary readers, because it led her to question even the ostensibly liberating category of "culture" itself. In questioning the fluid modern term that had come to serve as a measure of semiotic and identitarian indeterminacy, and in incorporating this restless inquiry into her "Joycean" narrative strategies, Hurston came to challenge the very category that, for many European American writers, had begun to harden the modernist antifoundationalist impulse into a sclerotic "American" project.

❖   Hurston's inquiry into the measures of cultural indeterminacy was fashioned in literary isolation from Moore's genetic inquiry into the deterministic measure of race. But it was shaped in dialogue with modern anthropologists and with African American philosophers who drew from and elaborated pragmatist axioms; through this lineage, Hurston's "caution" toward "culture" was of a piece with the intellectual heritage of even leading culture-bound literary modernists. Hurston's relationship to the European American modernists treated in this study is borne out by a complex historical genealogy, which scholars of modern American literature and culture have only recently begun to trace. In this genealogy modern history is driven by a series of exchanges between African American and European American intellectuals, including those between W. E. B. Du Bois and William James and between Hurston and anthropologist Franz Boas—who believed with Dewey that, once the modern sciences had reoriented themselves around the contingencies of "the pragmatic method," they would supply a basis for a millennial democracy based on indeterminacy and process.[91]

Boas was born a German Jew, but as an emigrant and a liberal scientist he was not immune to the exceptionalist longings that haunted the American social sciences in particular in the early part of the twentieth century.[92] The anthropologist should certainly be praised for his role in combating the racialist assumptions that swept American scientific and legislative communities in the teens and twenties. Nevertheless, his notion of "culture" was directed especially against those forms of racial essentialism that were dividing white America from within. Boas did try to destroy the notion that Americans of African ancestry were biologically inferior to those whose parents came from Europe. But he was also prone to invoking the physiological "difference" of "the Negro" as a means of illustrating the fundamental similarity between different types of white Europeans.[93] In Boas's writings "the Negro's" cultural parity was quickly sacrificed in an effort to unify a white European American body that had been fractured into "Nordic," "Alpine," and "Mediterranean" "sub-species." During the teens and twenties, this fracturing had been intensified by xenophobic and anti-Semitic Americans who feared that the nation's Nordic genetic legacy was being contaminated by new immigrants from Italy, Poland, and Russia. When Boas bolstered his notion of "culture" through the Archimedean interval between "blackness" and "whiteness," he exposed his term as an abstract and evasive solution to the deeper racial conflicts that were masked and even intensified by the rifting and the reconciliation of "old" and "new" European immigrants. In his blindness to his own racist premises, the anthropologist stood together with those white pragmatists who failed to note the divisive historical divide that W. E. B. Du Bois called "the color-line." In suggesting that democracy could be healed or whitewashed through a miscegenistic erasure of racial differences, Boas exposed the white liberal reformist aims of the contingent and "metonymic" conceptions of identity that he supported.[94]

Through her contacts with leading intellectuals including Boas and Alain Locke, Hurston was versed in modern ideas regarding the nature of identity; and many of these new currents of thought contained within them traces of the anarchistic and Darwinist conceptual premises that drove the metaphoric and metonymic procedures of modernists of European American descent. By carrying these premises across the 1920s, and across the Du Boisian "color line" as well, Hurston recontextualized and thus reoriented the distinction between competing modernist strains of immediacy and contingency. And though Hurston brought her reevaluation of guiding modernist premises to fruition in the thematic and narrative premises of *Their Eyes Were Watching God* (1937), her earlier anthropological writings provided a proving ground for her assault on the developing foundations of American modernism.

It was in her work as an anthropologist that Hurston began to apply widespread "modernist" concerns to her representation of the rural southern African American folk. Before beginning her career as a novelist, Hurston had engaged in an ongoing anthropological study of traditional African American speech and speaking practices. This study had alerted her to fundamental differences between "Negro expression" and the more standardized speaking practices of the European American majority. In her 1934 essay "Characteristics of Negro Expression," Hurston attributed these differences to the fact that African Americans spoke a language that had been "transplanted" on their "tongue[s]." Because the English language was more foreign to them than it was to European American speakers, Hurston wrote, black Americans were inclined to "add action to it to make it do." "We have 'chop-axe,' 'sitting-chair,' 'cook-pot' and the like because the speaker has in his mind the picture of the object in use. Action. Everything illustrated. So we can say the white man thinks in a written language and the Negro thinks in hieroglyphics." Rehearsing a pervasive modernist desire for relational immediacy, Hurston went so far as to liken the semiotic composition of Negro word pictures, or "hieroglyphs," to "barter," or purer forms of economic exchange ("NE," 24). In so doing she appeared to ally herself with white European American modernists like Pound, who identified "primitive" forms of language—Chinese ideograms and African "drum languages" among them—as curative mediums that might restore vitality and even referential fidelity to overly refined Western abstractions. Hurston can be distinguished from her European American modernist peers, however, in that she resisted not only the universalizing imperatives of "*kulchur*" but also the more contingent measures of "culture" that seemed to generate this curative language. She wrote of forms of "folk expression" both as vehicles for the ongoing invention of traditions that were, in her own Jamesian phrase, "*still* in the making" and as static vessels, as axioms that transmitted a stifling "tangle of Reconstruction phrases and concepts."[95] Partaking of a nominalistic suspicion of "easy generalization," she viewed the "contingency" (in her words, the "caution") that governed the concept of "culture" as an abstract category that was no more liberating to rural southern African Americans than was the category of "nature," or the "determinism" that was associated with the race-based forms of identity that the folk should supplant.[96]

Hurston made her best-known contributions to modern American literary expression not as an anthropologist but as the author of such "folklore fictions" as *Jonah's Gourd Vine* (1934) and *Their Eyes Were Watching God* (1937). As Henry Louis Gates, Jr., has suggested, Hurston's second novel is particularly distinctive as one that merges European-based techniques of "free indirect discourse" with the idiom-based medium of the African American "speakerly text." As a modern novelist, Hurston shared with Joyce a belief that identities could not be captured through conventional idiomatic expressions and narrative forms. Rather, a "speakerly text" could be generated only through nonrealist narrative techniques that set contrasting strands of discourse in motion. As a later African American novelist, Hurston faced these questions about the nature of storytelling and identity differently from the way the Irish author of *Ulysses* approached them. Joyce's assault on realism began in Europe during the second decade of the twentieth century. But by the late 1930s, "culture" had emerged as an orthodox American term for the very fluid sorts of identities that could be mapped by a narrative merging of intrinsic and extrinsic voices. Resulting in part from the work of American pragmatists and in part from the antifoundationalist writings of Franz Boas, the very identitarian indeterminacy that Joyce and others had associated with anarchist revolt had come to serve the interests of a fundamentally racist status quo.

Joyce had not based his aesthetics on pragmatist or Darwinist premises. Rather, he had found in Stirner and Nietzsche a means of rendering processual conceptions of identity through experimental narrative techniques. Joyce's collapsing in *Ulysses* of the distinction between "word" and "world" marked his narrative as an anarchistic production, and his refusal to extend the grounds for this collapse beyond the confines of individual libidinal experience prevented the more processual and indeterminate conceptions of group identity—racial, national, cultural—from hardening into products. In America, however, "culture" had become an axiomatic premise that had laid a foundation for indeterminacy itself. In the hands of pluralists it had come to stand for something essentially "American"; and in the hands of Boasians it had come to stand for something that was attractively modern and processual. In both cases it served the predominantly white liberal interests that controlled the channels—philosophical, scientific, artistic—through which it was produced. And Hurston, as a writer well positioned to recognize this, identified "culture" as an emerging American orthodoxy. She adapted some of the signal modern narrative techniques that Joyce had helped to refine, and she turned them against the very orthodox assumptions that narrative indeterminacy had come to support in America. In this sense she can be viewed as a modernist who applied the technos of immediacy to challenge the "first principles" that immediacy had come to assert.

❖ Writing to Ezra Pound in London in 1915, T. S. Eliot warned his fellow avant-gardist not to "hitch up" his new dynamic aesthetics to the modern Jamesian philosophy that provided a complement to vorticism (*LTSE*, 87). As a Ph.D. candidate who was working toward a Harvard doctorate in philosophy, Eliot was well positioned to see the similarities between James's transactional "mosaic philosophy" and Pound's vorticist account of the image as "a node" through which "ideas are constantly rushing" (*GB*, 91–

92).[97] Eliot's caution to Pound was an avant-gardist's distinction between an academic temper of reflection and an artistic one of invention. But in terms of the oppositional vitality of the new set of artistic practices that were being embraced by Pound and his circle, James's American philosophy in particular would come to pose a serious threat. In shifting the premises of anarchist appeals to immediacy from spatial to temporal models, James facilitated the gradual transfer of the traditional village barter economy to modern American soil.[98] He thus enabled pluralists like Dewey and Williams to locate the basis of antifoundationalism not in the radical and reactive grounds of a utopian economy but rather in the progressive grounds of an industrial nation of immigrants. This shift was a productive one for the poet Williams, who used it as a basis for imagining that an improvisational form of measure might be wedded to the democratic "metal" of American speech; and it provided an inviting climate for the metonymic procedures of Marianne Moore's poetry as well. From the standpoint of American writers who, like Hurston, were well positioned to see that processual conceptions of Americanness were not as elastic as they appeared, it led to yet another set of literary innovations, including the invention of a narrative form that refused to rest on the measure of culture.

TWO

Imagism and the Gold Standard

I n late 1912 a London social worker named Harriet Shaw Weaver answered
a call for donations from a financially troubled feminist journal. Dora
Marsden, editor of the *Freewoman,* wrote back to her new benefactress in
early 1913. Marsden's exchange with Weaver led to friendship and to the joint
production of a pair of magazines that became an archive of modern poetry,
starting with the imagist movement. A handful of recent literary and cultural critics have begun to use the *New Freewoman* and the *Egoist* to investigate a correspondence between Edwardian radical political thought and a
contiguous discussion and practice of the arts. The political material of the
early issues of the magazines was indeed often harder and sharper than the
artistic content. Marsden, for her part, was a former suffragette whose early
journalistic efforts stirred controversy among European and American feminists. As the editor of the *Freewoman,* the *New Freewoman,* and early issues
of the *Egoist,* she also earns a spot in the history of anarchism as an "individualist" in the tradition of Max Stirner. Given the rare political atmosphere of
their first correspondence, Marsden's letter to Weaver is remarkable for the
prominence it assigns to a topic not commonly associated with imagism,
feminism, or anarchist politics: "I should like very much to have a talk with
you. I was extremely interested to read of your personal attitude in connection with 'usury.' It made me feel that the New Era—the Free Era—is nearer
than most of us imagine."[1]

Weaver and Marsden's discussion of usury stemmed from a series of *Free-*

woman articles written by an economist named Arthur Kitson.[2] Kitson's articles on usury and the gold standard appeared in the summer of 1912, toward the end of the magazine's one-year life. During that year Marsden had grown increasingly absorbed in British, French, and American strains of anarchism; and she weighed their premises and objectives against the mid-nineteenth-century nominalist criteria of the German Max Stirner, whose critique of generalizing humanist concepts such as "freedom" and "rights" had spoken to the former suffragette when she encountered them in 1911. The *Freewoman*'s variety of anarchistic or libertarian feminism initially shaped itself around attacks on the parliamentary objectives of the campaign for franchise from which Marsden had broken. But the magazine's political horizons soon encompassed a broader philosophical critique of liberalism and reform-oriented Fabian socialism. Kitson's articles on economics seemed to amplify the *Freewoman*'s growing antistatist politics. By September 1912 Marsden was convinced that it was not her magazine's frank discussion of sexual issues but rather its new "anti-capitalistic" slant that had inspired recent boycotts of the *Freewoman:* "The animosity which we rouse is not roused on the subject of sex-discussion. It is aroused on the question of capitalism. The opposition in the capitalist Press only broke out when we began to make it clear that the way out of the sex-problem was through the door of the economic problem."[3]

The "economic problem" that so concerned Marsden and Harriet Shaw Weaver in 1912–13 may not appear to have preoccupied those writers—Ezra Pound, Rebecca West, Richard Aldington—who were featured in the more literary *New Freewoman*. But neither were these artists indifferent to what Kitson and his associates were promoting. The socialist West, for her part, came to argue vigorously against the removal of state safeguards from the golden-age agrarian societies that Marsden came to advocate in her editorials.[4] And Marsden and Weaver were not alone in their concern for the social implications of the gold standard and usury. As early as 1908, A. R. Orage, the editor of the *New Age,* London's leading left-wing journal, had published articles advocating underconsumptionism, a theory of the economy dismissed as crankish by the Ricardian orthodoxy. Between 1910 and 1912 Orage published a spate of articles and letters, as many as his backer would allow, from underconsumptionists such as the anarchist Winthrope Donisthorpe and the radical economists Henry Meulen and Kitson.[5] In British radical circles before the war, currency reform had come into its own as a controversial instrument of social and political change.

Kitson's prewar writings on the gold standard and usury served as more than a lively discussion point for London's radical intellectuals. They also contributed, both directly and indirectly, to the development of Ezra Pound's poetry. Through Dora Marsden's writings, they provided a conceptual bridge between semiotic and aesthetic concerns and the Stirnerian "individualist" forms of anarchism that were fashionable in British and American radical intellectual circles before World War I. In this they lent a gloss of social urgency to Pound's imagist campaign to "true" poetic language through an aesthetic call for "direct treatment of the 'thing.'" Rooted in a second strain of anarchist thought, moreover, Kitson's writings helped Pound to formulate a more sophisticated aesthetic program—one that replaced imagism almost as soon as imagism was established. Linked in the poet's mind with Ernest Fenollosa's contemporaneous analysis of "The Chinese Written Character," Kitson's study of Britain's "Gold Fetish" finally contributed to the textual collage practice that Pound called the "ideogrammic method."

The historical French anarchist roots of Kitson's writings were not apparent to Pound when the poet read his economic treatises in 1912.[6] But Pierre Proudhon's notion of an innately ethical "economic organism" was at that time a touchstone for heretical currency theorists, including Kitson, who sought to recapture directness not by revaluing money per se but by restoring through it the sort of primitive barter transactions that were inhibited by all forms of "nominal" currency. Pound absorbed these foundational Proudhonian premises in two stages. He encountered them first in 1912–13, through his own readings of Kitson and through Marsden's contemporaneous essays on the "economic problem." His second, more knowing exposure came much later, in the 1930s. By that time Pound had made a long and careful study of unorthodox economic writings, beginning with the postwar Social Credit treatises of Major Douglas. By the 1930s he was able to recognize the importance of Proudhon's thought to the currency theories of Silvio Gesell and to Kitson himself, whom Pound had finally come to embrace as an economic colleague and correspondent. Between the early teens and the late thirties, Pound wove Proudhonian economic premises ever more explicitly into his "rose in the steel dust" vision of poetic assemblage (C, 463). And though early modern British calls for currency reform predated his stated efforts to recover, through the poetic "word made perfect," those very ethical social pathways that were traced by "righteous" forms of monetary exchange, these calls nevertheless came to play a defining role in the development of twentieth-century American poetry (468). And they can also be said to have prepared Pound to intuit, in 1938, the historical kinship between modern collage poetry, and Proudhon's vision of a relational economy, and American pragmatist efforts to construct a "mosaic philosophy" in which "ideas are true as they go into action."[7]

1. Imagism and Economic Nominalism

Pound had been an appreciative reader of British and American anarchist journals, including the *New Freewoman* and the *Revolutionary Almanack*, in 1913–14; but it was not until the mid-1930s that he came to acknowledge Proudhon's centrality to "live" forms of radical economic thought—and to related movements in American poetry and philosophy (*SP*, 440). By that time the poet's vision of a textual collage practice had been long in the making. And it had long been rooted in the Proudhonian tenets that had funded Kitson's discussions of the gold standard and usury. More immediately, however, Kitson's critique of the gold sovereign reached the poet through a radical "individualist" British milieu—one that appreciated not its historical but its *conceptual* affinities with Stirnerian anarchist critiques of enervating collective forms of identity. Because Pound's primary introduction to Kitson came in 1913, through the promptings of the "individualist" Marsden, Kitson's writings influenced him first as a model for his imagistic program of directness and social efficacy in writing. More than a reluctant "follower" of the politically and philosophically sophisticated editor Marsden, however, Pound had also been a firsthand reader of Kitson in 1912. And as the poet himself later intimated, this direct exposure had equipped him to absorb something of the French anarchist implications of underconsumptionist theory, even if he had not been able to recognize the importance of Proudhon's ideas at the time.

Working to make a name for himself in 1912 London, Pound encountered currents of British radicalism in T. E. Hulme's and Orage's political and artistic circles and in the pages of the *New Age*, where his own letters and columns appeared alongside Kitson's in 1912.[8] Pound was certainly aware of Kitson's essays on the gold standard. Years later, in a letter that he wrote to Kitson in 1933, the poet introduced himself to the economist as a former reader of his early contributions to Orage's journal. In his correspondence with the author of "The Gold Fetish" and other essays, Pound was defensive regarding his initial failure to have grasped through Kitson an idea that later came to dominate his political and aesthetic horizons. Holding his editor,

Orage, responsible for his "late" arrival to the world of radical economic thought, Pound complained to Kitson that "music criticism [was] the ONLY topic which was safe enough for Orage to permit me to write on it often [sic]."[9]

Pound was stretching the truth when he said that music criticism was the only writing that Orage would accept from him on a regular basis. And he was rewriting history when he suggested that it was his editor who had prevented him from cultivating his youthful inclinations—predilections that would have otherwise led him straight to "econ/ and politics."[10] If anything, the frustrated "music critic" of 1912 was the more recalcitrant defender of the continental divide between politics and the arts. But this early aesthete's posture soon showed signs of strain. By early 1913 Pound's writings about poetry and poetic language had begun to reflect at least the rhetoric of Kitson's condemnation of Britain's "gold fetish." And by the summer of that same year, when Kitson's ideas reached Pound a second time through the rarefied mixture of philosophy, politics, and economics that Dora Marsden wove into her *New Freewoman* commentaries, Pound was using the rhetoric of the gold standard and usury to fashion new claims for the social significance of poetic technique. Prompted by Marsden's variety of individualist anarchism, which was laced with the nominalistic elements of Kitson's critique of "commodity money," Pound began to investigate the relationship between forms of political and economic and semiotic representation; and it was during this period, in the months leading up to the August 1914 outbreak of war, that the poet began to address a range of current political topics, including woman suffrage, syndicalism, and state socialism. Despite the consensus among Pound scholars that the poet's introduction to economics did not take place until the end of World War I, it was at this moment, in this body of prewar writings, that radical economic theory began to shape modern poetry.

In letters to colleagues, Pound dismissed Marsden as a remote polemicist who addressed an isolated band of readers. "Miss Marsden . . . has her own clientele who look for her," Pound wrote to the poet Amy Lowell in 1914. Portraying Marsden as insignificant to the literary content of the early issues of the *Egoist*, he suggested that she wanted only "her corner or some corner to let loose in."[11] If anything, however, Marsden had come to challenge Pound by asking him to clarify his own political beliefs and to "define the relation of the arts to economics."[12] Cornered by Marsden in the summer of 1913, the poet had at first been less than effusive in professing the allegiance to "individualism" that his employer had demanded of him. Assuring his new editor that the addition of a new literary page would not "queer the editorial columns" of the *New Freewoman,* Pound reluctantly squared himself with the egoistic credo that decorated the masthead of her "Individualist Review." "I suppose I'm individualist," Pound wrote back to his superior, "I suppose I believe in the arts as the most effective propaganda for a sort of individual liberty that can be developed without public inconvenience."[13]

Pound's alliance with Marsden's brand of individualism, however, would soon run deeper than either these brusque deferrals or later dismissals might suggest. Over the months ahead, Marsden's challenges to Pound, together with her own editorial writings, would provide the poet with a sharply contemporary context—that of modern British antistatist politics—in which to place his growing condemnation of forms of verbal "usury" in language. By the fall of 1913, Pound had come to credit Marsden for prompting his essay "The Serious Artist," which was now appearing in two installments in the *New Freewoman. "You done it,"* Pound wrote, referring to the *ars poetica* that contained the "root" of what he later called "the ideogrammic method": "You axed me questions. And I'm not through yet."[14] "The Serious Artist" was indeed only the beginning of Pound's answer to Marsden. Shortly after Marsden had issued her challenge, Pound began to augment his nominalistic analyses of "interest" and "abstraction" with antistatist political views. By 1914, when the poet wrote of the artist as a rebel who has "dabbled with democracy and now is done with that folly," he was beginning to ally poetry with the "public inconvenience" of anarchist "direct action."[15] In placing modern poetry on a continuum with live forms of radical political action—forms such as the syndicalist strikes, riots, and gun battles that were threatening Britain's Liberal government between 1908 and 1914—Pound was following Marsden's lead.[16] It was through her example that he began to tally the linguistic and aesthetic significance of radical economic and political thought.

Through his own reading of Kitson, Pound appears to have begun to grasp the philosophical if not the political implications of radical economic theory even before Marsden issued her challenge to him. It was in early 1913, following his initial exposure to Kitson's *New Age* analysis of money, that Pound began to express a nominalistic contempt of abstraction in language. Shortly before his introduction to Marsden, Pound had written of self-referential varieties of poetic language as being akin to incest and to monetary interest, or coins bred from coins. In a January 1913 essay published in

Poetry, Pound criticized Yeats's sensual and highly "associative" language as a decadent aesthetic variety of endogamy. " 'Works of art,' " Pound wrote of Yeats's "glamorous" verses, " 'beget works of art.' "[17] The timing of Pound's resonant indictment of his "symbolist" contemporary suggests that Kitson's condemnations of the gold fetish and of monetary interest may have held a broader philosophical significance for the *Imagiste* who began calling for "direct treatment of the 'thing' " in a March 1913 edition of *Poetry* magazine (*LE,* 3). But it was the Stirnerian anarchist Marsden who would awaken Pound to the radical political significance of such monetary and linguistic forms of inbreeding. As the first of Pound's London contemporaries to have conceived of both economic and linguistic varieties of abstraction as impediments to social revolution, the anarcho-feminist helped Pound to convert a colorful trope, which linked language and money as mediums of exchange, into a full-blown aesthetic. This aesthetic would prove central to the imagist technical procedures that Pound introduced and eventually modified in 1914, before bringing them to fruition in his long collage poem, *The Cantos.*

In letters in which she challenged Pound "to define the relation of the arts to economics" and in a series of *New Freewoman* leaders written in 1913, Marsden merged poetry and politics, subjecting both linguistic and political systems of representation to Stirnerian scrutiny.[18] Invoking Stirner's suspicion of all species of universals, Marsden argued that the practical value of words, political causes, and gold sovereigns alike was corrupted by the "decaying sweetness" of the ideas or the nominal values to which they referred.[19] It was here that the "cleansing" of poetry, politics, and money came to assume aesthetic and social revolutionary proportions. When Marsden suggested that the poet's "real" words should be modeled upon the heretical economist's "real" currency as an instrument of social change, she encouraged Pound's early adaptation of economic theory to poetic technique. Through her conceptual assimilation of Kitson's writings on currency and value to a larger antistatist political and philosophical platform, Marsden showed Pound how the imagistic if not the ideogrammic method might become a medium for restoring social efficacy to poetry.

❖ Following Pound's own lead, scholars have unanimously asserted that modern poetry absorbed nothing of economics until 1919, when Maj. Clifford H. Douglas made his debut at the *New Age.*[20] It was during the months that followed Pound's introduction to Douglas—whom Orage called "the Einstein of economics"—that the poet claimed to have been struck by the "blindin'" force of Douglas's underconsumptionist credit theories.[21] By Pound's account, Douglas had catalyzed "the acute phase" of the poet's own millennial "battle with ignorance." Before his exposure to Douglas's *Economic Democracy* (1920), Pound recalled, all "political" and "social theory had lain outside [his] view."[22] In quieter venues, however, Pound acknowledged that his conversion to underconsumptionism had been less than immediate and that he may have absorbed the writings of other radical economists before Major Douglas. In a letter to Pound written during the early 1930s, the underconsumptionist Kitson accused Douglas of having stolen his ideas from Kitson's own earlier, unheralded writings.[23] In answer, Pound suggested that Douglas, as a self-taught economist, had most likely read Kitson's work during an early period of his self-training and absorbed it incrementally, and then later reformulated it, having forgotten his source. "Having got my own economics a bit late," Pound confessed, "I can understand Doug/ thinking the moon hadn't been discovered it [*sic*] until he saw it there on the horizon."[24]

Pound may have fashioned this revision of the origins of Social Credit in an effort to soothe an ally who was jealous of Douglas. But this was not the first time that he had intimated that Douglas's insights—and his own quick conversion to them—may have owed something to unattributed sources. Writing in an obscure London arts journal in 1920, Pound claimed that with a single reading of Douglas's *Economic Democracy,* he had been able to grasp a network of related economic ideas. He went on to explain this experience as an outgrowth of his and Douglas's shared familiarity with a "single unobserved source." "What people do not understand," Pound wrote, "is that from a certain perhaps 'incomprehensible,' perhaps 'unconspicuous' or apparently unimportant *seed* of idea sprout vast crops of leaves and fruits of idea."

> You hear talk of "simultaneous discovery" of telephones, etc. These things probably proceeded from a single unobserved source. To get to personal example.
>
> Having read a certain amount of [Rémy de] Gourmont I write in criticism of him not merely an "idea" which is found in one of his books which I had not read, but I use the very words in which he expresses that "idea."
>
> Having read a single book by Maj. Douglas, I evolve a complete currency-arrangement identical with an evolution which he had already written but not published. In neither case were the books which I had read specifically *about* the subject on which my "constructive" thought had proceeded.[25]

In this passage Pound is vague as to what he means by a "single unobserved source"; but he is talking about something firmer than an ambient variety of influence. In the first example that he gives, Pound is not recounting an instance of mystical dictation when he speaks of having independently formulated not just Gourmont's " 'idea' " but the "very words" that Gourmont had inscribed into a book that Pound had not seen. Rather, he suggests that he and Gourmont both drew from an additional "source," or a text, that was familiar to both. And in the example of his reading of Douglas, his reference to a "complete currency-arrangement" suggests an additional text authored by a money theorist like Kitson. Pound himself did not begin to systematically link monetary and linguistic reform until the calamities of the Great War and the economic crisis of the 1930s had combined to awaken him to the apocalyptic consequences of the "muddying" of these analogous mediums.[26] But he does appear to have absorbed the conceptual premises of Douglas's Social Credit theories through Kitson's and Marsden's essays; and he appears to have adapted those premises to his poetry several years before he began to think about economics per se.

Pound's reluctance to acknowledge an economic source prior to Douglas may have been an outgrowth of his own failure to have seen "the moon on the horizon." This sort of blindness, moreover, would have been a blessing to a writer who wished to revise modern literary history. Despite his early aestheticism, Pound was from the beginning an organicist who believed that the related matters of economic and linguistic reference had been equally determined by a network of social and ethical concerns. If Pound was in fact remembering a specific body of essays that were " 'incomprehensible' " to him in 1913—and remembering them well enough to recognize their affinity with Douglas's writings—his failure to name Kitson, and perhaps Dora Marsden as well, suggests that at an early date he had chosen to construct an organic genesis for his poetic method—one that would require him to illustrate an independent flowering of artistic innovations along a course that was homologous to, but not causally dependent upon, contemporary economic "breakthroughs." From the standpoint of such a myth, it would have been a convenience for the poet to have misplaced the earlier economic "*seed*" that set him on his own ostensibly independent aesthetic course—a course that would eventually bring him into a conceptual alliance first with economic "Mahatma[s]," including Major Douglas and Silvio Gesell, and then with the pragmatist philosophers who seemed allied in their efforts to orient empiricism around relations.[27] Whatever Pound himself was willing to say or to see about the significance of economic theory to modern philosophy and to new methods of poetry, however, Kitson's prewar discussions of the ethics of monetary reference do share a marked structural correspondence to the discussions of semiotics and reference that soon preoccupied the poet. Registering in Pound's aesthetic pronouncements and practices alike, this correspondence should encourage his readers, together with readers of the many poets who have drawn from Pound's work, to consider the historical significance of prewar underconsumptionist thought to the modern practices of discursive directness and of the disjunctive collage method in poetry, as well as to Pound's eventual recognition of a kinship between these practices and modern pragmatist philosophy.

As early as February 1913, Pound's developing sense of how, and why, poems should acquire "a sane valuation" was being more or less directly shaped by the technical and ethical concerns of British underconsumptionist economists.[28] Underconsumptionism was, by John M. Keynes's coinage, an "underworld" theory of currency and credit that measured the strength of an economy according to its expediency of consumption rather than its accumulation of surplus.[29] The word *underconsumption* describes the condition to be remedied by a reorienting of value. The notion that value should be based on consumption, or on the relation between consumption and production, rather than on production alone, ran counter to an axiom known as Say's Law, which had dominated mainstream British and American economics until the Keynesian revolution of the late 1930s.[30] In *The General Theory of Employment, Interest, and Money* of 1936, Keynes had based his call for "direct state intervention" as a means of "escape from prolonged and perhaps interminable depression" on a refutation of Say's Law, or the conventional belief that "the whole of the costs of production must necessarily be spent in the aggregate, directly or indirectly, on purchasing the product."[31] (As a production-oriented measure, Say's Law reflected and perpetuated an economy of scarcity by placing a permanent limit on purchasing power.) To economists whose traditional beliefs had been shaken by a decade of economic depression, Keynes had "proven" that price should reflect more than merely the costs of production.

The classical notion that price should be determined by the costs of production results in what economists call a labor theory of value. Before the Keynesian revolution, a handful of late-Victorian economists had begun to challenge the labor theory by suggesting that price should also be based on the supply of money and credit available for purchase.[32] In league with both British and American "individualist" anarchists, these economists held that value should be a function not only of production but also of consumptive utility. A product's value should not be prescriptive but should be descriptive of its use to the individuals who made up the market. Drawing from the unconventional conceptions of value that had been put forth by these anarchistically inclined Victorian economists, a more politically eclectic group of economic renegades emerged in England in the 1880s. Calling themselves "underconsumptionists," this group proposed to break the stifling grip of the labor theory's price-production correspondence by increasing the availability of money or credit to the consumer. The overdrawing of credit would be held in check by the buyer's own concern for his or her reputation on the market. Freer access to credit would benefit producers by increasing circulation, and a healthier society would spring from a wider access to goods.

Kitson's study of the British gold sovereign in the *New Age* and the *Freewoman* reflected the politically eclectic spirit of these late-nineteenth-century underconsumptionist challenges to the labor theory of value. In his writings of 1912–13, the inventor-turned-economist displayed a liberal confidence in the possibility of economic reform. But he traced his underconsumptionist analysis and remedy to French anarchist sources. In a letter published in Marsden's 1912 journal, the *Freewoman*, Kitson distinguished between "money," which was "a *social* instrument," and "gold," which was "a commodity, and the subject of private ownership"; he credited this distinction to "P. J. Proudhon, one of the greatest minds in the economic world" ("MCI," 256).[33] Kitson and Proudhon both despised gold as a medium that fostered a commodity theory of money and hence a labor theory of value. When currency laws require that notes and checks be redeemable in gold, they believed, money is then anchored as itself an article of value. Endogenous gold-standard money reinforces the labor theory of value. The price of goods remains centered on production because the availability of money is determined by a factor estranged from consumptive demand. As an economist who vacillated between liberal and anarchist sympathies, Kitson proposed not to destroy the capitalist state but to repair it by substituting a variant of a "quantity" theory of money for the gold-backed commodity theory, so shifting the Ricardian emphasis on production, or surplus, to a more social emphasis on consumption.[34] (Whereas "quantity" money is often conceived to enhance the issuing state's control of the economy, Kitson viewed it as a means of destroying those financiers' monopolies with which the state was complicitous.) Recognizing that elements of a quantity theory of currency as a circulating medium were already present in England's surplus economy, Kitson proposed to purge the sovereign of its fetishized value by abolishing the gold standard ("GF," 94).

Kitson's writings against the gold fetish came to complement the nominalist critique of liberal democracy and socialism that Marsden and others were sounding in the early teens; and they elaborated this critique through an analysis of money that bore a structural resemblance to Pound's concurrent analysis of verse. Pound's condemnations of Yeats's "symbolist" poetry as a form of verbal usury and his concurrent plea for a harder, more compact type of poetry surfaced shortly after Kitson had begun contributing to the *Freewoman* and the *New Age*. Herbert Schneidau sees that Pound's imagist phase broke suddenly from "a dogged rear-guard action," which the poet had previously maintained against the Fordian principles of direct, presentational writing (*EP*, 13). Pound's conversion was rapid and thorough. By early 1913 he was even criticizing the interpretive excesses of passages from the early work of his new mentor, Ford Madox Ford. "Don't use such an expression as 'dim lands *of peace*'. It dulls the image. It mixes an abstraction with the concrete. It comes from the writer's not realizing that the natural object is always the *adequate* symbol" (*LE*, 5). For Hugh Kenner, the technical upheaval of imagism was a reaction against the excesses of a generation of British postsymbolist poets (*PE*, 180–91). Writers such as Arthur Symons, Ernest Dowson, and John Gray were at the center of a turn-of-the-century group of "pictorial" poets in London. Pound objected to the wavering between presentative and interpretive discourses in such postsymbolist poems as Symons's "On the Beach," which dissolves lines like "Night, a grey sky, a ghostly sea" into abstract formulations such as "The shoreline of infinity" (180). The Ford poem from which Pound drew "dim lands of peace" was similarly inconsistent in its diction. To Pound, Ford's 1904 "On a Marsh Road: Winter Nightfall" committed the postsymbolist error of hesitating between subjective and objective relation, or of combining incompatible approaches to reference (181).[35]

Pound's campaign against abstract diction in poetry was based on his belief that interpretive "comment" detracted from presentative "constatation of facts" ("AP," 662). His formula for a more direct poetry, however, was not simply an aesthete's call for fresher description. Imagism was more than a matter of taste. The two discursive modes distinguished by Pound in his criticism of Ford's poem differ in their referential character. The overinvested Yeatsian symbol "'*of peace*'" veils, or "dulls," the straight-spoken thing, "'dim lands.'" Pound equates the concrete part of Ford's phrase with the "natural object" itself. By removing the symbolist veil and placing the object directly in the poem, Pound asserted the possibility of referential transparency. Properly trimmed, the sign could be made true to the thing signified. The imagist call to "Go in fear of abstractions" has long been viewed as the expression of an essentially "disciplinary" or "hygienic" aesthetic program, but it was also bound to a more positive struggle for a direct correspondence between words and the things they represent.[36]

As an underconsumptionist advocate of currency reform, Kitson believed that gold was damaging to society because it was torn between two incompatible functions.[37] He provided a memorable description of the competing functions of gold money in his 1912 *New Age* letter captioned "The Gold Fetish."

> I once saw a child deliberating on which of the two utilities presented by his possession of a chocolate soldier he would enjoy. As a toy soldier it was a plaything, but then he had to forget it was a sweetmeat. He could only enjoy one utility at a time. In short, it was not *both* toy and sweetmeat, but toy *or* sweetmeat. He saw he could only enjoy one utility by destroying or ignoring the other. My contention regarding commodity money is similar. Gold sovereigns may either function as money or commodities—they cannot do both. They cannot be both sovereigns and commodities at one time. ("GF," 94)

The problem with fetishized gold was like that of referentiality in postsymbolist poetry. Innately conflicted, its "abstract" commodity value ignored or, more pointedly, destroyed its "concrete" worth as an article of circulation. In Kitson's view, gold-backed currency was flawed because it corrupted the transactions it was intended to serve. As a token of exchange, the gold sovereign was to be pressed into circulation. But as a commodity it was an item to be hoarded. Kitson wanted to produce a truer, more exchange-oriented form of currency by purging the sovereign of the commodity value that inhibited its healthful circulation. Once the sovereign was cleansed of its fictional value, the British economy would cease to encourage the accumulation of surplus: it would revolve instead around the more ethical imperative of transactions between producers and consumers of goods. The structural similarity between Kitson's analysis of gold currency and Pound's critique of postsymbolist poetry does not necessarily reflect a conscious effort to model imagism on underconsumptionist money theory. But in light of

Pound's later admission that he had come to "evolve" his first "currency-arrangement" through "a certain perhaps 'incomprehensible' . . . *seed* of idea," it may reveal to us the germinal stage of the poet's eventual "vast crop" of economic-aesthetic hybrids.

The referential cleanness of Kitson's de-fetishized sovereign might itself seem analogous to the cleanness of language that Pound advocated in formulating his poetics of presence. But Kitson was important to the development of modern poetry more for the way that he related currency theory to the larger critique of the labor theory of value. By 1913 even the "individualist" Marsden had begun to grasp the linguistic and hence the "poetic" significance of Kitson's suggestion that clean money could restore ethical patterns of circulation and consumption; and Pound's imagist and later ideogrammic methodological innovations were at least partly spurred by her suggestion that he consider both the social and the aesthetic significance of underconsumptionist economic theory. Through Marsden's promptings, Proudhon's notion of a relation-based "economic organism" came to play an indirect role in Pound's abandonment of his overly "STATIONARY" imagist aesthetics.[38] In the progression from Pound's imagist to his ideogrammic aesthetics, social and economic iniquities would be corrected not only by the clear terms that were elicited by the "direct treatment of the 'thing'" but also by the ideogrammic relations that came to span these clear terms. Poetry would become meaningful to society, in other words, when it was made true both to things in the world and to the dynamic and foundational relations between them. By encouraging Pound to come to terms with the political and linguistic implications of underconsumptionist theories of currency and value, Marsden affected modernist aesthetics beyond the imagists' poetry of presence. In apparent concordance with the model supplied by underconsumptionist currency theory, the clamorous collage method of *The Cantos* emerged as a gradual outgrowth of what Pound called a decade of "poetical reform," one that turned not only on "the scrutiny of the word" but also on "the cleaning up" of the "syntax" that joined words together (*SP*, 321).

2. Pound's Early Politics

Like a number of left-leaning Edwardian intellectuals, and like James Joyce among the Italian anarchists during the first decade of the 1900s, Pound was dismissive of socialist initiatives but quick to identify himself with anarchist political programs.[39] In some ways it is not surprising that an ambitious young poet should have publicly declared his sympathy, as Pound did in 1914, with revolutionary "syndicalist" platforms.[40] As Raymond Williams has suggested, trade-based forms of alliance and rebellion were broadly attractive to modern artists who identified themselves both with aristocrats and with starving workers whose productions were too lightly rewarded.[41] Many innovative modern writers, Pound, Joyce, and William Carlos Williams among them, were in fact drawn both to syndicalist forms of anarchism and to the more rigorously antifoundationalist premises that individualists like Marsden set forth in the *New Freewoman* and the *Egoist*. Among those modernists who toyed with anarchist sympathies, however, it is Pound whose affiliations would eventually prove to be the most vexed. By the 1930s the poet's early "syndicalist" vision of "a guild of the intelligent poor and near-poor" had given way to more authoritarian calls for a centrally stabilized credit system—calls that Pound came to augment, in 1943, with radio appeals for the execution of Jewish financiers.[42]

Pound studies have gained much from poststructuralists who have begun to sort out the conceptual conflation of money, language, and anti-Semitism in a corpus that includes not only poems and translations but also the rambling transcripts of fascist propaganda that the writer broadcast to American troops in Italy during World War II. In the process of reconciling Pound's damaging anti-Semitic tirades with his celebrated lyrics, however, many contemporary critics have portrayed the imagist poetics of presence as an innately reactionary campaign against "difference," or forms of referential "excess" or uncertainty in language.[43] The left radical sympathies that surface in Pound's early writing begin to complicate the portrayal of imagism as an essentially "protofascistic" aesthetic program; for this reason, these sympathies have been largely missing from contemporary evaluations of the poet. Despite the volume of Pound scholarship, the traditional consensus among critics regarding the "unbroken line" from imagism to fascism has diminished our understanding of the historical genesis of the poet's fascist and anti-Semitic beliefs.[44] A recovery of the historical anarchistic political and economic contexts of imagism suggests that the imagist campaign for "presence" in language was not simply an innately oppressive or reactionary aesthetic appeal. Pound's development was in many ways more troubling. The poet's early exposure to anarchism and to underconsumptionist economic movements suggests that his gravest "error" was not his belief that writing should be mystically "true" to things or to relations. His mistake was rather a less partisan conviction that value and meaning should be restored to ethical uses by a knowing elite. This mistake has been repeated by post-structuralist critics who measure Pound's early aesthetics against the essentially liberating measures of semiotic "difference" and "play."

Pound was not an unswerving advocate of any single political or economic program or platform in 1913; but neither was he entirely an aesthete in his early aloofness from the sort of doctrines that came to commandeer his life and writings. Like his early aesthetic formulations, his "political" writings of the pre–World War I years turned on an unstable commitment to the preservation of individual differences through mechanisms of non-political reform. Political reform, Pound believed, was the medium of "the theorist," who "constantly proceeds as if his own case, his own limits and predilections were the typical case, or even as if it were the universal" ("SA," 163). Responding to the challenge that Marsden had put to him after her own encounter with Kitson's writings on the evils of "'interest'" and gold currency, Pound had called in "The Serious Artist" for a cleaner, more clear-eyed type of poetry, one that resisted the symbolist commodification of language and the overly theoretical "false report" that it engendered. "False report," Pound suggested, stemmed from a neglect of the local; this was an error that was endemic to both poetry and politics. Plainly, he suggested, the state in England based its laws on false report, on the application of "a code devised for one state of society" to "a different state of society" (162).

Addressing "the relation of the arts" to "econ/ and politics" in his 1913 essay, Pound indicted all authorities complicitous with the state, from the Fabian "Sydney Webbs" to the bishop of London, whom the poet labeled a "*souteneur*," a pimp, for his prohibition of birth control, his application of "morals designed for a nomadic tribe" to "a people crowded into the slums of a modern metropolis" ("SA," 161). The church's betrayal of its constituents to biblical law revealed its own fetishistic blindness to modern urban London. The vitality of the arts lay here in their production of a clearer social vision:

> As inequities can exist because of refusals to consider the actualities of a law in relation to a social condition, so can inequities exist through refusal to consider the actualities of the composition of the masses, or of the individuals to which they are applied.

If all men desired above everything else two acres and a cow, obviously the perfect state would be that state which gave to each man two acres and a cow.

If any science save the arts were able more precisely to determine what the individual does actually desire, then that science would be of more use in providing the data for ethics. (162)

Pound's 1913 push to revalue language, to restore an "equity" between the sign and the thing signified, then, was attended by a progressive belief in scaled reform and also by shadings of an "individualist" commitment to "difference" and autonomy among "men." But these commitments also hinged on a belief that true reportage and clear writing would be finally their own socially transformative ends. Here, Pound's aesthetic is as politically volatile as Kitson's Proudhonian belief that a properly aligned industrial economy will engender an ethical society ("GF," 94). The technical program of imagism, as well as that of the ideogrammic method that Pound extrapolated from imagism, in fact partakes of a mixed political heritage, one that in turn draws, either directly or indirectly, from the anarchism of Proudhon, the reactionary medievalism of early "underconsumptionist" intellectuals like John Ruskin, and the variously anarchistic and liberal tendencies of the modern money scientist Kitson.[45]

One of the more difficult questions posed by Pound's eventual turn to fascism and anti-Semitism is how a self-styled "individualist," or even an avowedly "syndicalist" proponent of a decentralized guild-based economy, might come to support a politics that is committed to the suppression of "difference." Though there are some strong historical ties between anarchists and fascists in modern Italy particularly, it is a long journey from the egoistic "individual" to the nationalist "subject" and from the Proudhonian village to the modern fascist state. Zeev Sternhell traces the route from radicalism to reaction in modern Europe, arguing that a small group of "radical" intellectuals succeeded in shifting the lines upon which socialist and left anarchistic struggle was premised. Believing that the Marxists' "proletariat" and the syndicalists' "trade guilds" had equally exhausted themselves as means of revolutionary change, these intellectuals shifted the objects of revolutionary resistance away from capitalistic owners and toward a new group of "parasitic" "nonproducers." "Nonproducers"—which included bankers and bureaucrats—were portrayed as outsiders who threatened an otherwise integral bourgeois economy. As outsiders, they helped to perpetuate the idea that revolution was a national affair, and not a matter of class or trade affiliation (*BF,* 196, 227–28, 248, 253). Although racialist anti-Semitic beliefs were not an integral component of European fascism, they were all too readily adapted to its emerging nationalistic models.

We can find stirrings of this nationalist and racialist rhetoric in the radical economic and political views that Pound expressed before 1915. The imagist Pound was certainly versed in archaic prohibitions against usury, for example, but he was also attuned to the xenophobic and anti-Semitic overtones of Kitson's and Marsden's discussions of money that breeds money. Marsden had acquired her own belief that the "Free Era" was contingent on the banishing of "usury" roughly a year before her professional association with Pound. Here, she displayed an unacknowledged debt to Proudhon, the anarchist whose vision of an ethical "Social Contract" society she had publicly rebuked as impractical.[46] It was during the summer of 1912, when Kitson's letters and articles dominated the pages of the *Freewoman,* that Marsden began to express through economics her disappointment with current radical political movements. In an article called "Why Revolt Drags," Marsden challenged socialists and syndicalists alike for their "arresting[ly]" "respectful attitude towards capital." The radicals' adherence to " 'Money-ism' " laid the "dead hand" of capital on revolution. Marsden espoused underconsumptionism, reiterating its central distinction between real consumable wealth (production "for the Mouth") and nominal surplus (production "for the Ground"). "If we define 'wealth' as 'that which tends to satisfy human needs,' we recognize as wealth, not money, but specific commodities, food, clothing, houses, railways, and so on, and upon considering the nature of the things which comprise wealth, we recognize an element which militates against accumulation, an element which makes the consumption, the using up of wealth, the lesser of the two evils for persons which have the itch to hoard" ("WRD," 165).

Marsden followed the Proudhonian logic of Kitson's "money problem" in her editorial, linking her critique of a labor theory of value to commodity money, or the gold standard, which she discussed as a cause of the hoarding that co-opted revolution. Proudhon's vision of a society based on innately ethical exchanges brought out reactionary as well as revolutionary faces of Edwardian libertarianism. When Marsden blamed fetishized gold for "usury—a state of affairs . . . which should properly be regarded as criminal, as it was in times when religions had moral force," she invoked an oddly essentializing rhetoric that, for many, would have signaled an archaic call for the scapegoating of Jews ("WRD," 165). Marsden's appeal to the anti-Semitic sentiments of many modern intellectuals might be said to spring from a reactionary alliance between Stirner's call to individual autonomy and the specter of racial degeneration that bolstered European nationalist impulses before the war. But this tendency toward anti-Semitic reaction was not specific to full blooded "egoists" like Stirner and Marsden. Anti-Semitic persecution also entered the twentieth century through modern Proudhonians as well, along with a range of other left radical thinkers.[47] Following a wave of Jewish immigration into late-nineteenth-century England, British radical camps of all stripes—libertarian, socialist, and medievalist alike—saw an influx of anti-Semites into their ranks. The utopian society that each group envisioned was at times shored by the fear of an international conspiracy among Jewish financiers.[48]

As Marsden extended her critique of "principles" from politics to the arts in the *New Freewoman*, she seemed to view imagism implicitly as an organic component of the impending "Free Era" that she had spoken about to Weaver. In this deeply Proudhonian social vision, "usury" and "interest" would be forbidden as forms of economic and semiotic nonproduction. More immediately and more explicitly, however, she viewed imagism as a potential Stirnerian literary program, one with nominalistic political and philosophical underpinnings.[49] Marsden gathered poetry into a Stirnerian indictment of sentimentalizing political rhetoric when she wrote of the suffragette leader Emmeline Pankhurst: "She has pinioned herself with words—words—words, and these, not her own. She ventured into the maze of the symbolists, whose vulturous progeny—the empty concepts—got her!"[50] In her writings on aesthetics in later issues of the *New Freewoman*, she blended Kitson's plea for de-commodified money into her nominalistic critique of universals and of the intoxicating referent in language. In an editorial entitled "The Art of the Future," for example, Marsden quarreled with her literary editor, Pound, on the politics of reference in poetry ("AF," 183). Pound was by this time using Marsden's "Individualist Review" to promote "presentative" verse, and he had recently contributed a serialized installment of "The Serious Artist" as a lead editorial. In her public exchange with Pound on nominalism and the arts, Marsden bemoaned the reluctance of poets to follow the example of modern scientists who, in attending to "the 'thing,'" have broken "the dominion of the guess": "The experimental method brought the scientific free-thought period to an end. Observation of the subject put verbal notions out of court. With art on the other hand, matters have but reached at their ultimate limit the 'interest' of the verbal treatment, the imaginative interpretation" (181).[51] Marsden's condemnation of literature, through " 'interest,' " as a form of verbal usury, was delivered in the context of her suggestion to Pound that the potent social consequences of poetry lay hidden in "the relation of the arts to economics." Now placed in the context of anarchist political theory, the metaphor of language as money came to mark something more than a mere rhetorical incursion of underworld economics into a discussion of the arts. Words that refer not to some real subject but to other words have become the articles of usury that wrest power from the real subject and contribute to the socially pernicious reign or "dominion" of words themselves. For Marsden and Pound, verbal interest had become a matter of immediate, and vexing, political significance.

The shifts in Dora Marsden's nominalist thought, from political to economic to aesthetic registers, trace the avenues through which contemporary strains of radicalism and reaction alike were channeled into Pound's formulation of a new kind of poetry. Marsden's association of poetry with usury had indeed been sounded earlier, with very different political overtones, by the poet himself in early 1913. Anticipating the nominalist logic of Marsden's criticism of the "symbolist" leader of the suffragette "Cause," Pound had indicted the "symbolist" Yeats, who "believes in the glamour and associations which hang near the words. 'Works of art beget works of art' " ("SR," 125). Herbert Schneidau points out that Pound's complaint here is against Yeats's "derivative" or excessively allusive style (*EP,* 16). But Pound's phrasing also appeals vaguely to the righteous authority prohibiting "money that begets money." Marsden would eventually struggle to enlighten Pound to the revolutionary political potential of verbal and economic forms of nominalism; and Pound's recognition of this potential would enable him to raise his push for presence in poetry from the realm of the aesthetic. But even before the presentative method came to acquire radical political overtones, the poet-critic's appeal to archaic moral injunctions—"Works of art beget works of art"—had been consistent with Marsden's 1912 reference to biblical law in her discussion of monetary interest, and with Kitson's, when the economist preached of usury in the *Freewoman:* " 'The children born of it are Fire and Sword, Red ruin and the breaking up of Laws.' "[52] Implicit in these Edwardian judgments against the opacity or the "glamour" of commodified money or words is an assumption that fetishism blocks the healthful circulation of goods in an economy, or of ethics in a society, or of truth in language. Pound's writings on poetic technique in 1913–14 would be bolstered by an anarchistic antistatism that viewed abstracting political mechanisms as impediments to the attainment of healthful social "economy." But these writings were poised to draw from a reactionary tendency to circumscribe such an economy as a besieged utopia. Through the radical anarchistic and reactionary currents that saturated the underconsumptionist recovery of the innate goodness of direct transactions between producers and consumers, Pound acquired his understanding of "the poem" as itself an overall referential system whose health finally depended not so much on the hardness of its components as on a free circulation among them.

3. The Ideogram and the Anarchist Barter Society

Pound's shift from imagism to vorticism to the ideogrammic method entails a rethinking of reference in language. The imagist poetics of presence gives way to a poetry not of things but of relations. From an economic standpoint, this new emphasis might be said to anticipate not only Pound's writings in the 1930s on the velocity of money—"Blood circulates in the veins"—but the Keynesian substitution in the late 1930s and the 1940s of the orthodox orientation on production for a "structuralist" economy based on the relationship between production and consumption.[53] The Keynesian revolution, however, can be viewed as a late-coming incorporation into economics of conceptual changes similar to those that had registered in the early twentieth century in abstract painting and in collage, in physics ("mass is energy"), in philosophy (Bertrand Russell and William James on "relations"), and particularly in Saussurean structuralist conceptions of language.[54] However broadly "modernism" might be construed, the historical relationship between modern poets and the anarchists who provided challenging ideological contexts for their work reveals that the shift from a poetics of presence to a more dynamic understanding of verse is ingrained in the logic of underconsumptionist currency reform: Kitson registers his complaint with opaque commodity money in the push for a dynamic economy based on healthful exchange.

In his study of late-nineteenth-century American money theory and the development of the naturalist literary subject, Walter Benn Michaels finds a contradiction in the logic of "goldbugs," or conservatives who defended the intrinsic monetary value of gold against both "silverite" advocates of a mixed currency and paper-money radicals. The materialist defense of the natural value of gold, suggests Michaels, is negated by its affirmation of the artifice of gold currency: "metals do not become money; they always were; hence they never are."[55] The hoarding of gold demonstrates not a love of nature itself but a love of nature's seeming representation of money. Mimesis in nature, Michaels points out, tests the logic of materialism. It implies the presence of a mind that fashions the artifice of mimicry from resemblance. Gold thus shows us ourselves as not mere material brutes but as imagining souls.

> In nature—which is to say, from the positivistic and material standpoint of the brain—objects may look like one another but never represent one another. Only the unnatural makes representation possible, and it makes it possible by imagining the natural as artificial. In a certain sense, of course, this proves to be a mistake; the objects we find on the beach aren't really mimicking other objects. But in imagining that they are, we imagine for the first time the possibility not just of other brains but of other minds. Indeed, we imagine for the first time the possibility of our own minds. The mistaken love of representation that makes representation possible must first appear as a mistake about itself, as when we take the magpie's love of beauty for the human love of mimesis. In this respect, the love of natural things that resemble artificial ones is itself an instance of that resemblance, epitomizing the immaterial distinction between what we are made of and what we are. Thus, our primitive love of natural things that look artificial turns out to be nature's way of revealing to our brains the existence of our minds. (171)

Michaels follows the logic of the gold standard here to "the potential discrepancy between material and identity, the discrepancy that makes money, painting, and, ultimately, persons possible" (169–70). Offering a reading that figures "resistance" as an outgrowth of the capitalist economy itself, he is concerned less with the ideological status of challenges to the gold standard than he is with the emergence through them of the economy as a "subject" that affirms "the possibility of persons" (176–80). Here, gold is valued as a constitutive element of its defenders and its detractors alike.

Michaels's work has been criticized for promoting a general political "quietism"; but his specific account of the tension in naturalism between material and identity offers us a provocative way of thinking about imagism and the modernist shift to the more dynamic aesthetics of vorticism and the ideogrammic method. The imagist claim that the "natural object is always the adequate symbol" also cues the discovery that matter is mind: natural objects do not become symbols; they always were; hence they never are. Imagistic presence, that is to say, posits in nature the very artifice of representation that it seeks to supplant. The natural object grows unsteady as a standard. Writing of Pound's 1913–14 vorticist period, Marjorie Perloff has suggested that despite the poet's quarrel with futurism, Italian manifestos calling for "the destruction of syntax" alerted him that "simultaneity" and "dynamism" were vital qualities for poetry in an age of advertising placards, mass transit, and radio.[56] Pound's own retrospective account of vorticism as a response to "the defect of earlier imagist propaganda," its inadequate identification with only "the STATIONARY image," suggests that it was "the natural object" that had been placed in crisis by Marinetti (*ABCR*, 52).[57] Insofar as the "logic" that links "the gold standard" to "literary naturalism" is a historical one, the revolution in poetry precipitated by technology might be seen to coincide with a crisis in the logic of materialism in economic thought.

In its particular economic context, Pound's moment differs from this theoretical "naturalist" moment in that gold was conceived by underconsumptionists like Kitson and Marsden not as itself "natural" but as an objectified impediment to a more organic conception of nature. Nature's yield was not metal but exchange. This dynamic understanding of natural systems and processes substitutes activity for material, evading the hard contradiction of the object as a symbolized construct of the mind. But the emphasis on relations does not vanquish that contradiction altogether. Underconsumptionists from Ruskin to Kitson to Pound looked from mechanical productionist economic models to natural, organic systems of generation and distribution. What they found in the primary systems of nature was the trace of intelligence itself. An economy that pulses wealth "like blood in the veins" flushes natural systems with subjective "mind" in the way that gold mints its subjective money from nature. This confusion of natural with invented intelligent systems is native to ethical anarchist thought. Appealing to immanent pathways of fair exchange, the mutualist Proudhon naturalized not laws but the early-nineteenth-century village economies of his native rural France. Subsequent underconsumptionist appeals to ethical production, distribution, and consumption provided a standard of naturalized relations in place of the classicists' precious metal. The money heretics' economy was anchored not by gold but by an unwritten golden age—an era that always was and therefore never is. Saussure's attention to differential relations between signs can be seen as a reckoning with this lingering materialist tendency to naturalize relations. The idea of immanent linguistic structures, like that of founding Keynesian relations between production and consumption, does not locate these systems in nature per se, but it still displaces "mind" from the perceiver of things to the closed field of their transactions.

Pound conceived the ideogrammic method and the mosaic compositional field of *The Cantos* through underconsumptionism, anarchism, and an inventive study of the Chinese written character, one that was begun when the poet came into possession of Ernest Fenollosa's lecture notes in late 1913. Pound's aesthetic transition from the nominalistic "hygiene" of imagism to the dynamic practice of the ideogrammic method corresponds conceptually to Kitson's assumption that a de-commodification of money will restore to the medium its circulatory properties, making wealth flow "like blood in the human body."[58] Whereas Marsden's contempt for the " 'interest' " of poetic language suggests a bolstering of her philosophical formulations with radical economic thought, Fenollosa's phrasing in his 1904–8 lecture notes on the Chinese character indicates an indirect seepage of radical discourse into his writings. Fenollosa was by no means an anarchist; but in his lifelong study of Hegel, and in his contemporary interest in William James's self-styled "anarchist" writings, the Boston art historian was not completely removed from currents of intellectual radicalism.[59] In his own late-1913 London milieu, Pound would have sensed the anarchistic overtones of Fenollosa's account of linguistic signs as vessels for the transmission of "direct action" (*CWC*, 22). The nominalistic implications of this international slogan would not have been lost on a poet who was soon to style himself a "syndicalist" during a 1914 vorticist campaign to fluster the utilitarian British spirit: "The artist has been at peace with his oppressors for long enough. He has dabbled in democracy and now is done with that folly" ("S," 254).[60] In Pound's reading of Fenollosa's analysis of language, the underconsumptionists' transparent currency and economy of unmediated exchange were invoked by this reference to a politics that abjures franchise and party agency in favor of direct action. For the nominalist who sought to resuscitate poetry by pushing for "equity" between words and things, the political and economic implications of the Chinese character were laid bare by this phrase.

Reaching Pound as it did alongside Kitson's and Marsden's writings, Fenollosa's description of intelligent commerce within the substrata of language was conceptually allied to the underconsumptionist notion that communities are meant to evolve their own organic systems of economic exchange.[61]

The whole delicate substance of speech is built upon substrata of metaphor. Abstract terms, pressed by etymology, reveal their ancient roots still embedded in direct action. But the primitive metaphors do not spring from arbitrary *subjective* processes. They are possible only because they follow objective lines of relations in nature herself. Relations are more real and more important than the things which they relate. The forces which produce the branch-angles of an oak lay potent in the acorn. Similar lines of resistance, half-curbing the out-pressing vitalities, govern the branching of rivers and of nations. Thus a nerve, a wire, a roadway, and a clearing-house are only varying channels which communication forces for itself. This is more than analogy, it is identity of structure. Nature furnishes her own clues. Had the world not been full of homologies, sympathies, and identities, thought would have been starved and language chained to the obvious. There would have been no bridge whereby to cross from the minor truth of the seen to the major truth of the unseen. (*CWC*, 22–23)[62]

Fenollosa contended that language was metaphorical and that metaphors were rich because they were homologous to transactions in nature. Distinctions between nouns and verbs were arbitrary. There was no activity without things; there were no things without activity. The "truth" of language, like the "truth" of nature, lay in the "*transference of power*" between moving things. It was relations, not terms, that were real.

Fenollosa's assertion that "relations are more real and more important than the things which they relate" does not come directly from Proudhon's writings; but it can be placed within a wider philosophical debate that developed in sympathy with anarchism and the anarchistic political underpinnings of the underconsumptionist complaint against hoarded money. The idea that "truth" lies only in the transference of power accords with Proudhon's emphasis on economic exchange as reflective of the "true order" of society.[63] Anarchistic antistatist movements such as syndicalism, which rallied around the notion of economic "direct action," sprang from this emphasis on economic exchange, as did underconsumptionist thought like Kitson's, which attributed industrial depression and broad social decline to interest and other impediments to transaction.[64] Fenollosa's contention that relations are more important than things complements the logic of Kitson's analysis of gold. The gold sovereign should be appreciated for what it does, not for what it is. Money that does nothing, is nothing. The linguist's claim that without the analogic transactions of metaphor, thought is "starved" and language "chained to the obvious" resounds the underconsumptionist belief that poverty amid plenty can be traced to nominal wealth and surplus, to "mildewed production for the Ground" and the pinched bourgeois thrift mentality that surrounds it (Ruskin, *UTL*, 219; Surette, "EPBR," 439).

❖ Pound believed with Ruskin that art could transform society; and Fenollosa's treatise provided the poet with a "neutral" foundation upon which to base his development of a politically and economically efficacious kind of writing. By the 1930s Pound was appraising his own prescient discovery of a compositional "method" that exhibited the truths that were later set forth in Major Douglas's timely postwar theories of credit. Pound's role as a poet was to have located these truths in the medium of language. For this reason he was eager to acknowledge Fenollosa, rather than the anarchists and underconsumptionists who had layered the ideogram with social and political significance in 1913, as the methodological founder of the modern collage poem. In his references to Fenollosa in a 1930 essay, however, Pound paid metaphorical homage to the original political and economic matrix of *The Chinese Written Character as a Medium for Poetry*. Fenollosa's writings were "profound and inestimable," the poet suggested, because they had been conceived without regard to secondhand valuations, or the concern for "trademarks" that made "shoddy" of most modern intellectual productions. Lamenting his publishers' neglect of the lecture notes that had been entrusted to him by Fenollosa's widow, Pound suggested that it had been the late professor's lack of truck with doctrines and trends, the fact that his brand of thought "didn't have a union label on it," that had inhibited the public reception of his epochal teachings about the nature of language (*MA*, 103–4).

That Pound came to assign such prominence to Fenollosa's writings and that he came to speak of them as pure, yet-uncirculated "goods" suggests that from the very beginning, the art historian's insistence on an objective and dynamic natural basis for language had resounded the anarchistic imperative of direct exchange between producers and consumers—an imperative that had alerted the poet to the limitations of imagism as early as 1913 (*MA*, 104). With its appeal to "direct action" in language, *The Chinese Written Character* had pushed Pound's imagistic faith in the "sane valuation" of the word toward a belief that whole poems could be trued to induce ethical structures. Radiant ideogrammic structures possessed the power to transform because they were more deeply analogic to the local than were the "universalizing" political constructs of "theorists" and the glamorous, chiming "prisons" of symbolist and postsymbolist poems.[65] In Pound's developing "structuralist" aesthetic, it was not words but whole systems of words that could be rendered transparent. The material basis of Fenollosa's dynamic theater of nature had provided the poet with a methodological equivalent of Proudhon's society of uninhibited commercial exchange. In the spirit of Marsden's application of economics to semiotics, Fenollosa had showed Pound how the anarchist call for a real, circulating economy through the mechanism of real money might engender a shift from stasis to dynamism in poetry.

4. "Volitionist" Economics and Pound's "Pragmatic Aesthetics"

In Kitson's and Marsden's writings of 1912–13, Pound encountered at an early date a series of anarchistic solutions to "the economic problem." This exposure facilitated the poet's speedy assimilation of Major Douglas's Social Credit theories after World War I; and it provided a deep foundation for his embrace of American pragmatist philosophy in the late 1930s. Imbibing the currents of radicalism that coursed through the *New Freewoman* and the *New Age*, American modernists in World War I–era Britain were well positioned to recognize the affinities between anarchism and American pragmatist philosophy. At the fringes of London's vorticist movement, T. S. Eliot perceived an affinity between Pound's appeal to "the image" as a "node" of "unthroned" "ideas" and William James's "pluralistic" conception of "Experience" as a "mosaic" held together not by "Absolutes," but by the "live" "transitions" between its "pieces."[66] Recognizing this affinity at a time when the avant-garde spirit ran high in London, Eliot cautioned Pound not to compromise his dynamic aesthetics by affiliating them too closely with overly academic philosophical complements. Writing to Pound from Oxford, where he was reading for a Harvard philosophy degree in 1915, Eliot expressed an iconoclastic contempt for the sort of "contemplative" "easy-chair aesthetics" that might overrule "the aesthetics of the person who is about to do something"; and he expressed his relief that Pound had refused to "hitch [vorticism] up" to "some philosopher" like "Bergson" or "James" (*LTSE*, 87).[67] As a reader of Bergson and as a former student of Santayana at Harvard, Eliot could see that, like Bergson's conception of "creative evolution," James's vision of "experience" as a "living" "graft" that supplants its "fossilized" "antecedent" offered a theoretical framework for Pound's efforts to make the image dynamic.[68] At that time Pound had little concern for anything quite so institutional as American philosophy; but by the mid 1930s, when he proposed collaborative projects with Dewey, and then with Santayana, he seemed eager to undertake the sort of hitching up that Eliot had advised against.

Beginning in 1939, Pound struck up what became an extended correspondence with the Spanish-born American philosopher George Santayana.[69] Together with John Dewey, with whom the poet had corresponded during the mid-1930s, Santayana was one of the pragmatist philosophers that Pound had tried to procure as potential collaborators on books about economics and curriculum reform.[70] Out of the literal material of his letters to and recorded conversations with Santayana, the poet attempted to formulate a collage-style poetic statement that he called his "Pragmatic Aesthetics." Fenollosa's writings were "*fundamental*" to this little-known and never finished effort of Pound's (*MA,* 157); and the poet's equation of pragmatism with not only the Chinese ideogram but also underconsumptionist money theory marks a momentary coming together of European anarchist and American pragmatist strains of modernism. During the period of his growing fascist engagement, Pound had acknowledged that his own brand of underconsumptionism—which he now referred to as "volitionist economics"— had been rooted in the writings of the anarchist Proudhon. (Although Kitson and Marsden had both acknowledged Proudhon in their *New Age* and *New Freewoman* essays, Pound took his time in discovering the French mutualist's importance to underconsumptionist economic theory.) As Pound wrote in "In the Wounds," his 1935 memorium for A. R. Orage, "Proudhon will be found somewhere in the foundations of perhaps all contemporary economic thought that has life in it" (*SP,* 440). For Pound, this realization coincided not only with his growing conviction that the "left wing" fascist Mussolini was a leader who shared Pound's economic views (Mussolini had himself demonstrated both anarchist and socialist sympathies early in his political career) but also with his recognition of an affinity between Proudhonian anarchism and American brands of philosophy.

In his *Guide to Kulchur,* which he wrote in 1938, during the brief period between his contacts with Dewey and Santayana, Pound linked anarchistic currency theory directly to philosophical pragmatism. In an essay entitled "The Proof of the Pudding," Pound outlined his own "volitionist" conception of money as not a static commodity but a medium of living exchange; and he offered it as living proof of pragmatist "sanctions," like Dewey's, which called for an enrichment of static forms of "knowledge" with socially embodied varieties of "experience." "Ideas are true as they go into action," Pound summarized.

> I am not resurrecting a pragmatic sanction, but trying to light up pragmatic PROOF. The thread going through the holes in a coin . . . is a necessary part of a thought system.
>
> The moment man realizes that the guinea stamp, not the metal, is the essential component of the coin, he has broken with all materialist philosophies. (*GK*, 188)

In this passage Pound demonstrates a working familiarity with the fundamental tenets of pragmatist philosophy. Reiterating that "an idea" is "not *true*" until it "go[es] into action" (*GK*, 188–89), Pound sounded out the sanction that had guided the pragmatists' "experimental" temper since 1878, when Charles Peirce published his essay "How to Make Our Ideas Clear." Peirce had written there that a full apprehension of reality was contingent on measuring the "effects," or the consequences, of ideas and the fruits of actions (*PWP*, 31). As "PROOF" of this abstract pragmatist sanction, Pound submitted a Proudhonian critique of commodity currency, one that was based on the contemporary writings of the currency theorist Silvio Gesell and one that greatly resembled Kitson's critique of Britain's gold sovereign in the *New Age* in 1912.

The "PROOF" of the sanction that "an idea" should "go into action" lay in the hole in the "volitionist" coin. Through this hole the metal token would be sewn into the transactional tissue of society. By Pound's reading, the coin with the hole differs from the whole coin in the way that a circulating currency, which is marked by a "guinea stamp," differs from commodity money, which claims its value in metal. In this way Pound gilded the atomistic and overly static "materialist" belief systems that the pragmatists hoped to invigorate. Insofar as the problem with traditional modes of "materialism" (or "empiricism," as the pragmatists called it) could be reduced to the problem of the gold fetish, Pound had found a simple mechanical means of reorienting conceptual systems around "conjunctive relations"—relations that were, in a phrase that James coined in 1905, "[held] to be as real as the terms united by them" (*PU*, 789).[71] "Volitionism," Pound suggested, was something more than a synonym for the experimental set of methods that William James had described as a kind of "mosaic philosophy." It was the very "PROOF" that ran through the hole of the pragmatists' sanctions.

In one of the first serious attempts to consider Pound as a "pragmatist" poet, Frank Lentricchia places him in a canon of writers who, lacking viable poetic predecessors, turned to turn-of-the-century Harvard philosophers for their sources. Wallace Stevens, Robert Frost, T. S. Eliot, and Gertrude Stein, notes Lentricchia, were among the many who studied in Boston at the hands of pragmatists including William James, Josiah Royce, and George Santayana. As a poet who was educated in Philadelphia and then immersed in London circles, Pound was geographically and culturally removed from this circle. But Lentricchia suggests that Pound absorbed the Emersonian "individualist" components of William James's pragmatism and that he came to express it through his "theory of the image": "It was as if in his reading of Henry James he had at last discovered for himself the latent William Jamesian pragmatist politics and ethics of his two key imagist directives—'Direct treatment of the thing' and 'Go in fear of abstractions'" (*MQ*, 30). James's pragmatist directives certainly do share a nominalist impulse with Pound's early poetry, and they also share an individualist predisposition that is bound to the imagist's fear of abstractions. But the deepest affiliation between pragmatism and Pound's poetry lies in their shared conception of a dynamic form of nominalism, or an emphasis on the recovery of "true" relations or conjunctions. For both Pound and James, moreover, this relational emphasis was rooted in Proudhonian conceptions of an "economic organism"; it was for this reason that Pound sought in the 1930s and 1940s to form alliances with philosophers who were more or less loosely affiliated with the modern call for a "mosaic" conception of reality.

❖ In Pound's *Cantos* an imagistic "presence" lingers in the "bedding," or in the ideogrammic relations between episodes. Like the goldbug's precious metal, this presence naturalizes and displaces the intelligence that isolates and arranges the material of history. In the politics of Pound's later writings, as in the marginal yearnings of politics at large, the brightness of golden-age utopias—the village barter economies hailed by anarchist intellectuals, or the "pure," pre-Keynesian currencies idealized by contemporary economists—come to dazzle the lonely scavengers who declare them of value.[72] Noting the "endless agglutination" in *The Cantos* of images of purity and impurity, Bob Perelman reads Pound's displacement of genius onto the "steel dust" of his medium as an attempt to cleanse language of its inevitable social contingencies.[73] For Perelman, apologists who distinguish Pound's lyrical moments from his tirades against "kikery" reproduce in their own aesthetic systems the "split in Pound's work that continually produces" not only "diamond and mud" but also "Mussolini and Jews; the extraordinary individual and the masses; the genius and the diluting poets" (38). Displaying a poststructuralist awareness of the binary logic that engenders distinctions between pure and impure forms of language, Perelman's reading of Pound is both ethically and theoretically driven.

Perelman is right to contest the divide between poetry and politics. But his suggestion that Pound's early writings were "founded on the need for the kind of social authority that Fascism seemed to represent" provides an inadequate account of the young "syndicalist" who located the future of the arts in "a guild of the intelligent poor and near-poor."[74] Like a range of recent accounts of the politics of modernism, Perelman's reconciliation of Pound's aesthetic and social dimensions is not only historically misinformed. It also hinges on an innate contradiction. Imagism becomes continuous with fascism when critics negatively identify Pound's early aesthetics against enlightened contemporary stances toward language and politics. And insofar as the innately "authoritarian" notion of semiotic presence is fundamental to its "emancipatory" poststructuralist critique, such a sweeping distinction between open and closed spheres of reference must itself prove "unclean." Writing of the dialectical relationship between the avowal and the disavowal of presence in language, Richard Rorty has suggested that "the notion of 'hard fact' " is a constitutive component of the very "notion of intertextuality," of writing that glorifies "writing itself" (*CP*, 136). Applied to theories of currency, Rorty's philosophical assertion yields Michaels's suggestion that gold money, like semiotic certainty, lingers on in the less literal forms of fiduciary currency that come to replace it. In the constitutive mistake that "nature's money" reveals to those who see that money is minted by people, it is the very premise of presence, of natural hardness in language, that funds the semiotic equivalent of the repeal of the gold standard.

Rorty and Michaels share a belief that "presence" is constitutive of the very thinkers who deny it; and it is through this assumption that discussions of reference in Pound's poetry come to bear on the politics of poststructuralist critique. In dialectical accounts of the ascension of "new" over "old" systems of reference, the intrinsic "hardness" or "softness" of language or money is not really a determining factor. What matters more is the way that, in the relationship between opposed systems of reference, the immanence of one system gets conjured through the "mistake" of the other. Immanence can be ascribed equally to either "hard" or "soft" mediums. Pound, for example, exhibits the mobility of this property by shifting it first from "terms" to "relations" and then finally, in the last of *The Cantos*, to the now fully disclosed "subject," the broken genius who emerges through the discrepancy between words and the worlds that they fail. For many of those critics who condemn his poetics of presence, Pound's later writings are "authorized" not only by discourse itself but also by a penitent speaker whose presence wells from his admission that it is not truths but identities that float in the ether of language (*GD*, 333). In readings that locate the "subject" of Pound in his poetic recantation of the hardness of both politics and language, the constitutive mistake of representation in nature, the very mistake that is central to the indictment of presence in language, continues its immanent magic.

❖ Taken together with the anarchist sources of Pound's early aesthetics, the historical pragmatist sources of Pound's late recantation of economic and poetic authority provide further testimony to the idea that linguistic "presence" is not bound to authoritarian politics. The more "humane" voice that emerges at the end of *The Cantos* was shaped not by Kitson or Proudhon but by the very American philosophers who had rejected Pound's "volitionist" "PROOF" of their pragmatist "sanctions." In particular, the later writings of George Santayana contributed to the "sincerest" of Pound's readerly pleas.

> I have tried to write Paradise
>
> Do not move
>   Let the wind speak
>   that is paradise.
>
> Let the Gods forgive what I
>   have made
> Let those I love try to forgive
>   what I have made.
>   (*C*, 816)

In his own copy of Santayana's *The Idea of Christ in the Gospels* (1946), Pound made a special note of one particular passage, recording its page number in the book's flyleaf. In this passage Santayana had described "the nostalgia for paradise" as a "perennial" "sentiment" "in the human mind." "The garden of Eden," Santayana wrote, "is an inverted image of aspiration . . .; not, however the image of a wise aspiration. We may fancy that children are happy, or that we should live better like the animals, but this is hardly the case. There is the seed of something else within us, and we cannot be so easily satisfied" (*IC*, 167). Santayana was not exactly dismissing the utopian ideal that had anchored Pound's long search for a "righteous" social and poetical order. Rather, the philosopher preserved the idea of a generative garden in the notion that false paradises were "inversions" of real ones. A real paradise, he suggested, would not be a static and backward place like Eden. If it was anywhere to be found, it would be located in living social practices. As Santayana wrote in another passage that Pound highlighted in his book: "Better, much better, for human morality to be humane than to be sublime" (208).

By the time of Pound's reading of Santayana's book in the late 1940s, the poet's vision of a fascist millennium, one that was to have resurrected generative forms of economic and literary currency, had already begun to falter. In view of this, Pound's attention to Santayana's conceptions of "paradise" and "morality" sheds some light on the cryptic fragment that Pound later penned and kept in mind for use at the end of *The Cantos*.

> Two mice and a moth my guides—
> To have heard the farfalla gasping
>   as toward a bridge over worlds.
> That the kings meet in their island,
>   where no food is after flight from the pole.
> Milkweed the sustenance
>   as to enter arcanum.
>
> To be men not destroyers.
> (*C*, 817)

Against the excesses that attended his utopian belief that poetry could be as nourishing as "strong" "mountain wheat," Pound suggests that writing reaches meaning only through the metonymic accidents of language. Poetry produces nothing more essential to society than the "monarch" that crowns the butterfly, or farfalla, and the "milk" that colors the floating weed that is eaten by "kings." In deference to the idea of a "humane morality," Pound gestures toward surrendering the "inverted aspiration" that had long guided the *Cantos*—the belief that by making words "true" again, a poet can quell "the voice of famine unheard" (*C*, 810). As Pound well knew, however, Santayana was a "religious" philosopher who believed that "morality" was immanent not in the Gospels, nor in a freely circulating currency, but rather in the vaguely "generative order" that was cultivated by a political "dictatorship."[75] Following the example of a compatriot who had been wise enough to soften his appeals to the "surgical" imperative of "Fascism," Pound came to gather his "Paradise" through a softer, more improvisational set of pathways. The wispy politics that enveloped Pound's penitent "milkweed" indeterminacy, then, may have been a good deal "harder" than the politics that attended his imagist phase.

❖   Those strains of Edwardian political and economic radicalism that surface in Pound's early work represent more the predisposition than the partisanship of the imagist poet. Pound wanted to fix society for and through the arts, but the absorption of the radical left's Labour Party by the Liberals in power had made socialistic radical political affiliations seem complicitous with the state. Although Pound did not openly advocate underconsumptionism before World War I, he absorbed and appreciated its political, philosophical, and linguistic implications as early as 1912–13, through his own readings of Arthur Kitson and through radical anarchist contacts in T. E. Hulme's, Orage's, and Dora Marsden's circles. Pound's account of poetry as a medium that could be purged of its opacity in order to restore its healthful inductive qualities was at least indirectly derived from the same "underworld" currents of economic thought that the poet later appreciated in Major Douglas, in the Proudhonian money "heretic" Silvio Gesell, and in the underconsumptionist tracts of Kitson himself, when Pound "rediscovered" his writings in the 1930s (*EPIF,* 126, 252). Pound encountered what he himself called the "*seed*[s]" of a nominalistic currency theory well before his conversions to Douglas and Mussolini. These seeds enabled him to assimilate, and to relate to poetry, many of the anarchistic political sentiments that were allied to early radical economic programs. What this new poetic genesis suggests is that fascism and institutionalized anti-Semitism can be elaborated from an economic approach with roots in both progressive and radical anarchist politics. By fastening rhetorical and monetary hardness too directly to a politics that forbids difference and play, contemporary critics have managed to overlook one of modern literature's more unsettling narratives. Pound's totalitarian excesses did not stem from a commitment to sameness. Rather, they were rooted in anarchist political movements like Proudhon's and Marsden's that were sympathetic not only to the interests of a reactionary elite but also to those of historically marginalized groups such as workers and women.

During the late 1930s, as Pound came to embrace fascism as a political vehicle for a volitionist economy, he dismissed "race prejudice [as] red herring," describing it as a peripheral phenomenon that detracted from the real matter of economic corruption (*SP*, 299). Pound's "red herring" is not a qualifier that exonerates him for his role in a crime whose enormity might best have rendered him speechless. Rather, it is a dismissive disclaimer that gives the nod to grave social injustices. It reveals the cast of mind that enabled the poet to support racist eugenic purges in the name of institutionalized free credit. In coming to terms with this reprehensible alliance, critics have branded as essentially reactionary Pound's decades-long criticism of the political and rhetorical leveling of local and individual differences. In *The Genealogy of Demons*, Robert Casillo voices a tacit consensus among critics that values such as Pound's "suspicion of abstraction" cannot be removed from the "fascist constellation" of the poet's overall thought (*GD*, 328). Casillo's conclusion that "Bacigalupo is entirely correct when he describes *The Cantos* as 'the sacred poem of the Nazi-Fascist millennium' " expresses a well-founded wish to place the constructs of "image" and "ideogram" on a plane with the death camps at Auschwitz and Dachau.[76] The early historical context of Pound's aesthetic of presence, however, suggests that the poet's universe was not quite so ordered. The confusion of early-twentieth-century leftist and right-wing critiques of liberalism and socialism shows that Pound was not so much swept on a current of semiotic reaction as backed awkwardly, but no less unforgivably, into fascism and anti-Semitism through an adherence to outworn radical and progressive beliefs.

Pound's radical "syndicalist" moment reared up suddenly from the quieter "scientism" of "The Serious Artist." By 1914 the progressive program that was to carry the poet into modern society had begun to carry him away. What got lost early in Pound's and Kitson's "scientific" practice was the local: the induced "natural object" and its relations; the "real" sovereign and the communal, and constitutive, basis of exchange. This loss is not intrinsic to the sciences of money and language per se; it was rather a product of Kitson's and Pound's scientistic defense of their social visions in a historical climate of derision and indifference. Underconsumption drew its initial model for industrial England from eighteenth- and nineteenth-century rural Scotland, just as Proudhon drew his antistatist "mutualism" from early-nineteenth-century French villages (*SCEO*, 18; *RS*, 15). What the liberal Kitson did was to claim the literal authority of science and progress for a scheme that was metaphorically utopian. The neomedievalist Ruskin was similarly skewed in his hope that a coinage based on bread, iron, and silk would lead to a world that honored "NO WEALTH BUT LIFE."[77] Underconsumptionists erred in assuming that with a few simple adjustments to mechanisms such as the labor theory of value, the richly evolved ethics of village societies would flower forth in the modern industrial world. The communal spirit of the village guild found no foothold in the crowded sweatshops of London, nor did the medieval spirit lingering beneath Ruskin's call for "production for the Mouth."

Proudhon's, Kitson's, and Ruskin's utopias each referred to societies as remote from modern England as Ezra Pound's Cathay was from literary London. More damagingly, they referred to worlds that had hardened as outposts of provincialism for intellectuals disenchanted with bourgeois capitalism and its stifling socialist alternatives. The complaint against the Ricardian economy's betrayal of the individual blends easily into the conservative hue and cry over the erosion of culture. Ruskin's image of mildewing stockpiles of grain confuses concern for the industrial poor with concern for the status of the arts in an economy clenched by commercialism. Pound's condemnation of the slumlord bishop of London appeared beside his comment in the *New Freewoman* that heretics once burned at the stake were now sentenced to "starvation, or at least forced and irregular fasting."[78] Underlying Pound's twin indictments of fetishism and the bourgeois "thrift" mentality is a merging of left-wing and right-wing radical perspectives. Beneath his distinction between the medieval burning and the modern starving of heretical artists is an account of alienation. Pound was suggesting that the modern industrial state practices a passive persecution of "individuals" such as underworld economists and poets. But the isolation he describes is also that of a progressive who discovers he has been left behind. Defenders of "culture" who do not recognize the culture around them must seek refuge in preserves like rural Scotland or medieval England or the paradoxically progressive "sciences" of money and language. These utopias seem more authentic to their occupants than does the surrounding bourgeois society, which threatens to destroy or ignore them. The imagist appeal to the thing, to the local, was itself an appeal to a glamorous fetish. It led to a sharper, more compact style of writing, and it ultimately contributed to an opening of the compositional field of the poem. In its own local political context, however, imagism troubles us—not as a stirring millenary beast but as a repository of stalled radicalism and progress, where sour defenders of real money and sane valuation contrive boundaries that can be no more essentially oppressive than those traced by the later precedent of semiotic play.

THREE

Syphilis and James Joyce's *Ulysses*

In medical surveys published at the turn of the century, Irish asylums were shown to contain strikingly low percentages of patients suffering from a degenerative neurological condition called General Paralysis of the Insane (*TS*, 47–48). Long associated with the advanced stages of syphilis, "G.P.I." had been established as a tertiary complication of the disease in the mid-1890s (*DR*, 208–9).[1] The low statistical incidence of neurosyphilis in Ireland was surprising in light of the high rate of deaths from infectious diseases in that nation's densely populated capital city. But the idea that even "Dear Dirty Dublin" was awash with a spirit of chastity was in keeping with native myths of the moral purity of the sons and daughters of Erin. Beginning in the late nineteenth century, and gathering momentum in the years leading up to the Free State of the early 1920s, Celtic Revivalists were among those who "deluged" Ireland with "boastings of the purity of [its] women" and the "inviolable honour" of Irish men.[2] They countered long-standing European stereotypes of the Irish as disease-ridden sexual predators (*PHI*, 81). In lectures and handbills, many of them reprints of newspaper essays suppressed by English authorities, nationalist leaders portrayed the Irish as a "pure and virgin" race whose strength and vitality was to be defended against the withering "touch" of the English empire.[3]

The campaign to de-Anglicize Ireland took a sharply defensive turn in 1906, when the nationalist journal *Sinn Féin* ran a series of articles on venereal disease among English soldiers stationed in Ireland. Here, in a three-part essay titled "Ugly England," the Irish poet Oliver Gogarty adapted the eugenical specter of racial degeneration to the home soil Revivalist cause. Ireland's genetic constitution, Gogarty suggested, was not primarily threatened by the emigration of the country's fittest young citizens, nor by the alcoholism, prostitution, and poverty faced by many who stayed home. The greatest danger to Ireland's future lay rather in a visiting British army, whose overseas contingent in India was "'already more than half leprous from venereal excess.'"[4] "Ugly England" made plain what the nationalist leader Maud Gonne had implied in her O'Connell Street handbills, controversial entreaties advising young Irish women to avoid contact with the "enemies of their country."[5] In an era marked by cries of race suicide, Ireland's bourgeois citizenry had been inundated with warnings against English infection. But Dubliners closer to the wellsprings of disease knew that Ireland was more than a mere passive victim in the dangerous syphilis outbreaks of the early twentieth century. Suggesting that the imperatives of national purity might themselves have contributed to the suppression of neurosyphilis in Ireland, modern tenement dwellers spoke of Ireland's venereal immunity as an outgrowth of falsified diagnoses and of the medical mercy killing of advanced syphilitics, unfortunates allegedly "smothered" or given "a needle" in Dublin's Townsend Street Lock Hospital.[6]

Early in his career, James Joyce conceived of literature as a means of cleansing the "brutal" "atmosphere" of purity that poisoned conventional images of both the Irish family and the Irish nation (*LJJ2*, 191–92). Lamenting the continuing cry of "venereal excess" in *Sinn Féin*, the young author distanced himself from his former friend Gogarty and from a movement that he supported in principle, claiming now to be "nauseated" by the Irish nationalists' "lying drivel about pure men and pure women and spiritual love and love forever . . . I don't know much about the 'saince' of the subject but I presume there are very few mortals in Europe who are not in danger of waking some morning and finding themselves syphilitic. The Irish consider England a sink: but if cleanliness be important in this matter, what is Ireland? Perhaps my view of life is too cynical but it seems to me that a lot of this talk about love is nonsense" (*LJJ2*, 191). An apostate, an expatriate, and a self-styled "sinner" who is believed to have contracted gonorrhea and possibly syphilis at a Dublin "Nighttown" brothel in 1904, Joyce railed against the suppression not only of sexual efflorescence but also of the "venereal ill-luck" that should inevitably attend it.[7] "I wish some unkind person would publish a book about the venereal condition of the Irish," Joyce insisted in 1906, "since they pride themselves so much on their immunity" (*LJJ*2, 170). To his brother Stanislaus, Joyce had referred to *Dubliners*, his early collection of stories, as a "series of studies" of Dublin's "syphilis contagion"; he had described the same book in a letter to his publisher as "a moral history of my country," exposing Dublin as the "centre of paralysis" (*DSJ*, 51; *LJJ*2, 134). Years later, in 1922, the writer's efforts to overthrow the myth of Irish purity would culminate in the publication of *Ulysses*, a novel praised by some as ascendantly "naked" and damned by others as a book that "canalised" "the secret sewers of vice."[8] Among the Joycean excesses that troubled readers of *Ulysses* was the novel's irreverence toward interwoven standards of racial and sexual purity, standards challenged in the novel by a character named Leopold Bloom, the sexually "stained" Irish Jew at the heart of the novel, and by the rambling soliloquy delivered by Leopold's wife Molly, a Dublin adulteress whose speech brimmed with libidinal pleasures (*U*, 14.1218–19, 18.567).

Joyce's knowledge of the hidden venereal condition of the Irish is suffused throughout the content and the challenging form of a novel that is as relentlessly improvisational as Pound's *Cantos*. That the ravages of morality might be central to the story of *Ulysses*, as well as to Joyce's developing sense of how this story should be told, is suggested by the novel's history as a book censured for being as difficult as it was dirty. Buried in one of the "filthiest" and most wildly experimental portions of the novel, for example, amid a riot of political and sexual satire that debunks the "drivel" of the Irish as a "pure and virgin" race, is an ephemeral venereal casualty that tallies the cost of Ireland's talk about nation and love. In a disturbing and ambiguously worded passage in "Circe," the Nighttown prostitute Kitty Ricketts recounts the tale of "Mary Shortall that was in the lock with the pox she got from Jimmy Pidgeon in the blue caps had a child off him that couldn't swallow and was smothered with the convulsions in the mattress" (*U*, 15.2578–80). Kitty's is plainly a story about a baby who died from a seizure brought on by congenital disease; but it is also a testament to the ways in which language can cover and uncover truths. Deploying a passive construction, one that effaces the nominal "subject" from her account of the child that "was smothered with the convulsions," Kitty muddies the identity of the smotherer. The ostensible inadequacy of the prostitute's language alludes to the historical underpinnings of the confusion of two sins. In Dublin's Townsend Street Lock Hospital, as in *Ulysses* itself, the medical consequences of sexual "excess" are entwined with the ravages of "a lot of this talk about love."

The Madonna and Child of the lock hospital in "Circe" occupy only a small moment in the epic tale of Leopold Bloom, the middle-class advertising canvasser who attributes the death of his infant son Rudy, and his subsequent inability to make "natural" love to his wife, to a regrettable premarital encounter (*BD*, 53–58; *U*, 14.1068–77, 17.2283, 18.1400–1401). But Kitty Ricketts's account of the death of Mary's baby reveals something about the nature of Joyce's formal innovations. Bound to the question of how Mary's child dies—whether from disease or from the desire to contain it—is a series of historical questions about how words structure experience. *Ulysses* can be difficult to read because so much of its story is leaked to readers through defective grammatical and narrative structures. One of the narrative laws that Joyce so devilishly twisted was the premise that a nominal author, like a definite grammatical "subject," should exist prior to the characters and events in a novel. In a conventional realistic novel, the author's knowing presence is most keenly felt in those "transparent" or "unspoken" strands of narrative that seem to hold sway over the characters and action (*RW*, 14–15). Joyce's novel can be distinguished from Pound's epic poem insofar as its claims to discursive transparency, and hence its related claims to authorial command, are repeatedly relinquished. Refusing to conjure discursively the nominal ground of *Ulysses,* the voiceless narrative of the novel insinuates itself into the voices and personalities of the very characters it describes.[9] The narrative that swells with the bluster of the nationalistic Citizen in "Cyclops," for example, comes to mimic Gerty's pulp-fiction treacle in "Nausicaa" (*JJ*, 367). At times *Ulysses'* narrative goes so far as to echo the characters in the novel, weaving their speech into the narrative fabric that contains them. When the young poet Stephen Dedalus describes "the errors of [Shakespeare's] genius" as "portals of discovery" in "Scylla and Charybdis," for example, the narrative that follows quickly parrots the poet (*U*, 9.229–30; *JJU*, 84–85). Here, Stephen's defense of authorial integrity is deflated as the narrator of this episode invokes new "portals of discovery," or, more literally, a set of library doors, that open to admit another character into the surrealistic scene.[10]

As the events depicted in Joyce's novel come increasingly to unfold from the apparently incidental words spoken by its characters, *Ulysses* seems to be driven more by language than by an author. In portions of the middle chapters, it is not only the characters but also increasingly their "masks," and eventually their speech organs, that enter into dialogue with one another. The talking "face" of the intruding librarian and the talking "lips" of the barmaids at the Ormond Hotel come to supplant the characters who speak through them, much as the medium of the novel appears to overwhelm Joyce as the reckless genius of *Ulysses*.[11] Joyce's efforts to undermine the authority of the realistic narrator, and with it the transparency of authorial language, accord with poststructuralist challenges to the integrity of the author and to the related metaphysics of presence in language, the belief that words can be true to a free-standing world of meaning beneath them. In *Ulysses*, however, Joyce's textual innovations were rooted less in anachronistically intuited poststructuralist truths than they were in nineteenth-century writings on language and morality, writings by the anarchist Max Stirner and the philosopher Friedrich Nietzsche. Joyce's absorption of these newly current theorists, moreover, occurred in the historical context of a "revolt" that the author called "the greatest revolution in our time": that "of women against the idea that they are the mere instruments of men."[12] At a critical juncture in his career as a novelist, Joyce was exposed to feminists who applied Stirner and Nietzsche to discussions of disease and identity, and it was through modern feminist writings that he discovered the significance of anarchist assaults on "beginnings, origins, and principles" to a story about the failure and recovery of generational transmission.

1. The New Morality, British Feminism, and the Narrative of *Ulysses*

Joyce's merging of authorial narrative voices with the voices of characters begins in the opening pages of *Ulysses*, in the scene where a young Irish "medical" named Buck Mulligan, a character modeled on Oliver Gogarty, holds a mirror to the face of Stephen Dedalus, a character modeled on the author in his youth. Here, as Stephen encounters his reflection in "the cracked lookingglass of a servant," his thoughts are initially blended into the narrative that contains them (*U*, 1.146). "Stephen bent forward and peered at the mirror held out to him, cleft by a crooked crack. Hair on end. As he and others see me. Who chose this face for me? This dogsbody to rid of vermin. It asks me too" (*U*, 1.135–37). "Hair on end" is the sentence fragment that begins one of the first of *Ulysses'* "interior monologues." Like many of the fragments contained within these monologues, however, this one emerges with no definite speaker attached to it. Neither fully Stephen's nor the narrator's, these words are rather suspended between the third-person perspective of the sentence that precedes them and the first-person voice of the sentence to come. That a defective mirror should engender such a moment of narrative uncertainty calls attention to the lettered material of *Ulysses*, to the linguistic refractions that give life to the characters who are contained by the very flawed medium that they hold in their hands. The mirror tells Stephen that the words that he thinks and speaks do not stem necessarily from his person; it tells the reader that the words that surround Stephen's thoughts do not follow necessarily from an authorial narrator. At this pivotal moment in *Ulysses*, Stephen, like the author who creates him, exists not through words or voices but through the changing alignment of interior and exterior narrative perspectives. Stephen, like his creator, lives in a restless narrative frame that gathers words into the image before him.

Asking "Who chose this face for me?" and watching his reflection return the same question—"It asks me too"—Stephen encounters himself as a literary creation in the opening pages of *Ulysses*, mirroring the author's self-encounter through the words that he writes. Stephen thus inaugurates a series of inquiries into origins that will reverberate through the form and content of the narrative that follows. Envisioning his own embryonic genesis in "Proteus," for example, Stephen will go on to fashion for himself a new point of origin, one that is more empirical and yet more ethereal than his narrative conception in an Irish servant's cracked mirror. Scripting himself as first "wombed in sin darkness," the young "embryo philosopher" will conclude that he was "made not begotten," providing a mythic materialistic counterpart to his identity as a character begotten by words (*U*, 3.45, 14.1295). In *Ulysses* the foundational crisis that is keyed by Stephen's glimpse into the mirror will gather cultural resonance in the Jewish Bloom's annihilating vision of his ancestral origins. Pained by the death of his infant son Rudy and by the subsequent dissolution of his marriage to Molly, Bloom glimpses the "barren land" that "bore the oldest, the first race": "Dead: an old woman's: the grey sunken cunt of the world" (4.219–28). Bloom will eventually describe the loss that rocks him as an explicitly "racial" phenomenon: "No son. Rudy," is how Bloom telegraphs his tragedy: "[I am the] [l]ast of my race" (11.1066).

Syphilis imagery was instrumental to Joyce's "modernization" of the literary narrative, and it was essential to modern feminist efforts to reconceptualize identity, because it vividly illustrated the idea that activity could be as fleshily foundational as matter and because it gathered together modern anxieties about racial degeneration. Joyce's portrayal in *Ulysses* of degeneration as an outgrowth of brittle conceptions of gender and race, and his notion that the health of future generations hinged on a revitalization of these static categories, registers in his highly complex portrayal of the "soiled" "wanderer" at the center of *Ulysses*. Bloom is a hero whose marked status as a syphilitic and as a Jew in Catholic Dublin enables him to see that modern identity is not fixed after the fact in an imaginary genealogical amber; rather, it is continually fashioned in the internationalist flux of modernity. In the story of Molly's cuckolding of Bloom, moreover, *Ulysses* plays to the nationalistic belief that Ireland's racial integrity rests on the sexual containment of Ireland's pure women. As Mr Deasy explains to Stephen in "Nestor," "a faithless wife first brought the strangers to our shore here" (*U*, 2.392–93). But Joyce's "Penelope" finally shatters the icon of the "dishonoured wife" whose infidelities are blamed by others for Ireland's "misfortunes" (12.1163–64). Molly is a modern Irishwoman who speaks wisely of love and of the foundations of identity; it is her active transgression of national and marital conventions, of laws cemented by conventions of syntax and narrative, that enables her unpunctuated soliloquy to embody the elusive truths of *Ulysses*.

❖   In late 1914, as Joyce was finishing the final chapter of *A Portrait of the Artist as a Young Man* and starting work on *Ulysses*, he began thinking of narrative technique as a tool for combating the ravages of bourgeois morality, a degenerative malaise that he had earlier diagnosed as "the general paralysis of an insane society."[13] Complaining of the "unreality" of the conventional distinction between authorial narrative voices and characters' voices, and implying in the process that authors' and characters' minds were "full like everyone else's of borrowed words," Joyce began to imagine the novel as a medium driven not by autonomous speakers or writers but by language itself.[14] At this time, in the closing pages of *A Portrait of the Artist*, Joyce began toying with new ways of thinking about the author. In the narrative of that work, against Stephen Dedalus's inflated vision of the artist as a mastering agent whose every whim has the power to enlighten, Joyce implanted an image of the modern writer as "a vital sea" that "flow[s]" "round and round the persons and the action" in a novel (*PAFM*, 1047). Through Stephen, his pompous young poet-protagonist, Joyce proceeded coyly to figure this fluid conception of authorial consciousness, together with the vapory "interior monologues" that it would surrender, as a kind of eugenic tonic, one that would prove critical to the broadly conceived modern "race" that the cosmopolitan artist should set forth "to forge in the smithy of [his] soul."[15] As a modern artist, Stephen's task would be to reverse the spiral of racial degeneracy, to awaken "the conscience" of his complacent contemporaries, and to "cast his shadow over the imaginations of their daughters, before their squires begat upon them, that they might breed a race less ignoble than their own" (*PAFM,* 1151).

Occurring during the formative period between his first and second published novels, Joyce's half-mocking conflation of aesthetic with eugenic imperatives coincided with a resurgence of interest among feminists in England and Ireland in venereal diseases, and particularly in syphilis, which had long been viewed as a poison to women and to the modern European "race" as a whole. New Moralist writings on disease and identity came into Joyce's possession in early 1914 and helped to shape the thematic and even the formal contours of Joyce's fiction. As an innovative writer who viewed the modern women's movement as the cornerstone of all meaningful political struggles, Joyce used feminist discussions of women, race, and venereal disease to chart a narrative solution to problems posed by conventional forms of racial, national, and gendered identity. Joyce's conception of the author as a vital sea flowing through the novel had been conditioned by contemporary formulations of the "unitary stream" of the new woman's identity—a construct designed to "denominalize" and so revitalize women, immunizing them from the ravages of morality that attended the rhetoric of the syphilis contagion.[16] In his curative refashioning of the modern literary narrative, Joyce borrowed from feminists who challenged the damaging social and linguistic structures that facilitated the subjugation of even those progressive women who sacrificed their sexual autonomy on behalf of the suffrage cause. Joyce's salubrious expansion of the agent that anchors the text of *Ulysses,* together with his erasure of the formal textual markers that distinguish unspoken narrative voices from the voices of characters, marks a playing-out of the aesthetic and eugenic imperatives that Stephen had sounded in the closing pages of *A Portrait of the Artist.* The conceptual contours of these narrative innovations, as well as the local historical shadings that attended them in the story of Bloom, Rudy, and Molly, derived from contemporary anarcho-feminist efforts to refashion the reactive identity not only of "Woman" but also of the very " 'virgin' civilization" that recoils from syphilitic invasion.[17]

Joyce was living in Trieste when Dora Marsden published her essay "The Chastity of Women" in the 2 February 1914 edition of the *Egoist;* but his letters to Harriet Shaw Weaver indicate that he had "read . . . with great pleasure" that year's issues of the journal until he "ceased to receive them" after the August outbreak of World War I.[18] As Jean-Michel Rabaté has shown, Joyce was a particularly thoughtful reader of Marsden's early *Egoist* essays ("JE," 45–65).[19] Joyce paid late tribute, in *Finnegans Wake* (1939), to Marsden's early radical journals; furthermore, in a 1919 portion of his earlier novel *Ulysses,* he entered into a cryptic dialogue with one of her 1914 editorials.[20] In the "Scylla and Charybdis" episode of *Ulysses,* Stephen Dedalus begins a long philosophical discussion with a librarian who has materialized through the novel's "portals of discovery." During this debate Stephen refers to an unspecified group of "Egomen." "I believe, O Lord, help my unbelief. That is, help me to believe or help me to unbelieve? Who helps to believe? *Egomen.* Who to unbelieve? Other chap" (*U,* 9.1078–80). Joyce is said to be alluding here to the *Egoist* group—Weaver, Marsden, Pound—that supported his work during a time when "other chap[s]" would not.[21] (Among these others would have been the forty publishers who, by Joyce's own account, had refused to print his early collection of stories, *Dubliners.*) Rabaté, however, has noticed that the language surrounding this reference to the *Egoist* group also bears a direct semantic correspondence to an *Egoist* editorial of 1 August 1914—written by Marsden on the subject of belief and authority ("JE," 46–47).[22]

Joyce had been sufficiently captivated by Marsden's writings on belief and authority to have incorporated the rhetoric of one of her editorials into a later episode of *Ulysses.* But a historically contextualized study of the writer and the editor reveals a more extensive intellectual exchange: Marsden's contemporaneous writings on disease and identity played a role in determining the very form and content of Joyce's experimental novel. In columns adjacent to the first serialized installment of Joyce's own *Portrait of the Artist,* columns written during the same year as Marsden's essay on authority, the anarchist editor had sharply criticized a treatise on venereal disease written by Christabel Pankhurst, the leader of the militant British suffragettes ("CW," 44–46). Marsden's review of Pankhurst's notorious *Great Scourge and How to End It* (1913) drew together the network of social, political, and philosophical issues that informed Joyce's contemporaneous aesthetic appeal to the salvation of "the race." The former suffragette's response to the essentialized conceptions of race and gender that surrounded Pankhurst's discussion of the syphilis contagion provide an overlooked conceptual blueprint for Joyce's formal experiments in *Ulysses.*[23] And in displaying the relevance of Stirnerian and Nietzschean conceptions of language to contemporary notions of racial and gendered identity, the arguments set forth in

"The Chastity of Women" and other related essays by Marsden also contributed to the novel's thematic explorations of semantic and generational transmission.

In her challenge to Pankhurst, Marsden mustered an anarchist critique of the principles adhered to by a seemingly "radical" wing of the woman suffrage movement. Together with her mother, Emmeline, Christabel Pankhurst was a guiding light of the Women's Social and Political Union, the militant suffrage group that the Pankhursts had founded in 1903. By the time of the publication of *The Great Scourge* in December 1913, the WSPU had gained world notoriety with a series of sensationally orchestrated assaults on the foundering Liberal administration of Prime Minister Asquith. Ranging from window-smashings and fire-bombings to the slashing of paintings in art galleries, suffragette "outrages" represented an adaptation of anarchist "direct action" to the parliamentary cause of votes for middle-class British women. In 1912, during a police raid on the WSPU headquarters, Christabel Pankhurst fled England to escape the conspiracy charges that had landed her mother and other suffragette leaders in jail (*HWV*, 203–16). Assuming "solitary command" of the militant movement while hiding in Paris, she wrote the series of articles that spearheaded the WSPU's Moral Crusade, a propaganda campaign designed to distinguish the suffragettes' parliamentary objectives from the more radical class-based initiatives that were being increasingly associated with the suffragettes' tactics.[24]

As the textual centerpiece of Pankhurst's Moral Crusade, *The Great Scourge and How to End It* worked to temper the suffragettes' militant image by blending it with the more traditional icon of the womanly woman as a chaste moral exemplar. Shifting the suffrage campaign away from political or economic issues and onto the issue of "sexual vice," *The Great Scourge* coupled "Votes for Women" with a call for "chastity for men" (*GS*, ix, 37). Far from a matter of money or class, the suffragettes' militancy was a gendered call to arms against the "ranks of the vicious"—"rich men," "poor men," "men of moderate means" (46). Here, the specter of venereal disease served to distance the militant suffragettes from the dangerous "lower class" "hordes," revolutionary syndicalists whose strikes and uprisings in pre–World War I England and Ireland posed a threat to what many derided as the WSPU's "frail" bourgeois "hot-house blooms."[25]

In claiming that up to "80 per cent" of men "have before marriage been infected with one form of venereal disease" and that "three out of five" wives were unwittingly infected by their dissembling husbands, Pankhurst had exaggerated a social and medical problem that was a serious matter in London and especially in Dublin.[26] *The Great Scourge* was a popular tract in Ireland among feminists who knew themselves to be threatened by more than the leprous advances of Great Britain's army; but in England a growing contingent of feminist proponents of the "new morality" and "free unions" were disturbed by the suffragettes' reactive appeal to the innate chastity of women.[27] Like her more "humanist[ic]" feminist associate Rebecca West, Marsden believed that the "sex instinct" was no less wholesome than the "instinct of activity" itself; and in the spirit of this belief she complained that Pankhurst had robbed women of their vital sexual assertiveness by rendering them the passive victims of unbridled male lust.[28] Marsden detected an aura of self-annihilation in Pankhurst's assertion that " 'there can be no mating between the spiritually-developed women of this new day and the men who in thought or in conduct with regard to sex affairs are their inferiors.' "[29] Exposing the "unconscious expression of self-contempt" at the heart of this righteous call to arms, she disparaged *The Great Scourge* as a tract that fashioned women as the reluctant objects, rather than as the active pursuers, of sexual gratification ("CW," 46).

Criticizing Pankhurst's appeal to the disabling image of the woman in recoil, the anarcho-feminist Marsden used the invasive powers of the syphilis spirochete to suggest that women were threatened less by men who violated their sanctity than by the socially and linguistically constructed identities that the Victorian reformers and the modern suffragettes had embraced; and it was in this context that Joyce discovered the significance of Stirnerian and Nietzschean conceptions of language to the formal body of a literary narrative. Marsden objected to the defensive nature of Pankhurst's argument that women needed the vote in order to defend the integrity of their bodies; she claimed that the fear of syphilis was more debilitating than the disease itself. For Marsden, vitality was the only living tissue that the modern woman need defend. Since disease "can only be overcome by increased vitality," Marsden reasoned, "it is more important to heighten vitality than it is to combat disease." "There *can* be no disease of 'matter': it can be broken but it is incapable of contracting disease." Matter, like the body, and like identity itself, was a static concept and as such inconsequential. The only significant thing that could be violated was the process through which matter was assimilated into a vital, functioning identity: "There can only be such a breaking down of the spiritual unitary stream," Marsden wrote, "as to render it incapable of penetrating the material which it has assimilated and organized into a body" ("CW," 46).

2. Stirner's Egoism and the "Empty Concepts" of "Woman" and "Race"

To neutralize the invasive threat of the spirochete, Marsden applied to the syphilis contagion nineteenth-century ideas regarding the role played by language in the withering of the race through the suppression of individual instinctual vitality. Marsden's understanding that linguistic processes posed a greater danger to modern women than did disease derived from her reading of the German anarchist Max Stirner, the author of a book that "changed everything" for the one-time suffragette when she encountered an English translation of his work shortly before 1912 ("LI," 66). First published in Germany in 1844, Stirner's critique of liberal humanism in *The Ego and His Own* had gained renewed currency among early modern artists and intellectuals who shared Marsden's—and the young Joyce's—belief that contemporary forms of parliamentary representation had served to co-opt revolutionary initiatives by assimilating them to the aims of the state.[30] Stirner's anarchist classic had been translated from German into English in 1907; six subsequent editions of the book came to circulate among readers in London and New York during the years preceding the publication of *Ulysses* ("LI," 65). Although *The Ego and His Own* was missing from Joyce's extensive collection of radical political texts in Trieste, Dominic Manganiello has argued that Joyce was well versed in Stirner and that the German anarchist's doctrines proved central to the novelist's conception of the egoistic artist Stephen Dedalus.[31]

Whether or not he read the work of Stirner firsthand, Joyce, the artist who chafed against forms of state influence, is known to have studied contemporary writings, including those by the anarchist editor Benjamin Tucker and by the historian Paul Eltzbacher, which dealt extensively with the egoist's "scientific" analysis of the individualistic "foundation[s]" of "political liberty."[32] While he was living in Trieste in 1914, moreover, Joyce received back issues of the *New Freewoman* from Ezra Pound (*PJ*, 17–19). (The *New Freewoman* was the short-lived but widely acclaimed journal in which Pound had introduced imagism to radical "individualist" intellectuals in 1913. Edited by Marsden, this was the very magazine that would foreground its Stirnerian slant as the genderless *Egoist* in January 1914.) The issues of the *New Freewoman* that Pound mailed to Joyce featured a smattering of poems and essays by aesthetically inclined "individualists" like Pound, Allen Upward, and Richard Aldington, along with columns in which Marsden critiqued both the suffrage campaign and a range of other reform-based political movements and initiatives, from an avowedly Stirnerian standpoint.[33]

Although hardly a champion of religious thought, Stirner viewed the "immanent" imperatives of secular morality as a chief mechanism in the stifling of the modern individual's revolutionary vitality. Freed from the shackles of the "transcendent" authority of God, the liberal subject was now enslaved by "fixed" humanistic conceptions of what he or she ideally should be (*EO*, 59–62).[34] In *The Ego and His Own*, Stirner portrayed the modern tendency toward abstraction in language and toward generalizing nouns in particular as a corollary to the ascendancy of idealized conceptions of humanity. "With so many a man," Stirner wrote, "a thought becomes a 'maxim,' whereby he himself is made prisoner to it, so that it is not he that has the maxim, but rather it that has him" (*EO*, 81).[35] The liberal humanist subordinated his or her "actuating," "fleshly" appetites to the more "renunciative" appetite for "fixed" maxims and nominal "essences or concepts" like "Rights" and like "Man" (*EO*, 79–80, 225, 232, 236). The renunciation of self-actuating appetites served to weaken the modern subject, enabling the state to break down the individual's will and to adapt it to its own. In *The Ego and His Own*, Stirner implicitly gendered this modern malaise, invoking the image of the "chlorotic" young woman estranged from her nourishing instincts as an emblem of the individual whose vitality was paralyzed by the call to conformity with nominalized humanist ideals (79–80).

> There sits a girl opposite me, who perhaps has been making bloody sacrifices to her soul for ten years already. Over the buxom form droops a deathly-tired head, and pale cheeks betray the slow bleeding away of her youth. Poor child, how often the passions may have beaten at your heart, and the rich powers of youth have demanded their right! When your head rolled in the soft pillow, how awakening nature quivered through your limbs, the blood swelled in your veins, and fiery fancies poured the gleam of voluptuousness into your eyes! Then appeared the ghost of the soul and its eternal bliss. You were terrified, your hands folded themselves, your tormented eye turned its look upward, you—prayed. The storms of nature were hushed, a calm glided over the ocean of your appetites. Slowly the weary eyelids sank over the life extinguished under them, the tension crept out unperceived from the rounded limbs, the boisterous waves dried up in the heart, the folded hands them-

selves rested a powerless weight on the unresisting bosom, one last faint "Oh dear!" moaned itself away, and—*the soul was at rest*. You fell asleep, to awake in the morning to a new combat and a new—prayer. Now the habit of renunciation cools the heat of your desire, and the roses of your youth are growing pale in the—chlorosis of your heavenliness. (*EO*, 79–80)

Although Stirner's sexualized championing of the natural vitality of the unfettered "ego" provided a volitional complement to Proudhon's dynamic community of producers, the individualist's was a far more rigorous assault on foundations or "first principles."[36] The shadowy ethical imperative that modern collagists like Pound had sought in Proudhon's naturally circulating economy was submerged in the free-ranging "individual" that dodged the nominal tyranny of the fixed, empty noun.

Taken together with Joyce's anarchistically inflected belief that "a woman's love is always . . . egoistic," the novelist's portrayal of Molly Bloom as a rapacious sensualist who touches herself and thinks "I wouldnt mind being a man and get up on a lovely woman" suggests a modern regendering of the masculine egoist who refuses to be paralyzed by the seductive maxims that circumscribe national and sexual feelings (*LJJ*2, 191–92; *U*, 18.1146–47). Enjoying her feverishly illicit liaison with the "savage brute" Boylan and taking her pleasure in songs about Kipling's England, Molly sings her libidinal agency rather than claiming her voice through conventional national or gendered representational channels (*U*, 18.594, 18.377). Unrestrained in the confines of her bedroom, Molly remembers "coming for about 5 minutes" with her legs wrapped "round" Boylan, wanting to "shout out all sorts of things fuck or shit or anything at all"; and her public voice is explicitly linked to her direct sexual expression: "loves sweet sooooooooooong Ill let that out full when I get in front of the footlights again" (18.587–89, 18.877–78). In fashioning Molly's ravenous vitality as a half-parodic counter to the modern ailments suffered by "jaundiced politicians and chlorotic nuns," Joyce follows the Stirnerian contours of Marsden's anarcho-feminist writings on the renunciative spirit that undergirds the institutional oppression of both women and innovative modern artists (14.1290–91).[37]

In Molly's soliloquy, as in Marsden's critique of the British suffrage campaign, political shoptalk and romantic talk about "love forever" are both linked to the suppression of passion and vitality. In the opening lines of her soliloquy, Molly bemoans the wordy idealism that withers "progressive" women like Mrs Riordan, whose "methylated spirit" has been poisoned by "chat" about "politics and earthquakes" (*U*, 18.6–10); she later disparages the "skitting" chatter of "sparrowfart" young feminists who lack "passion" and so adopt causes to "make themselves . . . interesting" (18.879–87). Molly is as put off by Leopold's dreamy political natterings—"trash and nonsense"—as she is by her negligent husband's "nonsensical" proclamation that everything that falls from her "glorious Body" "is a thing of beauty and of joy for ever" (18.383–88, 18.1177–78). Wary of her husband's taste for etymological "jawbreakers," she associates Poldy's erudite verbal displays with his taste for pornography and his related desire to photograph his wife and so to touch her from a representational remove: "I asked him about her ['that dirty bitch in the Spanish photo'] and about that word ['metempsychosis']" (18.241, 18.563–65).[38] For Molly, men's words are, like dirty books and pictures, alienating mediums; as she voices her telling suspicion of her gynecologist's jargon, she imagines herself pinioned by his invasive medical queries. Of that "dry old stick Dr Collins," she remembers him "asking me had I frequent omissions where do those old fellows get all the words they have omissions with his shortsighted eyes on me cocked sideways I wouldnt trust him too far to give me chloroform or God knows what else" (*U*, 18.1153, 18.1169–72). Mistrustful of masculine political, romantic, and medical lexicons, Molly associates language itself with a violation of the body. In her suggestion, moreover, that this linguistic violation is precipitated not by violence but by an anesthetized surrender of the victim, Molly exhibits the trace of contemporary anarcho-feminist writings on language and identity.

For the anarcho-feminist critic of Pankhurst's *Great Scourge,* and for the novelist who claimed that "the greatest revolution in our time" was "the revolt of women against the idea that they are instruments of men," the allusions to "venomous" male "secretions" that surfaced within the rhetoric of suffrage compromised the campaign for franchise, suggesting that the vote itself was a negative medium, intrinsically disabling to women (*CJJ*, 35; *GS*, 61). For Marsden, the vote, like the marriage contract, led to the insidious enslavement of the women who would speak through it to appeal for parliamentary protection; and for the self-styled "anarchist" Joyce, it was a mechanism that pulled the "eccentric" individual into the absorptively "concentric" orbit of state interests.[39] By appealing to images of women in full "muscular" recoil against invasive medical practices and diseases alike, reformers and suffragists eclipsed images of women engaged in the activity of feeding their appetites, an activity that anarcho-feminists, like the syndicalists whom the young Joyce had admired, equated with forms of direct economic empowerment.[40] In so doing, advocates of women's rights worked to enslave women by denominating them not as active producers but as the passive owners of properties to be sold. As long as women conceived of themselves as inherently valuable properties, and as long as they demanded that these properties be protected by husbands and by the paternalistic state, they would be discouraged from taking the aggressive actions that would confer vitality and hence true worth.

Tracing the etymology of "worth" to the Anglo-Saxon root " 'Weorthan,' " meaning " 'to become,' " Marsden had asserted in the *New Freewoman* in 1913 "that the question of worth, [of the] power indwelling in the individual" was "the heart of the problem": "Power, humanly speaking, means ownership, which in turn means the power of using one's possessions in the service of one's own satisfactions."[41] An attention to one's own satisfactions, rather than to one's ability to satisfy others, would be the salubrious key to "becoming" for Marsden's vigorously individualistic new woman. Marsden followed both Stirner and Friedrich Nietzsche in associating the ascetic or reactive renunciation of instinctual satisfactions with the Platonic devotion to static "concepts" and "ideals."[42] The inherently inviolable sanctity of the womb that the suffragists defended was indeed the very sort of nominalization that Stirner associated with "chlorosis" and that Nietzsche associated with the ascetic ideal, "with its fiction of an afterlife, of a 'true world' possessing all the characteristics contrary to the world of 'life,' [an ideal that] represents the means of achieving this death at the heart of life."[43]

Marsden's extraordinary claim that the suppression of sexual instincts posed a greater threat to the health than did syphilitic infection derived from her application of Stirnerian and Nietzschean studies of language and asceticism to the campaign for franchise at a time when a variety of feminists sought to ally their causes with the modern fight against race suicide.[44] In *The Great Scourge,* Pankhurst had attempted to marshal eugenic imperatives to the cause of woman suffrage by suggesting that as long as women lacked the political leverage to hold men to women's standards of chastity, men would be continually "infecting and reinfecting the race with vile disease, and so bringing about the downfall of the nation!" (*GS*, x–xi). Unlike their more conservative English and Irish counterparts, German feminists of the early teens shaped their moral directives to the needs of a nation that was gaining in military and industrial strength. National imperatives of expansion, rather than appeals to the preservation of an archaic order, enabled some German women to speak of racial degeneration as a function not of male sexual excess but of the institutional reigning-in of women's sexual instincts ("BM," 6). Alluding to the Darwinian imperative of the physical superiority of the love-child, for example, advocates of motherhood and marriage reform suggested that the illegitimate offspring of unions based on passion were often fitter than those engendered by state-sanctioned partnerships.[45] Marriage unions that were driven by unnatural economic imperatives, they reasoned, encouraged among men and women the "misrepresentation" of the natural "sexual impulses" "which are in our blood." Conventional marriages were thus smothered by an aura of "dissimulation and secrecy," a stifling miasma "which forms the most propitious soil for the development of ['sexual maladies' and] diseases" ("IMW"). Among German feminists in the years immediately preceding World War I, individual vitality and the health of the race were spoken of as being contingent on "natural" sexual expression (Weindling, *HR*, 252–57).

Modern advances in the medical treatment of syphilis bolstered German and later British feminists who challenged the belief that sexual incontinence posed a threat to the health of the race.[46] "606," or "Salvarsan," the new arsenic compound that provided a "magic bullet" syphilis cure, was not widely used in England until World War I, but its German discovery in 1909 strengthened the vitalistic rhetoric of the Motherhood Protection and Sexual Reform League that emerged in Dresden in 1911.[47] Marsden had been exposed to these German strains of feminist thought through her correspondence in 1912 with one of this group's founders, Helene Stöcker. Marsden's brief but timely editorial collaboration with the Nietzschean feminist Stöcker, together with her own firsthand reading of Nietzsche, enabled her to transfer the notion of racial vitality to the more foundational imperative of the health of the egoistic woman who follows her instincts.[48] Although Marsden ultimately objected to Stöcker's appeals to the "faked-up authority" of nominal categories including "Woman" and "Race," as well as the reformable "State," she abstracted from Stöcker's advocacy of "natural" sexual passion the notion that individual sexual initiative was a vital key to new expansive forms of identity, forms desperately needed by a modern " 'virgin' civilization."[49]

The notion that unfettered sexual expression might be a vitalistic racial tonic registers ambiguously in the content as well as the form of *Ulysses*. In Joyce's novel, sexual freedom leads to deadly diseases, but it is also an emancipatory practice linked to the recovery of salubrious truths regarding the nature of racial and gendered identities. For example, it is not just Mary

Shortall's baby who displays the literal symptoms of *tabes dorsalis,* or neuro-syphilis. It is also the conspicuously abstinent father of the infant Rudy, yet another child who, infected with "morbous germs," "disappeared" through "an arrangement" that was "beneficial to the race" (*U,* 14.1279–85). Kathleen Ferris has recently argued that strong evidence for Joyce's lifelong medical struggles with syphilis has been downplayed by scholars who draw from an archival base sanitized by the novelist's survivors (*BD,* 2–5). In a reading of *Ulysses* informed by modern medical history, Ferris offers as evidence of Leopold Bloom's syphilitic infection not only the fact that the grieving father and husband blames his heirlessness on a youthful liaison with "a daughter of night" but also the intermittent impotence that Bloom is said to experi-ence in the novel, along with the leaky incontinence of his "waterworks," the telling "lightning" pains that shoot through his stomach and lower ex-tremities, and the distinguishing stiff-legged gait that signals the syphilitic symptom called "locomotor ataxia" (58, 60, 60–61, 59). Ferris has uncovered as well in the manuscripts of the closing "Penelope" chapter of *Ulysses* references to "syphyllis" together with Joyce's teasing admission that "L.B. had clap."[50] Questions as to whether Joyce actually suffered from syphilis, like questions as to whether Joyce's epic hero should be read as a literal or a metaphorical carrier of the syphilis spirochete, are finally ancillary to the larger issue of the impact of historical writings about disease and morality on Joyce's conception of the stream of consciousness narrative. But the parallels between Joyce's and Bloom's symptoms and histories enhance our understanding of how and why modern feminist discussions of syphilis enabled Joyce to adapt Stirnerian and Nietzschean premises to the content and form of *Ulysses.*

By fashioning Bloom as both a Dublin Jew and an avowedly "soiled" and "stained" "wanderer," Joyce constructed a character whose marked status as a religious and cultural outsider and as a bearer of the stigmata of venereal "ill-luck" enables him to cut through "a lot of this talk" about purity and nation and love (*U,* 14.1218–19). In the "Cyclops" chapter of *Ulysses,* for example, Bloom's resistance to what he decries as "national hatred among nations" contains a tautology that addresses the circularity of his compan-ions' disdain for English "syphilisation" (12.1418, 12.1197).[51] By slandering Britain as an empire administered with "more pox than pax," Bloom's com-panions lend credence to the very premises of foundational purity that enabled the English to type the Irish, together with European Jews, as syphi-litic degenerates (*U,* 12.1400–1401).[52] In the "Cyclops" and "Circe" episodes of *Ulysses,* Bloom further combats the derivative "drivel" that links bodily purity to genealogical conceptions of the Irish as a "pure and virgin" race. As an internationalist who links political tolerance and pluralism with the practice of "mixed marriage," he faces the taunts of racialists, anti-Semites among them, who question his national allegiance (*U,* 15.1699). Affirming himself to be Irish for the simple reason that "I was born here," Bloom exhibits a more viable concept of national identity than that displayed by compatriots who naturalize Irishness through the ghostly medium of bloodlines (12.1431). Bloom's identity as a Jew, and as a wanderer who is stained by signs of disease—his embodiment of features that modern racialists paired as signal markers of degeneracy (*PHI,* 81)—help to inscribe him as a "truer" Irishman than his reactionary companions. Smarting from the failure of his marriage and from his failure to have sired an heir, Bloom's struggle in *Ulysses* will be to come to terms with his wife's betrayal of him and to reconfigure himself as the "limp father of thousands," the herald of an internationalist future (*U,* 5.571).

If Bloom speaks as a modern literary character fashioned against racialist conceptions of national identity, his adulterous wife Molly gives formal testimony to the changing historical relationship between race talk and talk about love. Through the Irish nationalists' linking of racial imperatives with the imperatives of male control over women's sexuality, Molly's betrayal of her husband becomes a complicated affair. In "Cyclops," when the Citizen proclaims to a round of drunken companions that it was "the adulteress and her paramour [that] brought the Saxon robbers" to Ireland, he echoes Mr Deasy's suggestion to Stephen in "Nestor" that the island's racial purity has always been bound to the fidelity of its women (*U,* 12.1157–58, 2.392–93). Overhearing the Citizen's allegory in the pub where he hides from thoughts of his wife's infidelity, Bloom is stung by the implication that he himself is a bastard. Bloom's father, Virag, was not a Saxon invader, but as a Hungarian Jew he was an illicit paramour to the very Irish adulteress whom the nationalists scorn. The Citizen's reference to the iconic "dishonoured wife" hurts Bloom doubly, moreover, as a tangible reminder of the tryst that Molly has just enjoyed with her lover (12.1163–64). Because Molly's Irish pedigree is no purer than Bloom's, however, her liaison with Boylan both embodies and confuses allegorical accounts of the racial dissolution of a nation that excludes both her and her husband.

The closing chapters of *Ulysses* testify to Joyce's understanding of the linguistic and narrative significance of changing attitudes toward the relationship between sexuality and racial degeneracy. As Molly emerges in "Penelope" as a spokesperson for the healthful expansion of women's sexual prerogatives, her soliloquy cuts across the grain of the very sort of linguistic and narrative structures that, for theorists like Marsden, had worked insidiously to contain even feminists who followed conventional parameters by linking franchise to the imperatives of "race"—be they implicitly exogamous appeals to racial "vitality" like Stöcker's or more endogamous appeals to racial "purity" like Pankhurst's. Molly's soliloquy in *Ulysses* is set in contrast to the masculine forms of language that dominate what Joyce called the "dry rocky" syllogisms of "Ithaca."[53] In this penultimate chapter, as Bloom crawls into bed beside Molly, he rehearses her liaison with Boylan in a series of passages that parody the ways in which language polices the borders of personal and national equilibrium. Now "abnegated" and "equanimious," or so "Ithaca's" "narrator" informs us, Bloom meditates on the significance of grammar to sex.

> . . . the incongruity and disproportion between the selfprolonging tension of the thing proposed to be done and the selfabbreviating relaxation of the thing done: the fallaciously inferred debility of the female: the muscularity of the male: the variations of ethical codes: the natural grammatical transition by inversion involving no alteration of sense of an aorist preterite proposition (parsed as masculine subject, monosyllabic onomatopoeic transitive verb with direct feminine object) from the active voice into its correlative aorist preterite proposition (parsed as feminine subject, auxiliary verb and quasimonosyllabic onomatopoeic past participle with complementary masculine agent) in the passive voice . . . (*U*, 17.2212–23)

In his mock-heroic attempt to master what remains of his marriage, Bloom suggests that sexual agency can be determined and even undermined by grammar. The "natural grammatical transition" that Bloom imagines to flow from "selfprolonging" arousal and "selfabbreviating" detumescence is one that involves a mechanical switching of partners from an active-voice union to a passive coupling that places Molly physically on top. (Bloom's repeated assurances to inquirers that Molly has been "tiptop" suggest that he has been wrestling with this transition throughout his very long day [*JJU*, 41, 101].) This grammatical exercise is as close as Bloom can come to asking whether Molly liked it with Boylan; and despite his lip service to "the fallaciously inferred debility of the female," Bloom's masculine solace is that whether his wife is on top or beneath, grammar itself will prevent her from answering Boylan's thrusts. Boylan can fuck Molly, and Molly can be fucked by Boylan. But through a series of skillful grammatical maneuvers, Molly is prohibited from fucking Boylan back. Bloom's dry formulations make light of the idea that, through grammatical processes that nominalize lovers into fixed parts of speech, racial and marital integrity can be shored and restored. Here the law of the sentence prohibits Molly from taking pleasure in her treasonous violation of her husband.

In fashioning such a stark contrast between Bloom's grammatical containment of his wife and the sexualized rush of Molly's unpunctuated reminiscences in "Penelope," Joyce pokes fun at modern nationalists and at dreamy proponents of "free unions" as well. After Marsden, Joyce suggests that conventional structures of language can come to "paralyze" even champions of "mixed races and mixed marriage" like Bloom. In "Ithaca," the cuckold's grammatical contortions serve less to arrest Molly's sexual agency than they do to expose the thinness of Bloom's utopian pluralism. Here, the imperatives of marital and racial integrity are compensatorily restored to those who think they own language. Because Bloom is hurting and because, as a masochist, he hungers to savor his pain, he seizes control in a manner that exposes the inadequacy of language to the very "instinct of activity" that drives the actions of the characters in the novel. But if Bloom's hair-splitting pedantry now fumbles to repair the genealogical ruptures that *Ulysses* has so vividly thematized in the limp body and the warmed bed of its hero, Molly's linguistic unruliness points to a further utopian grounding of culture and language in libidinal drives.

> the rosegardens and the jessamine and geraniums and cactuses and Gibraltar as a girl where I was a Flower of the mountain yes when I put the rose in my hair like the Andalusian girls used or shall I wear a red yes and how he kissed me under the Moorish wall and I thought well as well him as another and then I asked him with my eyes to ask again yes and then he asked me would I yes to say yes my mountain flower and first I put my arms around him yes and drew him down to me so he could feel my breasts all perfume yes and his heart was going like mad and yes I said yes I will Yes. (*U*, 18.1601–9)

By the end of the long soliloquy that closes *Ulysses*, Molly's memories of a series of encounters with men have led her not away from her husband but rather back to a foundational moment with Bloom, a union rooted in a landscape whose resplendence pays tribute to the riotously generative graces of nature. Evading grammatical and narrative constraints, and erasing national and racial boundaries along with the names of the lovers she remembers, Molly has sung passionately of the flowers that God spills from Ireland to Gibraltar and of the beauty of originary unions engendered among them.

> I love flowers Id love to have the whole place swimming in roses God of
> heaven theres nothing like nature the wild mountains then the sea and the
> waves rushing then the beautiful country with the fields of oats and wheat
> and all kinds of things and all the fine cattle going about that would do your
> heart good to see rivers and lakes and flowers all sorts of shapes and smells
> and colours springing up even out of the ditches primroses and violets na-
> ture it is as for them saying theres no God I wouldnt give a snap of my two
> fingers for all their learning why don't they go and create something I often
> asked him atheists or whatever they call themselves go and wash the cobbles
> off themselves first then they go howling for the priest and they dying and
> why why because theyre afraid of hell on account of their bad conscience ah
> yes I know them well who was the first person in the universe before there
> was anybody that made it all who ah that they don't know neither do I so
> there you are they might as well try to stop the sun from rising tomorrow the
> sun shines for you he said the day we were lying among the rhododendrons
> on Howth head . . . 16 years ago my God after that long kiss I near lost my
> breath yes he said I was a flower of the mountain (*U*, 18.1557–76)

In "Penelope" Joyce invests Molly's language with libidinal primacy by modulating the narrative techniques that reflect his conviction that all words are borrowed words. Joyce has insistently blended the narrator's voice into the voices of characters in earlier chapters of *Ulysses*. "Penelope" differs from these chapters, and from other writings of Joyce's, in that the torrent of its speaker's reminiscences overwhelms any trace of an authorial narrator. Lacking a narrative voice to blend into the voice of its characters, "Penelope"'s mergings aspire to something other than an assault on the realistic novel's "transparent" narrative voice. By refusing to "pervert" Molly's language with commas or with "unreal" quotation marks, Joyce fashions the "clou" of *Ulysses* as an antidote to the varieties of linguistic paralysis that have afflicted other characters in the novel.[54] "Penelope" counters not only the nominalism that "contains" Molly in "Ithaca" but also the paralysis that follows from the sudden displacement of nominal foundations, a phenomenon vividly illustrated by Stephen's glimpse into the bottomless mirror. It does so by portraying Molly's language as a medium that is true to libidinal experience.

If we were to edit one small portion of "Penelope," for example, adding internal quotation marks to the well-known sequence that closes *Ulysses*, we would likely place them around the "one true thing" that Molly remembers Bloom saying, that she was "a flower of the mountain" (*U*, 18.1577, 18.1576).

and then I asked him with my eyes to ask again yes and then he asked me
would I yes to say yes my mountain flower

With Bloom's words so isolated, we hear his voice within Molly's as she remembers him asking her to " 'Say yes my mountain flower.' " But Molly's syntax also asks us to demarcate as an integral speakerly phrase an overlapping set of words that she herself breathes: " 'then he asked me [would I yes] to say yes.' " Molly's third-person reminiscence, " 'then he asked me . . . to *say yes*,' " has been absorbed and completed by Leopold's voice: " '*say yes* my mountain flower.' " In the conjunction of these two spoken phrases, there is not an absence but rather a richly doubled presence attached to the hinge words "*say yes*." Molly's ambiguous syntax reveals a foundational moment of passionate union wherein lovers feed one another with the desire that unites them, a union that is prohibited by laws of grammar that subordinate women to the prerogatives of patrilineal and national purity. In what Joyce referred to as the "Weib" of "Penelope's" syntactic interstices, Molly's soliloquy becomes a generative force, not as *féminine écriture* but as a graceful disclosure of identity as a fluidly mutual process, one that escapes the identitarian confines of gender and race.[55] In contrast with Stephen, whose very "substance" has been drained into a crack in a mirror, Molly solidifies herself through Bloom's eyes and words. Among the flowers of Ireland, Andalusia, and England's Gibraltar, she finds herself fashioned by the hand of her maker.

In her memory of her original union with her husband at the close of the novel, Molly illustrates the mutually constitutive process through which a lover becomes a lover through the eyes and words of another who shares in desire. In "Penelope" this process of mutual self-constitution is fashioned into an explicit metaphor for the modern author's assumption of identity through the eyes and words of his literary creations; and as a robust and well-traveled adulteress, Molly feeds this new vision of constitutive narrative foundations back into the novel's revisioning of the foundations of gendered and racial identity. In a rambling soliloquy that was praised by Joyce's contemporaries for its "X-ray" fidelity to "ordinary human consciousness" and by poststructuralist critics for having unleashed suppressed truths about the nature of discourse, Molly seizes what Joyce called the "sane full amoral" authority of a new literary narrative.[56] Joyce's understanding of how to challenge brittle conceptions of nominal identity through the words and bodies of Leopold and Molly, and his reassessment through these characters of conventional marital and genealogical structures, derives from Stirnerian and Nietzschean studies of language and morality, studies that were applied by modern feminists to the most "revolutionary" cultural movement of Joyce's day.

3. Nietzsche's Writings on Language and Identity

If Molly gains body through Stirnerian inquiries into the emptiness of nominal categories such as "Woman" and "Race," her soliloquy gains its dynamic representational authority, its capacity to embody the ravenous richness of identity, through Nietzschean conceptions of the bodiless "will" as a foundation that flashes through sentences and substances. Amid the growing ranks of political and intellectual "individualists" in the early modern English-speaking world, Stirner and Nietzsche had been linked as the tandem "prophet" and "poet" of the doctrine of egoism.[57] The revival of Stirner in England and America during the first decades of the century has been attributed to the interest of political radicals and intellectuals in contemporary translations of Nietzsche's writings; and through the influence of W. B. Yeats and Arthur Symons, early modern Dublin had become a world center of the cult of Nietzsche.[58] Joyce's brother Stanislaus has written of Nietzsche's significance to Joyce's writings during the period of *Dubliners;* in the opening chapter of *Ulysses,* Joyce portrays Buck Mulligan, a character modeled on his former Nighttown companion Oliver Gogarty, as a "hyperborean" adherent to the Nietzschean cult of the "new paganism," a movement that flamboyantly shirked religious and middle-class moral constraints (*U,* 1.92, 1.176).[59]

In their respective investigations of the genesis of bourgeois morality, and in their appeals to the unfettered "wills" of egoistic women and artists, Marsden and Joyce made no secret of their indebtedness to Nietzsche's writings on the origins of the ascetic ideal.[60] Nietzsche's alleged celebration of even the power of the tyrant had proved too rigorous for a number of the modern radicals who had come to embrace Stirner ("I," xiv). But the anarcho-feminist Marsden, whose writings were deemed dangerous to mainstream feminist interests, together with the novelist whose "cool assaults" on "Morality" she admired and defended, followed Nietzsche in believing that the priestly Judeo-Christian "turn[ing] inward" of man's "animal" "instincts" had produced "the *true fate* in the sanitary history of European man," the "ascetic ideal" that Nietzsche himself viewed as more damaging to the "health and race-vitality" of Europe than even the rival ravages of alcoholic and syphilitic blood poisoning.[61] In suggesting that it was the suffragettes' " 'purity' atmosphere" that endangered the future by engendering a "dull" and "petrified" " 'virgin' civilization," Marsden localized Nietzsche's theoretical portrayal of the stultifying contagion of morality ("CW," 46). Joyce did much the same, invoking contemporary discussions of disease and morality in his portrayal of the native integrity of a "stained" Jewish wanderer and in his foregrounding of a lusty adulteress as the source of the strongest and least corrupted language in *Ulysses*. But Nietzsche's particular significance for the lingual philosopher Marsden and for the novelist who overturned the structures of linguistic and narrative necessity in a formal revolt against the "syphilized" constraints of nation and gender lay in his analysis of the grammatical foundations of asceticism.

Nietzsche attuned Marsden and Joyce to the broadly pathological significance of the necessary relationships between subject and predicate and between substance and attribute. Marsden's championing of vitality as a more solid ground of identity than the body itself was derived from Stöcker's writings on motherhood and marriage reform and from Nietzsche's conception of the ontological priority of becoming over being, or of the deed over the doer; and her feminist application of Nietzsche's genealogical critique of the "metaphysics of substance" provided a model for Joyce's historically bound conception of an experimental literary narrative as a means of overcoming cultural and aesthetic inanition—degenerative phenomena that were thought to have stemmed from a modern turning inward of the instincts. For feminist critics of bourgeois morality, the newly "masculinized" spirochete represented a biological extension of the invasive speculum, an instrument used by state doctors in the involuntary screening and segregation of English and Irish prostitutes in the 1870s and 1880s.[62] Both were social instruments that damaged women not only by violating their bodies but also by staging relations between men and women as exchanges between active subjects and passive objects. The Victorian speculum or "steel penis," the feeding tubes later forced upon hunger-striking suffragettes, and the modern specter of the syphilitic husband all worked to reinforce the necessary priority of aggressive male action over female reaction.[63] But Nietzsche's belief that "philosophical systems" were "dominated" and "directed" by the "grammatical functions" upon which they were elaborated enabled Marsden and Joyce to see that among these modern instruments and images of subjugation, language was a particularly insidious medium that contributed not only to the historically gendered suppression of the agency of "the Sex" but also to the subjugation of the feminists who sought to reverse it.[64]

In *A Genealogy of Morals*, Nietzsche viewed the Judeo-Christian tradition as fostering a modern "*slave-revolt in morality*," which overturned the Greek aristocratic equation of goodness with dominating strength (*AGM*, 31). Nietzsche believed that "modernity" was characterized by a mass embrace of poverty and political weakness. In the "judaîse[d], christianise[d], vulgarise[d]" world of the last two millenniums, forms of defensive reaction had come to supplant vigorous "deeds" as the medium of virtuous expression (*AGM*, 31, 34): "Whereas on the one hand, all noble morality takes its rise from a triumphant Yea-saying to one's self," reads the Haussmann translation of *Genealogy* with which Joyce was familiar, "slave-morality will, on the other hand, from the very beginning, say No to something 'exterior,' 'different,' 'not self;' *this* No being its creative deed" (*AGM*, 35; *CJI*, 123). For Nietzsche the new slavish notion that the identity of a "strong" person can be claimed through his or her weak, renunciative activities entails a divorce of identity from the actions that should define it. It was this divorce that led Nietzsche to conceive of "the doer," or the pure self, as a "fiction." And the sickly lineaments of this fiction were perpetually rehearsed through causal relations that grammar assigns to subjects and predicates.

Nietzsche's conception of the grammatical origins of the reactive modern subject laid a foundation not only for Marsden's erasure of the diseased bodies of the woman and of the "feminized" race of the *mal du siècle* but also for Joyce's related dissolution of the author as a nominal presence in *Ulysses*.[65] In *Genealogy* Nietzsche suggested that grammar cleaves, affects a clean division between, subjects and predicates. In so doing it necessitates the construction of a causal relationship between two parts of speech that are themselves incomplete expressions of a dynamic and continuous conceptual ground. It was this dynamic, prelinguistic foundation that Nietzsche conceived as the "becoming," or the grammatically and materially unchained "fulguration," of the unembodied will (*AGM*, 47).[66] For modern egoists who viewed Stirner and Nietzsche as champions of individualistic resistance against the incursions of the modern state, Nietzsche's dynamic, bodiless "will" was a construct that dispersed and so preserved the atomistic authority of the Stirnerian "ego." In *A Genealogy of Morals,* Nietzsche appeared to have elaborated Stirner's conception of the liberal subject's enslavement to abstract humanist concepts into a critique of the grammatical conception of the subject itself.

> To demand of strength, that it should *not* manifest itself as strength . . . is as absurd as to demand of weakness that it should manifest itself as strength. A quantum of power is . . . equal [to a] quantum of . . . action. More correctly speaking, it is even this . . . acting itself, and nothing else,—and it is caused to appear otherwise only through the seduction of language (and of the cardinal errors of reason, fossilized in language), which takes and mistakes all action as conditioned by something acting, by a "subject." Even as the people will separate the lightning from its flash and take the latter for the *doing,* the effect of a subject called lightning, so popular morality will sever strength from manifestations of strength, as if behind the strong man there existed an indifferent substratum which is *free* to manifest strength or not. But there is no such substratum; there is no "being" behind doing, acting, becoming. "The doer" is merely a fictitious addition to the doing—the "doing" is all. (*AGM,* 46–47)

For modern individualists who linked Stirner and Nietzsche as founders of the egoist creed, the critique of grammar upon which Nietzsche founded his notion of the "metaphysics of substance" was a strategic extension of Stirner's critique of nominalization in *The Ego and His Own.* In the mid–nineteenth century, Stirner had attacked humanistic idealism, suggesting that a devotion to abstract maxims and terms suppressed an individual's true appetites, resulting in the chlorotic condition of the starved liberal subject. More than forty years later, Nietzsche carried Stirner's argument a step further, suggesting that appetites themselves were not attributes of the individual subject but rather the foundational phenomena that produced the traces of agency upon which the false notion of a static subject was based. In terms of grammar, Stirner's anarchistic project had involved a scaling back of the generalized nominal categories upon which political and religious structures were built. Beneath the calcified general nouns of the state could be found the more germinal particular nouns of the subject that the state had come to smother. Nietzsche appeared to have devised a more thoroughgoing grammatical purge that avoided the dependence of the Stirnerian construct of the "ego" upon the exhausted false subject that it came to replace. Nietzsche conceived general and particularized nominal subjects themselves as fictions produced by false assignations of causality to the foundational expression of appetite. For Nietzsche there was from the very beginning no thing that grows hungry. There were rather expressions of hunger, and these expressions were falsely contoured by grammar.

Joyce conceived *Ulysses* as a formal literary tonic to modern appeals to the sanctity of "race" and "nation" through those lines of Stirnerian and Nietzschean thought that Marsden displayed in her analysis of the suffragettes' appeals to the inviolability of women and modern races. Christabel Pankhurst's injunction "Never again must young women enter into marriage blindfolded" was a eugenically shaded appeal to self-possession on behalf of a constituency that had long been designated as "the Sex."[67] In *The Great Scourge and How to End It,* Pankhurst used the urgency of syphilitic contamination to spur women into becoming something more than the reactive objects of autonomous male subjects: the modern woman's medically and morally sanctioned refusal to enter blindly into unions with men, suggested Pankhurst, would challenge the male notion that "women are sex-beings and nothing more" (*GS*, 111). Pankhurst's own allusion to women in blindfolds suggests that "the Sex" was a social construction that perpetuated the notion that women's minds were innately more limited than men's. Pre-Victorian conceptions of "the Sex" as an unseeing constituency enjoyed a renewed currency in early modern Europe, a phenomenon indicated by the enormous popularity of psychobiological studies of gender differences such as Otto Weininger's 1903 book *Sex and Character.*[68]

Weiningerian adherents to traditional notions of "the Sex" held that because men's identities derived from spheres of activity other than the sexual sphere, men acquired an objective purchase in sexual and other relations that enabled them to see the world more clearly and completely than women could (Weininger, *SC*, 90–92). Women's perspectives were more subjective and hence more limited than men's because, as creatures whose primary purpose was believed to be the procreation of the species, their identities hinged utterly on transactions associated with sexual reproduction. Embracing the very deeply ingrained philosophical premises that facilitated this conception of women as beings who lacked "the power of making concepts" (194), Pankhurst argued that as long as women continued to view their identities as contingent on their sexual and reproductive activities and not on their activities as the guardians of their bodies and the health of the race, they would be poisoned, and the broadly conceived "race" they belonged to would be poisoned, by the more self-contained men to whom they turned for fulfillment. For Pankhurst, women would gain equal standing with men as creatures in command of their own sexual functions only by refusing to be the passive "objects" of the knowing "subjects" who willfully invaded their bodies.

In fashioning this call to women to transcend their debilitating status as members of "the Sex," Pankhurst attempted to reverse the poles of a traditionally gendered dichotomy that empowered men as seeing "subjects" over the "blindfolded" sexual "objects" upon whom they willfully exhibited their agency. But however it was gendered, the dichotomous relationship between actors and reactors hinged on the notion that a "substance," such as a "man" or a "woman"—or even the wider body of the degenerative modern "race"— could be distinguished from its "attributes," or the activities that it mastered or failed to master in acquiring its status as either a subject or an object. And the very premise that a substance might be distinct from its attributes was one that Nietzsche had encouraged modern intellectuals to reject. In terms of the very philosophical investigations of language that Marsden and Joyce applied to politics and aesthetics, the innately chaste womanly woman was an entity who was both conceptually and grammatically masculinized through the imperatives of widespread sexual disease. Rejecting the reactive nature of "the Sex," she acquired a nominal status as a self-contained subject whose activities centered not on her couplings with men but on the guarding of the nominal integrity of her body.

In a 1971 essay, "Nietzsche and Metaphysical Language," Michel Harr notes that for Nietzsche it is "the belief in . . . the truth of grammatical categories," particularly that of "the structure of subject and predicate," that conditions the ontological priority of substance and attribute, the Cartesian belief, in other words, "that 'I' is the subject of 'think,' whereas it is rather the thoughts that come to 'me'" ("NML," 17–18). Claiming that "at bottom, faith in grammar simply conveys the will to be the 'cause' of one's thoughts" (18), Harr's investigation of the metaphysics of Nietzsche's "lightning flash" exposes the historical intellectual kinship between Marsden's strategic ontological erasure of the modern woman's syphilitic body and Joyce's narrative solution of the modern author. For contemporary feminist critics of identity politics like Judith Butler, Nietzsche is useful as a modern thinker who suggests that the notion that an autonomous masculine "substance" determines its "attributes" is as much written into grammatical processes as into the social rituals through which men have traditionally staged their mastery over women (GT, 16–25).[69] To modern feminists who recognized that a central premise in the subjugation of women was the belief that, in contrast to "the Sex," men possessed a substance that was innately distinguished from its attributes, Nietzsche suggested that the institutional erasure of male *and* female agency might run deeper than the gendered rituals—like the historical speculum examinations and the syphilitic infection of women by men—that appeared to brutally display the prerogatives of male mastery. Even the men who mastered their sexual "attributes" at the expense of the fully sexualized women who were compelled to submit to them were finally subjugated by a larger process of nominalization that severed them from the dynamic libidinal foundations that were their true sources of power.

Marsden's appeal to the impenetrable "unitary stream" of identity that lay beneath the syphilitic's diseased body reflected her understanding of the theoretical weakness of Pankhurst's appeals to women—and to poisoned modern "races"—as self-contained "subjects." Similarly, Joyce's refusal to distinguish a knowing authorial narrative perspective from the more limited perspectives of his characters, and his attendant claims that all words are borrowed words, reflects his understanding of the theoretical weakness of the idea that knowing speakers lie beneath the words that are spoken. In *Ulysses* Joyce adapted to literary form not the theoretical premises of post-structuralism but the very nineteenth-century studies of language and morality that Marsden had so vividly illustrated in contemporary essays like "The Chastity of Women." He conceived of the novel as a medium immune to the ravages of morality by fashioning the authorial "I" not as the nominally insular subject of "think" but rather as the "vital" unitary stream into which thoughts are drawn. By modulating his narrative techniques in the scandalous soliloquy of a character who returns the "word" to the "flesh," Joyce channeled the stream of *Ulysses* into that of a lover who shines through the eyes and words of another (*MU*, 272; *U*, 18.567).

❖ In the opening pages of *Ulysses,* Stephen's recognition of his linguistic constructedness in the mirror of an Irish servant is an impure disclosure that leaks through a faulty narrative structure. Representing the inadequacy of English literary and linguistic forms to the Irish poet who inherits them, the cracked mirror of "Irish art" is said to display Stephen's knowledge of himself as a necessarily defective colonial subject, one whose image has been "distorted" by the English "interpreters" who sentence the Irish "at the bar of public opinion."[70] Before raising the mirror to Stephen, Buck Mulligan, a character modeled on the heretical nihilist who led Joyce through his Nighttown debauches in 1904, adopts words of the colonist who nominalizes and hence paralyzes his Irish subjects in the way that grammar freezes women: "That fellow I was with in the Ship last night, said Buck Mulligan, says you have g. p. i. . . . General paralysis of the insane! . . . Look at yourself, he said, you dreadful bard!" (*U*, 1.127–134). Here, Stephen's image of himself as infested with "vermin" expresses the systemic poisoning of the Irish through the imported linguistic and literary forms that contain them.

In *Ulysses* the condition of the subjugated colonial is likened to the condition of the woman further subjugated within the reaches of Irish society. As Mulligan pointedly tells Stephen, the Irish servant's mirror that portrays him as bestialized belongs to a "skivvy," or a maid. But if this image of a "dogsbody" covered with "vermin" is one that harkens to nationalist and women's struggles, it is equally an expression of revolt on the part of an author who believes himself to be nominalized, and hence paralyzed as an effective advocate of these struggles, by the very words that he puts to paper. In Mulligan's mirror, Stephen's author sees himself not as diseased but as contained by the structures of language, by the crippling grammatical and semiotic conventions that curtail his retrieval of what Joyce called the liberating "water," the true libidinal experience that melts the nominal conceptions that hold even the rebel in thrall (*LJJ*2, 191). The words that engender the author of *Ulysses* are conditioned by necessary relationships between subject and predicate, between substance and attribute, and between the author and the text—a series of conceptual structures whose rigid necessary relation will paralyze the very identities that they engender.

❖ Ezra Pound wrote in 1935 that the French anarchist Proudhon would "be found somewhere in the foundations of perhaps all contemporary economic thought that has life it." As early as 1913–14, "Proudhonian" theories of "volitional" currency had in fact helped the poet to replace the gold standard of worldly presence in words with a more structuralist standard of reference, one that was based on innately ethical exchanges between producers in a golden-age economy. The novelist Joyce drew from a different set of anarchist traditions in formulating his innovative narrative practices. Nineteenth-century critiques of language and morality, critiques that circulated widely among early modern anarchist intellectuals, enabled him to divine the libidinal authority of language and identity that pulsed beneath the structures of necessity that covered it. Like the anarcho-feminist Marsden, Joyce came to recognize that the processes that Nietzsche illuminated in his analysis of the metaphysics of grammar, the distancing of the "I" from the activity that defined it, fostered not mastery but an estrangement of the Stirnerian liberal subject from his or her "true" libidinal sources of power. Steeped in Stirner and Nietzsche, and prompted by Marsden's application of their tenets to discussions of the very syphilis contagion that had captivated him since his visits to Nighttown in 1904, Joyce devised the narrative experiments of *Ulysses* in an effort to release a richer account of libidinal experience than that afforded by conventional grammatical and conceptual structures. In terms of a fictional narrative, sexuality and racial vitality alike could be most fully represented, and most fully effected, through a gradual merging of borrowed and original words.

FOUR

William Carlos Williams, Prohibition, and Immigration

I nterviewed by a Dutch paper upon returning from the United States in 1921, Albert Einstein praised the neighborly "we" ethic of American philanthropists and the "solidity" of American manufactured goods. But the German-born physicist was disturbed by the isolationism of "the most powerful among the technically advanced countries in the world" (*IO, 7*). For Einstein America's trade tariffs, together with its disdain for the Versailles Treaty as an instrument of disarmament, betrayed an "anxious" and even "irrational" fear of international engagement (5). Not only did the United States hinder its own economic growth with prohibitive tariffs; its shrinking diplomatic profile in a world "where there are no longer any barriers between the continents" was "bound in the end to lead to disaster" (7). The lack of taverns in America was another thing that troubled Einstein. "The public house is a place which gives people the opportunity to exchange views and ideas on public affairs," he said. In its second full year of existence, the prohibition against making and selling liquor in America was threatening to implode America's isolationism, dividing American citizens one from another. Dry laws both dampened the democratic exchange of ideas and fostered contempt for the institutions of democracy. There is nothing "more destructive of respect for the government and the law of the land than passing laws which cannot be enforced" (6).

When William Carlos Williams accepted the Dial Award for poetry in 1927, he raised an empty gin flask and spoke of "a degradation/ticked off daily round me like the newspapers." For Williams, the Dial prize was a consolation, a momentary "lifting" of "the prohibition/we all feel." Toasting the Eighteenth Amendment as an empty "Senate's egg" that testified to "the motions of drinking," he implied that the closing of the saloon in the 1920s had cast a shadow over his work (*CP1*, 267). Prohibition had indeed contributed to Williams's refashioning of the American artist as the vibrant inhabitant of his own local experience; and it had helped to found his invention of a "hand to mouth" poetry whose "difficult form" derived not from "imitation" but from a resolute "clinging" to "the vernacular" (267).[1] The dry laws that reigned in America from 1920 to 1933 shaped the development of modern American poetry by enabling Williams to conceive his struggle against restrictive poetic traditions as an outsider's struggle against the "prohibitive" puritanical inheritance of modern America (*IAG*, 128). In a nation "befouled by Volsteads and Bryans," artists like Williams came to identify with the very invasive foreign "hordes" against whom temperance was pitched.[2] For Williams, as for Joyce, who had written of the modern Irish poet's flight from the degeneratively inbred nationalist factions that engulfed him, nativity had assumed a special meaning and urgency at a time when it was most difficult to stay at home.[3]

Einstein was right in noting that prohibition served to isolate Americans from one another. For many proponents of dry laws, isolation was precisely what the Eighteenth Amendment should accomplish. And the champions of the amendment that had been ratified in 1919 "with a speed that . . . left the country gasping" made little effort to conceal who it was that prohibition would outlaw.[4] William Jennings Bryan exposed the xenophobic undercurrents of the movement in 1918 when he confused the dry cause with the allied cause in Europe. Speaking to members of the Anti-Saloon League just months before the passage of an amendment banning "the manufacture, sale or transportation of intoxicating liquors" within the United States, Bryan linked as "two evils" the "kaiser" and the "brewery autocracy" that was losing its grip on the American home front (*ASL*, 69). The popular evangelist Billy Sunday was more inflammatory in his demonization of drink: "The Prussian beast and her whelps have been caged, now we are on the trail of King Alcohol and his brood" (12). Wartime prohibitionists had been quick to kindle the nationalism of a cause that pitted rural fundamentalists against the Old World immigrants—and particularly the immigrants from Germany—who managed a large number of America's urban saloons.

"Look what Prohibition has done for us," spoke the Reverend R. A. Hutchinson: "It has taken the saloon out of state after state. . . . It has taken one of the sins out of Cincinnati, and it has taken the 'toot' and the 'tonic' both out of the Teutonic brewer" (90).

The association of alcohol with German Americans was certainly an outgrowth of wartime anti-German hysteria, which led to bans on pretzels and Beethoven, as well as to righteous crusades to rename sauerkraut as "liberty cabbage" and German measles as "Victory Measles."[5] But anti-immigrant sentiment was not entirely a product of the war. By the early years of the twentieth century, the Prohibition Party had drifted away from its original progressive affiliations toward support of the Bible as the "Magna Carta of . . . national safety" and toward promotion of the large-scale "Americanization" of unassimilated immigrants (EE, 84, 87). Dry laws came to target "Besodden Europe," who "sends here her drink-makers, her drunkard-makers, and her drunkards . . . with all their un-American and anti-American ideas of morality and government"; prohibition was increasingly linked to calls for immigration quotas by temperance advocates who warned that "hundreds of thousands of foreigners . . . come here . . . not for freedom to worship God, as our fathers did, but for freedom to raise the devil."[6] By the early teens, race-conscious prohibitionists were portraying the new wave of eastern European and Italian immigrant laborers as the sodden objects of their reforms (WD, 36, 87). Statistically associated with "sex-sin" and syphilis as degenerate poisons to the American race, alcohol and immigration posed a tandem threat to America's moral and evolutionary inheritance (EE, 51–53).[7]

> We quarantine our ports of entry against cholera, yellow fever, the bubonic plague, smallpox and the like. Isn't it more important to protect our babies against alcoholism and the microbes of ignorance, superstition and prejudice, and thus prevent those who are nearest the level of the chimpanzee and the baboon from establishing the intellectual, social and political inheritance and environment of the baby? Isn't it about time that those of us interested in and aware of the power of the government, the opportunity and responsibility of the state, should awaken to a sense of realization that it is our duty to give, at least, as much attention to the breeding and rearing of babies as we do to the breeding and raising of Percheron horses, Holstein cattle and Berkshire hogs?[8]

The national prohibition of January 1920 coincided with a campaign to stabilize America's "racial" identity through the passage of increasingly restrictive immigration quotas, an effort culminating in the Johnson Act of 1921 and then finally in the severely restrictive Johnson-Reed National Origins Act of 1924. Johnson-Reed ruled that the admission of future immigrants should be proportionate to the ethnic makeup of the nation. By determining this makeup on the basis of an 1890 census count, the National Origins Act favored a continued admission of British and northern European immigrants while reducing the flow of the New Immigration from eastern and southern Europe to roughly one-fifth the annual number that had been admitted during the first decades of the century.[9] Dry laws and immigration were allied as prohibitive measures for Americans who wished to defend themselves against virulently invasive threats to the integrity of the American race, a race with Anglo-Saxon genetic underpinnings (HA, 150).

Williams may or may not have followed the scandalous New York Times reports of Einstein's Dutch interview, wherein the popular scientist was alleged to have dismissed American men as the "toy dogs" of their immeasurably extravagant wives (ELT, 348–49). But the homebound poet who complained to his colleagues in 1920 "We live in bags" would have sympathized with Einstein's assessment of America's global isolationism and the internally isolating effects of prohibition.[10] It was in an alienating climate of "prohibitions," "fetishes," and "don'ts" that Williams called for American artists to "become awake to [their] own locality" by paying attention to the "immediacy of [their] own contact."[11] Here, Williams joined a call among American painters and critics for a "freshly evolved localized personality in modern poetics," one that pushed past "local color" toward a more universalizing "localized idea of modernism."[12] Bram Dijkstra has chronicled the nativist spirit that emerged before Williams among avant-garde visual artists in New York in the teens and the twenties. Waldo Frank, Marsden Hartley, and Paul Rosenfeld were among the colleagues who labored to adapt the particulars of American experience to the Continental aesthetics of cubists, surrealists, and dadaists. The "french orchid" that Williams wished to Americanize in 1920 included "dadaesque" random constructions and an aesthetic of opacity based on nonrepresentational renderings of the artwork as an impenetrable object.[13]

Walter Benn Michaels has suggested that Williams "Americanized" such aesthetics by adapting them to current "identitarian" conceptions of nativism: the nonmimetic poem's bald assertion of its identity as a poem became in the 1920s a formal enactment of the American's assertion of primary Americanness (OA, 83–84). But if an avant-garde celebration of the materiality of poetry contributed to the Americanization of Williams's own work,

Williams's prosodic invention of an American poetic idiom turned more on the writings of modern pragmatists and physicists—writings that emphasized process as the measure of identity. Reaching the poet through the arid medium of America in the 1920s, the new relative measures of John Dewey and of Einstein himself assumed a uniquely American poetic significance for Williams. Prohibition and the immigration quotas that the dry laws supported served to alter Williams's sense of the measure of poetry, encouraging a relative apportioning of a poetic line founded on the American idiom.

1. Williams and the Prohibitionary Climate of 1920s America

Prohibition and alcohol are associated with literary tradition and invention in Williams's aesthetic statements of the early 1920s. During this period he couched his invention of an idiomatic poetic measure amid a reversal of the terms of both restrictionist polemics against racial mixing and related prohibitionist polemics against alcohol. While prohibitionists were attempting to link alcohol and alcoholism to the immigrants who threatened America's Anglo-Saxon racial and cultural heritage, Williams portrayed alcohol as more a tonic than a poison. In his freewheeling poetic and prosodic experiments of 1923, Williams wrote of the avant-gardist's desire to "intoxicate" the "imagination" and to let "words" "get drunk" (*I*, 90–91, 159). Alcohol was a forbidden tool that enabled the avant-gardist not only to "crack" the "too stiff personal[ity]" of the artist, but to shatter the artist's medium: "Awu tsst grang splith gra pragh og bm."[14]

If "white mule" could be an intoxicating elixir to the modern writer and his medium, however, it could also be the enervating poison that sapped the "heat" and the "core" and the "drive" from the nativist effort to generate an indigenous American poetic.[15] Distinguishing himself from dry doctors who condemned drink as a corrosive to both somatic and national immunity, Williams linked the symptoms of alcohol poisoning not to the "invasive hordes" that threatened America's Anglo-Saxon racial identity but rather to the inbred sophisticates who imbibed too heavily in Anglo-Saxon literary traditions. The poet complained to John Riordan in 1925 that he himself could not begin to "compete" with Eliot "in technical knowledge of the conned examples of English poetry which he seems to know so well. . . . I'll be damned if I see why we need all of us fall into his trap . . . and by swilling his words into us arrive in the end at his brand of despair."[16] Williams sounds like a temperance advocate here in his condemnation of Eliot's plagiarism of Anglo-Saxon traditions. His dry-decade troping of *The Waste Land* with swill suggests that alcohol is a danger not because it speeds the invasion of new, foreign contaminants but because it leads to a hardening of the shell of tradition, a form of bourgeois rigor mortis akin to the malaise that James Joyce had earlier diagnosed as "the general paralysis of an insane society" ("PA," 85).

Taboos against drinking and racial mixing were twin evils for Williams in his avant-garde writings of the early 1920s. The writer began his dadaist jumble of poetry and manifestos in *Spring and All* by disclosing his own apocalyptic "monster project" of renewal: "Tomorrow we the people of the United States are going to Europe armed to kill every man, woman and child" (*I,* 90). A mere five years after the staggering casualties of the war, futurist calls for war as the world's only hygiene echoed with an absurdity that Williams readily embraced. Williams's break with tradition, like his break with the traditional bourgeois sanctity of life, was to be a deep one, deeper than the breaks effected by the nationalistic iconoclasm of the Italian futurist and the English vorticist avant-gardes. The American apocalypse would be evolutionary in scale: "First we shall kill them and then they, us" (90). Nationalistic and humanistic concerns are equally anathema for the artist who moves "chaotically about," "refusing or rejecting" the coherence of values or programs (115). Sparing only the Russians, for whom "we shall build a bridge from edge to edge of the Atlantic," Williams's apocalypse jabbed both at the isolationist paranoia associated with immigration quotas and anti-Communist sentiment during the Bolshevist Red Scare, and at the sticky humanist logic of the melting pot that finds the "human race, yellow, black, brown, red and white, agglutinated into one enormous soul," into a "horrid unity" that "boils and digests itself within the tissues of the great Being of Eternity that we shall then have become" (90, 91).

If Americanization programs attack the vigorous sources of the American language, assimilation itself produces a cancerous mass that is more dangerous than the virulent "invaders" that threaten its integrity. Williams makes a deathly specter of both restrictionists and assimilationists in *Spring and All,* suggesting that the nihilistic spirit of the avant-garde is built into the melting pot itself: "Why should we care? Children laughingly fling themselves under the wheels of the street cars, airplanes crash gaily to the earth. Someone has written a poem" (*I,* 92). The logic that perverts America's institutions of self-preservation turns the Eighteenth Amendment itself into a drunken debauch, making puritanical America a suitable spot for an artistic apocalypse: "The imagination, intoxicated with prohibitions," Williams admonished in *Spring and All*, "rises to drunken heights to destroy the world" (90–91). Williams's 1923 assessment of Poe as an original who wrote violently against "the indriving force of a crudely repressive environment" (111) helped the modern American to transplant European futurist and dadaist aesthetics of annihilation into the soil of American letters.

For Williams, the crudely repressive environment of America in the early 1920s was characterized by puritanical prohibitions against racial contamination in the forms of both temperance and eugenics. Williams recognized that even liberal Americanization programs buried anxieties about mongrelization in their cultivation of "the generic opalescence of humanity in . . . our immigrants."[17] Residual Lamarckian notions of the direct impact of environment on an organism's genetic makeup had suggested to some advocates of the melting pot that the American physical and cultural environment could genetically bend races to patriotic American designs.[18] Assimilationist enterprises could thus abstract and neutralize not only the cultural integrity of America's new immigrant population but even their genetic sources of foreignness. As the passage of the Eighteenth Amendment and the Johnson-Reed National Origins Act suggests, however, the years between 1910 and 1924 also witnessed a rise in more reactionary attempts at engineering American racial identity. During an era that was building toward unprecedented peaks of Ku Klux Klan membership, prominent American eugenicists like Henry H. Goddard were blending statistical studies with the findings of early modern geneticists to implicate miscegenation, and the venereal disease and chronic alcoholism that attended it, to the atrophying of the American race.[19] Prohibitionist and restrictionist sentiment gained increasing prominence in popular journals and in congressional debates, with authorities like Vice President Coolidge cautioning in *Good Housekeeping* against the dangers of racial mixing (*PAN*, 318, 395 n. 53). In both its liberal and its reactionary measures, the American milieu in the early 1920s was a crudely repressive background against which Williams labored to fashion a "dynamitized" native artistic identity.

In Williams's statements in *The Great American Novel* of 1923 on eugenic prohibitions against racial mixing, one can see that the repressive atmosphere of American anxieties about miscegenation provides a powerful background for Williams's sexualized views of the creative work of the poet. In the latter pages of the novel, his description of a surgery performed on an immigrant woman alludes to legislation that, by 1925, had led to mandatory sterilization of women on the grounds of "feeble-mindedness," a defect of distinct racial proportions, in twenty-five states (*HA*, 133–37). "There it is. It. Like some tropical fruit color of the skunk cabbage flower. There it is, that mystical pear, glistening with the peritoneum. Here the caverns. Alpha if not omega. Talk politely and obey the law. But do not remove it" (*I*, 194). Although this uterus "appears to be normal," the young intern in Williams's *Novel* is reminded that the patient is one of the new immigrants, one of those "expressionless" "modern messes"—"Jews and Polocks, Sicilians and Greeks"—who lack the character of the old immigrants from England, which is the source of "the kind of immigration we want." The woman on the table is praised as strong and courageous, but "she is a polock" (195), a member of that race whose "heads have no occiput" (197). "Her husband," moreover, "is good for nothing at all." "If you can find any reason for doing a hysterectomy doctor, do it" (195). The *Novel*'s doctor stands in the chill of America's eugenic imperatives: "Oh my country. Shall it be a hysterectomy? Arnold there is a wind with a knife's edge." The catgut slips out of the needle. The intern's hand trembles (194). The doctor's decision remains unclear. When Williams's narrative asserts later that despite prohibitive eugenic imperatives, and despite any number of "infiltration tactics from 'superior civilizations,'" "America will screw whom it will screw and when and how it will screw" (210), his phrasing resonates his answer in the prologue to *Kora in Hell* to Hilda Doolittle's complaint against the " 'hey-ding-ding' " mockery of his nearly "sacred" poems of the teens. Protesting that the concept of the poem as "sacred" binds the poet to stultifying traditions, Williams snapped, "I'll write whatever I damn please, whenever I damn please and as I damn please and it'll be good if the authentic spirit of change is on it" (13). Writing and screwing whatever one likes were pointedly American activities, combining breaks with authority and tradition with self-defining attempts at contact across prohibitionary barriers.

It is in this sterile American climate of prohibitions and taboos that Williams launches the formal poetic program of *Spring and All.* Read by Mike Weaver as a vigorous response to Eliot's *Waste Land*, a "blast" that hit Williams hard in December 1922, the opening poem of Williams's sequence also addresses the prohibition of alcohol and the immigration quotas that Congress had been rushing to tighten since 1921. Certainly no American institution better exemplified the strict prohibitionary spirit of the 1920s than the sanitarium that crowned Williams's American modernist aesthetic.

By the road to the contagious hospital
under the surge of the blue
mottled clouds driven from the
northeast—a cold wind. Beyond, the
waste of broad, muddy fields
brown with dried weeds, standing and fallen

patches of standing water
the scattering of tall trees
(*CP*1, 183)

By suggesting that the institution itself may be catching, the ambiguous name of the contagious hospital assigns a virulent pathology to the place of cure. In this way it partakes of the bottoms-up irony of *Spring and All*'s aesthetic of intoxicating prohibitions; and, through Dewey's pragmatist toppling of the American standard of "English," it partakes of William James's belief that "experience" unfolds like a tree grafted from genetically distinct scions—grafts that the founding pragmatist himself associated with local idiomatic forms of language.[20] Whatever this institution might be, the late-winter landscape that surrounds it in 1923 bespeaks the aftermath of war and the failure of progressivism in a world bereft of traditional standards—a world whose cold center might initially appear to invoke an Eliotic "absence or still point."[21] But for Williams the wasteland of March in New Jersey is not so much a culture of drift as one of containment, one that walls its microbes of disease and vitality alike within such institutions as the Eighteenth Amendment and the Johnson Act of 1921. The walls of the contagious hospital embody the restrictionism that underwrites the identitarian American spirit that Walter Michaels locates in Williams's prose of the late 1920s particularly ("AM"). Here, in the wake of Deweyesque notions of nativity and "contact," this containment itself is a contagion to be fought. The approach of spring in this poem, "Now the grass, tomorrow/the stiff curl of wildcarrot leaf," takes place as the poet-physician draws the early modern reader toward, and through, the very barriers against racial infection that the American legislature constructs.

2. Stirner and Proudhon in Williams's American Aesthetic

Formulated in 1920, Williams's aesthetic of "contact" was a call for American artists to shed the prophylactic imperatives of tradition and infect themselves with a direct experience of their own surroundings. The poet's confidence in the generative imperative of "contact" was rooted in Dora Marsden's early anarchistic framing of the imagist aesthetic of direct presentation. Williams had begun reading Marsden's essays in imagist forums like the *New Freewoman* and the *Egoist* as early as 1913–14.[22] A follower of the nineteenth-century German individualist Max Stirner, Marsden had championed individual experience and initiative, adapting the conceptual premises of Stirner's nominalist philosophy to politics, economics, and modern British and American poetry. A former suffragette herself, Marsden viewed modern programs of political reform as impediments to action, and she likened the effects of reformist rhetoric to the noxious effects of narcotics and liquor.

> What have we in mind when we say Freedom? . . . What is the relationship of the simple, normal, definable life-process of over-coming specific resistances which we call getting free to the vague symbolic indefinable thing called Freedom. The second is a blatant exploitation of the first. . . . [It] is not an action: it is a worked up atmosphere, secured by special nose-gays of 'freeings' . . . bunching them together and inhaling their decaying sweetness with exactly the same kind of pleasure as that which the drugtaker and the drunkard get out of their vices. As tippling is the vicious exploitation of the normal quenching of thirst so the following after 'Freedom' is the vicious exploitation of the normal activity of working oneself free of difficulties. ("VC," 3)

The idea of generative "contact" is implicit in Marsden's anarchistic championing of "direct action" over a numbing adherence to principles. (For the New Moralist Joyce, Marsden had literalized such a call to contact by suggesting that even in a disease-ridden city like London, the key to health and vitality lay not in abstaining from sexual congress but in repossessing libidinal drives.)[23] But Williams's notion that "contact" should fund a particularly American identity shades away from Stirnerian anarchist appeals to individual initiative in favor of the more processual conceptions of an "ongoing democratic experience" that were popularized by postwar American advocates of a dynamic and heterogeneous national unity.[24] In the early 1920s, John Dewey was promoting a belief system contingent "upon consequent" rather than "antecedent phenomena" and "upon the possibilities of action" rather than upon "precedents"; and the pragmatist stirred Williams by writing in 1920 about the potential significance of modern immigrant populations and of a dynamic American cultural identity to the development of the arts in America.[25] Dewey suggested that "Americanness" itself might be a viable relational measure, a measure recently authorized by modern physicists and astronomers; his notion of a relatively apportioned national identity spurred Williams to conceive that a relationally measured poetry might stem more or less directly from the American idiom.

Marsden's rigorous nominalism had served as a conceptual springboard for the imagist Williams in his efforts to distance himself from the abstract "humanist" traditions that the puritans had imported from Europe to America. For the poet, these were the very disembodied "federalizing" traditions that had silenced the congress of American saloons and stifled the dynamic rhythms of American identity by demanding conformity to falsely apportioned racial standards (*IAG*, 128). For the fashioning of a new American identity and poetic, however, Williams required a more inclusive standard of measure than the one that Marsden had extended in her individualistic critique of humanism. Stirner's "ego" was itself a "tight tied" little renunciation of all but the inviolable measure of the individual "soul" (110). It was Williams's more expansive search for an idiom drawn from "the speech of Polish mothers" and for a poetry christened with "champagne and semen" that drew the American poet closer in 1920 to pragmatist conceptions of a forward-looking reciprocity between experience and its encompassing measure.[26]

As a philosophical nominalist, Marsden had rebuked the "empt[iness]" and the "faked-up authority" of the category of "Race" as vigorously as she had rebuked the category of "Woman" ("VC," 5). Distributed throughout a series of editorials in the New Freewoman and the Egoist, her diatribes against the dangers of essentializing words reached a range of modern literary innovators, including Pound, Joyce, and Williams. The pragmatist Dewey, in contrast, showed Williams that an essentializing notion of American identity might serve as a necessary component of an American aesthetic ("AL," 684–87). As a "cultural pluralist," Dewey suggested that the measure that was most "essential to an America" was not the fixed standard of "Anglosaxondom" but rather the ongoing measure by which Americans "assimilat[ed]" themselves "*to one another.*"[27] In imagining such a measure, he fashioned a pluralistic conception of Americanness as a profoundly "natural" form of identity, one that was more attuned to the processual universe that modern scientists were unmapping than were the calcified Newtonian identities of more racially stable nations.[28] Dewey's introduction of a fundamentally relational conception of American identity spurred Williams to envision a native poetry that was open to local contingencies. The vitality of an American aesthetic of words that were "drunk," words "plastered over with muck out of the cities," lay less in its ability to wash itself clean of American experience than in its ability to drink heavily of the variety that an experience of America affords (*I*, 159, 175).

Like Williams's early poetry, Dewey's essentializing appeal to the "assimilation" of Americans "*to one another*" stands poised between radical and reactionary political impulses. In his study of American modernism of the 1920s, Walter Michaels views Williams's development of a nativist nonmimetic aesthetic as an expression of a new brand of American nativist thought. For Michaels the " 'opacity' " of much of Williams's poetry of the 1920s—the nonmimetic materiality of words therein—is an outgrowth neither of "the critique of representation" nor of "its defense" but rather of what he sees as the emergence during that decade of "identitarian" tendencies in American conceptions of race (*OA*, 83, 166 n. 150; "AM," 52–53). Michaels situates Williams's writings of that decade amid "pluralistic" variants of the more explicitly "racialist" sentiments that culminated in the restrictive immigration quotas of the Johnson-Reed Act of 1924. Couched in racialist rhetoric that distinguished between not only incoming "Asiatics" but also the "Nordic," "Alpine," and "Mediterranean" races from Europe, the so-called National Origins Act had been aimed at the "New Immigration" from Asia and especially eastern and southern Europe (*TE*, 177–78; *HA*, 155–57). Michaels notes that although restrictionists like Lothrop Stoddard had written in 1920 that the country was being " 'invaded by hordes of immigrant Alpines and Mediterraneans, not to mention Asiatic elements like Levantines and Jews,' " popular sentiment was already beginning to turn away from essentialist notions of "superior and inferior racial stock" and toward assertions of mere "difference" geared "to foster among the nativeborn a proper appreciation of their own Americanness" (*RT*, 160).[29]

By Michaels's reading, American nativists of the 1920s abandoned the racialist idea that one stock was better or worse than another in favor of the more pluralistic notion that difference itself was a "bedrock" criterion for American identity (*OA*, 13–14; 64–66). Reading Williams's early work as an expression of this shift, Michaels joins a growing number of critics who have tallied the literary and cultural significance of the modern notion of cultural pluralism. As Werner Sollors has shown, the idea that America might compose a pluralistic "mosaic" rather than an assimilationist "melting pot" of national identities was first sounded within the early-twentieth-century "pragmatist" circles that centered around William James at Harvard ("CPP,"

257–58, 267–73). Within these very circles, however, the pluralistic directives that have since shaped debates regarding the American literary canon can be traced back further still, to nineteenth-century French anarchist sources.[30] As a historical term, *cultural pluralism* was coined and theorized during the teens and the twenties by a second-generation pragmatist, Horace Kallen. Kallen had studied closely with William James between 1905 and 1908; and the historical conceptions of "pluralism" that support Michaels's vision of American modernism in the 1920s were first explored by a series of leftist intellectuals—Kallen, Dewey, Alain Locke, Randolph Bourne—who responded variously to James's "pluralistic" assault on "the notion of a[n] . . . Absolute of any sort."[31] As an ingredient of the philosophical pragmatism that James formulated during the middle years of the first decade of the twentieth century, "pluralism" was an account of "individual" "experience" that James linked explicitly to "*Anarchy* in the good sense."[32]

By sounding out the significance to American identity of James's abstract "anarchist" and "pluralist" models, Kallen and Dewey conveyed to Williams the domesticated shell of not Stirner's but Pierre Proudhon's variety of European anarchism. In the opening decades of the twentieth century, the "mutualist" tenets of the founding French anarchist lingered on in syndicalist labor movements in continental Europe; and they circulated among a small but vocal band of radical economists and "philosophical anarchists" in modern England and America. In his writings of the 1850s, Proudhon had sought to recover not the atomistic individual as the instrument of social change, but rather the more expansive, relational entity that he called the "economic organism." Modeled on the example of a decentralized village guild economy, Proudhon's "economic organism" was ruled not by democratic or socialistic political directives but by innately ethical pathways of exchange, pathways formed by unmediated economic contact between producers and consumers.[33] This construct reached American social theory— and American poetry—through the writings of pragmatists, such as James, who suggested that the anarchists' "economic organism" was of a structural and temperamental piece with his own pragmatist's "pluralistic universe." For James these entities, one political in nature and the other philosophical, were linked insofar as they supplanted antecedent "first principles" with improvised foundations of their own making.[34]

The powerful structural affinity between Proudhon's "economic organism" and James's "pluralistic universe" gains a historical dimension through the philosopher's claim in 1903–4 that his "pluralism" was an outgrowth of

"*Anarchy* in the good sense." But the cultural pluralist notion that American immigrants should, as Dewey put it, "assimilat[e] *to one another*" rather than to an abstract standard of "Anglosaxondom" was not in and of itself immanently radical. Abstracted from its radical political contexts by both James and Dewey, Proudhon's image of an innately ethical society—one in which the needs of the individual were mystically reconciled with the needs of the community—blended handily into exceptionalist conceptions of American democracy as an ongoing, unifying process.[35] Adapted to lingering visions of America as a nation that carried its own unique potential, cultural pluralism could, and did, assume a variety of political guises. As Michaels has shown, in the 1920s the call to cultural pluralism was neither radical nor unique to an enlightened liberal intelligentsia.[36] It was also sounded by racialist Americans who were eager to cushion their calls for immigration quotas with a call for the removal of the "syntax" of racial hierarchy from American identity.[37] Giving voice to the current "desire" shared by Americans who wished "to become supremely American," Calvin Coolidge was among the advocates of what might be described as a nonhierarchical, "mosaic" conception of identity, one that would hide real divisions, lending an aura of solidity to a deeply divided national body.[38]

According to Michaels, Williams's distinguishing achievement as an American modernist was his adaptation of an identitarian nativist aesthetic to literary form. This identitarian formalism was based on the poet's notion that "the poem will express America by embodying it" (*OA*, 84). Williams's modernist-materialist notion that poems should be what they are, which is poems—and his nativist-materialist notion that American poems should be what they are, which is American poems—turned nonmimetic varieties of writing into American writings. The standard against which writing was to be called American was removed from European literary standards or models when that standard became a question of generic identity. If poems could be poems by being nonrepresentational, by their materialism's being a nonrepresentational form of materialism, then they could be American poems by adhering to the identitarian logic of American nativists. Hence Williams's praise of Poe—a writer concerned less with representing American subjects than with letting "the real business of composition *show*"—as a foundationally "American" writer, who was both "original" and "abstract."[39]

By situating Williams's nonrepresentational aesthetic amid the nativist rhetoric of identity, Michaels locates Williams's aesthetic appeal to the "local"—"No ideas but in things"—not in the metaphysically destabilized "centerless center" of language but in the pluralistic gesture toward generic identity that is afforded by the suspension of mimesis.[40] This identitarian gesture, however, is a static one that does not account for the dynamic tension in Williams's work between representational and nonrepresentational aesthetics or between the aesthetics of cleanness and that of contamination underlying the ethic of "contact" that Williams devised in the racialist shade of the Johnson Act and the Eighteenth Amendment.[41] Pound had written to Williams in 1917, " 'It is opacity that saves your work' " (*I*, 11). But colleagues like Marianne Moore in New York saw that "opacity" was not really the distinguishing feature of Williams's poems. "With the bee's sense of polarity," Moore noted, "[Williams] searches for a flower and that flower is representation."[42] In a similar vein, Wallace Stevens remarked that the "imagist" Williams wrote as though he were "polishing" "a lens by which he hopes to see clearly."[43] What may be most characteristic of Williams's writing, in fact, is its commitment not only to the materiality of language that frees writing to become writing—or American writing to become American (*OA*, 83, 166 n. 150)—but also to the cleanness of a residual imagist aesthetics of writing. When Pound wrote to Williams that " 'opacity is NOT an American quality' " (*I*, 11), Williams would later counter that, beyond the " 'fizz, swish, gabble, and verbiage' " that had characterized American writing for the expatriate author of *Cathay*, it was a nominalistic clarity of vision that would prove most essentially American: "It has been by paying attention to the thing itself that American plumbing, American shoes, American bridges, indexing systems, locomotives, printing presses, city buildings, farm implements and a thousand other things have become notable in the world. Yet we are timid in believing that in the arts discovery and invention will take the same course."[44]

Williams's Deweyesque notion that American racial identity was a forward-looking process suggests that if there was an identitarian "difference" affirmed anywhere in Williams's writings of the early 1920s, it was a difference that turned on a distinction between motion and stasis rather than on a distinction between "us" and "them." If Williams's early poetics can be said to have participated in identitarian nativist conceptions of Americanness, in other words, they did so by asserting that Americanness was more an ongoing event than an afterward-gathered condition.[45] In its merging of processual with static nominal conceptions of identity, Williams's notion of a distinctly American form of measure restores contemporary writings on the relativistic nature of nations (and, through Einstein, on the relativistic nature of the heavens as well) to the anarchist premises that funded both Dewey's and James's pragmatist assaults on philosophical "first principles." Rooted in Dewey's writings on the dynamic nature of identity, the improvisational imperative of "the speech of Polish mothers" preserves within it an anarchistic germ of the "*graft*-theory" that James had gathered to his pluralistic assault on "the notion of a[n] . . . Absolute" (*ML*, 311). Dispensing with the static antecedent of the parent stock, the grafted tree that James invoked as an emblem of both pluralism and anarchism was a kind of living mosaic, one that claimed its "dynamic" identity, as James put it, in "the moment," or in "the line of fire" that was generated by the immediate relation of its "parts" (310–11). Through this emblem, the anarchist and pragmatist sources of Williams's "nativist modernism" can be distinguished as they began to diverge.

Williams's notion of a relational measure for American poetry did more than preserve the anarchistic structure of James's graft and mosaic, however. It also helped to domesticate that structure. For James, the graft and the mosaic had both signaled the generative possibilities of a still plastic universe. Allied to a variety of "individual" "experience" that carried an implicit nationalist content, moreover, they finally served to impose a dynamic American variety of experience over the anarchistic "society," or the pulsing, relational entity that Proudhon had advocated when he proposed to replace mechanistic political structures with the organic "*Reciprocity*" that lit the immediate pathways of exchange between producers and consumers.[46] As pragmatists, James and Dewey allied their respective "exceptionalist" appeals to individual and collective American experience with the anarchist imperative of a deregulated barter economy.[47] Williams would eventually restore this exceptionalist appeal to American experience back to the anarchist economic roots from which it was drawn. Following Pound's lead, he came to support the Proudhonian idea of a relational economy first in the form of the American Social Credit Movement and then as an advocate of the radical currency theorist Silvio Gesell (*AB*, 103–14; *AWCW*, 385; *SP*, 440).

Williams's earliest attempts to flavor his avant-gardist and imagist poetics with Stirnerian appeals to individual experience and with Proudhonian appeals to a society based on direct exchange can be found in the manifestos of *Contact*, the journal that he and Robert McAlmon started in 1920. In the opening manifestos of the first issue of the magazine, Williams declared his "faith in the existence of native artists who are capable of having, comprehending and recording extraordinary experience."[48] In Williams's manifestos, the "native" capacity to make powerful art hinged on two related practices. One was a disavowal of sentimentality, the "intelligent" cultivation of an "emotional vigor" that would be free from the drain of "humanitarianism." The other was the writer's ability "to express perceptions rather than to attain standards of achievement"—standards meted out through the gold currency of "information," or bookish culture, and "past art" (1).[49] Tradition, high culture, and humanitarianism were linked in Williams's manifesto as impediments to "contact" with "indigenous" "experience," which was a necessarily American experience for those artists who live in America: "We will be American," Williams affirmed here in a nascent identitarian spirit, "because we are of America."[50]

Although Williams's nominalistic appeals to contact and to relational forms of identity were supported by a range of anarchist tenets, it was the pragmatists' "domestication" of anarchistic assaults on static "first principles" that enabled Williams to Americanize his avant-garde project. John Dewey's June 1920 *Dial* essay on the importance of immigrant culture to American artists gave depth to Williams's belief that the vitality of American experience was threatened by "standards of achievement" associated with the past.[51] In the January 1921 issue of *Contact,* Williams included a quotation from Dewey's essay "Americanism and Localism": "John Dewey: We are discovering that the locality is the only universal."[52] Dewey's dictum referred specifically to the failure of progressive "Americanization agencies" to assimilate American immigrants to poorly conceived standards of national identity. Newly arrived immigrants cannot be made into Americans, Dewey insisted, because they are too busy determining what being American means. The best immigrants resist institutionalized efforts to assimilate them, in other words, because they have more pressing indigenous interests. "They are chiefly concerned with what goes on in their tenement house, their alley, their factory, their street. If a 'trained mind'—like the writer's, for example— can't tell . . . just what Americanization is, probably the absorbed denizens of the locality are excusable for not trying to find out more about it. One gathers of course that Americanization consists in learning a language strangely known as English. But perhaps they are too busy making the American language to devote much time to studying the English" ("AL," 685).

Dewey's essay was instrumental to Williams's conception of a native American art based on an aesthetic of contact because it linked immigrants to both a dynamic conception of American identity and to an authentically local experience of America that was channeled directly into the American idiom. "Nation-wide" concerns, which included "prohibition" as well as the molding of new steerage to empty cultural and linguistic standards, were not only ill-defined for the educationalist; they were pathological as well: Dewey wondered whether the immigrants who are denounced for their resistance to Americanization "may not also be infected by the pervading spirit of localism" that he finds evident in American newspapers, "the only genuinely popular form of literature which we have achieved" ("AL," 685, 686). Inverting the terms of restrictionists and prohibitionists who linked immigrants with alcohol and venereal disease as virulent threats to the vulnerable body of the American race, Dewey gave an answer to Williams's complaint against the prophylactic nature of American society. In the prologue to *Kora in Hell,* Williams had hinted at the loneliness of homebound artists in an age of American expatriates: "It is seldom that anything but the most elementary communications can be exchanged. . . . We live in bags" (*I,* 17); and he wrote to Kenneth Burke in 1921 of his and McAlmon's journal as an attempt to put American artists in touch with one another, to make "CONTACT with the Americans we want to meet."[53] Dewey's conception of the immigrant's spirit of the local as a contagion that might threaten such national interests as prohibition and the standard of the curiously named "English" language suggested to Williams that institutionalized walls of defense were themselves symptoms of a fear of vitality that weakened American identity. "Americanism and Localism" helped Williams to conceive his avant-garde treatment of poetry in the early 1920s as a specifically American endeavor. The nativist walls of defense against immigrant culture and alcohol alike became measures for Williams of the importance of localism in his aggressive campaign for an indigenous American art.[54]

3. Williams's Prosody in *Spring and All*

The little lyric poems that Williams interspersed throughout the rambling prose treatises of *Spring and All*—poems later anthologized as "For Elsie," "The Red Wheelbarrow," and the eponymous "Spring and All" itself—have long been viewed as landmarks in the development of a modern American poetic. Many of the poems are crisply accessible; some seem almost documentary in their detailed fidelity to the landscapes and vernacular phrases and cadences of New York and northeastern New Jersey. Others pay an oblique sort of tribute to surrealist and dadaist aesthetics of randomness and the opacity of language that Williams championed in the early 1920s. In terms of prosody, the poems in *Spring and All* represent a formal departure from Williams's earlier work; this departure was as crucial to Williams's perception of the "Americanness" of the collection as the language and the images that the poems contain. In conjunction with the shortening of Williams's poetic line and his increasing tendency to drop end-line punctuation, Williams's radical deployment of enjambment in *Spring and All* changed the identity of the poetic line itself, enabling the American poem to enact formally the aesthetic of contact that was prohibited both by restrictive legislation and by traditionally apportioned metrical schemes.

John Hollander and Steven Cushman have both written of the "systematic" use of enjambment as a distinguishing feature of William Carlos Williams's verse, with Cushman identifying enjambment itself as "the main principle of prosodic organization" of much of Williams's poetry from the 1920s onward.[55] Cushman sees the gradual shortening of Williams's line in his early poetry as a key to his developing use of enjambment as a principle of prosodic organization.

> In a poem where enjambments occur at the ends of ten- or twelve-syllable lines, those enjambments work locally, strongly affecting the beginnings and endings of lines, while exerting little immediate pressure on the middles. In a systematically enjambed short-line poem this changes. Suddenly, there is little left in a line that can be called its "middle." Instead, it has a head which inherits a syntactic remainder from the previous line and a tail where the next enjambment waits. The short-line poem is in a state of constant enjambment. In non-metrical verse short-line enjambments determine lineation directly, unlike their metrical, long-line counterparts. They have the immediate power to influence the grouping of successive words into successive lines. This grouping of successive elements (words) and events (lineations) becomes the basis of prosody in non-metrical verse.[56]

Cushman's description of poems that achieve a "constant state of enjambment" can be applied to many of the poems in *Spring and All,* poems in which Williams began experimenting with extremely short lines. The "middles" of the opening lines of this surrealist jumble, for example, are as evasive as the images that they spill.

> The sunlight in a
> yellow plaque upon the
> varnished floor

is full of a song
inflated to
fifty pounds pressure

at the faucet of
June that rings
the triangle of the air
(*I*, 109)

Relying on Hollander's definition of enjambment as the nonalignment of
syntax and lineation, Cushman approaches enjambment as an organizing
principle by gauging the levels of resistance elicited by different types of
nonalignment.[57] Context certainly conditions a line's resistance to enjambment, but as a rule resistance grows stronger as lines divide progressively
smaller, more integral, syntactical units. A clause, for example, offers less
resistance to being divided than does a phrase within a clause. Words themselves, divided into phonemes, offer the greatest resistance to enjambment.
The line endings of poems written around the time of the poem eventually
anthologized as "The Faucet of June" distinguish the poems of *Spring and
All* from those with more conventional or "strong" line endings, poems like
those gathered for publication in *Al Que Quiere!* in 1917 and in *Sour Grapes*
in 1921. In the stanzas quoted above, many of the lines end with articles and
prepositions rather than with nouns or verbs. Regular heavy enjambment of
this sort ruptures the syntactic integrity of the poem, making an ongoing
display of syntactic imperatives that would otherwise be concealed by an
alignment of syntax with lineation. Movement is one of the overall effects of
such a foregrounding of syntax. The lines of the poem begin to turn on their
often deferred fulfillment of syntactic imperatives. Sunlight is released from
the opening line of this poem, for example, only to be caught in some
unspecified container—some indefinite "a." The opening lines and stanzas
of "The Faucet of June" flow one into another, with the undressed imperatives of syntax determining their movement.

Though its lines are not as dramatically shortened as those of many of the
poems that followed it in *Spring and All,* the opening stanza of "By the road
to the contagious hospital" shares the prosodic makeup of what Cushman
calls short-line nonmetrical verse.

By the road to the contagious hospital
under the surge of the blue

mottled clouds driven from the
northeast—a cold wind. Beyond, the
waste of broad, muddy fields
brown with dried weeds, standing and fallen

patches of standing water
the scattering of tall trees

The first line of the poem stands whole as a dependent clause made up of two prepositional phrases. Since little of the syntactic force of the opening sentence spills over from the first line to the second, the enjambment that occurs between the first two lines of this poem is relatively weak, or unresistant. In contrast to the first two lines of the poem, however, lines 2 and 3— "blue/mottled clouds"—are strongly enjambed across a fairly integral syntactic unit, a phrase within an encompassing clause. John Hollander has noted that for many readers of this poem, "blue" first appears as a nominal parallel to the "hospital" in line 1 (*VR*, 111). It is only the gradually unfolding necessity of syntax and the blatant phrasal enjambment of "from the/northeast" and "the/waste" that combine to slip "blue" into its less summery adjectival setting. If Williams's enjambed bending of the semantic status of "blue" owes something to poets like Milton, who practiced species of "sense variously drawn out" in his heavily enjambed blank verse poems of the seventeenth century, however, there was little prosodic precedent in 1923 for the harsh enjambment that followed the second line of this stanza, with lines 3 and 4 severing definite articles from their nouns.

Enjambment imbues "blue" with a nominal substance that lingers on after "blueness" is conditioned by an overcast sky; but it is another type of wrenching that takes place in the clouds that appear in line 3. Clouds materialize here only to evaporate into a phrase that draws them into relation to an unsupplied term. Here, the relation itself assumes the semantic force of the unspecified material that it fails to convey. There is no "middle" of the line to contain the clouds because the subject of the line is neither "clouds" nor "northeast" but rather the flow of perception itself, "driven from the/northeast—a cold wind." Insofar as enjambment contributes to the "breathless budding of thought from thought" that Moore praised in Williams's poetry—or to what Hugh Kenner calls the "tractorlike" cadences of the poet's flatly "attributive" "Jersey speech rhythms"—its dramatic appearance on the road to the contagious hospital exhibits Williams's prosodic rendering of Dewey's writings on the infectious spirit of the local in America's immigrant culture.[58]

The movement or the breathless budding of Williams's heavily enjambed poems is the fruit of a prosodic system that turns not on quantitative standards of measure but rather on the locally determined standard of "contact." Cushman's account of the relation in nonmetrical verse between words as "elements" and lines as "events" is a useful one for understanding the significance of Dewey's notion of the local orientation of immigrant culture to Williams's prosodic innovations of the early 1920s. Poetic lines can be described as events because lines of poetry score time. Apart from marking time, however, the nonmetrical line is an event determined by its relation or its "contact" with syntactic contingencies. Heavily resistant enjambment of the sort that characterizes many of the poems in *Spring and All* lays bare the otherwise hidden fibers of syntax by continually skewing its alignment with the poetic line. In poems characterized by short lines and by an absence of end-line punctuation, each line comes to make a graphic display of its coincidence or lack of coincidence with a particular stretch of an ongoing stream of syntactic modulation. In a short-line nonmetrical poem, the succession of elements that the line contains appears to be uniquely determined by the contingencies of the syntax that runs through it. Syntax is foregrounded as the sinuous genius of the very truncated line that breathes it to life.

By claiming that "in nonmetrical verse, short-line enjambments determine lineation directly," Cushman suggests that the standard that dictates each line is both local and dynamic. It is perpetually set and reset by the moment that the semantic chain provides it. The third and fourth lines of "By the road to the contagious hospital," then,

> ... of the blue
> mottled clouds driven from the
> northeast—a cold wind. Beyond, the
> waste ...

do not seem violently shortened by the imperatives of quantitative measure. Nor are they sheared by what Hollander calls the "rough" dictates of "typographical width" (*VR*, 111). They appear rather to be determined by the changing local contingencies of syntax as it slips variously in and out of alignment to feed the elements of one line meaningfully into the elements of the lines that surround it. In "By the road to the contagious hospital," enjambment becomes the engine that fuels the approach to the hospital and the approach of spring. The "tail" of the clouds that emerge in line 3 is in the momentarily indeterminate "blue" of the line before it; and their "head," which is the movement that smears them across the sky, is in "the/north-east" that straddles into line 4, which in turn points to "the/waste" tipping into line 5. Rather than serving to illustrate either a correspondence or a randomly delineated noncorrespondence between quantitative measure and meaning, this poem's nonmetrical prosody—its system of alignments and nonalignments—propels a rush of perceptions that Williams described as "a force, an electricity, or a medium, a place" (*I*, 150). The dynamic locality of the line is as much the native material of *Spring and All* as America's hospitals or wheelbarrows or its pure products gone crazy.

Prohibition and the immigration quotas of the early 1920s encouraged Williams to orient his standard of poetic measure around the changing contingencies of "contact" between syntax and lineation. Such a dynamic conception of measure was itself prompted by the sclerotic forms of American identity that the Eighteenth Amendment and the Johnson Act were meant to uphold. John Dewey's writings on American identity and immigrant culture in 1920 enabled Williams to conceive of a relational measure as an intrinsically American phenomenon, one that was elusively fused to the American idiom itself. Implicit in Dewey's objection to the standard of the "English" language—an objection that Williams would second in his appeal to educators to ban the teaching of "English" in American schools (*EK*, 146)—was a pragmatist notion that knowledge owes as much to the future as it does to the past. It is better, Dewey went on to elaborate, "for philosophy to err in active participation in the living struggles and issues of its own age and times than to maintain an immune monastic impeccability, without relevancy and bearing in the generating ideas of its contemporary present" (*PC*, 55).[59] By adhering to received standards of Americanness, champions of Americanization were guilty of overwashing. They scrubbed out the living sources of the standards that they claimed to uphold. Assimilationists were destroying the American language on behalf of the English. The idea that Americanness is produced by the very contaminants from which Americanization agencies sought immunity suggests that identity is destroyed by attempts to preserve it. It suggests that standards of Americanness should be made of those very things that the measure of Americanness prohibits.

Acknowledging that immigrants were busy "making the American language," Dewey provides a local historical foundation for the pragmatist emphasis upon "consequent" rather than "antecedent phenomena" and "the possibilities of action" rather than "precedent" (*PC*, 24). Pragmatism, Dewey claimed in 1922, was a "revolutionary" "extension of historical empiricism," based on a conception of a "still plastic" "universe," one that "is still, in James's term 'in the making,' 'in the process of becoming'" ("DPA," 421; *PC*, 25).[60] The changing makeup of America's burgeoning immigrant population across the late nineteenth and early twentieth centuries may have contributed to the pragmatists' sense of a still plastic universe. As a young man in the 1890s, Dewey himself was associated with some of the humanitarian agencies designed to "assimilate and acculturate" "into the American mainstream" the fourteen million Europeans and Asians emigrating to America between 1860 and 1900; he came to question the assimilationist enterprise during the boom that admitted an additional fourteen million during the first two decades of the twentieth century.[61] However Dewey regarded the humanitarian management of the melting pot, the image itself contained a powerful progressive notion of an American race-in-formation. This notion of race-in-formation was an integral component of "the progressive and unstable character of American life and civilization" that Dewey in 1922 held to be crucial to the development of "a philosophy which regards the world as being in continuous formation," one that holds "a place for indeterminism, for the new, for a real future" ("DPA," 428; *PC*, 33). If the "progressive and unstable character" of America's racial identity gave a nationalistic flavor to the newness and "indeterminism" of a "world" "in continuous formation," however, America's dynamic and forward-looking racial identity rested finally on the universal authority of "the lessons of physics and biology concerning moving energy and evolution," lessons which teach everyone that "reality . . . itself" is "in transition" (*PC*, 39, 40).

4. Williams, Dewey, and Einstein

Williams "discovered" in Dewey's writings in 1920 a modern scientific foundation for the idea that America's fluxional racial identity was constitutive of the American idiom and its relational measure. When Albert Einstein told readers of the *London Times* in November 1919 that "inert mass is simply latent energy," he laid a popular conceptual foundation for a universe of events that existed neither in space nor in time but in "interval" relation to one another (*IO*, 230).[62] Einstein's relational account of the "'curvature of space'" posed a challenge to the descriptive utility of such fundamental Euclidean measures as the " 'straight line' " and " 'the plane' " (*IO*, 231); it was a challenge that had gained worldwide attention in May 1919 when the British astronomer Arthur Eddington observed that rays of starlight were themselves bent by the gravitational field of the sun (*ELT*, 284–99). The rise in the 1920s of popular American interest in quantum mechanics may well have been conditioned by the identitarian nativist thought that Michaels sees as integral to Williams's appeals to the material of the poem as an object. In 1926 Williams himself went on to draw from a popular physics primer, *Four Lectures on Relativity and Space,* in fashioning an account of "Modern Prosody" with the writer and mathematician John Riordan.[63] But this identitarian species of relativism appears to have reached Williams most forcefully through Dewey's writings on immigrant culture. When Williams affirmed through Dewey in the second issue of *Contact,* "We are discovering that the locality is the only universal," the poet himself "discovered . . . quite by chance" Dewey's relation of American nativist identity to Eddington's heavenly confirmation of a world of relational measures.[64] "We are discovering that the locality is the only universal," Dewey wrote. "Even the sun and the stars have their own times as well as their own places" ("AL," 687). It was equations like this one that placed relativity at the heart of Williams's indigenous American poetic, one that was grounded in "the speech of Polish mothers."

Dewey's essay "Americanism and Localism" helped Williams to see that a relativistic rendering of the poetic line was a uniquely American imperative with universal, and universalist, dimensions. Einstein had presented his 1905 Special Theory of Relativity as an attack on the fixity of measure. What we think of as absolute values of time and space—"the shape of measuring devices and the speed at which clocks move"—were in fact relative values (*IO*, 230). They were contingent "on their state of motion with respect to the coordinate system," or the "second body to which the movement of the first is referred" (229). Dewey adapted Einstein's notion of relativity to the immigrant standard of American "English," crowning his localist credo in "Americanism and Localism" with the discovery that the anchoring stars have their own times and places. As a fellow "revolutionary" philosopher whose lingering Hegelian sympathies left him less resistant than James to forms of "abstraction," Dewey went on to acknowledge the necessity of theoretical measure, as uncertain as measure must certainly be (*LO*, 19, 291–92; *CP*, 72–89). "The truth" of the relative measure of both stars and Americans, Dewey wrote, "is first discovered in an abstract form, or as an idea" ("AL," 688). The German physicist's vision of the curved path of starlight had originated not from a clean imagistic delineation of the "natural object" but from a theorized continuum between local and universal identity, one that set into relative motion the authority of the imagists' empirical aesthetic of "witness." Einstein's was a theoretical displacement of the nominalistic stasis of imagism that encouraged Williams's aesthetic displacement of the "natural object" with a nativistic sense of "place" as an "electricity" generated by the productive nonalignment of the "object" with measure itself.[65]

Comparing his own work to the work of modern astronomers, Williams went on to acknowledge the importance to modern poetry of Eddington's confirmation of the relative measure of the universe, likening his own poetic medium to the medium of modern astronomers: "Were we to scrape the words from the paper, or the stars from the sky, they would mean alike, nothing" (EK, 128).[66] Williams's adaptation of relativity to the measure of American poetry was to be gradual and unsystematic; but the poet appears to have intuited with Dewey in the early 1920s the nativistic significance of the "curvature of space." Just months after the scientist's celebrated first visit to America, Williams published "St. Francis Einstein of the Daffodils" in the June 1921 issue of *Contact*. Though this early American poem does not take enjambment as its dynamic organizing principle, it exhibits a stirring recognition of the significance of relativity to identitarian conceptions of American measure.

> In March's black boat
> Einstein and April
> have come at the time in fashion
> up out of the sea
> through the rippling daffodils
> in the foreyard of
> the dead Statue of Liberty
> whose stonearms
> are powerless against them
> the Venusremembering wavelets
> breaking into laughter—[67]
> (CP1, 130)

Einstein would not himself emigrate to America until 1933, but Williams crowned him the happy genius of the immigrant masses "at the time in fashion" when American restrictionists were closing ports of entry to refugees from the war. Here, the nativist imperative of the General Theory of Relativity surges like new steerage from Europe and Russia before the Statue of Liberty—a symbol ossified by backward-looking prohibitions and quotas. The newcomers streaming in from the east overpower America's restrictive traditions and institutions in much the same way that Dewey's immigrant culture overpowers the decadent standard of the English language. In the wake of Eddington's discovery that starlight is bent by the gravitational field of the sun, the "Venusremembering wavelets" of America's identity assume a heavenly resonance. American immigrants bring their identities with them in the form of cultural traditions that, like light waves, are transmuted, or curved, by the event of immigration itself. Institutional measures of identity can no longer contain new Americans, not because immigrants are recalcitrantly identified with their sources of origin but because these sources are the sources of the energy that nourishes their invention of newer, more "exceptional" forms of nativity.

When Einstein arrived in New York, a crowd of five thousand Zionists, many of them refugees from eastern Europe and Russia, gathered to welcome him in the plaza outside City Hall (*ELT*, 470, 475).

> Sweet Land of Liberty,
> at last, in the end of time,
> Einstein has come by force of
> complicated mathematics
> among the tormented fruit trees
> to buy freedom
> for the daffodils
> till the unchained orchards
> shake their tufted flowers—
> Yiddishe springtime!
> (*CP*1, 130)

For Lisa Steinman, the praise that Williams lavishes here upon Einstein's "complicated mathematics" is vague and inflated (*MA*, 103–4). More than celebrating the exalted physicist, "St. Francis Einstein" serves to excoriate an American press and public that overvalue theoretical scientists as much as they undervalue artists.[68] And though there is an undercurrent of irony in Williams's portrayal of St. Einstein as a liberator of the daffodils, the "Yiddishe springtime" that he engendered was a genuinely liberating elixir for Americans who were parched by the imperatives of racial selection—imperatives supported in early modern America by an antiquated vision of an Anglo-Saxon racial heritage. By the sort of "popularized" reading that carried Einstein to Williams in the 1920s, energy was the new generative source of changing American standards of identity; and a mathematics that converts solids to light waves taught that when one pulse of energy dies, another is already there to replace it. Einstein's postulate that mass is energy applies to the masses that constitute America and Americanness: the patron saint of energy

> has come among the daffodils
> shouting
> that flowers and men
> were created
> relatively equal.
> (*CP1*, 131)

And it is a postulate that itself becomes an original fund of identity. "Old-fashioned knowledge is/dead under the blossoming peachtrees" (*CP1*, 131). It is no longer the calculus of any "Venus"—or "England," or even any "Russia" or "Poland"—that is constitutive of American identity; it is rather the physicist's fluid conception of origins as "a force, an electricity, or a medium, a place" that fuels the ongoing process of identity.

Williams and Dewey and Einstein together recognized that if there was a disease rampant in America in the 1920s, it was not a sickness that threatened Americans from without. It was more the renunciative malaise that surfaced both in the "anxious" "prohibitive" spirit that Einstein criticized in the *Nieuwe Rotterdamsche Courant* and in the isolationism that Dewey attributed to America's fear of "contamination through contact" in *The New Republic* in 1920.[69] The "prohibitive" "essence" that Williams himself discerned in America's "federalizing," "lack of touch" European legacy had now turned in on Americans, isolating them from their own skins and surroundings and closing them off from their dynamic racial and linguistic and literary foundations (*IAG*, 128). Williams found the literary outgrowth of such a hothouse aesthetic in the writings of Eliot, which displayed a withering adherence to European traditions.

In his essay "Americanism and Localism," Dewey had shown Williams that the concerns of the nation, those of Americanization and prohibition, were not progressive American concerns but rather backward-looking ones associated with the overattention that American artists paid to European traditions. In so doing, Dewey provided a powerful template for Williams's modern nativist break with literary convention. Concurring in "Americanism and Localism" with James Oppenheim's assessment that American poets were discovering how to overthrow traditional measures in order to create a more native American art, Dewey gave a national historical moment to the modern American poets' invention of tradition. He suggested that when Americans begin to discover that the coordinate heavens are apportioned of their own times and places, then "the novelist and the dramatist will discover [with the poet] the localities of America as they are, and no one will need to worry about the future of American art. We have been too anxious to get away from home. Naturally that took us to Europe even though we fancied we were going around America" ("AL," 688).

Appearing as it did in 1920, Dewey's essay on immigrant culture suggested to Williams that energy itself was the cornerstone of American identity; it also suggested that such a relativistic identity could be adapted to the material of poetry. Williams was to fashion gradually his own nativist aesthetic along Dewey's own lines, aligning his measure with Einstein's and affiliating his American idiom with the speech of Polish mothers. The American idiom that Williams brought to his poems of the early 1920s was foremost a formal enactment of the poet's nativist aesthetic of local contact. Williams's aesthetic of contact is expressed in the prosody of many of his poems from the early 1920s. In poems that are now commonly associated with the development of a distinctly American poetic idiom, Williams organized his prosody around degrees of alignment and nonalignment of syntax and lineation. Thus he set syntax and lineation into relative motion, locating the standard of Americanness in the movement and flux of their perpetually changing relations. The local contact of syntax and lineation that determined the standard of the line itself was a challenge to the quantitative measures of classical meter as well as to the Newtonian standards of identity upheld by the Eighteenth Amendment and the National Origins Act. Williams's aesthetics of cleanness are conceptually rooted in anarchist nominalist tenets—tenets that were telegraphed to Pound and Joyce through the writings of Dora Marsden and through the writings of anarchistic economists who sought fidelity not to "things" but to "relations." A range of anarchist tenets—both Stirnerian and Proudhonian—were energized and made contemporary by avant-garde aesthetics of randomness and the object-status of art, but it was finally the pragmatist conception of a "still plastic"

American identity that pushed Williams not only beyond the "tight tied" little measure of the egoist's "soul" but also beyond the "small, sweet forget-me-not" measure of the dadaist poem as an American thing.[70] Like the pragmatist conception of a plastic American universe, Williams's invention of a dynamic poetry rooted in the American idiom was finally a relational event, occasioned by the local matter of racialist immigration quotas and by the lonely, renunciative dry laws that Einstein lamented after his 1921 visit to America.

FIVE

Marianne Moore and Eugenics

I n June 1912, members of the American Academy of Medicine gathered in Atlantic City for a conference on medical problems of immigration. Among the papers presented that year was a Marine Hospital officer's account titled "The Medical Examination of Arriving Aliens," in which Dr. Leland E. Cofer described the screening procedures administered to the three thousand to five thousand immigrants—mostly Italian, Russian, Slovak, and Polish—landing daily at Ellis Island. "In the case of the large stations," Cofer wrote, ". . . it has been necessary to effect an organization by which the mentally sound immigrants can be eliminated from the line."

> On the average line . . . there are never less than two men on duty, and usually three or four. . . . If one of the medical examiners sees one of the stigmata of mental degeneracy, a certain mark is put in white or colored chalk on the immigrant's clothing. Every other medical examiner noticing this as the immigrant comes down the line knows the meaning of it. The next medical examiner may discover some deformity, in which case another check mark is placed on the clothing of the immigrant. Finally the examiner detailed for the eyes may discover a . . . defect . . . in which case another mark is placed on the clothing of the immigrant, so that when he is presented later in a private room for further examination, no less than three men are called upon to demonstrate the presence of the disease. (*MPI,* 34, 36)

Examiners scanned aliens for defects of both body and mind, but screening practices were most keenly focused on "the stigmata of mental degeneracy." In private booths set off from the main queues at Ellis Island Station, intelligence tests involving flags, playing cards, and wooden puzzles awaited those who had been tagged for further scrutiny as mentally unfit.[1]

❖ When asked about her attention to layout and typography in her poetry, Marianne Moore claimed never to have planned the odd shapes of her trademark syllabic stanzas: "Words cluster like chromosomes, determining the procedure."[2] The genetic metaphor is certainly an important one for the kind of poetry Moore was writing during the first decades of the century; but her answer to Donald Hall was an artist's evasion. Moore's verse was crafted. By the early 1920s the poet was known for her practice of sifting through various printed materials—natural histories, travel guides, Protestant divine tracts, magazine ads and feature articles—and singling out sentences and phrases, circling words that rhymed and then connecting these with penciled lines. From splices in paraphrase and in quotation she sometimes then patterned out rhymed syllabic stanzas and sometimes buried her rhymes in free verse. As Patricia Willis describes it: "When the poem reached a stage that pleased her, she turned to the typewriter, often making multiple carbons of a draft. Each carbon was an opportunity for revision, some bearing signs of six or seven reworkings with different colored inks and pencils. Colored pencils had another role: Moore often marked her 'a,' 'b,' and other rhymes with different colors to facilitate proper repetition of the pattern throughout a poem" (*VV*, 29–30). Even at its unruliest, as in this passage from "In the Days of Prismatic Color" (1919), Moore's verse was always carefully pieced together from a variety of sources:

> . . . Principally throat, sophistication is as
>   it al-
>
> ways has been—at the antipodes from the init-
>   ial great truths. "Part of it was crawling, part of it
> was about to crawl, the rest
>   was torpid in its lair." In the short legged, fit-
> ful advance, the gurgling and all the minutiae—we have the
>   classic
>
> multitude of feet.
> (*O*, 49–50)

Moore's poetic "sampling" of quoted passages from both literary and popular sources is a practice with intricate historical roots, particularly insofar as its democratic inclusiveness is tempered with a countervailing claim to what the poet called "the eagle's perch" of artistic selectiveness. But this habit of mixing the common with the highbrow is one of the traits that distinguished Moore from her modernist peers. Early detractors like the poet-critic Pearl Anderson, who branded Moore's poems "hybrids of a flagrantly prose origin," objected to the classical prose locutions that filled out her stanzas; but critics were equally disturbed by her quirky variety of diction.[3] Colleagues like T. S. Eliot, on the other hand, admired Moore for her "impeccable" rendering of "clenches and clevelandisms" into an "aristocratic" "American language" that merged "the jargon of the laboratory and the slang of the comic strip."[4] For William Carlos Williams, the metrical and syntactic dexterity with which Moore combed seventeenth-century English prose rhythms toward modern journalism's "promotional prose" was rendered vital with a "swiftness" of "transit" through an "intensely, intentionally selective" manipulation of materials.[5] Democratic but not indiscriminate, Moore's red-pencil habit of picking and choosing from among "all these phenomena" was from the beginning portrayed as a radical aesthetic reconfiguration of the place and the practice of the modern American poet.

By referring to clustering chromosomes as a structuring principle for her stanzas, Moore was not locating the origins of her modernist technique and aesthetics in such contemporary political practices and issues as immigrant screening and eugenics. But her reference to genetics does suggest that the poet's work was shaped in something other than a purely personal and idiosyncratic remoteness from her time. Moore's most distinguishing formal hallmarks, including her broadly inclusive diction and her overburdened syntax, were rather the outcome of self-conscious reflection about the nature of language and poetry, reflection grounded in an ongoing engagement with a network of contemporary debates about genetics, immigration policy, and the nature of "American" language and identity in her time. Moore's poems and essays, and her reading notes from the late teens and the early twenties, evince an unusually acute knowledge of the life sciences as well as an awareness of modern efforts to extend these sciences into the realm of social management. But Moore's poetry is also marked by a deliberate effort to adapt the conceptual premises of modern genetics to language and semiotics. In developing her own modernist aesthetic of "contingency,"

Moore was explicitly concerned with how the generational transmission of life-forms might provide new models for the transmission of meaning in language.

Moore's manner of elaborating formal practices from contemporary social debates challenges some widely held critical assumptions about literary modernism. These assumptions include not only the conviction that modernist aesthetics were developed in isolation from public concerns but also the belief that some strains of modernism are worth preserving because they seem to anticipate poststructuralist conceptions of language and identity. Modernist attitudes regarding the nature and function of language varied widely. One end of the spectrum was crowded by the Poundian fantasy of the poetic "word made perfect"; at the other end lay a competing—and yet in some cases complementary—conviction that words bear only a remotely contingent relationship to the things that they represent. Because this latter conviction appears to anticipate late-twentieth-century theoretical assumptions regarding the fundamental instability of language, those writers who seem most devoted to an aesthetics of "accident"—writers such as James Joyce, Gertrude Stein, and Marianne Moore—have gained in stature among critics at the turn of the twenty-first century.[6]

Moore's case is a special one because her writings display an otherwise hidden facet of the historical antifoundationalist roots of modernist conceptions of contingency. Like many American modernists, including Williams in his early avant-garde jumbles and Pound at the wispy, confessional close of *The Cantos*, Moore bolstered her aesthetics of "accident" through readings of early-twentieth-century American philosophers. But whereas Pound's and Williams's writings reflect some of the historical and conceptual affiliations between pragmatist and anarchist varieties of antifoundationalist thought, Moore's illuminates more the connections between pragmatism and evolutionary theory and genetics. Guided by her formative readings of pragmatists like William James and John Dewey, Moore derived from modern genetic theory an aesthetic of wayward semantic leaps that enabled her to uniquely confront the essentialist logic of modern eugenics, or the science of racial engineering. In the generative instability of language itself, Moore found something other than a deconstructionist's challenge to conventional structures of meaning and power. In the 1920s and 1930s, contingency showed her that ethical positions could be powerfully significant not when they were written in stone but when they were adopted as choices.

Guided in part by her careful study of pragmatists including James and

Dewey, Moore's readings in natural history and genetics provided her with a unique perspective on immigration and American identity. During the second and third decades of the century, as steerage from eastern and southern Europe continued to climb, the issue of immigration and attendant questions regarding the nature of race and heredity became leading topics of debate in both popular and intellectual circles. Moore did not devise her poetic practice of inclusive selection in direct response to this debate. But this aesthetic was accompanied by a set of distinguishing technical features—elaborate stanzas, complex nominal compounds, abrupt lineation, and a strong tendency toward punningly metonymic modes of reference—that can be usefully seen as a biologist-poet's response to the nativist controversy over immigrant selection. Merging her studies of evolution, genetics, and eugenics into a modernist aesthetic through the conceptual lenses of philosophical pragmatism, Moore strayed from garden varieties of modern poetry, devising an aesthetic of accident that was both widely admired and largely misunderstood.

1. Moore's Poetry and the National Origins Act

As Dr. Cofer went on to describe them, medical checks at Ellis Island in 1912 were both a liberal cultivation of "the generic opalescence of humanity in . . . our immigrants" and an exercise in racial selection.[7] In an effort to streamline mass screenings, examiners scanned aliens for those "racial characteristics" that might index potential diseases (*MPI*, 37–38). According to the Marine Hospital doctor, "proven" and "trustworthy" physicians knew that "dangerous and loathsome diseases preponderate" in the citizens of particular European countries. The "ability to recognize nationality immediately upon the line" was pronounced to be "a necessary factor in this examination" (39, 38). With a premium placed on the spot detection of ambiguous "Class A-I diseases"—"idiocy, imbecility, feeble-mindedness, epilepsy, insanity and tuberculosis" (32–33)—the screenings mandated by 1907 law appear to have been driven by racial concerns.

Distinguishing among the "racial characteristics" even of various European immigrants, Cofer invoked a modern conception of race that divided Europeans into several distinct categories: long-headed Teutonics; stocky, round-headed Alpines from central and eastern Europe; and slender Mediterraneans. Cofer's polygenist conception of European races was rooted in essentializing taxonomies of multiple racial stocks such as those set forth in 1899 by the American economist William Ripley in *The Races of Europe*.

Popular racialist schemata like Ripley's were attractive to Americans who wanted to distinguish between the modern New Immigration from eastern and southern Europe and the old one from the British Isles, Germany, and Scandinavia (*RCE,* 58–62; *PAN,* 154). If the Marine Hospital doctor was shading his talk on immigrant screening with racialist assumptions, however, the medical screening procedures he spoke of could only have been applauded by his colleagues as gestures at racial selection. During the first two decades of the twentieth century, steerage swelled to nearly a million newcomers per year. Physicians' chalk marks were cosmetic in the face of such numbers. With immigrant families accounting for up to 80 percent of the populations of America's largest cities, demographers began to speculate that the declining birthrates of "old stock" Americans might be due to the belief that children born in modern America would someday face the painful struggle of unchecked economic competition.[8]

Newly discovered genetic principles—such as the law of hybrid reversion—were hastily adapted to polygenist notions of race, feeding a growing nativist fear of American "race suicide" in the early twentieth century. Popular studies such as Madison Grant's *Passing of the Great Race* of 1916 charged that the new immigration was weakening the nation's gene pool in a biological analog to America's democratic transfer of power from old-stock "Nordic" Americans to inferior European races (*HA,* 150). Tabulations from immigrant intelligence tests and from two million Alpha and Beta tests administered to army recruits would soon confirm a widespread tendency toward feeblemindedness in the swarthier European races.[9] Vice President Coolidge added fuel to the racist restrictionist campaign in 1921, writing in *Good Housekeeping* of the proven degenerative effects of mongrelization on America's Nordic genetic legacy (*PAN,* 318). Economic unrest, combined with postwar isolationism and the statistical fruits of eugenicists like the mental tester Robert Yerkes, provided a potent summons for more comprehensive port restrictions. In 1924, with the issue of racial engineering debated openly in Congress, the National Origins Act was passed and signed into law by Coolidge, implementing quotas that maintained a constant influx of Nordic stock while cutting to less than one-fifth the numbers previously flowing from countries populated by Mediterranean and Alpine races (*TE,* 177–78; *HA,* 155–57).[10]

❖   During the late teens and early twenties, amid controversy over quotas and Bolshevism and labor agitation, the nativist literary critic Van Wyck Brooks railed against the "weak and sickly" condition of the arts in America, complaining that commercialism and an attendant "immigration from without the Republic" had wrecked efforts to build a cultural "nest" for literary development.[11] "Cultural pluralists" like Randolph Bourne were meanwhile cautioning against the puritanical foundations of the "cultic" "superstition" of "eugenics" and "racial perfection."[12] John Dewey's pluralist writings on immigrant culture as a source for American art suggest that early modern calls for the renewal of language through "a freshly evolved localized personality in modern poetics" may have sounded as a reaction against the popular "middle class" nativism that pushed Ku Klux Klan membership to peaks of 2.5 million after World War I.[13] But however American writers and intellectuals of the teens and twenties positioned themselves with respect to issues of nativity and immigration and race, the National Origins Act leads us to some important extraliterary sources for the distinctive verse that Moore and her colleagues wrote during this period. The work of geneticists and eugenicists caught Moore's attention and shaped her understanding of how meaning is transmitted in poetry. Poets like Williams championed a localized idiom not only through appeals to American identity as an ongoing process but also through a soil-bound aesthetic of "contact" with indigenous cultural and racial material that, "rich/in savagery," could maintain a "primal and continuous identity with the ground itself."[14] Under the pressure of immigration and eugenics, Moore developed a less essentializing nativist aesthetic by adapting modern theories of heredity to semantic transmission. Genetics grounded her belief that America's material and racial foundations were in fact hard to locate. Indigenous essences could not be fixed in words, or even in fluid poetic forms, but they flashed instead like meaning through language, trailing "zigzag inscriptions" across series of word accidents and biological puns (*MM*, 35). The new discipline of "experimental biology" showed Moore that the very contingency that determines the generational transmission of life-forms might serve as an enriching and constitutive force in language itself.

Granted an immediate political significance by the issue of immigration, early modern models of genetic transmission might be considered as sources for the branching metonymic associations that critics have noticed in Moore's poetry and prose both (*LL*, 206, 233).[15] In his 1956 study of language, "The Metaphoric and Metonymic Poles," Roman Jakobson drew from aphasia research in formulating a distinction between the substitutional semantic principles of romantic poetry and the contiguous ones of realist prose. The Russian formalist recounts "a well-known psychological test" in which children linked words of their own choosing to the key word *hut* (*FL*, 90). These children exhibited predilections toward words that were either semantically "substitutive" of or "contiguous" to the object in question. Substitutive, or broadly metaphoric, reactions to *hut* ranged from synonyms like *hovel* to antonyms like *palace* to metaphors themselves like *den* and *burrow;* contiguous, or metonymic, responses included *thatch litter* and *poverty* (91). Situating Jakobson's antinomy within the framework of a larger discussion of semantic transmission, Paul de Man elaborated the formalist's "substitutions" and "contiguities" as metaphoric "necessities" and metonymic "contingencies" (*BI*, 274; *AR*, 3–15, 63). For many critics, de Man's writings on metaphor and metonymy are more eccentric than definitive; and his elaboration of Jakobson's terms should not be seen to mark a progressive aesthetic continuum against which Moore can be graded as a precociously poststructuralist modernist poet. But "contingency" is nevertheless an apt term for the accidental procedure of Moore's associative writing.

The patchwork quotational collage surface of "In the Days of Prismatic Color," for example, helps to structure a text that turns on "contingent" semantic procedures.

> . . . Principally throat, sophistication is as
>> it al-
>
> ways has been—at the antipodes from the init-
>> ial great truths. "Part of it was crawling, part of it
> was about to crawl, the rest
>> was torpid in its lair." In the short legged, fit-
> ful advance, the gurgling and all the minutiae—we have the
>> classic
>
> multitude of feet.

Metonymy unfolds this deeply creased statement about the seductiveness of poetry. In the first of the passage's three segments, the floating "principle," "throat," finds its synechdochic body as the instrument of the smooth-voiced sophisticate. *Throat* and *sophisticate* stand in a contiguous part-for-whole relationship much as do Jakobson's *thatch litter* and *hut.* Through a metaphor of physical structure, this throated sophisticate then becomes a serpent uncoiling from inside its lair. Yet again, a set of synechdochic substitutions—"short legs" and "feet" for a centipede—trigger the insect that gurgles from the snake's skin. Lacking a central stated metaphor that links the arthropod to the slinky medium containing it, few of the terms in this semantic chain stand in necessary mutual relation. But the whole passage flows as an account of how language deceives.

De Man contends that the terms of the part-for-whole and whole-for-part substitutions of synecdoche are organically fused, rendering them "borderline" tropes that convey essences as well as contiguous relations (*AR*, 63). Every throat, by this reasoning, is honeyed with the sophisticate's oil. But if contiguous synechdochic relations convey shades of necessity, Moore qualifies the necessity of this poem's terms by predicating their synecdoche on puns. All of the tropes in this passage—whether metonymic, like the sophisticate's throat, or metaphoric, like the throat's serpent—turn on the short legs of the centipede that springs from the snake. The bug's multitudinous feet are themselves contiguous to the sophisticate-snake's shadowy abode, which is fixed at the footless "antipodes" of great truths. Only through the most flagrant linguistic coincidences—through the pairing of "antipodes" with "centipedes"—do this poem's metrical feet flutter the shadows of verse. Accidents of word morphology insure that contingency rules Moore's contiguous semantic sequences.

The accidents that govern the particulate shuffle of biological heredity might be said to provide an abstract conceptual ground for the metonymic and punning procedures of "In the Days of Prismatic Color." In other poems written during this same period, however, Moore undertakes a thematic investigation of the relationships between language, life-forms, and native identity. As she does so, she directs her readers toward the local political sources of her emerging aesthetic. In her 1920 poem "England," for example, Moore raises questions regarding essences and accidents in linguistic and biological forms; and she suggests that in these questions lies evidence of the hidden kinship between semantic and genetic forms of transmission.

> . . . . The
> letter "a" in psalm and calm when
> pronounced with the sound of "a" in candle, is very
> noticeable but
>
> why should continents of misapprehension have to be ac-
> counted for by the
> fact? Does it follow that because there are poisonous
> toadstools

which resemble mushrooms, both are dangerous? In the
    case of mettlesomeness which may be
  mistaken for appetite, of heat which may appear to be
    haste, no con-

clusions may be drawn.
  (*O*, 57–58)

In this poem about American landscape and language, meaning, like poison in lookalike plants, does not cling to the literal warp of a word. Common sense and a knowledge of mushrooms should tell readers that despite the leatherbound conventions that stabilize them, messages are always inflected by local semantic and social occasions. Calling in a 1920 *Dial* essay for an awakening of the arts in America, the pragmatist John Dewey had championed a democratic localism over empty nativist standards that demanded that immigrants "be either Americanized or . . . go back where they came from." Dewey looked to immigrant quarters for a renewal of the American tongue, claiming that semantic vitality was not dissolved but rather hardened and faceted in a melting pot where citizens are "too busy making the American language to devote much time to studying the English" ("AL," 685). The poet Moore did not carry a localist imperative to the lengths of Williams's new idiom of "the speech of Polish mothers." But hidden among the toadstools and mushrooms of "England" is a complaint against the essentializing "Americanism" of racist restrictionists. The poison-fearing enemies of dialect in Moore's poem speak pointedly to American advocates of new standards of language and breeding. By posing a nominalistic spirit of occasional identity against floating linguistic and biological forms, "England" challenges the essentialism that underlies nativist visions of a distinctive American race.

❖   Moore held long to a belief that language and life-forms provided keys to the fluxional nature of identity itself. Her reading diaries from 1907 onward track the studies in biology and natural history that served to counterpoint her readings in philosophy, aesthetics, and the arts. In notes from her readings of 1919, shortly before "England" first appeared in the *Dial*, Moore copied passages from an 1889 edition of Darwin's *Variation of Animals and Plants under Domestication*. The New World plant and animal forms—the "dark-brindled" caterpillars with their "tiger-like" markings, the "candlestick-like opuntias" and the "dirty door-mat" fleeced goats—that

Darwin featured resemble the metaphors and compounds soon to crowd the poet's lexicon, suggesting Moore's stylistic debt to this admirably "businesslike" Victorian expositor of phenomena.[16] Of special interest to Moore as she read *Variation* were accounts of New World floral and faunal nativity. "When I visited the Galapagos archipelago . . . . [Moore's ellipses] about 500 miles fr. S. America I found myself surrounded by pecul. species of birds reptiles & plants existing nowhere else in the world. Yet they all bore an American Stamp. In the song of the mocking-thrush, in the harsh cry of the carrion hawk, in grt candlestick like opuntias I clearly perceived the neighborhood of America" (1250/2). Moore's further attention to Darwin's comparisons of New World dogs, cats, and boars with their counterparts in England and Europe suggests that questions of native identity and biological form were linked for the poet throughout her reading of *Variation*.

Among Darwin's writings, *Variation of Animals and Plants* offers an uncharacteristically evasive response to questions about heredity and determinism in life-forms. Although the monogenist "one-stock" implications of evolutionary theory did provide a logical counter to those notions of fixed racial types that were cherished by many early-twentieth-century scientists, *Variation* seemed to point in a different direction. In this work Darwin searched among domesticated life-forms for evidence of the direct genetic inscription and transmission of environmentally derived traits. The dirty door-mat fleece on the goat-backs that Moore culled from *Variation* was a feature browned "directly" into generations from parental exposure to the Antigua sun (1250/2; *VAP* 1:103). Such notions of the inheritance of acquired characteristics—a belief that had been set forth by the early-nineteenth-century French zoologist Jean-Baptiste de Lamarck—were passed from *Variation* and other nineteenth-century sources into the twentieth century, where they provided American polygenists like Ripley and Grant with a new means of determining racial essences. Modern Americans could be classified and arranged in hierarchies by scientists who identified the genetically cast stamps of the ancestral environments that determined who these Americans might be.

Moore did not look to the Lamarckian Darwin as a source for polygenist conceptions of race, but she noted something akin to a "hereditarian" aesthetic foundation in Darwin's rendering of accounts such as "Mr. Blyth's" on the origins of goldfish in China. "The Chinese are just the people to have selected a chance variety of any kind and to have matched and paired for it. . . . [Moore's ellipses] In an old Chinese work it is said that the fish w/ vermilion scales were first raised in confinement during the Sung Dynasty (960 AD). & now they are cultivated in families everywhere for the sake of ornament" (1250/2). Predating the young poet's fondness for brilliant "Chinese vermilion" ("People's Surroundings," 1922) and " 'Chinese cherry' " ("Picking and Choosing," 1920), Moore's attention to Blyth's account suggests that for her, aesthetic essences like purity of color might have been linked to the practice of selective breeding. Blind to the contemporary racial political implications of this quaint and slightly exotic anecdote, Moore might have found in it a metaphor for the poetic breeding of language toward painterly truths. But if there are racialist overtones to the breeding of decorative goldfish toward stable aesthetic essences, the example of the MacKenzie River dogs in Darwin's *Variation* can be said to have supplied Moore with sporting evidence of the hollowness of racial determinism. Dewey's nominalistic scolding in the *Dial* of essentializing nativists who hold immigrants to an "Americanizing" standard of proper English can be teased from Darwin's account of that North American dog species which, "when brot. to Eng., never learned to bark properly." Anglicization was happily marked for one river pup "born in the Zoolog. Garden" who soon learned to make "his voice sound as loudly as any other . . . of the same age and size" (1250/2).

Moore's attention to the story of the MacKenzie River dogs marks her playful awareness that locally bound traits, such as habits of "dialect," are not as easily graded as the redness of fish scales. The continuum of variation that Darwin charts in his study, along with the zigzag genetic contingency of hybrid production, helps to unravel the ill-conceived terms of fixed formal essences. Comparisons of New World with European dog species suggest that, lacking the gold standard of red fish from China, local "cultural" norms are fluid, ever shaped and reshaped by accidents of transmission and by the changing complexions of locales. Race-conscious Americans who worship the imperatives of "Anglosaxondom" are an offshoot of the stiff-lipped imperialists who believe that their subjects should bark like the queen. When filtered through Moore reading Dewey and Darwin, "England's" rendering of "pure English" portrays the habit of invoking ancestry as a practice lacking in "culture."

2. Pragmatism as a "Genetic Theory of What Is Meant by Truth"

Through her readings of Dewey and Darwin, Moore gathered evidence against notions of linguistic and biological determinism. But in her poetry of the late teens and the early twenties, she developed her own unique means of recreating, through chains of words, the instability of generational transmission. If the thematic content of "England" helps us to situate Moore's writings amid the National Origins Act, the metonymic unfolding of the poem's lesson about resemblance and identity helps us to see how she attempted to adapt modern genetic theory to poetry. "England" is prismatically a poem about America, with its musings on the nature of wild and tame forms splintered from an overall account of nation and nativity. Toadstools and a New England accent and temperament follow from an evaporating catalog of American character and tone.

> . . . and America where there
> is the little old ramshackle victoria in the south, where cigars
>   are smoked on the
>   street in the north; where there are no proof readers,
>   no silkworms, no digressions;
>
> the wild man's land; grass-less, links-less, language-less
>   country in which letters are written
>   not in Spanish, not in Greek, not in Latin, not in short-
>   hand
> but in plain American which cats and dogs can read! The
>   letter "a" in psalm and calm . . .
>   (O, 57)

Cats and dogs; psalms, calm, and candles; mushrooms and poisonous toadstools; heat, haste, mettlesomeness, and appetite. All these phenomena materialize here not as the conceptual components of a guiding metaphor of identity and resemblance but as surveyed and surveying features of a national character and landscape. Meaning proceeds by fundamental leaps and skips in Moore's poetry; and these are leaps both of contiguous surveillance and of accidents of language. The same punning directive that pushes contiguity to contingency in the metered centipede of "In the Days of Prismatic Color" conditions the metonymic logic of "England." Does it follow from the 'a' in candle that because there are poisonous toadstools, mushrooms are dangerous? Yes, but only because, scaled against "continents of misapprehension," toads perched on stools describe an attitude of purists who watch over "calm." The literal frog in Moore's mushroom is yet another false poison, but it is one that affects a fortuitous identity in "England."

❖ William Carlos Williams might have been speaking of the frog-pedants of "England" or of the "humbug"-"hummingbug" of "Picking and Choosing" when he described the "unbridled leaps," the semantic collisions that result in Moore's verse from "a multiplication of impulses" "crossing at all eccentric angles" ("MM," 59, 53). Modern visual art forms like cubism and collage set edges and fragments into arrangements that sharpened particular qualities by foregrounding distinctness rather than blending parts into a whole (*FL*, 92). A similar crispness resulting from Moore's "lack of connectives" led Williams to describe her work as a procedure geared to restore a natural freshness to fragments of language. Moore's poetry was predicated on a radical removal of word pieces—"cutting them clean out"—from their disease-ridden sources. Removed "bodily" from the "greasy contexts" of sense and sentimental attachments, old words were then "treated with acid to remove the smudges" and reassembled into structures that invigorated them as resonating terminals of artistic intelligence ("MM," 57–58). It was in the "porcelain garden," the "primitive masonry" of Moore's apple-edged, "unstandardized" "units" that new meaning moved "easily and completely," enabling "the thought" to reveal "the 'thing' " otherwise masked by the stale fragrance of reason (55–59). In his 1925 appraisal of Moore, the imagist Williams implied that words were somehow innately vibrant and meaningful but that they lost their discrete vitality within the rationalist thought systems that support the enervating principles of humanism. Poems performed a service to words by wrenching them from common conventional sense. A textual collage practice like Moore's worked both to restore the intrinsic vitality of words and to juice them with life by placing them within the artist's intuitive new circuitry of relations (52–54, 58). The freshness of Moore's language was both natural, or necessary, and accidentally, or contingently, wrought.

With its habit of burrowing into " 'the particulars of experience,' "[17] philosophical pragmatism supported the imagistic standard of "things" that the poet Williams is said to have brought to Moore's "insoluble" writings (*LL*, 161; "MM," 58). For Moore, however, pragmatism served as another sort of conceptual conduit: it also channeled Darwin's theories of evolution and even Mendelian genetic theory into the aesthetics of semantic collision at work in her writings. Charles Molesworth reads Dewey as a source for the poet's broadly modern concern with "the dialectic between tradition and innovation, between the stable form and the individual act" (*LL*, 161). But pragmatism was especially valuable to Moore because it mapped for her a conceptual route between Darwinian notions of species and fluid Emersonian appraisals of language. Moore shared something of Williams's imagist aesthetic of presence in poetry; and her imagist tendencies and her later collage practices were supported by the nominalistic and the more relational "pluralistic" components of James's and Dewey's philosophies. The more rigorous attention to semantic contingency that distinguishes Moore's writing from that of other modernists, however, can finally be traced to the pragmatists' philosophical and semiotic adaptation of the lessons of natural history and genetics.

Moore's favorite teacher at Bryn Mawr was Theodore de Laguna, a philosophy and government professor who wrote on the impact of evolutionary theory on pragmatism (*LL*, 41, 54).[18] Around 1910, shortly after she graduated from college, Moore made a note of de Laguna's new book *Dogmatism and Evolution* in her reading diary (1250/1); and then seven years later she made careful study of the pragmatist Dewey—as if in prelude to her 1919 reading of Darwin's *Variation*. Pragmatist tenets bear directly on the relation between Moore's aesthetic and those of Williams and Pound. Passages from Dewey's *Essays in Experimental Logic* and *Democracy and Education* that Moore noted in her reading diary of 1917 give voice to an imagist poet's contempt for literalists who assume " 'that wherever there is a name there is some reality corresponding to it' " (1250/2). Moore saw that the Dewey of *Essays* blamed reason for the pettiness and pedantry of literalists. Engulfed in abstract thought systems, those who trafficked excessively in theories reduced "truth," or the "correspondence of idea and fact," to a " 'static, inert relation,' " wanting a pragmatist's attention to the "lead[ing]" and "guid[ing]" function of thought (1250/2). The colorful dig at Bertrand Russell that Moore had earlier copied from an issue of the *Nation* echoes a pragmatist emphasis on the mechanics of contingency that momentarily joins Moore with her avant-garde American peers but finally distinguishes her from them: "I should say that the symbolic reals are about as truly representative of life and experience as a bishop whose activities were confined to diagonal squares would be representative of the archbishop of Canterbury" (1250/1). For Moore, the verbal sorcery that swaps the archbishop for a chess piece is an illuminating lesson itself, one that beams on Dewey's nominalist caution: " 'the barest glance at human history shows that mistakes have been the rule' " (1250/2).

If Moore found philosophical support for the imagist aesthetic of presence in her 1917 reading of Dewey, it may have been because she was able to situate Dewey's nominalism within the context of an earlier and more formative study of pragmatism and language. During her student years at Bryn Mawr, the young poet read William James appreciatively, absorbing more or less directly his Emersonian vision of a language not of substantives but of fluxional relations (*LL*, 50, 70–77).[19] In his 1890 essay "The Stream of Thought," James contrasted the syntactic parcels of Western language with his vision of a unity between the "substantive" and "transitive" aspects of fluxional thought (*PP*, 243). Asserting that the "transition between the thought of one object and the thought of another is no more a break in the *thought* than a joint in a bamboo is a break in the wood," James reckoned that we "ought to say a feeling of *and*, a feeling of *if*, a feeling of *but*, and a feeling of *by*, quite as readily as we say a feeling of *blue* or a feeling of *cold*" (*PP*, 240, 245–46). "There is not a conjunction or a preposition, and hardly an adverbial phrase, syntactic form, or inflection of voice, in human speech, that does not express some shading or other of relation which we at some moment actually feel to exist between the larger objects of our thought . . . the relations are numberless, and no existing language is capable of doing justice to all their shades" (*PP*, 245).

In poems of the "National Origins" period of the late teens and early twenties, techniques from the visual arts enabled Moore to aesthetically realize James's substantiation of the transitive tissue of speech. Moore's collage poems of this period hinged on the insertion and tight juxtaposition of short quoted passages; insofar as these passages emerged as associatively, but not syntactically, linked semantic units, they contributed to a compression of the syntax that governed the poem.[20] Compression of syntax is a distinguishing characteristic of much American poetry written during the period after World War I, and its debt to avant-garde visual and conceptual arts has been discussed at some length.[21] Partly from a wish to obscure and partly in an effort to foreground what James called the "shadings" of conceptual conjunctions, poets like Mina Loy wrote dense poems that eliminated the pragmatist's *and, if, but, by*, so that reading her work was, in one poet's words, like "walking through granite instead of air."[22] In her free-verse collage poems of the early 1920s, however, Moore restores transitive shadings to language through more complicated varieties of compression that extract not just the connective tissue of speech but even such integral indexes to meaning as subjects and verbs. Amid the breakdowns of syntax that attend the densest of Moore's documentary collages (in poems like "An Octopus" and "Novices"), dislocated phrases—many of them wrapped in quotation marks—themselves emerge as the Jamesian linguistic "substantives," assuming the semantic burden of key syntactic referents. The quotational object-poems that Moore composes in this manner are deceptive. Retaining many of James's *and*s, *if*s, *but*s, and *by*s, they have the tendrilly appearance of syntactically overfed prose. But they are as conceptually austere as many imagist verses. Set in forbidding juxtaposition, Moore's "substantive" quotational phrase-objects are rendered "transitive" not by syntax but by the raw performance of metonymic and metaphorical transactions among them.

❖ The stamps of natural selection and modern genetics that distinguish Moore's collage practice and her nativist aesthetic from the work of her peers can be partly deciphered through James's and Dewey's appeals to Darwin and to his modern genetic successors. In *Dogmatism and Evolution*, Moore's teacher de Laguna wrote explicitly of the impact of Darwin on the pragmatist philosophers Peirce, James, and Dewey;[23] as a student of biology, the young " 'Individualist' " Moore must have been particularly intrigued by James's Darwinian polemic against Spencerian environmental determinism in her reading of *The Will to Believe* (*LL*, 50, 70–71). James saw natural selection as a powerful antidote to the enervating belief that individual identities and destinies were utterly conditioned by societal and environmental factors. For him, Darwin had made a powerful contribution both to natural history and to social theory by distinguishing between the causes that produce variation and the causes that maintain it in the process of selection (*WB*, 221). Environment played a small role in selection, but the greater generative production of variables, a bounty based on "internal molecular accidents," was itself an unknown (223).

> You know about the invisible factors of fermentation, and how the fate of a
> jar of milk—whether it turns into a sour clot or a mass of koumiss—depends
> on whether the lactic acid ferment or the alcoholic is introduced first, and
> gets ahead of the other in starting the process. Now, when the result is the
> tendency of an ovum, itself invisible to the naked eye, to tip towards this di-
> rection or that in its further evolution,—to bring forth a genius or a dunce,
> even as the raindrop passes east or west of the pebble,—is it not obvious that
> the deflecting cause must lie in a region so recondite and minute, must be
> such a ferment of a ferment, an infinitesimal of so high an order, that surmise
> itself may never succeed even in attempting to frame an image of it? (225)

James's free-falling ovum is an antiquarian oddity, but his account of biological reproduction as determined by an infinitesimal ferment of a ferment anticipates the variable shuffling and reshuffling of modern genetic combination. In his 1906–7 lectures on pragmatism, the philosopher went on to blend language study with life sciences in appraising the evolutionary findings of "geologists, biologists and philologists" (*P,* 59). Here James argued that natural history, and studies of natural selection especially, had engendered wide philosophical and linguistic repercussions. By showing us "the power of chance happenings to bring forth fit results," "Darwinism has once and for all displaced design from the minds of the 'scientific,' " recommending to the "contemporary imagination" "some kind of an immanent or pantheistic deity working *in* things rather than above them" (111, 70). Lecturing just as cytologists were beginning to demystify Darwin's account of natural selection, James tagged pragmatism itself "a genetic theory of what is meant by truth" (65–66).[24]

Dewey's account of Darwin's intellectual legacy was specifically concerned with life-forms and the rationalist underpinnings of teleology. In a 1909 *Popular Science* essay titled "Darwin's Influence upon Philosophy," Dewey historicized the significance of biology to philosophy and ethics. For Dewey, nature itself, with its tendency to generate like forms "distant in space and remote in time," implanted and cultivated notions of "type" in the minds of the Greeks and the scholastics: "the conception of *eidos,* species, the fixed form and final cause, was the central principle of knowledge as well as of nature" ("DIP," 92). Perceptions of orderly biological design supported an Aristotelian faith in intelligent systems of classification; and modern thought, Dewey cautioned, still glints with a garden variety of reason. "We dispose all too easily of the efforts of the schoolmen to interpret nature and mind in terms of real essences, hidden forms and occult faculties . . . by laughing at the famous gentleman who accounted for the fact that opium put people to sleep on the ground that it had a dormitive faculty. But the doctrine, held in our own day, that knowledge of the plant that yields the poppy consists in referring the particularities of an individual to a type, to a universal form . . . [is] a survival of precisely the same logic" (92–93). By replacing creationist notions of fixed species with natural selection, *The Origin of Species* "cut strait under" the lingering Ptolemaic legacy of the scholastics, supplying radical proof that human experience, and hence the instruments of inference themselves, are also in flux (92, 95). Like James, Dewey reflected the tenor of the decade by locating the future of philosophy in evolution and genetics. In Dewey's view, the life sciences, entrenched before Darwin in universalizing notions of species, had been a drag on Copernican revolution.

The impact of the new scientific method upon life, mind, and politics, had been arrested . . . because between these ideal or moral interests and the inorganic world there intervened the kingdom of plants and animals. The gates of the garden of life were barred to the new ideas while only through this garden was there access to mind and politics. The influence of Darwin upon philosophy resides in his having freed the new logic for application to mind and morals by conquering the phenomena of life. When he said of species what Galileo had said of the earth, *e pur se muove*, he emancipated once and for all genetic and experimental ideas as an organon of asking questions and looking for explanations in philosophy. (93)

James's and Dewey's grafting onto pragmatism of "genetic theory" and "experimental ideas" in 1906 and 1909, respectively, is noteworthy considering that the term *genetics* had not been adapted to modern usage until the biologist William Bateson garnered it for the new science in 1906 (*GTG*, 35). Dewey's allusion to "genetic and experimental ideas" suggests that natural selection for him, as for James, was filtered through the fresh discipline of "experimental biology" sweeping Europe and America just after the turn of the century (*TE*, 15–25).

3. Moore, Luther Burbank, and Eugenics

Moore's understanding of the fluidity of plant and animal species, and hence of the contingency of racial identity, was bolstered by her readings of James and Dewey. Like her pragmatist guides, she was steeped in Darwin's writings; but she also possessed a keen interest in the post-Darwinian genetic theories that had become central to modern discussions of heredity, environment, and identity. In his 1897 book *The Will To Believe*, William James displayed what looks in retrospect like a prescient predilection for those theories of genetic "contingency" that emerged after 1900. Discussing the importance of Darwin to philosophy, he lightly glossed over the evolutionist's regrettable attempt to theorize the direct biological reproduction of accidentally acquired features. Darwin's theory of "pangenesis," James suggested, represented only a momentary lapse in an otherwise cogent account of the primacy of accident and indeterminacy (*WB*, 221–22). In the notes that she entered into her reading diary of 1919, Moore had seemed to take no notice of Darwin's startling accounts of the transmission of acquired mutilations—somatic changes that included cracked cow horns and circumcised foreskins (*VAP* 1:466–70). But lecture notes from biology courses at Bryn Mawr do indicate the poet's familiarity with "pangenesis" and "gemules," baroque components of the somatic "blending" theory of heredity that Darwin elaborated from antiquity in *Variation of Animals and Plants under Domestication*.[25] From an early date, Moore showed a particular interest in the mechanics of the transmission of life-forms—a subject that played a central role in debates surrounding the American eugenics movement of the early twentieth century.

Had Darwin possessed a more "modern" understanding of the mechanism of genetics, he might have been spared from having to account for the apparent inheritance of acquired characteristics. Eight years after the 1859 publication of *The Origin of Species,* Darwin had been challenged by colleagues to explain how single mutations might survive the swamping that awaited their mixture with the mass of population (*DC,* 209–11). At this time Gregor Mendel's statistical study of hybrid inheritance, though published in 1865, was still awaiting wide readership. A Moravian monk isolated from Europe's scientific circles, Mendel spent two years crossing and re-crossing the offspring of twenty-two varieties of garden peas.[26] Tracking the disappearance and reemergence of isolated traits—greenness, yellowness, wrinkles, roundness—he concluded that physiological characteristics were not actually fused in sexual reproduction but that they were in fact particulate, preserved intact and passed on as discrete entities, in dominant or recessive forms, to subsequent generations. Lacking such a handy defense as Mendel's against the swamping challenge to natural selection, Darwin reverted to a Lamarckian notion of the inheritance of acquired traits: environment, he would argue in *Variation,* played a direct and persistent role in producing variations in species.

The rediscovery of Mendel's theory in 1900 did not put an immediate end to Lamarckianism. The neo-Lamarckian view that life-forms were categorically determined by ancestral environments was still used to support American polygenist conceptions of race like Coolidge's in his Nordic miscegenation tract in *Good Housekeeping.* Conservative social planners struggled against the conceptual challenges provided by the notions of variational contingency that James and Dewey located in *The Origin of Species.* They sought instead to preserve the socially stratifying imperatives of environmental determinism. Disparities of wealth and station were justified by the idea that natural stresses strengthened a people's genetic fiber, weeding out failures and programming successes directly into future generations. And for Americans like Coolidge and Madison Grant, the polygenist implications of environmental origins provided modern racial fodder for the red tooth of "fitness." If the inheritance of acquired characteristics fostered social visions that were narrowly programmatic in the eyes of "individualists" like William James in *The Will to Believe,* contrary hypotheses, like August Weismann's 1890 theory of the germ plasm as an inviolate reproductive material, threatened even colder extremes of biological determinism. The notion that acquired characteristics might be more or less directly inherited had at least supplied turn-of-the-century Americans with a theoretical basis for melting-pot visions of race-in-formation. In the image of the melting pot, Lamarckianism provided a progressive outlook on what was seen as a necessarily mixed racial American heritage and future: immigrants of various shapes and shades could be both socially and biologically "Americanized," with their material adaptation to the New World leading more or less directly to their genetic assimilation into a single "American race" (*RCE* 245).

After the turn of the century, American eugenicists emerged to adapt current biological and sociological imperatives, as well as the principles of engineering, to this new race-in-formation. Lacking the mediating term that Franz Boas would gradually formulate as "culture," Lamarckian eugenicists "tended to assume the physical inheritance of . . . complex mental characteristics" (*RCE*, 251). Habit was embedded and passed forth as instinct (247). Culture was conveyed in the blood (253). Yet Weismann's theories of the germ plasm and the rediscovery in 1900 of Mendel's study of hybrid garden peas did not precipitate an immediate dismissal of Lamarckianism in American biological sciences. Rather, in the first two decades of the century, biology was caught between extremes of holdover Lamarckian environmentalism and the early biological determinism of geneticists who had yet to map what Hamilton Cravens calls the "contingent" effects of populations and surrounding environmental factors on the process of genetic combination (*RCE*, 253–54; *TE*, 171). Not only did hereditarian biologists lack the mediating findings of later population geneticists from within their own discipline; they were also resistant in a growing climate of nativism to the more sophisticated models of biological and cultural identity that eventually emerged in the 1920s and 1930s in the form of Boasian cultural anthropology (*RCE*, 299–302). The eugenics movement, which flourished in leading universities during the first decades of the twentieth century, sprang from what we recognize now as an improbable hybridization of Lamarckian social thought and hereditarian biological tendencies. But in the pre-Boasian climate of the times, its innate contradictions were not so immediately apparent.

The idea of particulate inheritance held special appeal to early modern scientists who wished to merge biological with social sciences under the technical aegis of engineering. Charles Davenport was sanguine regarding the utilitarian implications of a particulate genetic constitution when he addressed members of the American Association for the Advancement of Science in 1904. "As the qualities and behavior of molecules are determined by their constituent atoms, so the essence of the individual is determined by its constituent characteristics. And as we may construct new substances at will by making new characteristics of atoms, so we may produce new species at will by making new combinations of characteristics."[27] At the turn of the century, Davenport campaigned to bring to America the statistical approach to nature study that was developed by British biometricians like Karl Pearson and Sir Francis Galton, Charles Darwin's cousin. Appointed as secretary of the Committee on Eugenics of the American Breeder's Association, Davenport accelerated the activities of members, including popular luminaries like Alexander Graham Bell and Luther Burbank, as well as leading biologists, sociologists, and psychologists—including the mental tester Yerkes—known for their pioneering work in mental inheritance, feeblemindedness, and criminology (HA, 62, 64–65). Among the committees that Davenport oversaw was one on immigration headed by Prescott Hall and Robert DeC. Ward, leaders of the elite and influential Boston-based Immigration Restriction League. Fellow Brahmins and former Harvard mates of the pedigreed puritan Davenport, Hall and Ward posed the issue of immigration in starkly polygenist terms. They drew from Ripley and from the New York society lawyer Madison Grant in adapting to racial engineering distorted "Mendelian" principles such as the notion that cross-breeding inevitably leads downward toward reversions to more "primitive" ancestral types (RCE, 68, 324 n). At immigrant stations like Ellis Island, Ward and Hall argued, Americans must choose between preserving a "progressive" and "energetic" Nordic nation peopled by immigrants of "British, German and Scandinavian stock" or creating an " 'atavistic' " composite of "Slav, Latin, and Asiatic races."[28]

Moore's own writings in fact show that she managed a deliberate application of the new science to her poet's aesthetics; and it is through a close study of particular notes, essays, and poems that we can more precisely appreciate her understanding and use of eugenics. In poems like "The Labors of Hercules" (1921), for example, Moore spoke out directly against such patrician proponents of Nordic supremacy as Hall, Ward, and Madison Grant, likening the barrenness of elite restrictionists to the emptiness of the truisms that they exploited. It is an effort, Moore begins, "to popularize the mule," teaching it the democratic "principle of accommodation . . ."

> to prove to the high priests of caste
> that snobbishness is a stupidity,
> the best side out, of age-old toadyism
>
> . . . .
>
> to convince snake-charming controversialists
> that it is one thing to change one's mind,
> another to eradicate it—that one keeps on knowing
> "that the negro is not brutal,
> that the Jew is not greedy,
> that the Oriental is not immoral,
> that the German is not a Hun."
> (O, 63–64)

Versed in nature, Moore knew that mules were bred by mating donkeys with mares. Engendered at the limits of hybridity, these mixed creatures were as vigorous and powerful as they were sterile. If such an emblem as the mule in "Hercules" interrogates equally the purity and the fertility of "the high priests of caste," it embodies a flaw in the character of nativist appeals to Nordic supremacy. When read in the context of restrictionist debates over race, the excerpted sermon that closes this poem does more than dismiss empty rhetoric and bigotry on principle: it challenges eugenicists like Grant, Hall, and Ward by closing with a World War I–era nationalist's slur against German Americans, "hyphenated" citizens of divided loyalty who had fallen from favor as the first-born tribesmen of the great Nordic race (PAN, 197–98). Sowing their future American race with disaffection, the restrictionists are like Moore's mythical bird of statecraft who will go

> staggering toward itself and with its bill
> attack its own identity, until
>   foe seems friend and friend seems
>   foe.
> (MM, 35)

The spiteful and contradictory logic of eugenics seems indeed to concentrate those themes of internal divisiveness that color Moore's 1916 address "To

Statecraft Embalmed." Compiling tables of quantifiable data, the new breeders of nativity engender nothing but diffusely malicious clichés.

If Moore showed a principled disdain for the flagrant racist clichés exploited by many eugenicists in the teens and twenties, however, she may still have been drawn to the essentialist premises of the eugenics movement. In a 1925 editorial for the *Dial*, Moore splashed praise on the horticulturist Luther Burbank, posing him as a modern replacement for Newton in Professor Emeritus Dr. Charles Eliot's pantheon of Western history's great educators. In Moore's view, Burbank was not a champion of the contingent "mosaics" celebrated by philosophical and cultural pluralists but a careful shaper of new generations. "Has one consciously been . . . less in debt to Luther Burbank whose witchcraft we are told is merely the suncraft of an observer, than to Sir Isaac Newton? Since, having been made to understand how five hundred kinds of fruit may be produced on one tree, how white blackberries, stoneless plums, spineless cactus, and sweet lemons may be successfully 'designed,' one cannot but understand somewhat of the water, of the air, and of the sun which contributed to produce these curiosities" (*CPMM*, 154). Written shortly before Burbank's death in 1926, Moore's paean to the wizard of Santa Rosa crowns a popularity that ranged widely among modernist writers, from Pound in his essay "Cavalcanti," to T. S. Eliot in "Burbank with a Baedeker," to Williams in *The Great American Novel* and John Dos Passos in *U.S.A.* As a naturalist poet who admired both the "businesslike" prose of Charles Darwin and the "unbusinesslike" "fondness of nature" of the practical Henry Ford (1250/1), Moore seems almost to have made an aesthetic study of the vegetable inventions of the celebrated modern breeder. Burbank's crossing of peaches with almonds, of apples with quinces, of potatoes with tomatoes—and his christening of hybrids like "Elephant Garlic," "The Paradox Walnut," "The Pearl Prune," "The Blood Plum," and "The Sunberry"—might be considered as sources for the proliferating compound nominal hybrids that distinguish Moore's diction.[29] Praised by fellow botanists as a hands-on hybridizer with an unschooled but judicious eye (*GTG*, 118–20), Burbank with his suncraft provides a demystifying model for the eclectic collage poet who affected to map her own handiwork with quotations and notes. As a "designer" of nature who believed that his methods offered models for racial engineers, however, Burbank places Moore in another kind of light.

Moore's praise of the colorful Burbank in 1925 as a great modern "educator" appeals to the racist foundations of the National Origins Act not only through the metaphorically volatile concept of horticultural "design," but also through the celebrated hybridizer's direct involvement with the eugenics movement. A national hero during the early decades of the century, Burbank was sought by journalists for his views on subjects ranging from diet and meditation to evolution and school reform. The California gardener was an early advocate of Chinese immigrant exclusion, and his only book-length publication was on the subject of eugenics·(GTG, 160, 156). Appearing initially in 1906 as a long essay in *Century Magazine* (then edited by the young poet William Rose Benét, a childhood neighbor and lifelong friend of Moore's), *The Training of the Human Plant* won praise from temperance advocates like the poet Ella Wheeler Wilcox, who proposed that the government distribute a copy of Burbank's book to every mother in the nation (GTG, 161). The tract began with a chapter titled "The Mingling of Races," which contained a demographic breakdown of the 752,864 immigrants who entered the United States in 1904. In the face of such a "colossal example of the crossing of species," Burbank proposed to adapt "the principles of plant culture and improvement in a more or less modified form to the human being" (*THP*, 6, 5). An admirer of Darwin's *Variation of Animals and Plants under Domestication*, Burbank was at this time an anomaly as a eugenicist who believed that "environment is the architect of heredity"; and his prescription for the melting pot buried racist and classist anxieties beneath vague calls for "supervision and selection" and a glowing emphasis on nurturance and educational reform—namely fresh air and sunshine and no school for children under ten.[30]

Moore may or may not have had the hybridizer-educator Burbank in mind when she wrote, late in life, of students as "foster plants of scholarship";[31] but she was clearly tracking his horticultural and sociological innovations in her reading diaries of the early 1920s. During the 1922 family trip to Mount Rainer that led to her long twin poems "Marriage" and "An Octopus," Moore copied passages from an interview with Burbank from the July 16 *Seattle Times*. "In nature we find varied an & inanimate forms of life many of wh have motion Some of wh in the higher forms we call emotions. Education and environment can never make any appreciable progress in producing a better race of human beings. Perm. results can only be obtained by the selec of the best individuals for continuing the race this selec being continued thru a series of generations." Apparently trying to lighten up the interview, the *Times* writer then asked Burbank, "What do you think of the Climate of S. California." "Wherever you can grow oranges it is no fit place for a white man to live . . . [Moore's ellipses] I would rather have a grave at Santa Rosa than all of Southern cal. Then why does S.C. attract so many people I interposed Because it is better advertised than the N. part of the State. They all flock to the place they're told to go. Less than 15% of our own people do any orig. thinking on any subject. Our army tests showed that" (1250/3). Among the scientific periodicals that Moore skimmed during the National Origins fervor was the *Journal of Heredity*, the leading forum for American eugenicists throughout the second and third decades of the 1900s. Noting articles with such titles as "Inheritance of Mental Traits," "Twinning in Brahma Cattle," and "The Ancestry of Abraham Lincoln," the poet copied passages such as this one on heredity and criminality from a 1924 article "Behavior and Gland Disease": "In disease as in health, the man of the gutter will behave according to his world and the man of the peaks in keeping with his."[32] Moore's interest in heredity and hereditarians may have been as aesthetic and as skeptical as sincerely scientific, but in the context of praise for Burbank it seems to signal at least a tacit support for eugenics. If Moore partook of the sanguine spirit of racial engineers like Davenport, indirectly celebrating new racialist steerage restrictions with her praise of stoneless plums and sweet lemons, however, she also anticipated flaws intrinsic to the science of human selectivity that Burbank set forth. In the margin of her transcription of the *Seattle Times* interview with Burbank, Moore queried "(What about recessive traits [indecipherable mark] Elizabeth Tuttle [indecipherable mark] Edward's grandmother)" (1250/3).

Moore's cryptic dialogue with Burbank can be read in two ways. On the one hand, eugenicist judges were soon to use "Mendelian recessives" as grounds for the mandatory sterilization of the promiscuous daughters of feebleminded mothers—the same poor and uneducated women who were sterilized by court order in twenty-five states (*HA*, 138–39, 133–37). In light of the apparent persistence of hereditarian dangers, Moore's quarrel might have been with the softness of the plant breeder's program of selection. The hybridizer who had called in *The Training of the Human Plant* for laws "to prohibit in every State in the Union the marriage of the physically, mentally, and morally unfit" seemed now to be peddling an overly positive program, one that accented "selection of the best" while evading the question of how to eliminate the worst (*HA*, 58). In the context of Moore's pragmatist leanings and poetic practice, however, her own reference to recessive traits seems to constitute a more fundamental criticism of Burbank the eugenicist. By using Mendelian terms to challenge the horticulturist's naive hereditarian approach to social issues, the poet aligned herself with the more contemporary views of population geneticists.

By breeding fruit flies in milk bottles during the teens and twenties, the population geneticist Thomas Morgan established that genetic transmission was a far more complex and contingent affair than eugenicists like Davenport—and the *Seattle Times*'s Burbank—had conceived it to be (*TE*, 171). Mendelists had erred first by assigning single corresponding genetic units to discrete somatic features: one gene unit for eye color, one for hairline, another for width of jaw. They assumed that biological reproduction involved a one-on-one matching up of gene units that resulted in various combinations of dominant and recessive traits. Eugenicists then elaborated from this miscast framework a similar correspondence between genetic units and particular character traits, such as laziness and wanderlust (*TE*, 164, 172; *HA*, 67–68).[33] The second mistake of the Mendelists—their hereditarian determinism—was related to the first. In order that heredity might be arithmetically cast, the process of genetic combination was abstracted from contaminating local environmental contexts. Morgan's fruit fly populations showed that environmental pressures did indeed play a role in the pairing of chromosomes (*TE*, 171–72). One of the fundamental contradictions of racist eugenicism was its joining of a Lamarckian polygenist essentialism—which used geography and climate as grounds for racial essences—with a neatly manipulable hereditarian determinism (*PAN*, 152–53; *RCE*, 324 n). In her eugenic reference to recessive traits, Moore asks Burbank how trait selection can engineer the many randomly hidden units of genes. Although the question itself reflects a unit conception of genetic material that was already under challenge by Morgan, the poet was implicitly suggesting that the designing of Americans might be a chancier enterprise than the designing of roadsters. Against deterministic selection, Moore invoked the sort of Jamesian fermentation of environment and heredity that population geneticists now saw as a necessary component of biological reproduction.

4. Genetics, Metonymy, and Moore's Modernism

If Moore's poetic interest in horticultural design and in genetics seems somewhat heady and remote, it gains explicit political dimensions in light of her poetic indictment of the restrictionist authors of the National Origins Act. And if her writings of the late teens and the early twenties hint at an awareness of the relationship between forms of language and forms of identity, Moore later testified through her poetry not only to her concern for the modern science of racial engineering but also to her conviction that a modern metonymic brand of poetry might provide a response to one of the most pressing political issues of her day. Bonnie Costello has noted that a great number of Moore's poems treat questions of aesthetic representation through the thematic lenses of biological and artistic reproduction. In Moore's "Nine Nectarines," for example, the genealogical impulses attendant on natural history and art history provide, in their "infinite regress," a formal account of Moore's own multiply authored quotational poems.[34] Moore's crossing of natural history with mythology in her 1935 poem about a Chinese porcelain painting, however, suggests that modern genetic theory had come to supply her with an imperative that was at once ethical and aesthetic.

> Arranged by two's as peaches are,
> at intervals that all may live—
>   eight and a single one, on twigs that
>   grew the year before—they look like
> a derivative;
>   although not uncommonly
> the opposite is seen—
> nine peaches on a nectarine.
>   Fuzzless through slender crescent leaves
>   of green or blue or
>   both, in the Chinese style, the four
>
>   pairs' half-moon leaf-mosaic turns
> out to the sun the sprinkled blush
>   of puce-American-Beauty pink
>   applied to bees-wax gray by the
> uninquiring brush
>   of mercantile bookbinding.
> Like the peach *Yu*, the red-
> cheeked peach which cannot aid the dead,
>   but eaten in time prevents death,
>   the Italian
>   peach-nut, Persian plum, Ispahan
>
>   secluded wall-grown nectarine,
> as wild spontaneous fruit was
>   found in China first. But was it wild?
>   Prudent de Candolle would not say.
> (*MM*, 29)

Moore knew from readings of Darwin and the Swiss botanist Alphonse de Candolle that the origins of the peach and the nectarine were a subject of nineteenth-century contest. Among the more tantalizing clues to the origins of hybridized, or specifically crossed, plants like Victorian nectarines were accounts of sudden reversions to aboriginal forms (*VAP* 1:398, 439). Darwin's *Variation of Animals and Plants under Domestication* cites many reports of nectarine trees springing from peach parents, as well as abundant instances of "sports," or mutated nectarine clusters on peach tree limbs, and occasional "half-and-half" fruits. But seed reversions and bud variations pointed the other way too, with cases of "nine peaches on a nectarine" providing evidence for each tree as the specific parent of the other (1:361). Through centuries of back-and-forth crossing, the hybridization of nectarines and peaches seemed so thorough that neither fruit could remember where it began. If there was anything to be learned from genetics, it may have been located in the humility of the meticulous de Candolle: "I laid stress, in 1855, on other considerations in support of the theory that the nectarine is derived from the common peach; but Darwin has given such a large number of cases in which a branch of nectarine has unexpectedly appeared on a peach tree, that it is useless to insist any longer upon this point, and I will only add that the nectarine has every appearance of an artificial tree."[35]

Mendelian "recessives" and Darwinian "bud-variations" are important components of Moore's modernist aesthetic because they illustrate the fundamental instability of life-forms in transmission. By naturalizing accidents in generational carriage, the wayward leaps of particulate inheritance enrich the modern poetic relational aesthetic in the same way that postmodern semiotics gives depth to the formalist distinction between substitutional and contiguous tropes. Admired through the gates of Dewey's "garden of life," the blushing contrast between nectarines and peaches grafts its still-life contiguity onto the tree of knowledge itself. The nectarine beside the peach becomes the nectarine behind the peach, displacing the conceptual agency that determines the genesis and transmission of both life and meaning. Within the framework of biological transmission, "substitution" becomes generational "necessity," and positional "contiguity" becomes a variety of transmissive "contingency." The very particulate contingency of modern genetic combination that accounts for such marvelous sports of hybrid reversion as Darwin recorded in *Variation* is what enables Moore to transfer the laws of genetics to both the particulate nominalist and the relational aesthetics of modern imagist and ideogrammic poetry. Applied to poetry, genetic contingency shakes the semiotic burden of natural generation not only from the primitive index of things in words but also from the structuralist standard of foundational relations upon which collage poems like *The Cantos* and *Paterson* come to rest. Developing her own metonymically strung semantic chains toward the contingency that conditions hybrid production, Moore used an image of nine nectarines on a peach tree as a metaphor for the generative displacement of meaning that marks her poetry for contemporary readers.

❖ When the DNA molecule was finally "solved" in the 1950s, its codings revealed a relational complexity far greater than counts of garden peas or even fruit flies had revealed (*HA*, xi). Scientifically minded Americans commonly recognized that, notwithstanding new ethical imperatives, nature was so full of surprises, of tics on the order of recessive traits and bud variations, that eugenicists were left finally as helpless in their attempts to fix future races as were Victorian botanists in their efforts to trace the origins of fruit. Early-twentieth-century population geneticists who mapped the contingency of chromosome pairing, discovering that its chemical intricacy was then further tensed by environmental pressures, had constituted a sort of modernist vanguard in recognizing that, as a science, eugenics could offer at best a succession of natural and unnatural accidents. "The facts in themselves are curious," wrote Darwin, concerning "evidence on the origin of the nectarine" (*VAP*, 1:361).

Accidents were never anathema to Moore; and her praise for "prudent de Candolle" should probably not be read as a retrospective swipe at an American scientific movement that was beginning its retreat in the 1930s (*TE*, 180). The examples of peaches and nectarines in Moore's poem, however, show that it is not only the mechanics but also the premises of racial engineering that are flawed. As "Nine Nectarines" ends with an image of a mythological creature eating one of the fruits hanging from the branch in the porcelain, a complex correspondence between biological and cultural transmission begins to emerge.

> A Chinese "understands
> the spirit of the wilderness"
>   and the nectarine-loving kylin
>   of pony appearance—the long-
> tailed or the tailless

            small cinnamon-brown, common
        camel-haired unicorn
    with antelope feet and no horn,
        here enameled on porcelain.
            It was a Chinese
            who imagined this masterpiece.
    (*MM*, 30)

Laurence Stapleton has resourcefully accounted for the Chinese kylin as the mythological Asian unicorn that emerged from the Yellow River with the first Chinese written characters on its back.[36] As a "small cinnamon-brown, common/camel-haired unicorn," Moore's hornless pony is itself an ideogram composed of linguistic components as fresh and as impure as that of the "puce-American-Beauty pink" blush of the nectarine, a derivative fruit that adapts to the "hardiness" of the North American vernacular and climate alike (*VAP*, 1:360). Browned into the Chinese unicorn, "cinnamon" and "camels" map the history of the animal's hybridization, the ancient east-west trade routes along which legends and fruit stocks moved, linking points from old Rome to Ispahan to Pekin.[37] Language, like peach stones, confuses the East with the West and the Old World with the New. It serves as a barrier to origins and as a local social frame. There are no essences to be found in the philological substance of words; but language roots those who use it in its half-moon arcs of inflection. Moore's Chinese are pragmatist sages. They make stories, not studies, of origins.

❖ Genetic variability provides the semiotic ground that distinguishes Moore's modernist imagist aesthetic from that of European American colleagues like Williams and Pound. If a pragmatist resistance to syntactically braced systems of language supports the semantic freshness that Moore achieves through compression, hyphenation, and slip-disc lineation, this freshness is animated by semantic renderings of principles like Mendel's recessives and Darwin's aboriginal reversions. "Nectarine" holds the nectar that feeds the animus of language.[38] This is not a painterly pun native to the peach-eating kylin but an accident of nature and of translation that structures Moore's vision of language. In the best of Moore's writing, an aesthetic of accident and semantic collision keeps her ever-awakening phrases away from the snares of truisms and clichés. Like the imagist poets of the early modern period, Dewey recognized the power of the modern Ptolemaic tendency toward universalization, and he grounded its political register in the "Americanizing" imperative of racist restrictionists. Moore too saw the local political stakes of the snake-charming lure of racist truisms, and her poetics are perhaps all the more radically Copernican for her own work's witness to such common flaws in herself. "It was a Chinese/who imagined this masterpiece." Didacticisms like this one display Moore's own susceptibility to disembodied essences and "truths," a common weakness that marks the language and politics of even the most sophisticated of her contemporary readers. Paired with her admiration for eugenicists like Burbank, Moore's predilection for the very commonplaces against which she wrote pushed her outside the realm of common aesthetics toward an aesthetic of renewal. Life sciences provided a semiotically enriched dadaist model for semantic transmission that was as yet unconquered by aestheticians. Emerging ever so slowly, the laws of genetics were rawer and yet more rigorously antirationalist than the Continental aesthetics of Marinetti or Tristan Tzara. Fundamentally fluid, yet sharply particulate, and immediate yet complex in their admission of local environmental influence, genetics gave Moore a ground that was more vividly indeterminate than the founding economies of Pound's *Cantos* or the libidinal pulses of Joyce's *Ulysses* or even the new "relative" measure of Williams's American idiom. Attuned to a pragmatist's insistence on the leading and guiding function of accidents themselves, however, Moore was not merely the most rigorous of the modernist harbingers of indeterminacy. More than her European American modernist peers, and more than many of her postmodern followers, she found in semantic contingency—and in the attendant "mistakes" that rule both natural and social history—a practical foundation for the declaration of ethical truths.

SIX

Zora Neale Hurston and "The Races of Europe"

Zora Neale Hurston's *Their Eyes Were Watching God* (1937) is filled with side characters who share little with Janie Crawford, the horizon-bound heroine who has lately been absorbed into the American literary mainstream. Drawn loosely from the author's own anthropological field notes, the fleeting exchanges between these characters make up a lexicon of what Hurston's contemporaries called an "unconscious" folk culture (*ET*, 11). Typical of these exchanges is a discussion between a group of "big picture talkers"—Lige, Sam, and Walter—on the relative importance of "nature" and "caution." "Whut is it," Lige asks Sam, "dat keeps uh man from gettin' burnt on uh red-hot stove—caution or nature?" Insofar as this question can be made to shine back onto the speaker who asks it, Lige's inquiry into the roles played by caution and nature resembles Stephen Dedalus's self-reflexive query in the opening chapters of *Ulysses*. Is the artist born consubstantially, "begotten" by words—or is she "made" in the loom of language that nets her in flight? Are the porch-sitters themselves the knowing inventors of the authentic stratum that they embody in the novel, or are they an unconscious expression of a larger cultural body to which they already belong? "Ah'm gointuh tell yuh," Sam answers. "It's nature dat keeps uh man off of uh red-hot stove."

"Listen, Sam, if it was nature, nobody would have tuh look out for babies touchin' stoves, would they? 'Cause dey just naturally wouldn't touch it. But dey sho will. So it's caution."

"Naw it ain't, it's nature, cause nature makes caution. It's de strongest thing dat God ever made, now. Fact is it's de onliest thing God ever made. He made nature and nature made everything else."

"Naw nature didn't neither. A whole heap of things ain't even been made yit."

"Tell me somethin' you know of dat nature ain't made."

"She ain't made it so you kin ride uh butt-headed cow and hold on tuh de horns."

"Yeah, but dat ain't yo' point."

"Yeah it is too."

"Naw it ain't neither."

"Well what *is* mah point?"

"You ain't got none, so far."

"Yeah he is too," Walter cut in, "de red-hot stove is his point." (*EWG*, 226–27)

As a vernacular scoring of the heredity versus environment conflict, the debate regarding nature and caution was a pointed one during an epoch of scientific racism. But like the author of the surfacey "folklore fiction" that contains them, the picture talkers seem incapable of enlarging the topic toward its full social and political significance.[1] The argument about nature and caution seems rather to exist as a local social moment that enables one speaker to paint his adversary atop the wrong end of the wrong kind of vehicle. In adapting a leading scientific controversy to the competitive realm of "the dozens," the porch-sitters seem to have frittered away "the point" of the discussion.[2] But as Walter reminds us, it is through the speakers' side-winding evasions of the very thesis of the controversy—contained within the abstract parameters of "nature" and "caution"—that the point of the exchange begins to come clear. It is "de red-hot stove" that finally matters. However he accounts for his agency, whether through "nature" or "nurture," "race" or "culture," the black man, and the black man's children, will inevitably be burned. It does not matter what the outcome is because "dese white folks," as one of the porch-sitters eventually speculates, "got ways for tellin' anything dey wants to know" (*EWG*, 228).

❖ By late 1933 the science of racial engineering had engendered organizations like the Human Betterment Foundation, a California-based group whose pamphlets provided models for mass sterilization programs in Germany.[3] Historians have only recently begun to reconstruct lines of direct collaboration between Nazi scientists and American eugenicists during the years leading up to the installation of modern crematoriums in Auschwitz-

Berkinau and Dachau; and the Roosevelt administration's refusal to aid Jewish refugees during the worst years of European persecution is now spoken of as something more than a tragic outgrowth of American isolationism. Within the United States in the 1920s and 1930s, however, the gradual ascendance of "culture" as an ostensibly "contingent" measure of identity does appear to have slowed the advance of racialist legislation. In the National Origins Acts of 1921 and 1924, Congress had passed race-based immigration quotas; during the years surrounding that same period, legislators in twenty-five states had followed California in calling for the sterilization of women deemed "feebleminded" by local courts. As a growing number of studies of modern American literature and culture have begun to suggest, the measure of "culture" gained widespread currency in America as a counter to such racialist fervor.[4] Granted a scientific validity by population geneticists like Thomas Morgan and by anthropologists including Franz Boas, Melville Herskovits, and Zora Neale Hurston, "culture" was ideologically cushioned by pragmatist champions of an American "universe" that was "still . . . 'in the making.' "[5] The idea that identity was derived more from the "caution" of "cultural bonds" than from the "nature" of fixed "physical types" helped Americans to articulate a fitful opposition to emerging fascist movements in Europe; and it laid a groundwork for the Civil Rights movements that gathered force during the second half of the twentieth century.[6]

The modern American embrace of culture was a tonic for a handful of innovative "native" American writers. Weathering the reactionary onslaughts of eugenicists and immigration restrictionists, stay-at-home European American modernists like William Carlos Williams and Marianne Moore fashioned new kinds of poetry by adapting changing conceptions of native identity to changing views and uses of language and art. Drawing from pragmatist philosophers who mapped a new universe of "possibility" and from social theorists who imagined America as a "mosaic of peoples," these poets succeeded in converting anarchistically based modernist aesthetic tenets into newer "American" varieties of modernism—varieties that were meted out according to the fluid dictates of "cultural" forms of identity. During the 1920s and 1930s, however, there was another group of artists and intellectuals in America whose more searching conceptions of "culture" led to an altogether different set of literary innovations. The very category of the Harlem Renaissance is rightly criticized as one that singles out a series of intellectual and artistic inquiries among African Americans only to preserve them as contained, or silenced, by the collapse of patronage and by the rise of class-based inquiries among African American intellectuals of the early

1930s (*MHR*, 91–92). As a period-based phenomenon, the Harlem Renaissance may well need to be redressed; but beginning in the 1920s, a number of social and economic factors did contribute to a resurgence of interest in the question of what African Americans were made of. Among these factors was the very divisive racialist climate that divided white Americans into "subspecies," or competing members of what was widely referred to as the biologically stratified "races of Europe."[7] Culminating in a call among white Americans for a conciliatory form of "cultural pluralism," one that sought to unite Americans of English, Polish, Italian, and other forms of European ancestry, the race scientists' stratification of white European racial identity played a role in the reinvention of African American identity.

❖ The idea of "caution," or learned behavior, was instrumental to the notion of "culture" that white cultural relativists like Boas used to combat racial determinism in the 1920s and 1930s; in Hurston's novel, the porch-sitters' irreverence toward "caution" suggests a "cultural" skepticism regarding the ultimate uses to which any such instrument might be put.[8] If "nature makes caution," as Sam rather shrewdly suggests, then the two terms are not so divergent as they might seem. Nature may or may not "make" caution, but the very suggestion that it does so points indirectly to a conceptual flaw at the root of many modern European American and African American literary innovations. In the philosophical displacement of one system for another—even in attempts like the anarchists' and the pragmatists' to replace a system with a reflexive refusal to systematize—the claim for "naturalness" itself is continually made new. Cultural anthropologists like Boas joined modern philosophers like James and Dewey in making a relativistic axiom of Darwin's vision of the instability of species; in so doing, they made caution more "natural" than nature.[9] Through such efforts, "foundations" remain integral to antifoundationalist critiques. And even the efforts of African American intellectuals to ground this dialectic in history, naturalizing the oppressed black's recognition of the constructedness of white laws, merely add natural fuel to the fire that burns the constituent that Hurston called "the bottom black."[10] What is voiced by the folk characters in Hurston's novel, then, is the author's recognition that modern conceptions of race and culture are equally inadequate to African American identity.

❖ As an accomplished folklorist who had participated in the Boasian invention of cultural anthropology, Hurston was familiar with the idea that "organic differences" between groups of people were "overshadowed by environmental influences" (*AML*, 49). Among contemporary critics, however, the historical affiliation between Hurston and Boas has contributed to misreadings of Hurston's variety of modernism. Although literary historians differ as to the nature and extent of Hurston's commitment to race and her related ideological embrace of Boas's culture, Hurston's poststructuralist readers share a tendency to judge her folklore fiction on the basis of its fidelity to the indeterminacy upon which culture seems to rest.[11] Poststructuralist assessments of *Their Eyes Were Watching God* have long turned on the idea that for Hurston the Negro is at once a cultural and a speakerly entity—a subject engendered through a wedding of identitarian and discursive varieties of contingency.[12] Dorothy Hale traces the avenues through which a range of leading African Americanist critics, readers of Hurston among them, have adapted Du Bois's historical notion of the American Negro's "double-consciousness" to formalist assumptions regarding "double-voicedness"[13] as an authenticating but fundamentally "negative" seat of consciousness, one that "possesses no positive content of its own" (448). In a similar vein, Shamoon Zamir views the contemporary African Americanist critical "preoccupations" with "parodic doubling" and "signification and indeterminacy" as direct outgrowths of the "notions of supplementarity and *différance*," axioms set forth by Derrida in his study of "the history of the ideas of speech and writing" (*DV*, 212).[14] Through these and other conflations of epistemological and discursive measuring criteria, the double-voiced subject that graces African American texts like Hurston's has gained a special sort of authenticity, allied to the authenticity claimed for the unspeaking subaltern subject who, in Gayatri Spivak's view, remains uncorrupted by the imperialistic mechanisms of "expressive subjectivity."[15]

Hurston has been a welcome subject for these sorts of conflations because she was both a folklorist and a modern novelist who deployed destabilizing narrative strategies. In her work poststructuralist conceptions of discursive authenticity—conceptions associated with spoken language in particular—seem borne out by the contingent forms of identity that the folk embody as representatives of an autonomous oral culture. The priority that culture acquired over race during the modern period, in other words, appears to complement the priority that has been granted to speakerly over written texts by critics who value performative identities and the subaltern constituencies that are associated with them. In their laudable if anachronistic efforts to fit Hurston to their "progressive" poststructuralist paradigms, many of these critics have neglected to see that culture was a construct that she approached with great caution.

Hurston's "individualist" politics have perplexed more than a small number of the contemporary readers who try to situate her as a modern champion of progressive poststructuralist causes.[16] And though she can hardly be dismissed as a reactionary who aligned deterministic notions of racial identity and direct reference in language, neither can she be identified as a progressive writer who identified "culture" as a social outgrowth of the principles of narrative and semiotic free play. Hurston distinguished herself not as a conventionally reactionary or radical author but as a writer who was reluctant to naturalize contingency by authenticating culture as an antidote to outworn notions of race. And it is only by disentangling her writings from the postmodern measure of progress, a measure that couples language and identity, that we can begin to appreciate the full historical and literary significance of this gesture. In her refusal to embrace the foundations upon which antifoundationalist thought had come to rest in America, Hurston conceived of a fictional narrative in which racially and culturally bound forms of discourse serve not as touchstones of identity but rather as discursive materials that facilitate the ongoing construction of identity through narrative modulation. By mastering an idiomatically marked variety of "free indirect discourse," in which identity was divorced from the new apportionings of authenticity that "culture" conferred upon raced, classed, and gendered varieties of voices, Hurston transformed what Henry Louis Gates, Jr., calls "diegetic" conceptions of racial identity into mimetic palimpsests that bore traces of identitarian processes. For Hurston this was not a presciently poststructuralist exercise but a historical response to a set of modern scientific phenomena ranging from the eugenics movement to advances in modern physics. As a modern African American novelist, Hurston drew from a unique network of social and intellectual circumstances to devise a narrative practice that dispensed with even the more process-based essentialism that has increasingly come to appropriate modernist textual practices to the construction of subaltern identity. She made "Negro" identity into a condition that could not be authenticated and hence that could not be co-opted by either reactionary or progressive movements.

1. Hurston, Pragmatism, and American Exceptionalism

Hurston's belief that language-making, and not language, was a cornerstone of identity is built into both the content and the narrative structure of *Their Eyes Were Watching God*.[17] Branding Hurston's novel a "speakerly text," Gates views it as a radical departure from other African American literary narratives ("ST," 65). Drafted in 1936, during an intense six-week span while Hurston was doing anthropological fieldwork in Haiti, the novel turns on a modernist blending of the narrator's voice with the voices of the characters. The characters in the novel, however, speak in a series of rural southern black dialects—dialects that many of Hurston's contemporaries, including Locke and Richard Wright, would condemn as insufficiently differentiated from the voices of minstrelsy.[18] The controversy raised by Hurston's first critics points to a feature that distinguishes her novel from other narratives that turn on varieties of free indirect discourse. Insofar as the interchanges between the novel's characters and its narrator shift the axis along which the novel's "color line" is drawn, *Their Eyes* charts a more complex set of discursive dynamics than other experimental modern narratives, including those, like William Faulkner's *Sound and the Fury,* that play "raced" strands of discourse against a fixed, or "normative," white narrative ground.

In assuming that Hurston's novel authenticates a true idiom by pitting black speakerly against false white writerly voices, or even by pitting dialogic against monologic voices, recent critics have made the same mistake as Hurston's contemporary readers. In Hurston's novel the absorption of characters' voices by the narrator of the book does not mark the ascendance of a more authentic, subaltern form of identity, which is somehow fundamentally allied to the notion of "double-voicedness" ("BA," 445–46). Rather, it marks Hurston's effort to convert the modern literary narrative into a stage upon which identity can be expressed through the interplay of discourses that are themselves finally inadequate to either "being" or "becoming." Like Hurston's historical detractors, poststructuralist critics who celebrate Hurston as a writer who restores cultural identity to, or even through, the speakerly voices that contain it have neglected the network of social and intellectual sources that encouraged Hurston to approach "culture" with "caution." Thus they have failed to locate the discursive interstices where *Their Eyes* speaks its piece. A full recovery of these interstices, and of the means through which they are engendered in Hurston's narrative, hinges not so much on a poststructuralist authentication of performative speech acts over written forms of expression as on a retrieval of the social and intellectual foundations of Hurston's modern African American narrative "hieroglyph" (445–48).[19] And insofar as they provide a formal foundation upon which to examine Hurston's literary adaptation of African American responses to pragmatist conceptions of language and identity, James Joyce's narrative innovations in *Ulysses* provide a starting point for assessing the historical politics of Hurston's narrative strategies in *Their Eyes Were Watching God.*

Ulysses is one of the first modern novels that uses not only characters but also an experimental narrative technique to address the question of how identity is constructed. Joyce's exploration of identity through the technique of "free indirect discourse" owes more to European anarchism and nihilism than it does to American philosophy. But as a novel that makes full formal and thematic use of antifoundationalist premises, *Ulysses* provides a framework for understanding the mechanisms through which Hurston used the writings of black and white American philosophers to fashion the modern narrative as a theater for the performance of Negro identity. In *Ulysses* Joyce's immersion of the narrative voice into the voices of the novel's characters bolsters his critique of deterministic conceptions of identity. One of the first pronounced blendings of the novel's omniscient narrative voice with a character's voice occurs in a passage where the protagonist, the Irish poet Stephen Dedalus, glimpses himself in an Irish handmaiden's mirror. Likening the distorting mirror to Irish art itself, Stephen testifies to the Irish subject's harsh encounter with the representational inadequacy of English words and conventional narrative structures. When Stephen suggests that Irish identity is distorted by the medium through which the Irish writer seeks to express it, Joyce's distortions in *Ulysses* come to assume explicit political dimensions. Through Stephen's story, and through the interrelated stories of Leopold and Molly Bloom, Joyce assaults a range of deterministic conceptions of identity, racial conceptions among them; and he subjects them to a thoroughgoing critique that is spearheaded by the very medium of the novel. Here, the dissolution of the harsh divide between quoted and unquoted words, or of the divide between "originary" narrative and "derivative" character voices, works to remove the linguistic and conceptual impediments that prevent a variety of characters—Irish, Jewish, female—from being adequately represented.

In *Ulysses* Joyce was working from the antifoundationalist premises of individualist anarchism rather than from within the relation-bound pluralistic confines of American pragmatism. And though later pragmatists like John Dewey came to chastise the author of *Ulysses* for reducing contingency to a series of "shocks" and "blind" narrative "jumps," the early William James of *The Will to Believe* (1897) and "The Stream of Thought" (1890) had himself explored the very axioms that drove Joyce's exploration of the relationship between linguistic and biologistic determinism.[20] James's reading of Darwin had led him to champion the free-falling and "infinitesimal[ly]" contingent nature of generational transmission; it had encouraged his application of this dynamic to a criticism of conventional forms of language and reason

(*WB*, 225). In *The Principles of Psychology,* James came to criticize the inadequacy of language and reason to the continuum, or "the unbroken stream," that characterizes individual "consciousness" (*PP*, 243–48). The accidents of identity and knowledge that issued from an individual's stream of thought could not be trained by any deterministic system of syntax or reason. They could only be released, in the way that generations could only be released, from the indeterminate tangle of variables that went into their making.

James himself had refrained from extending the implications of genetic indeterminacy to modern questions of racial identity; but his pragmatist colleague Josiah Royce did apply the idea of philosophical contingency to a critique of the hereditarian assumptions that drove the American eugenics movement. In *Race Questions, Provincialism, and Other American Problems* (1908), Royce had spoken to white Americans of the practical virtues of viewing race as more an "accidental" than an "essential" phenomenon.[21] He seems to have sensed in James's celebration of biological and semantic indeterminacy a conceptual challenge to the premises of eugenics—a challenge that was later eloquently spelled out by European American writers including Marianne Moore. Moore herself was not a reader of Royce's lesser-known pragmatist text, but *Race Questions* did win the attention of Franz Boas, as well as W. E. B. Du Bois, the influential African American intellectual who had studied under James and Royce at Harvard.[22] By the time of Royce's book, Du Bois had already begun to consider the significance of foundational pragmatist axioms like "essence" and "accident" to an analysis of the historical source of the very "problem" that his white mentors had been slow to identify.[23] In suggesting that "the problem of the Twentieth Century" was not a nakedly epistemological problem but rather a crisis that stemmed from the tangible "color-line" itself, the author of *The Souls of Black Folk* (1903) had mounted an implicit challenge to the very abstract axioms that enabled pragmatists, and also the poststructuralists who have followed them, to contain "race" within the frameworks of philosophy and semiotics (*SBF*, 359). In posing a historically based sociological challenge to the universalizing premises of James's and even Royce's writings, Du Bois laid part of a tentative foundation for Hurston's eventual critique of the static premises upon which modern American antifoundationalist thought had come to rest.

In her essays and novels, Hurston displays a clear grasp of both the conceptual power and the political limitations of James's understanding of the significance of Darwin to semiotics. James's attention to the "transitive" nature of the individual's stream of thought held Western syntax to the Darwinian standard of a syntax that was attuned to the "accidental" contours of experience, as opposed to a defective language system that froze experience into "substantive" components (*PP*, 243–48). In "Characteristics of Negro Expression," a 1934 essay that was based on her extensive study of African American speech and speaking practices, Hurston had rehearsed something of James's distinction between "transitive" and "substantive" varieties of language in her account of rural southern "Negro expression." In her etymological investigation of such Negro "hieroglyphs" as the colloquial "chop-axe," for example, she suggested that Negro culture had added "drama" to language by restoring tangible verbal qualities, like "chop," to "legal tender" nouns, like "axe." And in *Their Eyes Were Watching God*, the divide between static knowledge and dynamic experience becomes central to the identity of a black woman who learns that "talkin' don't amount tuh uh hill uh beans when yuh can't do nothin' else": "You got tuh *go* there tuh *know* there" (*EWG*, 332). The idea that a person's "going" might be somehow bound to folk culture or vernacular expression, however, is greatly complicated by Hurston's association of "folk expressions" with an antiquated "tangle" of "Reconstruction phrases and concepts."[24]

Janie Crawford's task in *Their Eyes Were Watching God* is summarized in a sentence that Hurston inserted into a later draft of the manuscript that she had roughed out so quickly in Haiti: Janie can acquire a vibrant modern identity only by breaking with her postslavery upbringing and "fit[ing]" "new words" to her "old thoughts."[25] Here, as in Hurston's colorful account of the vitality of "Negro Expression," self-invention is born from a struggle against outmoded forms of language. In *The Principles of Psychology*, James had fashioned the "self" that might revive language by fitting new words to old thoughts as an ahistorical "individual"—a "*me*" that was universally defined against an encompassing "*not me*" (*PP*, 289). In subsequent writings, however, this ostensibly apolitical axiom would come to display the "American exceptionalist" premises upon which it had originally rested. In *The Varieties of Religious Experience* (1904), for example, James echoed exceptionalists like Emerson in associating deterministic, substantive forms of language with the "sick soul" of Europe and indeterminate, transitive forms with the "healthy mindedness" of America.[26] And in his published lectures collected as *Pragmatism* (1907), James described the pragmatic synthesis of opposed European philosophical tendencies in terms of a distinctly American reconciliation of traditional class divides (*P*, 491–93). He revealed the deep correspondence between the pragmatist quest for free will and the long-standing objectives of exceptionalists who had asserted that because of its "republican government and economic opportunity," America "occupies an exceptional place in history," a place not tied to the fortunes of Europe (*SS*, xiv).[27] Hurston's was a "Du Boisian" quest for identity through language insofar as it challenged the implicit American "exceptionalist" divide between what Emerson called "sepulch[ral]" European rationalists and the more "transparent" American descendants who were capable of immediate and invigorating perception.[28] In *Their Eyes Were Watching God*, Janie's quest for "new words" abandoned the transcontinental divide in favor of a more historically focused desire to authenticate one set of American premises over another. Here dynamic Negro expression became an antidote to calcified and backward-looking white American standards of measure.

Although the "old thoughts" that shackle Janie in the novel do not issue directly from white mouths, they bespeak a white American set of values— values rooted in the institution of slavery—that have been internalized by African Americans. It is through her struggles with the grandmother who raised her and with the respectable black farmer that "Nannie" compels the adolescent to marry that Janie comes to understand that individual experience is prior to language. (In the novel, Nannie forces Janie to marry Logan Killicks because he is a landowner who can "protect" her from the dangers facing black women in Reconstruction America.) Here, Hurston's understanding of what it is to be an "individual" is less abstract than that of the early "psychologist" James, who asserts that "we all draw the line of division between [the halves of the universe] in a different place" (*PP*, 289). And though Hurston did express an ambivalence toward Du Bois as a leader who was so tangled up in "books and papers" that he failed to recognize the current needs of the rural southern "bottom black," she absorbed his critique of pragmatist axioms through disciples like Langston Hughes and James Weldon Johnson.[29] It was through a secondhand absorption of Du Bois's ubiquitous conception of "double-consciousness" that Hurston's modern narratives came to turn on a more historically grounded apportioning of the universe.[30] Du Bois's conception of the historical mechanism that had eroded the cultural contributions of citizens torn between two sets of standards—"an American, a Negro; two souls, . . . two warring ideals in one dark body" (*SBF*, 364–65)—represented an updating of James's evasive suggestion that the individual experience of the self-actualizing American might be a counter to deterministic European varieties of thought and language. From the standpoint of "the color-line," it was plain that the exceptionalist notion that Europe was the debilitating source of substantive varieties of language, and of the morbid resistance to action that substantive language brings about, contained within it a paradoxical reliance on the polar terms *Europe* and *America* as an inadequate pair of substantives themselves.

In *The Souls of Black Folk*, Du Bois had challenged his white pragmatist teachers by suggesting that it was not merely the American "individual" who was authorized to penetrate the veil of substantive measures of experience. An awareness of the falseness of "essential" truths and their static semantic corollaries hinged not on the intrinsic differences between static and dynamic truths, but rather on the recognition of a local racial division between two living constituencies, one of which had been empowered to hold a standard over the other. "Double-consciousness," Du Bois asserted, had endowed African Americans with the "gift" of "second sight," or the capacity to see the constructedness of all standards of measure (*SBF*, 364). Through the veil that separated black culture from white, it was evident that no measures were "natural" ones, not even the "transitive," contingent measures that the Darwinist psychologist James had opposed to the determinists' substantive substitutions. To overthrow old truths, as Darwin and Royce and Moore had done, by naturalizing new ones and illustrating them in action through "the gates of the garden of life" was to perpetuate the very capacity to naturalize that was itself a greater tyrant than either determinism or contingency per se ("DIP," 93). Determinism and contingency were in and of themselves empty instruments. They were equal as weapons that, once possessed, conferred real power and authority. Hurston's private denigration of "cheap" white folklorists, and even her vexed celebration of "enlightened" white anthropologists like "Dr. Boas, the King of Kings," who knew how to "make people work the hardest . . . of anybody else in creation," was based on her recognition that although "culture" was certainly preferable to "race," its ostensibly relativistic measures served as much to channel power and authority as did the more deterministic measures that it came to replace (*DT*, 683). What mattered was not only the theory itself, in other words, but also the ideological work that was performed by its formulation, its assertion, its implementation. And it was in the act of questioning the new lines of authority that the "the color-line" channeled that Hurston came to distance herself not only from American pragmatist assumptions but also from the conservative and oppressive offices of even the most progressive varieties of modern African American thought.

2. Historical Measures of "Negro" Identity

By 1934 W. E. B. Du Bois's ubiquitous notion of "double-consciousness" had enabled Hurston to maintain a fluid understanding of the folk materials that she had begun to weave into her novels. In accounting for the dynamic social contingencies that distinguished "Negro expression" from other forms of oral and written communication, Hurston took up the Du Boisian notion that local social and historical circumstances had rent asunder the identity of the American Negro; she wrote this rift not only into the structures of address that conditioned her narrative voices but also into the very genesis of the idiomatic discourse that her narratives featured. In this way she complicated the simple axiom invoked by the distinction between black and white, even as this outworn axiom was given new vigor through the mediating category of culture. The notion of culture as a foundational category of identity had served to replace outworn models of determinism with more modern models of contingency, but it had also worked to preserve racialist notions of "authenticity" by displacing them from genealogical to epistemological criteria. Because it was so clearly defined in opposition to the pervasive notion of the Negro as a racial subject, Negro culture was from the beginning founded on a shared recognition that identity was a socially bound construct. This epistemological boundary worked to reinvigorate the besieged notion of "authenticity," and with it the very essentialist conceptions that had hovered around racialist conceptions of whiteness and blackness.

Hurston attempted to empty American Negro culture of its vestigial claims to genealogical authenticity by describing its idioms as fundamentally derivative and performative. In "Characteristics of Negro Expression," Hurston suggested that African Americans have come to speak in "hieroglyph[ic]" word pictures only because the language they speak is not their own ("NE," 24). Distinguishing this claim from the racialist belief that black Americans had an innate affinity for "primitive" African languages as opposed to the "highly developed" languages of Europeans, Hurston suggested that it was not the Negro's "Africanness" per se that fostered his unique relationship to the English language. It was rather the relative disjunction of African and European cultures and languages that had rendered English as a language that was "not evolved in him but transplanted on his tongue" (24). Because the language the Negro speaks is not evolved in her mouth, she "must add action to it to make it do." The result of the Negro's alienation from English was a reconcretization, or a rerooting, of the very "detached" words that constituted the "cheque word" language of Anglo high stylists.[31] "We have 'chop-axe,' 'sitting-chair,' 'cook-pot,' and the like," Hurston wrote, "because the speaker has in mind the picture of the object in use. Action. Everything illustrated" ("NE," 24). For Hurston, double-consciousness, or the historical fact of two warring souls, was displaced onto the relationship between the black speaker's thoughts and his or her language. The split between experience and words served to denaturalize the English language for the African American speaker. The disjunction of African and European cultures makes the Negro a special kind of citizen, one who is uniquely equipped to restore vitality to the American language.

In this sense, then, it is Hurston's race-based distinction between evolved and transplanted varieties of language that appears to have laid a foundation for a performative conception of African American identity. In "Characteristics of Negro Expression," Hurston implied that it was the Negro's very lack of familiarity with the language that enabled him to restore to the English language qualities that were missing. It was through the act of restoring this language that Negro culture was born. Hurston placed a premium on the Negro's facility for imitation because it was through mimicking and remaking what did not belong to her that the Negro created her own identity. And in later writings like *Their Eyes Were Watching God,* the lexicon of materials to be mimicked and remade would eventually come to include the very identitarian conceptual schism—"race" and "culture"—upon which her careers as a folklorist and as a "Negro" writer had turned. Far from serving as the axiomatic poles through which the American Negro might be located, race and culture were materials through which Negro identity could be fashioned.

In *Their Eyes Were Watching God,* Hurston came to locate identity in the interstices of voices that called across a heavily conditioned Du Boisian divide. Gender and class were among the categories of identity that complicated Hurston's color line. But Hurston resisted Du Bois's influence by refusing to fix the voices that she deployed—and even the doubling intervals between them—as static markers of identity. Her absorption of "double-consciousness" was conditioned by her adherence to less reactive conceptions of "minoritarian" privilege. Hurston's belief that the Du Boisian "gift" of "second sight" might itself provide not a reactive epistemological ground for Negro identity but rather a vehicle for its ongoing performance drew not from more historically sensitive renderings of pragmatist conceptual axioms but rather from the more abstract, more process-oriented conceptions of identity that were set forth by a new generation of African American intellectuals. By the early 1930s, for example, Alain Locke was beginning to think of identity as a construct that was generated through an "Einsteinian 'frame of reference,'" a "relative" system of measure that provided "just what we want for social and psychic phenomena."[32] Here the abstract conceptual complement that modern physics offered to African American intellectuals was at least superficially similar to the one that it had offered earlier to European American free-verse innovators like William Carlos Williams.

By the time of Locke's discovery of Einstein's significance to a more relativistic measuring of identity in 1931, Williams had found in modern physics a scientific corollary to the notion that a white pluralistic apportioning of "the American idiom" might be gained through an improvisational form of poetic measure. In 1921, at the outset of his first experiments with heavily enjambed short-line free-verse poems, the poet had followed John Dewey in canonizing "St. Francis Einstein of the Daffodils" as a champion of the European immigrant masses ("AL," 687).[33] Exemplifying the interdisciplinary inquiries that had characterized early-twentieth-century American intellectual enterprise, Dewey had used first evolutionary theory and then relativity theory as scientific corollaries to the modern pragmatist search for more fluid, improvisational thought systems. As a social activist who had long been committed to the welfare of America's immigrant populations, moreover, he came to associate the dynamic immigrant challenge to the static standard of "Anglosaxondom" with Einstein's challenge to the Newtonian universe. Williams placed Dewey's sociologically and scientifically informed declaration that "the locality is the only universal" at the heart of his call for a distinctly American form of free verse in 1921; by the middle of the decade the poet had begun to draw from Alfred North Whitehead's discussion of Einstein's theory in *Science and the Modern World* (1925) and from Charles Steinmetz's popular physics primer, *Four Lectures on Relativity and Space* (1923), in formulating his notion of the "variable foot" as a measure wedded to the ever-changing contingencies of syntax and lineation (*AB*, 48).

Although modern physics had provided Williams and Locke with attractive analogues for their refashionings of "American" identity and "American Negro" identity, relativity was finally no more a source for the artistic outpourings of the New Negro than it had been for white pluralists who defined Americanness through the exclusion of the Negro idioms that were muted in service to it. In the contrast between African American and European American adaptations of the process-based imperatives of modern physics, however, lies the genesis of a new approach to "culture" that was central to Hurston's writings. For Locke the more process-based conceptions of identity that relativity seemed to bolster were rooted not in the ongoing imperatives of "St. Francis Einstein's" European immigrant masses but rather in an emergent interest in Negro folklore shared by African American artists and intellectuals who had emigrated to urban centers like New York and Washington. Responding in part to the efforts of white pluralists to reconstitute a white race that had been divided by a eugenically driven apportioning of "the races of Europe," African American thinkers of the late 1920s had begun to turn their attention to Negro folk traditions, conceiving them not as essentially black materials but as a series of practices that invoked real blackness only through their "unconscious" evasion of white Newtonian standards of measure. And the very rigorous variety of modern antifoundationalism that came to drive Hurston's narrative innovations in the 1930s can be traced through Du Bois and Locke to this modern "Renaissance" recovery of African American folk traditions.

❖   Locke was a leading light at Howard University when Hurston studied at the vibrant Washington D.C. institution between 1919 and 1921. During those years Hurston joined a literary club that was sponsored by Locke, a philosophy professor; and she associated with a number of leading black intellectuals and artists, including Locke and Du Bois, at a local literary salon led by Georgia Douglas Johnson. On the significance of the color line to modern thought, Locke concurred with Du Bois when he called for African Americans to intervene in the modern "scientific" study of "race." As a socially driven discipline, Locke claimed, "race science" was best understood by those groups who were least served by its orthodoxies. "Those who belong to a minority group and those who are victims of an assertive creed or race ought to consider that they have the point of vantage from a scientific point of view," Locke argued. "We see the garment, so to speak, from the seamy side and we ought to know how it is constructed." Citing Du Bois's "prophetic," if somewhat "cynical," foregrounding of " 'the color problem [as] the problem of the 20th century,' " Locke allied himself with the NAACP leader in identifying "race" as a construct through which power was channeled.[34] And he stood together with Du Bois in suggesting that the dynamic of such a channeling could be reversed. Writing in *Darkwater*, a 1920 book that "greatly influenced" Langston Hughes, for example, Du Bois had laid claim to a "singular" "clairvoyan[ce]" regarding "the Souls of White Folk."[35] "I view them," he stated ominously, "from unusual points of vantage. Not as a foreigner do I come, for I am native, not foreign,—bone of their thought and flesh of their language. Mine is not the knowledge . . . which servants have of masters or masses have of classes or capitalists of artisans. Rather I see these souls undressed and from the back and side. I see the working of their entrails, I know their thoughts and they know that I know."[36] Here, Du Bois and Locke stood together in celebrating what poststructuralist critics including Gayatri Spivak value as the subaltern, or minoritarian, perspectives that confer epistemological authority to those who have long been denied it. For both of these modern African American leaders, truth was negatively fashioned through a suppressed group's exposure of the constructedness of what seems natural to the oppressor.

The color line was a divide that granted agency to those who were positioned to police it; rather than wishing it away as an unjust construction, Du Bois and Locke sought to turn it to the black man's advantage, suggesting that African Americans were uniquely positioned to intercept the epistemological contraband that was smuggled across its divide. Where these two critics differed was in their understanding of the manner in which this interception lent authority to the Negro's perspective. Du Bois likened the African American's exposure of the racist social basis of "natural" laws—laws asserting that the black race was innately fit to be ruled—to an exposure of the "ugly, human" flesh of the white man himself.[37] In so doing, he parlayed a set of assumptions that remain questionable for contemporary critics who seek to locate authenticity and authority in subaltern perspectives and voices.[38] On the one hand, Du Bois suggested that white society had invoked such laws to cover its innate weakness, or its reliance on the very racist practices that had corrupted its humanity. In his negative portrayal of the innate superiority of the African American, Du Bois's racial essentialism mirrors that of the Irish nationalists in *Ulysses,* reactors who perpetuate the very binary logic that facilitates their own subjugation. On the other hand, however, Du Bois's less essentializing suggestion that white society has been corrupted by the fact of its long mastery begs the question of the corruption of those positioned to acquire a "mastery" of this knowledge.

As a canny political strategist, Locke appealed intermittently to the essential African grounds of Negro identity; but as a philosopher, he endeavored to escape such latent essentialism, as well as the slavish dependence on the master that had hampered "old school" black "thinkers" like Du Bois.[39] By grounding his race-based epistemology not in a galvanizing epiphany of pale skin but rather in a vision of the "seamy side" of the ideological "garment" that concealed this bareness, the younger leader ultimately emphasized the active means rather than the reactive object of the New Negro's vision. Locke thereby preserved Du Bois's emphasis on history while muting the old-school thinker's dialectical dependence on white mastery. Such an emphasis on epistemological process complements Locke's allegedly "aestheticist" de-lineation of the parameters of the African American renaissance of the 1920s. Du Bois's insistence that Negro art must serve a well-defined social purpose ensured that the Negro's consciousness would remain tightly bound to the white consciousness against which it remained negatively defined. In the 1920s Locke orchestrated an appeal for freer artistic expression with his anthology of *New Negro* writings and woodcuts. His desire to escape the Du Boisian bind by exploring a range of components of Negro identity—gendered, cultured, classed—was part of what led Hurston to propose an artistic alliance with a leader who seemed to her to be "different" from all others.[40] In her early years at least, up until Locke betrayed her by dismissing as politically superficial the "folklore fiction" of *Their Eyes Were Watching God*, Hurston claimed to find Locke's "work in Philosophy" "less confining" than that of Du Bois.[41]

Though Locke's process-oriented "Philosophy" laid a ground for less reactive conceptions of black identity, Locke and Hurston were in fact given to occasional outpourings of racial essentialism. These expressions suggest that even process-based conceptions of double-consciousness could recoil from time to time in dialectically driven assumptions regarding the authen-ticity of the Negro. Like many of her contemporaries, Hurston acknowl-edged that color was a central fact of both American history and American consciousness. In answer to Locke's warnings to her regarding the "absolute blindness" of "the Caucasian mind" "to the things that are really revolution-ary in Negro thought and feeling," Hurston wrote of her own belief "that white people could not be trusted to collect the lore of others."[42] In private letters to Locke, Hughes, and Charlotte Mason, Hurston questioned the capacity not only of old-school white folklorists (like Odon and Johnson, authors of the widely circulating *Negro Workaday Songs*) to grasp the mate-rial of black culture, but of new wave cultural anthropologists as well. In 1929, for example, she conspired with Mason and Alain Locke to keep Paul Radin, a progressive white disciple of "Papa Franz" Boas, from interviewing and appropriating the stories of Cudjo Lewis, a former African slave living outside of Mobile, Alabama.[43] (Lewis, who was also known by his African name, "Kossula," was the subject of the yet unpublished "Barracoon," Hurston's own first book-length anthropological study.)[44] And in a manuscript chapter of *Dust Tracks* that was censored by the book's publisher, she wrote that, in contrast to "the darker races" who "desire enough for [their] own use only," "the idea of human slavery is so deeply ground in that the pink-toes can't get it out of their system" (*DT,* 793).[45] The idea that blacks and not whites were innately qualified as guardians of black culture was shared by many black and white thinkers alike, but Hurston was unique in her suggestion that black insight was bound not to nature or caution but to the Negro's vernacular performance of new thoughts through old words. And it was through her understanding that racially bound conceptions of identity might be invoked and productively played against culturally bound conceptions that Hurston came to use the modern literary narrative as a vehicle through which identity could be performed through, rather than defined by, these mutually implicated categories.

In Hurston's literary narratives, identity is constructed not through the terms but through the interstices of vernacular and literary expression. Locke's exposure of the "seamy side" of the "garment" enabled Hurston to conceive that it was not constructed discursive strands themselves but rather their interplay that provided a foundation for identity; nonetheless, the use of vernacular voices to counter literary ones reflected a resurgence of interest among modern African American intellectuals in folklore as a new form of cultural material. And among the intellectual leaders who spearheaded this return to Negro folk sources, the movement had been negatively modeled on the historical fracturing of white racial identity. The urban sophisticate Locke was hardly an early devotee of Negro folk culture, but in 1925 he laid a demographic blueprint that complemented what Charles S. Johnson was heralding as a "new emancipation" of "folk materials" among African American artists and scholars (*ET,* 12). In his epoch-making introduction to *The New Negro,* Locke had written of Harlem as an intercultural and international "laboratory" that had been established by black "leaders" from various regions and countries; he declared that this cadre of professionals had not led, but rather followed, their "rank and file" constituencies to New York.[46] Locke's placement of uneducated rural blacks at the root of a modern cultural renaissance may not have engendered Johnson's reevaluation of African American folk culture.[47] But the class shadings of the philosopher's renaissance race map clearly supported the sociologist's call for a renewal of interest in the very vernacular materials to which Hurston herself was already beginning to turn.

Until the 1920s, Johnson wrote, black intellectuals had "bitterly oppos[ed] Negro dialect, and folk songs, and anything that revived the memory of slavery" (*ET,* 12). Long controlled by white artists, these materials were rightly associated with minstrel traditions that enclosed blacks within a damagingly narrow comic-pathetic range (*MHR,* 21–22). In accounting for a groundswell of receptivity toward this long suppressed folk legacy, Johnson invoked the very pseudoscientific parsing of the white race into "sub species" that Marianne Moore had criticized in "To Statecraft Embalmed" (1916). In a chilling metaphor that fused the fractious spirit of wartime nationalism with the rising racialist calls of American isolationists, Moore had fashioned "statecraft" as a mythical bird that will go

> staggering toward itself and with its bill
> attack its own identity, until
>> foe seems friend and friend seems
>>> foe.
> (*MM,* 35)

Racialist immigration quotas were anathema to white modernists like Moore, who would come to link genetic and cultural contingency to vibrant new verse forms governed by metonymy. But the example of the legislative division of the white race in modern America bespoke a different set of possibilities for a people already excluded from "statecraft" and hence from the righteous pluralistic appeals for new national unity. In the introduction to *Ebony and Topaz,* a 1927 anthology of African American art and scholarship that celebrated long suppressed "folk materials," Johnson suggested that the scientistic implosion of the white "race" had provided a means of altering contemporary perceptions of the black. "We are accustomed," he wrote, "to think of Negroes as one ethnic unit, and of whites as many,—the Nordics, Mediterraneans; or Germans, Irish, Swedes; or brachycephalics and dolichocephalics, depending on our school of politics or anthropology" (*ET,* 11). In appealing to the distinguishing morphological characteristics of a variety of European nations, Johnson implied that African Americans should at least comprise a multitude of ethnic units.

In *Ebony and Topaz,* however, Johnson refrained from engaging in the sort of scientific critique of classification that had fueled the cultural anthropologists' anthropometric assaults on the racial typing of the Negro.[48] Declining to even strategically parse the Negro along the biologistic lines that race scientists had used to divide the white race from within, he asserted that "the really valid distinctions between the races" lay not in biologically essential differences but rather in "dissimilar customs and culture patterns" (*ET*, 11). Significantly, Johnson believed that differences in customs and culture patterns were most fully articulated in those Negroes who were least likely to read his anthology of African American writings. For him, the strongest challenge to the essentialist category of the Negro race lay in the "unconscious," and hence relatively diversified, contributions of the "folk groups" rather than in the more "conscious," and hence more assimilated, contributions of the intelligentsia who had long suppressed these groups in their efforts to measure the American Negro against the standards of the dominant culture (11–12). Negro folk culture came into being not so much through an affirmation, or even a negation, of its genealogical proximity to ancestral hearths as through its apparent transcendence of the claims to a negative epistemological "authenticity" that the idea of "double-consciousness" contained. Neither holding the Negro back nor propelling the Negro forward along progressive but ultimately essentializing lines, folk traditions became a vehicle for more modern and less debilitating forms of identity.

Seeking less deterministic means of fracturing essentializing conceptions of the American Negro, African American intellectuals sought to avoid the mistakes of the modern race scientists who had divided the white race into "sub-species." From the standpoint of African Americans who, like Hurston, came to question the value and meaning of "culture," moreover, the newer, more fluid conceptions of identity that emerged to counter white racialism were also fraught with problems. For many black artists and intellectuals, these conceptions were not as attractive as they were to the progressive whites who sought to use them to reunify the races of Europe. Franz Boas, for example, had been among those who led the charge against the scientific racism that swayed American legislators during the early decades of the twentieth century. Yet the very mechanism of his assault revealed that "culture," too, could be used to relegate African Americans to the liminal positions to which race had confined them.

In his 1922 essay "The Measurement of Differences between Variable Quantities," Boas had argued that scientific racial categories reflected a "lack of clarity of concept" because they were based on "arbitrary" measuring criteria ("MD," 182, 181). To illustrate the instability of such categories, Boas invoked a pair of examples that underscored the role of arbitrarily selected reference points in the measurement of racial subjects. In his first example, Boas suggested that when compared without the benefit of a mediating term, a "pure White population" and a "pure Negro" population will appear to differ morphologically (184–85). When a reference point such as a population of baboons is interjected into the comparison, however, the initial differences between these groups appear to diminish. Boas then followed this "humanistic" illustration with a second example: "When we compare a group of blond, blue-eyed North Europeans with dark complexioned, brown-eyed South Europeans, their dissimilarities are the most striking feature. If we add a Negro community to these two groups the similarities between the North and South Europeans would be much more prominently in our minds" (185). By joining it to the baboon from the preceding example, Boas converted the "Negro community" into an arbitrarily selected reference point, one that serves to illustrate the Newtonian crudeness of conventional scientific racial categories. In the process, he rendered the white, and not the Negro, population as the beneficiary of the anthropological assault on the category of race.

In uncovering the instability of scientific conceptions of race, Boas relegated black Americans to the margins of "culture." So positioned, the Negro could serve to make vivid, through his difference, the very modernness of a new form of anthropological measure. And progressive European American modernists displaced the Negro in a similar fashion.[49] As an imagined amalgam of the speech rhythms of European immigrants, for example, the idiom that William Carlos Williams identified with "the speech of Polish mothers" acquired its relativistic "Americanness" as much through its exclusion of black voices as through its inclusion of new white ones. The cultured American idiom gave new currency to "meaningful" racial differences exactly by branding as "meaningless" the modern differences that it replaced. In his 1925 essay "Advent of the Slaves," Williams claimed to have known "intimately" a "colored [man]" whose "talk" quenched him like "water from a spring" (*IAG*, 210, 211). But the "loquacious" "Negro" himself had eluded the poet, who had found him, and others like him, to be "shy" and "resistant as an eel" (210, 211). "I wish I might write a book of his improvisations in slang," Williams wrote in this patronizing portion of *In the American Grain* (1925): "I once made several pages of notes upon his conversation—but I lost them" (211).

Whether due to the "colored man's" congenital evasiveness or to the caginess of the white writer who invokes the black vernacular for the purpose of dramatizing its disappearance, an African American presence emerges only to slip from the margins of Williams's writing. "Waggin', wavin', weavin', shakin'," this presence traces the implicit limits of the American idiom. In Williams's modern pluralist universe, African Americans do not contribute to modern forms of Americanness. "Saying *nothing,* dancing *nothing*" (*IAG,* 209), they serve rather as mute figures who supply the wordless patterns upon which whiter varieties of Americanness can be modeled. In the early poems that Williams modeled on "the American idiom," "loquacious" "colored men and women" provide voiceless links between the "relativistic," process-oriented imperatives of Americanness and indigenously American art forms. Lacking a voice of his own, the jazz musician who emerges in the middle of *Spring and All* (1923) sounds a markedly wooden note amid Williams's fluid early idiom poems. "Get the rhythm," mimes a white exceptionalist who paints Americanness in black-face.[50]

> That sheet stuff
> 's a lot a cheese.
>
> Man
> gimme the key
>
> and lemme loose—
> I make 'em crazy
>
> with my harmonies—
> Shoot it Jimmy
>
> Nobody
> Nobody else
>
> but me—
> They can't copy it
> (*I,* 130–31)[51]

African Americans were no more central to Williams's poetics in the early 1920s than they were to the project of cultural anthropology. They provide exotic examples through which process-based art forms, forms that imitate in a manner that makes them inimitable, can be identified as indigenously American. In their muteness, however, African Americans also mark the limits of the American idiom. They are allowed to model this idiom's processes, but they are forbidden to partake of, and hence to possess, its material.

The example of the racialist apportioning of "the races of Europe" had provided a negative model for modern African American intellectuals who, like Johnson, sought to emancipate "local" folk traditions from the shackles of minstrelsy. At the same time, "relativistic" and "pluralistic" amalgamations like those of Boas and Williams made it difficult to embrace folk traditions as cultural antidotes to overly deterministic conceptions of Negro racial identity. African American folk culture was attractive not as a contingent antidote to race but because, as an "unconscious" medium, it was apparently immune from the essentializing negative claims shared equally by white pluralists like Williams, for whom white Americanness depended on a veiling of blackness, and by sometime black nationalists like Du Bois, for whom black Americanness hinged on an exposure of the "ugly" white soul. Johnson's defining claim in *Ebony and Topaz* was that by attending to the varieties of customs and cultures secreted in "unconscious" folk songs and dialect, American Negroes might begin to collapse that part of their identity that Negro intellectuals like Du Bois had tended to measure against whites. Hurston had published a couple of stories in dialect in Johnson's anthology, and she had contributed to Locke's *New Negro* anthology the year before. Her contributions to these two compilations not only delineate her prescience as a Harlem Renaissance writer who was already committed to the vernacular "soundings" that would attain prominence in the 1930s, but they also trace the intellectual sources of her later narrative innovations in *Their Eyes Were Watching God* (*MHR*, 91–95; *SR*, 16). Drawing tentatively from Locke's less color-bound elaboration of Du Boisian tenets, Hurston formulated her notion that a conditioned variety of the color line, one that was intermittently inflected by both class and gender, had enabled *some* individual subjects, in *some* individual moments, to see that it was dynamic processes rather than static categories that lay at the root of identity. Johnson's conception of "unconscious" folk traditions, moreover, helped her to understand that modern blackness might be claimed not only through a refusal of deterministic genealogical channels but also from a refusal to reactively authenticate a "second-sighted" negation of the ideological premises that white determinists upheld. As Johnson imagined them, folk traditions were equally indifferent to determinism and contingency as premises that marked epistemologically based forms of identity, and the idea of such an "unconscious" body of Negroes helped to prevent Hurston from following the racialist paths of culture-bound European American modernists like Williams and Moore. Taking the unconscious folk as her model, the novelist was able to stop short of equating dynamic processes with culture and static categories with conceptions of race. For her these categories were valuable not because they worked to rechannel authenticity but because they provided new materials for the ongoing fashioning of identity.

3. Narrative Measures in *Their Eyes Were Watching God*

In her own celebrations of rural southern black folk culture, Hurston partook of Johnson's effort to free African American identity both from the shackles of white standards of measure and from the strictures of the very minoritarian epistemological communities that emerged in reaction to them. In portraying rural southern African Americans in "Characteristics of Negro Expression" as linguistic outsiders who possessed a unique grasp of language, Hurston *had* borrowed somewhat from Du Bois's valuation of a minoritarian perspective. Read alongside Ezra Pound's polemics on money and language as foundational social media, moreover, her celebration of black "barter" words over white "cheque" words seems to partake of the objectives of American exceptionalists. Here, an avowedly "primitive" American minority is coaxed forth to invigorate the language of a "more civilized" majority, staging a nativistic reenactment of the imperialistic appropriations of modern European painters who, following the examples of Picasso and Braque, had learned to assimilate vibrant African sculpture to decadent, overly refined European art forms. In the spirit of Du Bois's celebration of the power of vision from the far side of the veil, Hurston does seem to suggest that the African American picture word is somehow more truthful than the cheque-word language that has evolved in the European American mouth. But Hurston's veiled "insight" in *Their Eyes Were Watching God* does not finally turn on a reactive Du Boisian exposure of the dominant white culture's assumptions. And although it draws somewhat from Locke's and Johnson's more process-oriented glimpses of the constructedness of racial and even cultural identities, it finally refuses to authorize a minoritarian perspective on the basis of either its penetrating knowledge of, or even its naive indifference to, the measures of a dominant culture. In her novel, Hurston's dynamic understanding of "Negro expression" refuses to rest on her earlier folklorist's claims regarding the essentially communal and hence performative nature of rural southern African American language. It reflects a more "cautious" conviction that folk traditions, and the conceptions of "culture" that surround them, can be used to provide new and distinctly modern strata of material through which identity, which is at once black and individual, can be performed.

❖   As suggested by the big-picture talkers who approach culture with caution in *Their Eyes Were Watching God*, Hurston recognized that performative oral practices could serve to cut through the hegemony of universals like nature and nurture, and she eventually channeled this awareness into a new type of modern literary narrative. But she knew better than to simply submit to the kind of relativism that such an awareness might produce. "Culture," like the "empty *warmhearted*" humanist principles that Stirnerian anarchists had challenged, was an indefensible category to a modern "individualist" like Hurston; nonetheless, there were times when it provided an indispensable measure of resistance (*EO*, 31).[52] One such time comes just before the hurricane climax of *Their Eyes Were Watching God*, when Janie befriends a racist woman who threatens to poison her relationship with a man whom she has worked hard to find.

Janie's status as a "coffee-and-cream" colored woman with "luxurious[ly]" "cascading" hair has long been an affront to readers who believe that the novel bows to white standards of beauty. But Janie's "fairness" also serves to prepare for the conflict that places racial standards of any sort on a plane with the foundational standards that the porch-sitters debunk. When the widowed wife of the mayor of Eatonville meets and marries Tea Cake, a younger man who teaches her to play checkers, to hunt, and to swap stories with the bean-pickers on the Florida muck, she feels fulfilled in a way that she has not felt with either of her two previous husbands. One of these husbands had squinched his girl bride into the mule's harness of "safety," and the other had crushed her with "horizons" that sounded only his own single voice. In the Everglades with Tea Cake, Janie befriends a proudly "featured" local woman. Worshiping at the altar of "Caucasian characteristics for all," Mrs. Turner has internalized white racist beliefs about dark-skinned black men like Tea Cake, whom Janie has recently married; she tries to persuade Janie to "class off" with other mulattos by leaving her young husband for Mrs. Turner's own brother (*EWG*, 293, 289). Janie's response to Mrs. Turner follows the logic of the porch-sitters, who debunk both poles of the "nature" versus "caution" debate. Refusing to argue the intrinsic virtues of blackness or whiteness, or of nature or caution, Janie answers simply that she loves her husband, thus denying the ontology of skin tone as a significant category of identity. Janie's assertion that "we'se uh mingled people" with both "black kinfolks" and "yaller kinsfolks" derives from Hurston's pioneering work in anthropometrics with Boas, and particularly with Melville Herskovits, which had shown that because of "the amount of mixture represented in the American Negro population," "the use of the word 'Negro' . . . is without justification from a biological point of view."[53] It makes no sense to value white or black because both are equally foundational, and hence equally incidental, to the genetically hybridized creations that modern Americans must be.

Janie's claim "We'se uh mingled people" echoes the claims of cultural anthropologists who questioned the scientific validity of the category of race. But it differs from the anthropologists' claim in its refusal to invoke "culture" as a categorical alternative to the overly deterministic term that it replaces. Rather than providing an opportunity to summon the abstract touchstone of culture, Mrs. Turner's racism leaves Janie feeling "dumb and bewildered." Janie does not summon a formulated alternative to the category of race; instead, she offers wisely that she "ain't got no real head fur thinkin'" (*EWG*, 290). She stays with Tea Cake because she "loves 'im" (289). In light of the porch-sitters' assertion that it is neither "nature" nor "caution" but rather "de red-hot stove" that is the point of the controversy, Janie is justified in her refusal to think that neither race nor culture can account for the radiant truths that she feels with her mind, heart, and body.

Through Mrs. Turner, Hurston portrays racism as a deadly contagion that spreads across lines of color and culture. Mrs. Turner exhibits a racist self-hatred in her efforts to make mulattos "class off" against American Negroes whose ancestry is more purely black African. She thus models a variant of the white racialist division of European Americans into classes of "sub-species" of whites. And although the light-skinned Janie seems immune to Mrs. Turner's efforts to sabotage her marriage, the darker Tea Cake is literally sickened when he overhears the woman spewing her "poison" (*EWG*, 291). Publicly, Tea Cake responds to the racist threat to his manhood by beating his wife. (Among Tea Cake's male friends, Janie is valued because, as a light-skinned black woman, her welts and bruises make a ready display of her husband's brute mastery [94].) Privately, however, he internalizes Mrs. Turner's racism and allows it to literally poison his body. After Tea Cake refers to Mrs. Turner as a "heifer" who runs him down "to de dawgs," he is bitten by an actual dog as he rescues Janie during a devastating flood (291). The dog is rabid, and in the weeks that follow, Tea Cake loses his mind. He believes that Janie has poisoned him to incapacitate him while she sneaks around with Mrs. Turner's brother. When Tea Cake confronts his wife with a pistol and takes delirious aim, Janie shoots him to save her own life. The dark-skinned drifter who had once struck Janie as "a glance from God" closes his teeth into her forearm as he dies (261).

From the initial publication of *Their Eyes Were Watching God* to its academic discovery in the late 1970s, critics have been troubled by the scene in which Janie stands trial for the murder of Tea Cake. Richard Wright alluded to this trial when he condemned Hurston for catering to the "chauvinistic tastes" of "a white audience"; and Sterling Brown found it "surprising" that in spite of the "clear innocence" of the novel's protagonist, "all the Negroes [should] turn away from Janie at her murder trial."[54] In the late 1970s, as *Their Eyes* began to circulate in the academy, Robert Stepto sharpened the charges leveled by Hurston's literary contemporaries. At a critical juncture when Janie is asked to tell her own story, her courtroom testimony is delivered in a third-person narrative. Here, the absence of first-person testimony seems to undercut the illusion that Janie has gained a voice in the novel.[55] Critics have viewed this scene as an aberration in the novel because it complicates the claims to speakerly authenticity upon which the novel seems to hinge. But even feminists who defend Janie's right to maintain her silence have failed to hear what Janie does say through the narrative of this scene (xii). Janie's words in the courtroom go unheard for two reasons. They are spoken at the interstices of narrative "sayings" and "showings," and they are divorced from the conventional markers of identity that contemporary critics associate with voices in African American novels.

Hurston's ambivalence toward the category of "culture" has engendered a wide range of contemporary interpretations of *Their Eyes Were Watching God*. It is this ambivalence that has contributed to feminist readings of the scene in which Janie stands silent before the court. In many ways gender does seem to stand between Hurston and an embrace of the "unconscious Negro folk culture" that characters like Lige, Sam, and Walter seem to embody. In the trial scene, for example, the "Negroes," Tea Cake's male friends from the 'Glades, stand poised like "palm trees" awaiting storm winds in the back of the courtroom. The celebrated "godmakers" of culture hold "their tongues cocked and loaded," marshaling their censure of Janie as "the only real weapon left to weak folks" (*EWG*, 327). When one of this group tries to speak out publicly against the woman who is believed to have betrayed Tea Cake in his sickness, he is silenced by a white judge who calls on Janie to testify to a sympathetic white jury. Through the novel's narrator, Janie speaks and is quickly absolved of wrongdoing; and as the Negroes unleash their "tongue storm" of gossip later within earshot of the grieving widow, they unwittingly "signify" on Nanny's guiding axiom that the "nigger woman" is the "mule uh de world." "Aw you know dem white mens wuzn't gointuh do nothin' tuh no woman dat look lak her," one of the muck men complains as Janie walks free.

> "She didn't kill no white man, did she? Well, as long as she don't shoot no white man she kin kill jus' as many niggers as she please."
> "Yeah, de nigger women kin kill up all de mens dey wants tuh, but you bet' not kill one uh dem. De white folks will sho hang yuh if yuh do."
> "Well, you know what dey say 'uh white man and uh nigger woman is de freest thing on earth.' Dey do as dey please." (329–30)

Tea Cake's friends are right to suggest that a white jury might be quicker to convict a dark-skinned woman who killed a white man; but they are mistaken in claiming that because black men's lives are devalued, black women are therefore free to do with them what they please. The gendered veil that falls between Janie and the "godmakers" of culture seems more profound here than the racial veil that separates the black world from the white.[56] Folk culture may be a dynamic source of signifying play, but it does not in and of itself constitute a benign counterpart to the less racially stable voices of the dominant culture. And the widowed Janie's censure by black bourgeois women as she returns to Eatonville only further vexes the notion that Negro expression somehow constitutes an authenticating performative medium. Hurston's much-quoted celebration of African American oral traditions—"words walking without masters; walking altogether like harmony in a song"—assumes an added dimension when it is restored to the larger context from which it is often excerpted. Issuing from the mouths of the Eatonville women who condemn Janie Crawford, the harmony that gathers these words is revealed to be mastered by spite. "Seeing the woman as she was made them remember the envy they had stored up from other times. So they chewed up the back parts of their minds and swallowed with relish. They made burning statements with questions, and killing tools out of laughs. It was mass cruelty. A mood come alive. Words walking without masters; walking altogether like harmony in a song" (EWG, 175).

Janie's firsthand knowledge of the spiteful ministerings of patriarchal and bourgeois power structures complicates her portrayal of black life in the rural South; and it compromises Hurston's rendering of the color line in

Their Eyes Were Watching God. But readers critical of Hurston's sympathetic portrayal of the white courtroom hearing have tended to overlook the mimetic qualities of the modern narrative in this scene. When Janie wins the sympathy of the jury, she does so knowing that she speaks as a black woman to an all-powerful white audience. As she begins speaking to the jury, "they all leaned over to listen while she talked. First thing she had to remember was she was not at home. She was in the courthouse fighting something and it wasn't death. It was worse than that. It was lying thoughts. She had to go way back to let them know how she and Tea Cake had been with one another so they could see she could never shoot Tea Cake out of malice" (*EWG*, 328). In telling the truth of her life and her feelings for her husband, or so the narrator informs us, Janie must force herself to go "way back" and to tell the story of how she traded Eatonville for a life of drifting and gambling with a younger man—however this group of respectable middle-class white listeners might feel about her choice. But the "lying thoughts" that pose a greater threat than death are also the thoughts that crowd the head of a speaker who knows she is "not at home." The foreign place in which Janie finds herself is not just a courtroom where she is sworn "to speak the truth, the whole truth and nothing but the truth." It is an explicitly white institution; and as such, it is a place where her skin-gained knowledge of the color line tells her to evade her interlocutor, to offer "a feather-bed resistance" to the white man's "probings," if she wants to maintain possession of her own "say" and "song."[57]

In the courtroom, however, Janie cannot simply smother the binary terms set before her, as the "unconscious" picture talkers have done, when they restored "the point" of the "nature versus caution" debate to its "red-hot stove" origin—which is the only meaningful signifier in Jim Crow America. What Janie does in this scene is no less than to step across a deeply instituted discursive divide. As a cautious celebrant of Negro folk culture, Hurston came to understand that even the desire to locate an "unconscious" folk was an outgrowth of the white containment of African American identity. And Janie embodies this understanding in the courtroom. Expressing a historical "caution" toward the very "culture" that she herself stands for as a literary character, Janie comes to recognize that the folkish realm that is home to her is no more dependable, and finally no less constructed, than the more blatantly socially empowered realm of the court. Her "truth" is fashioned independently of the very conventions that dictate black "feather bed" evasions. In taking the step that she takes, Janie sheds both her biological identity and the cultural skin that is marked not only by her possession of the "gift" of "second-sight" but also by her "unconscious" refusal of such a gift—a refusal that she embodies when she tells the racist Mrs. Turner that she simply loves her dark husband. In doing that, Janie loses her claims to a community that is based on a knowledge of the illusion of biology, and even her claims to a feathery innocence of the specious standards that produce this illusion. It is because Janie rejects not only the terms of the race/culture axiom but also the range of available responses to these terms that she is able to acquire a coherent identity, one that lays a foundation for her successful self-advocacy.

Insofar as it succeeds in blending the vernacular voices of the novel's characters with an omniscient narrative voice, Janie's testimony in the white courtroom provides a window into Hurston's particular narrative innovations in *Their Eyes Were Watching God.* In an essay derived from his landmark study *The Signifying Monkey,* Henry Louis Gates, Jr., suggests that in this novel Hurston "introduced free indirect discourse into Afro-American narration" ("ST," 175). Drawing from a range of contemporary narrative theorists, Gates distinguishes between the "mimetic" and the "diegetic" components of Hurston's groundbreaking narrative. Mimetic voices, he argues, are voices that show characters. These include the quoted voices of individual characters in the novel as well as the more collective voices that issue forth, in quotation marks, from "the big picture talkers" on the general store porch or from "the great flame-throwers" in the work camps in the Florida 'Glades. Diegetic voices, such as the voice of the novel's narrator, do not so much show as *tell* readers about these characters from an omniscient remove. Hurston's blurring of the boundaries between mimesis and diegesis does not in and of itself constitute a literary innovation. Joyce was only one of a number of modern novelists who had experimented with this technique by the time of Hurston's merging of these discursive strategies in *Their Eyes Were Watching God.* And although Hurston's merging certainly advanced the frontiers of modern narrative invention, her signal achievement does not lie in what Gates views as her reconciliation of modernist claims for narrative indeterminacy with the performative nature of African American identity.[58] The relationship between "Negro expression" and modernist formal practices is not any more an essential connection than that between African American identity and poststructuralist discursive imperatives that give speakerly voices a priority over writerly ones. In their concern for a discursive stratum associated with a set of "unconscious Negro folk contributions," Hurston's own contributions do not turn on a divide between blackness and whiteness. They turn instead on a changing set of divides that serve not to displace race for gender or for class but rather to confound the binary relationship between dominant forms of discourse and any forms that might be defined as emergent in terms of this dominant. In the face of the failure of race and culture alike, Hurston believed that Negro identity lay in the discursive performance of materials upon which no firm claims to possession could be laid. It was this belief that enabled her to significantly extend the modern novel's narrative showings.

For critics who confuse "double-consciousness" with "double-voicedness" in linking African American identity to poststructuralist notions of the social constructedness of language, Hurston's merging of quoted and unquoted narrative portions is bound to Janie's assumption of a speakerly wisdom and identity. By Gates's reading of *Their Eyes Were Watching God*, for example, it is only when the grandchild of slavery begins to assert herself against the "big voice" of her second husband that Janie's vernacular voice begins to color the novel's narrative. At this point the narrative shifts more toward a vernacular expression through its use of an abbreviated syntax that corresponds to Janie's own. When the "big picture talkers were using the side of the world for a canvas," explains a narrator who seems to use Janie's own tongue, "Joe would hustle her off inside the store to sell something. Look like he took pleasure in doing it" (*EWG*, 217). In the bluesy interval between "it looked like" and "look like," the diegetic, or "telling," part of the story identifies sympathetically with the very speaking subject that it has previously "shown." In passages like this one, Hurston appears to have engendered the kind of authorial consciousness that Joyce had coyly described as "a vital sea" that "flow[s]" "round and round the persons and the action" in a novel (*PAFM*, 1047). Janie could indeed be speaking to us of the novel's narrative philosophy when she entrusts her own story, or "tongue," to the mouth of her friend Phoeby (*EWG*, 179). And the very pragmatist gospel that she asks Phoeby to preach, moreover, the "knowing" that she gains from "going" "tuh de horizon" and learning "de maiden language all over," is itself a kind of mirror to the novel's method of telling. From her experiences in Eatonville and in the Florida Everglades, Janie has learned that love is not a "grindstone dat's de same thing everywhere and do de same thing tuh everything it touch." It is instead "lak de sea. It's uh movin' thing," one that "takes its shape from de shore it meets" (332). Through such metaphors the story of Janie's coming into her own, and her acquisition of the speaking voice that narrates this coming, appears to be part and parcel with the changing form of the book that contains her.

In *Their Eyes Were Watching God*, Hurston's narrative modulations are geared to facilitate a variety of readings of the novel. Vernacular expression has no fixed discursive value or meaning. It is not linked fast to either cultural or racial identity per se; it is rather a stratum of discourse that Hurston manipulates to make showings out of tellings, forming literary "hieroglyphs" that were as vivid and as dramatic as the ones that she found in rural southern black speech. In her narrative display of Janie's assumption of a speaking voice, for example, Hurston combs not only the syntax but also the phonetic matter of Janie's blackness into the narrative that frames the long-suffering wife's story. When her oppressive husband is diagnosed with a terminal illness (Jody's acute kidney failure follows from Janie's verbal defiance of her husband ["ST," 177]), the force of Janie's sorrow interjects the vernacular into a thicket of rhetorically burnished biblical imagery. "So Janie began to think of Death. . . . What need has Death for a cover, and what winds can blow against him? He stands in his high house that overlooks the world. Stands watchful and motionless all day with his sword drawn back, waiting for the messenger to bid him come. . . . She was liable to find a feather from [Death's] wings lying in her yard any day now. She was sad and afraid too. Poor Jody! He ought not to have to wrassle in there by himself" (*EWG*, 242). In *Their Eyes*, Hurston plays to the reader's sympathy for Janie, who gains the strength that she will need to administer truthful last rites at her husband's bedside. Janie will confront her husband, telling him, "You changes everything but nothin' don't change you"; and she will accuse him of having spent his life "worshippin' " only his own "works" and "big voice" (244). As Janie explains to her husband that "you got tuh pacify somebody . . . if yuh wants any love and any sympathy in dis world," the narrative itself has begun to pacify and to sympathize with Janie's own voice. The modulated use of vernacular expressions like "wrassle" shades diegesis toward mimesis in Hurston's novel. The voice that "tells" begins to "show," to make a world-sided "picture" of the very lessons that have earned Janie her sorrowful ascendance over Joe.

Hurston's historical caution toward culture as a contingent category of identity is written into the narrative structure of *Their Eyes Were Watching God*. But it is easy to overlook this caution by assuming that vernacular speech lends a kind of authenticity to the body that possesses it. In Hurston's novel, rural black idiomatic expression does appear to lend a vexed sort of authenticity to the novel's protagonist. And insofar as *Their Eyes* is a modern novel, one that reverses conventional narrative polarities, turning the book's omniscient voice into a "hieroglyph" that illustrates the same laws of expression that Janie has been laboring to enounce, this authenticity seems linked to modern and even postmodern discursive strategies. In her handling of similarly "raced" idiomatic strands in her autobiography, however, Hurston suggests that there is nothing intrinsically authentic or authenticating about the idiomatic material of "Negro expression." For Hurston the vernacular acquires its transformative power not as a "signifyin(g)" instrument that "repeats" or "doubles" a dominant standard, but rather as a vivid measure that provides a constantly changing series of points of resistance to, and convergence with, other strands of expression. In her handwritten manuscript of *Dust Tracks on a Road*, for example, Hurston experimented with a variety of ways of combining "standard" white English and "bottom black" vernacular voices. Speaking to a racially divided audience of her belief that the black race must "pry loose the clutching hand of time" in order to "settle for some influence on the present," this now widely read "Negro" writer was careful to modulate her idioms.[59] "I am three generations removed from [slavery] and therefore have no experience of the thing," she wrote.

> From what I can learn, it was sad. No doubt America would have been better off if it never had been. But it was and there is no use in beating around the bush. Still there seems to me to be nothing but futility in gazing backward over my shoulder and buking the grave of some white man who has been dead too long to talk about. Neither do I see any use in button-holing his Grandson about it. The old man probably did cut some capers back there, and I'll bet you anything my old folks didn't like it. But the old man is dead. My old folks are dead. Let them wrassle all over Hell if they want to.[60]

It is the apparent political sentiments of passages like this one that have led a large number of critics to brand Hurston a conservative black writer. In these comments she begins by measuring the slave trade in terms of its cost to, not an African American constituency, but American society as a whole. She then trivializes the genocidal dimensions of slavery by likening the destruction of black families to a harmless "cutting of capers." And she ends by relegating to the Devil and antiquity an institution that she admits to be very much alive. ("The idea of human slavery," Hurston states toward the end of this chapter, is still "so deeply ground in" to the white race that they have not yet abolished "the slave quarters," but merely moved them "farther away from the house" [*DT,* 793].) In cleansing this passage of its initial vernacular locutions, Hurston appears to use "standard" diction to "class off" with the very "white audience" that her dismissal of America's slavery legacy seems geared to appease. As she did with other words and phrases that she was uncertain of, she underlined the colloquial form "buking" for reconsideration. She permitted the slave owner's black-faced "capers" to stand; but she crossed out the word "wrassle" and penciled in "wrestle" above it. By proposing that her black ancestors should not "wrassle," but "wrestle," "all over Hell" with the ancestors of her admiring white readers, Hurston distances her work, in both form and content, from the weary reminders of a conflict that should best be forgotten.

Hurston's politics in this passage are not quite as accommodating as they seem, however; and her deployment of standard white diction likewise serves something less than appeasement. In the sentences that follow her call for the burial of slavery, the writer suggests that the struggle between the "races" continues and that it takes place in a more earthly arena. "But the old man is dead. My old folks are dead. Let them wrestle all over Hell if they want to. That is their business. The present is upon me and that white man's grandchildren as well. I have business with the grandson as of today. I want to get on with the business in hand" (*DT,* 787). On the heels of her reference to wrestling angels in Hell, Hurston sounds an ominous note when she states that, like "the present," "that white man's grandchildren" are "upon me." The historical conflict between the races seems not to have ended. The crude depiction of struggle between the old man and the old folks has not been erased. It has instead been transmuted into a new sort of competition, one that abandons the idea of a reactive insurrection in favor of a more calculated variety of "influence," one that hinges on the possibility of an infiltration from within. Behind the "assimilationist's" wish not to "button-hole" the white grandson is a desire to do much more than cajole. Hurston's eagerness to "do business" is fueled by her conviction that she will beat him: "The game of keeping what one has," she had written in 1928, "is never so exciting as the game of getting."[61] The "getting" that motivates the writer is not just a matter of money. This "business in hand" is also a matter of vindicating the very ancestors whose clutches she has feigned to escape. Behind the ostensibly "conservative" politics of the writer who claimed to sympathize with the aims, if not the "horizonal" means, of both Communists and Race Men was a lingering anarchistic belief that social change is rooted not in words but in economic deeds.[62] A combative black ancestor lurks in the standardized form of "wrassle." The whitened "wrestle" glides on wheels into the heart of the modern market.

A glimpse at the holograph manuscript of a censored chapter of *Dust Tracks* gives readers what may be an unfair advantage in gauging the effects to which Hurston used the vernacular. But even without the directives offered by her penciled revisions, a careful reader can hear the wheels of the standardized wooden-horse "wrassle." In the expressions "buking" and "cut some capers," the widely heralded "Negro" writer laid a minstrel trail, one that would soften white readers toward the safely insular playfulness that the idiomatic form of "wrassling" should connote. By feathering white ears for idiomatic expression and then withholding the idiom in favor of the stronger standard form instead, Hurston's autobiographical speaker trades her capacity to claim discursive authenticity for the privilege of staging a stealthiness that she cannot engage in directly. She opens a complex rift between autobiographical sayings and showings, one that does not rely on the epistemological authority of an oppressed minority's "signifyin(g)" doublings. It was not Hurston's possession of black or white forms of speaking, or even of gendered or classed strands of discourse, that enabled her to construct a hieroglyph of either Zora's or Janie Crawford's Negro identity. In and of themselves, these strands are meaningful only insofar as modern axioms like "nature" and "caution," or poststructuralist ones like essence and indeterminacy, can fix their relation to a speaker's identity. The ascension of the indeterminate notion of culture over the overly deterministic notion of race, Hurston knew, had above all given new life to the axiomatic distinction between real voices and false ones. For this reason the author of *Their Eyes Were Watching God* and *Dust Tracks on a Road* saw fit to sever any connection between voice itself and identity, electing instead to portray Janie Crawford, and Zora Neale Hurston herself, as characters who perform blackness in the act of evading any sanctioned category that might come to mark it.

Hurston's commitment to performing "Negroness" through discourses that bore no direct relation to either racial or cultural identity is crucial to the courtroom scene in *Their Eyes Were Watching God*. The third-person account of Janie's testimony begins with a fine-tuned accession to the vernacular voice through which Janie has been "shown" to the reader of the novel: "First thing she had to remember was that she was not at home." In showing us a character who stands outside of herself, the narrative appears to paint a "Negro" picture of her self-alienation in the white courtroom.

Like Du Bois's black American subject, Janie comes to see herself "through the eyes of others" and to measure her soul "by the tape of a world that looks on in amused contempt and pity" (*SBF*, 364). At the same time, however, the subtle vernacular shading of this passage lends an aura of ease to Janie's feeling of displacement in the courtroom. Sweetened by the skin of the empty article that it grazes, "First thing" shows us a character who finds a home in remove; and it suggests Janie can do so because her experience of the color line, like that of the authorial narrator who speaks comfortably to a judging white readership, has taught her something about language. The remove that Janie has learned to master in the novel is a discursive remove, one that results not from a linkage but rather from a severance of speech—and even speech in its doubleness—from its immediate relation to identity. In light of Hurston's strategic willingness to "wrestle" with the folkish idioms that mark Janie's black speakerly ascendance, moreover, the vernacular shadings of the courtroom scene display the confidence that arises from Janie's knowledge that Negro identity can be pieced together on any ground, from any body of materials. Janie's comfortable displacement in the courtroom finally stems from her hard-won knowledge that an idiom does not constitute either a positively or a negatively defined self, that it is rather a tool that channels the makerly impulses, or the "going," that lies at the root of identity, which provides the basis for "knowing" who you are. In this sense high white cheque words are no more or less fundamental to "Negro expression" than are the bartered goods of the store porch picture talkers. Nature's voices are no less native to whiteness or blackness than are voices that are made out of caution. In a modern climate of cultural ascendance, it is the very rootlessness of Hurston's telling of Janie that finally turns *Their Eyes* into a novel about black cultural identity, an identity that hinges on a refusal to assign either nature or caution to different narrative strands or techniques.

❖ In her seeming refusal to honor race as a potent category of identity, Hurston was chastised by her peers as a writer who failed to sound the political depths of the African American novel. Increasingly, however, she has come to be viewed as a more or less adequate champion of culture by critics who have dispensed with race, substituting for its outworn genealogical premises newer, epistemologically based ones. For most of Hurston's postmodern readers, "authenticity" is not conferred by virtue of ancestry but by a variant of the Du Boisian "gift" of "second sight," or the capacity to see that identities are, as Stephen Dedalus was made to say in *Ulysses*, "made not begotten." In her use of modernist strategies such as those that worry the divide between narrative voices and character's voices, however, Hurston did not posit culture as an epistemological alternative to more explicitly deterministic conceptions of race. In the content of novels such as *Their Eyes Were Watching God*, culture is only a tactical category, one that is valuable only insofar as it can be used to mount a situational challenge to racial determinism. Janie's "mingled-people" resistance to Mrs. Turner's call for her to "class off" against dark-skinned African Americans is such an instance of Boasian intervention. But in Hurston's novel, Boas's conception of culture is also released as a damaging construction. It is unraveled in the modern folktales spun by the Eatonville porch-sitters, a constituency that, according to contemporary critical criteria, should stand to "benefit" from the notion that it is not nature, but rather caution, that keeps the baby from the stove.

In their offhand dismissal of both "caution" and "nature," Hurston's folk characters unconsciously testify to a late survival of a modern antifoundationalist aesthetic, one that faltered as critiques of "first principles" passed from anarchist to pragmatist hands, which mainstreamed and codified them according to the new dictates of "culture." In her resistance to the development of a modern American pluralist ideology that used "the 'Negro' " to mark "the limits of Americanization" (*OA*, 145 n. 22), Hurston refused to rest on an attractive category that was functioning not to dismantle Jim Crow but rather to unify a white race in opposition to a black one. By fashioning a novel in which culture was located neither positively nor negatively in voices themselves, but in the unpredictable play of the narrative through the registers of the many voices that were available to her, Hurston created culture as a phenomenon that is inseparable from its making. The culture that Hurston achieves comes to encompass the culture that she has received both from sympathetic modern colleagues and from the poststructuralist critics who equally seek to contain her as a voice from the far side of the veil. In practicing such an aesthetic, this much-sought-after black woman writer eludes not only her modernist peers but also those contemporary critics who have sought to press her into the service of a range of "minoritarian" premises and practices. In the context of British- and American-based literary movements, *Their Eyes Were Watching God* partakes of a larger antifoundationalist tradition that cultivates the modernist recognition of the constructedness of the "natural" and extends it beyond even those critical methodologies that champion "constructedness" as an end rather than as a means of expression. It was finally the backward-looking cast of "culture," a measure geared to unify "the races of Europe," that prompted an African American writer to identify and challenge one of the more powerful foundations that antifoundationalism had produced.

Afterword

Ezra Pound wrote, "The natural object is always the *adequate* symbol"; Marianne Moore wrote, "All these phenomena are important"; William Carlos Williams wrote, "No ideas but in things." In their credos these three writers joined together in calling for a poetry of presence. Modernist aesthetics of direct presentation brought first "the natural object," the phenomenal thing itself, into the poem; and by the early 1920s, collage methods of composition brought artifactual bits of history and material from other disciplines and discourses into poetry and prose works formed around fragmented documentary materials. There was an ostensible organic relationship between the mimetic body of the imagist or the documentary poem or prose piece and the gritty phenomenal or extraliterary material from which it was made. In modern fiction, as well, techniques of "free indirect discourse" collapsed the distinction between "interior" and "exterior" perspectives in the novel. In bringing the authorial narrator right into the story, the writers who used these techniques seemed to be drawing the story itself out of the material of actual experience. As Joyce expressed it, half-ironically, half-prophetically, through Stephen Dedalus in *A Portrait of the Artist as a Young Man,* the modern experimental novelist would become not a nominal entity, but rather "a vital sea" that "flow[ed]" through his or her medium. And in *Their Eyes Were Watching God,* Hurston reiterated and modulated this sentiment by suggesting, of the fluid narrative procedures that gave depth to her heroine, Janie Crawford, "You got tuh *go* there tuh *know* there."

❖   These new readings of Pound, Joyce, Williams, Moore, and Hurston suggest that the modernist desire to *embody* experience through language, rather than to represent it, was something more than a matter of aesthetics. Modernist appeals to immediate forms of expression stemmed from local social and intellectual sources including anarchist writings on the nature of monetary currency and anarcho-feminist theories of disease and identity; and they were shaped by the historical incorporation of nineteenth-century anarchist premises into an American brand of philosophy that provided a conceptual cradle for "cultural pluralism." Anarchism, pragmatism, and modern conceptions of "culture" provide us with a new account of the origins of modern formal innovations. In the process these sources also shed new light on some of the recent critical assumptions and methods through which modernism is now being reappraised. But there is yet another consequence of a recovery of anarchist and pragmatist sources for modernism's resistance to "beginnings, origins, and principles." Even within the very circumscribed literary spheres to which they must inevitably be applied, these sources call us to rethink the canonical divides that separate "high modernists" like Pound and Joyce from equally mislabeled "Harlem Renaissance" writers, including Zora Neale Hurston.

The writers gathered into this study partake of various cultural traditions; and it can be as unsatisfying to freely assemble these traditions as it is to reflexively segregate them. After World War II the Irish "high modernist" Joyce became the darling of English and American critics. These "New Critics" were largely indifferent to textual political contingencies; and for this reason Joyce was perhaps too often and too freely grouped with other English and European American literary innovators. Because of Joyce's early canonization by the New Criticism, his involvement with continental European, and even with London-based anarchist, writings does not dramatically alter our understanding of his place as a modern writer. Hurston's inclusion in this study is another matter. As the object of poststructuralist critics whose laudable political objectives have sometimes clouded their attention to textual and even social historical particulars, the African American folklorist and novelist has been largely set apart from European American intellectual traditions. Hurston's exposure, through Franz Boas, and particularly through Alain Locke, to anarchistically derived currents of American pragmatist thought asks us to reconsider whether current forms of identity politics, however politically efficacious they might be, can serve as adequate guiding measures for literary and cultural history.

As I argue for Hurston's centrality to the study of more traditionally canonical modern writers, I do so with an awareness of the dangers of appropriating cultural differences. That Joyce and Hurston were both ambivalent about their own racial and cultural identities does not negate their particular historical positions as Irish or African American writers. Academic literary study at the turn of the twenty-first century is eclectic and therefore difficult to characterize. But as a body, today's critics are by and large more acutely aware of social and political differences than were their more "universalizing" counterparts of the 1950s, 1960s, and 1970s. Among contemporary literary and cultural critics—critics from England, Ireland, and America alike—there should be few who fail to recognize that Joyce's social historical position as a "modernist" differed from the positions of his English literary counterparts. Similarly, most should know, and know well, that Hurston stood at a social historical remove from many of her European American "modernist" contemporaries. Although Joyce and Hurston may have each used the same words as their English or European American peers, they often used these words in ways that reflected a heightened awareness of the social constructedness of language itself. To ignore these differences in deference to these writers' resistance to categorization would be to ignore a good deal of the best critical work of the last twenty-five years. And it would be to fail to read fully two of the most rewarding novelists of the modern period.

Although I think it is important that we recognize Pound, Williams, and Moore as European American writers and Joyce and Hurston as Irish and as African American writers, respectively, I also believe that we should take seriously Joyce's, and particularly Hurston's, ambivalence toward the categories of "race," "nation," and "culture." Due to her own stated "caution" regarding claims to racial and cultural identities, Hurston has proved particularly vexing to critics who seek to view early-twentieth-century literature as a theater for contemporary conceptions of identity. It is this ambivalence, however, that makes her so central to a study of modernism's refusal of "beginnings, origins, and principles." Hurston's questioning of the modern substance of "race" is hardly newsworthy. Her critique of the newfound category of "culture," by contrast, distinguishes her as a modern writer with something pressing to say. For Hurston this critique emerged from a historical dialogue with the very European American currents and traditions from which she has been canonically barred. Her example compels contemporary critics to reconsider the ways in which our most cherished measures of identity can and cannot be made to measure literary and cultural history.

In evaluating large-scale literary and cultural moments like the one treated in this study, critics must certainly account for the national, racial, and "cultural" differences that distinguish those who labor at that moment's conceptual forefront. In order to prevent an endless recycling of theoretical axioms and the misapplication of ahistorical assumptions regarding "pluralism" and "diversity," however, critics must also turn to history in order to become more cognizant of the measure of the very "difference" that they employ. As readers we carry with us into the twenty-first century many modernist premises and axioms, including deeply consequential distinctions between race and culture, between "the one" and "the many," and between static and processual forms of identity. As our knowledge of the anarchist and pragmatist origins of modern literature sheds new light on the very terms that we use to measure difference in the twentieth-first century, our study of modernism becomes also a study of our own postmodern moments. In this way modernism speaks back to us not only as the subject of literary and cultural study; it speaks as well through the very terms and methods that we use to measure its matter.

ABBREVIATIONS

1250/1   Marianne Moore. Reading Diary 1907–15, notebook 1250/1 (VII 01 01),
Rosenbach Archive, Rosenbach Library and Museum,
Philadelphia.

1250/2   Marianne Moore. Reading Diary 1916–21, notebook 1250/2 (VII 01 02),
Rosenbach Archive.

1250/3   Marianne Moore. Reading Diary 1921–22, notebook 1250/3 (VII 01 03),
Rosenbach Archive.

AAN   Melville Herskovits. *The Anthropometry of the American Negro*. New
York: Columbia University Press, 1930.

AB   Mike Weaver. *William Carlos Williams: The American Background*.
Cambridge: Cambridge University Press, 1971.

ABCR   Ezra Pound. *The ABC of Reading*. 1934. Reprint, New York: New
Directions, 1960.

AEP   Cornel West. *The American Evasion of Philosophy: A Genealogy of
Pragmatism*. Madison: University of Wisconsin Press, 1989.

"AF"   Dora Marsden. "The Art of the Future." *New Freewoman* 1, no. 10
(1 November 1913): 181–83.

AGM   Friedrich Nietzsche. *A Genealogy of Morals*. Trans. William A.
Haussmann. In *The Works of Friedrich Nietzsche*, vol. 10. New
York: Macmillan, 1897.

"AL"   John Dewey. "Americanism and Localism." *The Dial* 68, no. 6 (June
1920): 684–88.

"AM"   Walter Benn Michaels. "American Modernism and the Poetics of
Identity." *Modernism/Modernity* 1, no. 1 (1994): 38–56.

AML   Franz Boas. *Anthropology and Modern Life*. 1928. Reprint, New York:
Dover, 1986.

"AP"   Ezra Pound. "The Approach to Paris . . . V." *New Age* 13, no. 23 (2 October 1913): 662.

AR   Paul de Man. *Allegories of Reading: Figural Language in Rousseau, Nietzsche, Rilke, and Proust.* New Haven, Conn.: Yale University Press, 1979.

ASL   Anti-Saloon League of America. *Proceedings of the Special Conference Called by the Board of Directors of the Anti-Saloon League of America for the Purpose of Launching a Movement for World-Wide Prohibition.* Westerville, Ohio: American Issue Publishing Co., 1918.

AWCW   William Carlos Williams. *The Autobiography of William Carlos Williams.* 1948. Reprint, New York: New Directions, 1951.

"BA"   Dorothy Hale. "Bakhtin in African American Literary Theory." *ELH* 61, no. 2 (1994): 445–71.

BBS   Les Garner. *A Brave and Beautiful Spirit: Dora Marsden: 1882–1960.* Avebury, Eng.: Aldershot, 1990.

BD   Kathleen Ferris. *James Joyce and the Burden of Disease.* Lexington: University Press of Kentucky, 1995.

BF   Zeev Sternhell, with Mario Sznajder and Maia Asheri. *The Birth of Fascist Ideology: From Cultural Rebellion to Political Revolution.* 1989. Trans. David Maisel. Princeton, N.J.: Princeton University Press, 1994.

BI   Paul de Man. *Blindness and Insight: Essays in the Rhetoric of Contemporary Criticism.* Rev. ed. Minneapolis: University of Minnesota Press, 1983.

"BM"   Bessie Drysdale. "Der Bund für Mutterschutz: A German League for the Protection of Mothers." *Freewoman* 1, no. 1 (23 November 1911): 6–7.

BSP   Henry Meulen. *Banking and the Social Problem.* London: Henry Meulen, 1909.

C   Ezra Pound. *The Cantos of Ezra Pound.* 1971. Reprint, New York: New Directions, 1991.

"CA"   Deborah J. Coon. "Courtship with Anarchy: The Socio-political Foundations of William James's Pragmatism." Ph.D. diss., Harvard University, 1988.

CC   Ross Posnock. *Color & Culture: Black Writers and the Making of the Modern Intellectual.* Cambridge, Mass.: Harvard University Press, 1998.

CD   Horace Kallen. *Culture and Democracy in the United States: Studies in the Group Psychology of the American Peoples.* New York: Boni and Liveright, 1924.

CJI   Neil Davison. *James Joyce,* Ulysses, *and the Construction of Jewish Identity.* Cambridge: Cambridge University Press, 1996.

"CJJ"   Georges Borach. "Conversations with James Joyce." Trans. Joseph
         Prescott. *College English* 15 (March 1954): 325–27.

CJJ   Arthur Power. *Conversations with James Joyce.* Dublin: Cahill, 1974.

CP   Richard Rorty. *Consequences of Pragmatism.* Minneapolis: University
         of Minnesota Press, 1982.

CP1   William Carlos Williams. *The Collected Poems of William Carlos
         Williams.* Vol. 1, *1909–1939.* Ed. A. Walton Litz and Christopher
         MacGowan. New York: New Directions, 1986.

CPMM   Patricia Willis, ed. *The Complete Prose of Marianne Moore.* New York:
         Penguin, 1986.

"CPP"   Werner Sollors. "Critique of Pure Pluralism." In *Reconstructing
         American Literary History,* ed. Sacvan Bercovitch, 250–79.
         Cambridge, Mass.: Harvard University Press, 1986.

"CSP"   John Dewey. "Some Connexions of Science and Philosophy." In *John
         Dewey: The Later Works, 1925–1953,* ed. Jo Ann Boydston, 17:402–
         14. Carbondale: Southern Illinois University Press, 1990.

CSW   Bram Dijkstra. *Cubism, Stieglitz, and the Early Poetry of William
         Carlos Williams.* Princeton, N.J.: Princeton University Press, 1969.

"CW"   Dora Marsden. "The Chastity of Women." *Egoist* 1, no. 3 (2 February
         1914): 44–46.

CW   James Joyce. *The Critical Writings of James Joyce.* Ed. Ellsworth
         Mason and Richard Ellmann. 1959. Reprint, Ithaca, N.Y.: Cornell
         University Press, 1989.

CWC   Ernest Fenollosa. *The Chinese Written Character as a Medium for
         Poetry.* San Francisco: City Lights Books, n.d.

DC   Loren Eiseley. *Darwin's Century: Evolution and the Men Who
         Discovered It.* 1958. Reprint, New York: Doubleday & Co., 1961.

"DIP"   John Dewey. "Darwin's Influence upon Philosophy." *The Popular
         Science Monthly,* July 1909, 90–98.

DM   Bruce Clarke. *Dora Marsden and Early Modernism: Gender, Individ-
         ualism, Science.* Ann Arbor: University of Michigan Press, 1996.

"DPA"   John Dewey. "Le développement du pragmatisme américain." *Revue
         de Métaphysique et de Morale* 29, no. 4 (October–December 1922):
         411–30.

DR   Sander L. Gilman. *Disease and Representation: Images of Illness from
         Madness to AIDS.* Ithaca, N.Y.: Cornell University Press, 1988.

DSJ   Stanislaus Joyce. *The Complete Dublin Diary of Stanislaus Joyce.* Ed.
         George Harris Healey. Ithaca, N.Y.: Cornell University Press, 1971.

DT   Zora Neale Hurston. *Dust Tracks on a Road.* 1942. In *Zora Neale
         Hurston: Folklore, Memoirs, and Other Writings,* ed. Cheryl A.
         Wall, 557–808. New York: Library of America, 1995.

DV   Shamoon Zamir. *Dark Voices: W. E. B. Du Bois and American
         Thought, 1888–1903.* Chicago: University of Chicago Press, 1995.

E   James Huneker. *Egoists: A Book of Supermen*. 1909. Reprint, New York: Charles Scribner's Sons, 1913.

EE   Andrew Sinclair. *Era of Excess: A Social History of the Prohibition Movement*. 1962. Reprint, New York: Harper & Row, 1964.

"EI"   Carl Watner. "The English Individualists as They Appear in *Liberty*." *Journal of Libertarian Studies* 6, no. 1 (1982): 59–82.

EK   William Carlos Williams. *The Embodiment of Knowledge*. New York: New Directions, 1974.

ELT   Ronald W. Clark. *Einstein: The Life and Times*. New York: Avon Books, 1971.

EO   Max Stirner. *The Ego and His Own*. Trans. Steven Byington. New York: Benjamin R. Tucker, 1907.

EP   Herbert N. Schneidau. *Ezra Pound: The Image and the Real*. Baton Rouge: Louisiana State University Press, 1969.

"EPBR"   Leon Surette. "Ezra Pound and British Radicalism." *English Studies in Canada* 9, no. 4 (1983): 435–51.

EPIF   Tim Redman. *Ezra Pound and Italian Fascism*. Cambridge: Cambridge University Press, 1991.

ET   Charles S. Johnson, ed. *Ebony and Topaz: A Collection*. 1927. Reprint, Freeport, N.Y.: Books for Libraries Press, 1971.

EWG   Zora Neale Hurston. *Their Eyes Were Watching God*. 1937. In *Zora Neale Hurston: Novels and Stories*, ed. Cheryl A. Wall, 173–333. New York: Library of America, 1995.

FD   Sandra Stanley Holton. *Feminism and Democracy: Women's Suffrage and Reform Politics in Britain, 1900–1918*. Cambridge: Cambridge University Press, 1986.

FL   Roman Jakobson and Morris Halle. *Fundamentals of Language*. 1956. 4th ed. The Hague, Netherlands: Mouton Publishers, 1980.

GB   Ezra Pound. *Gaudier-Brzeska: A Memoir*. 1916. New York: New Directions, 1970.

GD   Robert Casillo. *The Genealogy of Demons: Anti-Semitism, Fascism, and the Myths of Ezra Pound*. Evanston, Ill.: Northwestern University Press, 1988.

"GF"   Arthur Kitson. "The Gold Fetish." *New Age* 11, no. 4 (23 May 1912): 94.

GI   Pierre-Joseph Proudhon. *General Idea of the Revolution in the Nineteenth Century*. 1851. Trans. John Beverley Robinson. 1923. Reprint, New York: Gordon Press, 1972.

GK   Ezra Pound. *Guide to Kulchur*. 1938. Reprint, London: Peter Owen, 1952.

"GM"   Gertrude Stein. "The Gradual Making of the Making of Americans." In *Selected Writings of Gertrude Stein*, ed. Carl Van Vechten, 241–58. 1946. New York: Random House, 1990.

GM   Michael Levenson. *A Genealogy of Modernism: A Study of English Literary Doctrine 1908–1922*. Cambridge: Cambridge University Press, 1984.

GS   Christabel Pankhurst. *The Great Scourge and How to End It*. London: E. Pankhurst, 1913.

GT   Judith Butler. *Gender Trouble: Feminism and the Subversion of Identity*. New York: Routledge, 1990.

GTG   Peter Dreyer. *A Gardener Touched with Genius: The Life of Luther Burbank*. Berkeley: University of California Press, 1985.

HA   Mark H. Haller. *Eugenics: Hereditarian Attitudes in American Thought*. New Brunswick, N.J.: Rutgers University Press, 1984.

HH   Sheila Rowbotham. *Hidden from History: 300 Years of Women's Oppression and the Fight against It*. 3d ed. 1977. Reprint, London: Pluto Press, 1992.

HK   Sarah Schmidt. *Horace M. Kallen: Prophet of American Zionism*. New York: Carlson Publishing, Inc., 1995.

HR   George Hutchinson. *The Harlem Renaissance in Black and White*. Cambridge, Mass.: Harvard University Press, 1995.

HR   Paul Weindling. *Health, Race, and German Politics between National Unification and Nazism, 1870–1945*. Cambridge: Cambridge University Press, 1989.

HS   Morrison I. Swift. *Human Submission*. Pt. 2. Philadelphia: Liberty Press, 1905.

HWV   Christabel Pankhurst. *Unshackled: The Story of How We Won the Vote*. 1959. 2d ed. London: Cresset Women's Voices, 1987.

"I"   J. L. Walker. Introduction to *The Ego and His Own*, by Max Stirner. Trans. Steven Byington. New York: Benjamin R. Tucker, 1907.

I   William Carlos Williams. *Imaginations*. New York: New Directions, 1970.

IAG   William Carlos Williams. *In the American Grain*. 1925. Reprint, New York: New Directions, 1956.

IB   Benjamin Tucker. *Instead of a Book, by a Man Too Busy to Write One*. New York: Benjamin R. Tucker, Publisher, 1893. Reprint, New York: Arno Press and the New York Times, 1972. Page references correspond to the reprint edition.

IC   George Santayana. *The Idea of Christ in the Gospels*. New York: Charles Scribner's Sons, 1946 (author's collection).

"IMW"   Helene Stöcker and Dora Marsden. "Interpellation to Men and Women of All Civilized Countries." Dora Marsden Collection, box 4, folder 8, Princeton University Libraries.

IO   Albert Einstein. *Ideas and Opinions*. Trans. Sonja Bargmann. 1954. Reprint, New York: Crown Publishers, 1982.

ION	John Dewey. *Individualism, Old and New*. 1930. In *The Later Works of John Dewey, 1925–1953*, ed. Jo Ann Boydston, 5:41–123. Carbondale: Southern Illinois University Press, 1990.
"IPM"	Frank Lentricchia. "On the Ideologies of Poetic Modernism, 1890–1913: The Example of William James." In *Reconstructing American Literary History*, ed. Sacvan Bercovitch, 220–49. Cambridge, Mass.: Harvard University Press, 1986.
JD	Robert Westbrook. *John Dewey and American Democracy*. Ithaca, N.Y.: Cornell University Press, 1991.
"JE"	Jean-Michel Rabaté. "Joyce the Egoist." *Modernism/Modernity* 4.3 (September 1997): 45–65.
JJ	Richard Ellmann. *James Joyce*. 1959. Reprint, New York: Oxford University Press, 1965.
JJU	Vincent Sherry. *James Joyce, Ulysses*. Cambridge: Cambridge University Press, 1994.
JM	Ezra Pound. *Jefferson and/or Mussolini*. 1935. Reprint, New York: Liveright Publishing Corp., 1936.
JRE	Vincent Cheng. *Joyce, Race, and Empire*. Cambridge: Cambridge University Press, 1995.
KMA	Paul Thomas. *Karl Marx and the Anarchists*. London: Routledge and Kegan Paul, 1980.
LE	Ezra Pound. *Literary Essays of Ezra Pound*. Ed. T. S. Eliot. New York: New Directions, 1968.
LGS	Daniel Cory, ed. *The Letters of George Santayana*. New York: Charles Scribner's Sons, 1955.
"LI"	Robert von Hallberg. "Libertarian Imagism." *Modernism/Modernity* 2, no. 2 (1995): 63–79.
LJJ2	James Joyce. *Letters of James Joyce*. Vol. 2. Ed. Richard Ellmann. New York: Viking, 1966.
LL	Charles Molesworth. *Marianne Moore: A Literary Life*. New York: Atheneum, 1990.
LO	Brian Lloyd. *Left Out: Pragmatism, Exceptionalism, and the Poverty of American Marxism 1890–1922*. Baltimore: Johns Hopkins University Press, 1997.
LTSE	T. S. Eliot. *The Letters of T. S. Eliot*. Vol. 1, *1898–1922*. Ed. Valerie Eliot. New York: Harcourt Brace Jovanovich, 1988.
LWJ	Henry James III, ed. *The Letters of William James*. Boston: Atlantic Monthly Press, 1920.
M	Peter Nicholls. *Modernisms: A Literary Guide*. Berkeley: University of California Press, 1995.
MA	Ezra Pound. *Machine Art and Other Writings: The Lost Thought of the Italian Years*. Ed. Maria Luisa Ardizzone. Durham, N.C.: Duke University Press, 1996.

MA Lisa Steinman. *Made in America: Science, Technology, and American Modernist Poets.* New Haven, Conn.: Yale University Press, 1987.

"MCI" Arthur Kitson. "Correspondence: Money, Capital, and Interest." *Freewoman* 2, no. 39 (15 August 1912): 256.

"MD" Franz Boas. "The Measurement of Differences between Variable Quantities." *Quarterly Publications of the American Statistical Association* (December 1922): 425–45. Reprinted in Boas, *RLC*, 181–95.

MHR Houston A. Baker, Jr. *Modernism and the Harlem Renaissance.* Chicago: University of Chicago Press, 1987.

ML William James. *Manuscript Lectures.* Cambridge, Mass.: Harvard University Press, 1988.

"MM" William Carlos Williams. "Marianne Moore." *The Dial* 78, no. 5 (May 1925): 393–401. Reprinted in *Marianne Moore: A Collection of Critical Essays,* ed. Charles Tomlinson, 52–59. Englewood Cliffs, N.J.: Prentice-Hall, 1969.

MM Marianne Moore. *The Complete Poems of Marianne Moore.* 1956. New York: Penguin Books, 1986.

MP John Ruskin. *Munera Pulveris.* New York: Charles E. Merrill, 1891.

MPI American Academy of Medicine. *Medical Problems of Immigration.* Easton, Pa.: American Academy of Medicine Press, 1913.

MPM Franz Boas. *The Mind of Primitive Man.* 1911. Reprint, New York: Macmillan, 1931.

MQ Frank Lentricchia. *Modernist Quartet.* Cambridge: Cambridge University Press, 1994.

"MU" Rebecca West. "On Mentioning the Unmentionable: An Exhortation to Miss Pankhurst." *Clarion* 1138 (26 September 1913): 5.

MU Frank Budgen. *James Joyce and the Making of 'Ulysses' and Other Writings.* 1934. Reprint, Oxford: Oxford University Press, 1989.

"NE" Zora Neale Hurston. "Characteristics of Negro Expression." In *Negro: An Anthology* (1934), ed. Nancy Cunard, 24–31. Abridged by Hugh Ford, 1970. Reprint, New York: Continuum, 1996.

"NML" Michel Harr. "Nietzsche and Metaphysical Language." In *The New Nietzsche: Contemporary Styles of Interpretation,* ed. David Allison, 5–36. New York: Delta, 1977.

"NS" Ezra Pound. "The New Sculpture." *Egoist* 1, no. 4 (16 February 1914): 68.

NS George Mosse. *Nationalism and Sexuality: Middle-Class Morality and Sexual Norms in Modern Europe.* Madison: University of Wisconsin Press, 1985.

NWN Paul Mariani. *William Carlos Williams: A New World Naked.* New York: McGraw Hill, 1981.

O Marianne Moore. *Observations.* New York: Dial Press, 1924.

OA   Walter Benn Michaels. *Our America: Nativism, Modernism, and Pluralism*. Durham, N.C.: Duke University Press, 1995.

P   William Carlos Williams. *Paterson*. Rev. ed. prepared by Christopher MacGowan. New York: New Directions, 1992.

P   William James. *Pragmatism*. 1907. In *William James: Writings 1902– 1910*, ed. Bruce Kuklick, 480–624. New York: Library of America, 1987.

"PA"   James Joyce. "A Portrait of the Artist." In *A Portrait of the Artist as a Young Man: A Facsimile of Epiphanies, Notes, Manuscripts, & Typescripts*, ed. Hans Walter Gabler, 71–85. New York: Garland Publishing, Inc., 1978.

PA   James Joyce. *A Portrait of the Artist as a Young Man*. 1916. Reprint, New York: B. W. Huebsch, 1917.

PAFM   James Joyce. *A Portrait of the Artist as a Young Man: A Facsimile of the Final Holograph Manuscript, Chapters III, IV, & V*. Ed. Hans Walter Gabler. New York: Garland Publishing, Inc. 1977.

PAN   John Higham. *Strangers in the Land: Patterns of American Nativism 1860–1925*. New Brunswick, N.J.: Rutgers University Press, 1955.

PC   John Dewey. *Philosophy and Civilization*. New York: Minton, Balch & Co., 1931.

PE   Hugh Kenner. *The Pound Era*. Berkeley: University of California Press, 1971.

PH   Howard Zinn. *A People's History of the United States*. New York: HarperCollins, 1980.

PHI   Sander L. Gilman. *Picturing Health and Illness: Images of Identity and Difference*. Baltimore: Johns Hopkins University Press, 1995.

PJ   Ezra Pound. *Pound/Joyce: The Letters of Ezra Pound to James Joyce, with Pound's Essays on Joyce*. Ed. Forrest Read. New York: New Directions, 1967.

PP   William James. *The Principles of Psychology*. Vol. 1. 1890. Reprint, New York: Dover Publications, 1950.

PPEA   Jean Wahl. *The Pluralist Philosophies of England & America*. 1920. Trans. Fred Rothwell. London: Open Court, 1925.

PU   William James. *A Pluralistic Universe*. 1909. In *William James: Writings 1902–1910*, ed. Bruce Kuklick, 625–819. New York: Library of America, 1987.

PVS   Judith R. Walkowitz. *Prostitution and Victorian Society: Woman, Class, and the State*. 1980. Reprint, Cambridge: Cambridge University Press, 1994.

PWP   Charles Peirce. *Philosophical Writings of Peirce*. Ed. Justus Buchler. New York: Dover Publications, 1955.

"PWT"   Richard Sieburth. "In Pound We Trust: The Economy of Poetry/The Poetry of Economics." *Critical Inquiry* 14 (autumn 1987): 142–72.

QH   James Fairhall. *James Joyce and the Question of History.* Cambridge: Cambridge University Press, 1993.

RCE   George Stocking. *Race, Culture, and Evolution: Essays in the History of Anthropology.* 1968. New York: Free Press, 1982.

RLC   Franz Boas. *Race, Language and Culture.* New York: Macmillan, 1940.

RM   Vincent Sherry. *Ezra Pound, Wyndham Lewis, and Radical Modernism.* Oxford: Oxford University Press, 1993.

RP   John Dewey. *Reconstruction in Philosophy.* 1920. Boston: Beacon Press, 1957.

RS   Frederick F. Ridley. *Revolutionary Syndicalism in France.* Cambridge: Cambridge University Press, 1970.

RT   Lothrop Stoddard. *The Rising Tide of Color against White World-Supremacy.* New York: Charles Scribner's Sons, 1920.

RW   Colin MacCabe. *James Joyce and the Revolution of the Word.* New York: Harper & Row Publishers, Inc., 1979.

"S"   Ezra Pound [Bastien von Helmholz, pseud.]. "Suffragettes." *Egoist* 1, no. 13 (1 July 1914): 254–56.

"SA"   Ezra Pound. "The Serious Artist." *New Freewoman* 1, no. 9 (15 October 1913): 161–63.

SBF   W. E. B. Du Bois. *The Souls of Black Folk.* 1903. In *W. E. B. Du Bois: Writings,* ed. Nathan Huggins, 357–547. New York: Library of America, 1986.

SC   Otto Weininger. *Sex and Character, Authorized Translation from the Sixth German Edition.* 1903. Reprint, London: William Heinemann, 1906.

SCEO   John Finlay. *Social Credit: The English Origins.* Montreal: McGill-Queen's University Press, 1972.

SE   William Carlos Williams. *Selected Essays.* New York: New Directions, 1954.

"SHP"   William F. Bynum. "The Great Imitator: Syphilis in Historical Perspective." In *Fatal Attractions: AIDS and Syphilis from Medical, Public and Personal Perspectives,* ed. Ken Arnold and Fiona James, 4–9. London: Wellcome Institute for the History of Medicine, 1995.

SP   Ezra Pound. *Selected Prose 1909–1965.* New York: New Directions, 1973.

"SR"   Ezra Pound. "Status Rerum." *Poetry* 1, no. 4 (1913): 125.

SR   Lynda Marion Hill. *Social Rituals and the Verbal Art of Zora Neale Hurston.* Washington D.C.: Howard University Press, 1996.

SS   Dorothy Ross. *The Origins of American Social Science.* Cambridge: Cambridge University Press, 1991.

SSWL   Les Garner. *Stepping Stones to Women's Liberty: Feminist Ideas in the Women's Suffrage Movement, 1900–1918.* Rutherford, N.J.: Fairleigh Dickinson University Press, 1984.

"ST"   Henry Louis Gates, Jr. "*Their Eyes Were Watching God:* The Speakerly Text." In *Zora Neale Hurston: Critical Perspectives Past and Present,* ed. Henry Louis Gates, Jr., and K. A. Appiah. New York: Amistad Press, 1993.

SW   Lisa Tickner. *The Spectacle of Women: Imagery of the Suffrage Campaign 1907–1914.* Chicago, University of Chicago Press, 1988.

TC   Ralph Barton Perry. *The Thought and Character of William James: Briefer Version.* 1948. Reprint, Nashville: Vanderbilt University Press, 1996.

TE   Hamilton Cravens. *The Triumph of Evolution: American Scientists and the Heredity-Environment Controversy 1900–1941.* Philadelphia: University of Pennsylvania Press, 1978.

THP   Luther Burbank. *The Training of the Human Plant.* New York: Century Co., 1907.

TS   John Benignus Lyons. *Thrust Syphilis down to Hell and other Rejoyceana.* Dublin: Glendale Press, 1988.

U   James Joyce. *Ulysses: The Corrected Text.* Ed. Hans Gabler, Wolfhard Steppe, and Claus Melchior. New York: Random House, 1986.

UA   Don Gifford and Robert Seidman. Ulysses *Annotated: Notes for Joyce's* Ulysses. Berkeley: University of California Press, 1988.

UC   Frederick J. Down Scott. *William James, Selected Unpublished Correspondence 1885–1910.* Columbus: Ohio State University Press, 1986.

UTL   John Ruskin. *Unto This Last and Other Writings by John Ruskin.* Ed. Clive Wilmer. London: Penguin, 1985.

VA   Linda Leavell. *Marianne Moore and the Visual Arts.* Baton Rouge: Louisiana State University Press, 1995.

VAP   Charles Darwin. *The Variation of Animals and Plants under Domestication.* 1868. 2d ed. New York: D. Appleton & Co., 1894.

"VC"   Dora Marsden. "Views and Comments." *New Freewoman* 1, no. 1 (15 June 1913): 3–5.

VR   John Hollander. *Vision and Resonance: Two Senses of Poetic Form.* 1975. 2d ed. New Haven, Conn.: Yale University Press, 1985.

VV   Patricia Willis. *Marianne Moore: Vision into Verse.* Philadelphia: Rosenbach Museum and Library, 1987.

W   William Carlos Williams. *The Wedge.* Cummington, Mass.: Cummington Press, 1944.

WB   William James. *The Will to Believe.* 1897. Reprint, New York: Longmans, Green & Co., 1931.

WD   Wilbur F. Crafts. *Why Dry? Briefs for Prohibition: Local, State, National and International.* Washington D.C.: International Reform Bureau, 1918.

WIN Margaret Ward. *In Their Own Voice: Women and Irish Nationalism.* Dublin: Attic Press, 1995.

"WPE" William James. "A World of Pure Experience." 1904. In *William James: Writings 1902–1910*, ed. Bruce Kuklick, 1159–82. New York: Library of America, 1987.

"WRD" Dora Marsden. "Why Revolt Drags." *Freewoman* 2, no. 35 (18 July 1912): 164–65.

WST Cliona Murphy. *The Women's Suffrage Movement and Irish Society in the Early Twentieth Century.* Hertfordshire: Harvester Wheatsheaf, 1989.

NOTES

Introduction

1. In his well-known description of a poem as a "machine made of words," Williams associated vernacular speech with useful materials like "Babbitt metal," which was used in the production of ball bearings. Here, as elsewhere, he expressed a greater concern for materials and processes than for representation itself. Williams, *W*, 8–9.

2. The idea of a pluralistic "mosaic of peoples" was first set forth by the pragmatist and Zionist Horace Kallen. See Kallen, *CD*, 58.

3. The traditional Marxist distinction between "dominant," "emergent," and "residual" ideologies owes much of its currency to Raymond Williams. See his *Marxism and Literature* (Oxford: Oxford University Press, 1977), 121–27.

4. Ibid., 55–71.

5. For a study of anarchism and British modernist circles, see Clarke, *DM*. Clarke extends earlier work by Levenson, *GM*. On Boston pragmatists and white American modernist poets, see Lentricchia, *MQ*; and Richard Poirier, *Poetry and Pragmatism* (Cambridge, Mass.: Harvard University Press, 1992). On pragmatism and African American intellectual and literary traditions, see Hutchinson, *HR*; Posnock, *CC*. Hutchinson's and Posnock's studies both respond to West's pioneering work in *AEP*.

6. See Gayatri Chakravorty Spivak, "Can the Subaltern Speak?" in *Marxism and the Interpretation of Culture*, ed. Cary Nelson and Lawrence Grossberg (Urbana: University of Illinois Press, 1988).

7. Walter Michaels is among those "new historicist" critics who have experimented with "improvisational" varieties of historical scholarship. In his much-discussed book *The Gold Standard and the Logic of Naturalism* (1987), for example, Michaels works from analogies between different synchronic dis-

courses—late-nineteenth-century literature, painting, money, philosophy—which acquire a unifying "logic" amid a weakening of the theoretical frameworks that poststructuralist critics might use to contain them.

8. I take this phrase from a definition of anarchism set forth by the American anarchist Benjamin Tucker in *IB*.

Chapter One. Mosaic Modernism

1. Dorothy Ross discusses the late-eighteenth-century origins of the American "exceptionalist" belief that because of its "republican government and economic opportunity," America "occupies an exceptional place in history." Ross, *SS*, xiv. On exceptionalist tendencies in American pragmatist thought, see Lloyd, *LO*, 297–99. See also Ross, *SS*, 162–71.

2. The pragmatists William James and John Dewey were liberals and not anarchists, but they were familiar with, and at times attracted to, certain aspects of anarchist thought. James, who harbored a deeper interest in anarchism than did Dewey, acknowledged that his own brand of philosophical "pluralism" had been based in part on "*Anarchy* in the good sense." Dewey's interest in anarchism is more complicated; his comment regarding democracy as an "anarchic" program whose "theory" was "to be tested by experience" should be considered alongside his criticism of anarchist movements. Despite his aversion to anarchist appeals to "immediacy," Dewey joined in an effort to convert communitarian anarchist premises into new varieties of democratic social theory. Dewey was among a handful of post–World War I pragmatist intellectuals who drew directly from James's "pluralism," and hence indirectly from the anarchist premises that had helped to sustain it, in fashioning "cultural pluralist" conceptions of American identity. For James's remarks on anarchism and his philosophical pluralism, see James, *ML*, 310–11. See also James, "WPE," 1180–81. For Dewey's remarks on an "anarchic" democracy, see his *German Philosophy and Politics* (1915), in *The Middle Works of John Dewey, 1899–1924*, ed. Jo Ann Boydston (Carbondale: Southern Illinois University Press, 1976–83), 8:166–67. See also Alan Ryan, *John Dewey and the High Tide of American Liberalism* (New York: W. W. Norton, 1995), 192.

3. Max Eastman, "The Anarchist Almanac," *Masses*, March 1914, reprinted in *Echoes of Revolt: THE MASSES 1911–1917*, ed. William L. O'Neill (Chicago: Quadrangle Books, 1966), 47.

4. Describing the progressive scientific makeup of many turn-of-the-century radicals, the syndicalist Walter Lippmann wrote, "Men desire first, then they reason; fascinated by the future, they invent a 'scientific socialism' to get there." Walter Lippmann, *A Preface to Politics* (New York: Mitchell Kennerley, 1913), 215; quoted in Lloyd, *LO*, 228.

5. Tucker eventually allied his sweeping critique of liberal and socialistic forms of government with Stirner's founding egoist text *The Ego and His Own*

(1844), but his brand of individualist anarchism was most profoundly shaped by the writings of Proudhon. In 1876, early in his career as a leading anarchist publisher and spokesperson, Tucker translated and published Proudhon's first and best known book, *Qu'est-ce que la propriété?* (1840). It was in *What Is Property?* that Proudhon first proclaimed himself both an "anarchist" and "a firm friend of [natural] order." Defining "*Anarchy*" as "the absence of a master, of a sovereign," he argued that it was only "our accustomed habit of taking man for our rule and his will for law, [that] leads us to regard [anarchy] as the height of disorder and the expression of chaos." Proudhon contended that in an era whose democratic and nascent socialistic platforms perpetuated the fundamental iniquity of monarchy, anarchism was the only forward-looking political position. "The most advanced among us are those who wish the greatest number of sovereigns," he claimed. "Their most ardent wish is for royalty of the National Guard. Soon, undoubtedly, some one jealous of the citizen militia will say, 'Everybody is king.' But when he has spoken, I will say in my turn, 'Nobody is king; we are, whether we will or no, associated.' " Pierre-Joseph Proudhon, *What Is Property?* trans. Benjamin R. Tucker (London: William Reeves, n.d.), 2:260, 264–65. Throughout the pages of *Liberty,* Tucker echoed Proudhon's suggestion that the ghost of the "sovereign" (whose "most material and most abstract form" was gold currency) lived on in even the most enlightened of late-nineteenth- and early-twentieth-century democratic and socialistic programs. Pierre-Joseph Proudhon, *The Solution of the Social Problem* (1848–49), in *Proudhon's Solution of the Social Problem,* ed. Henry Cohen (New York: Vanguard Press, 1927), 60.

6. In *Spring and All* (1923), William Carlos Williams parodied this militant modern spirit by calling for the immediate annihilation of the people of Europe, Russia, and America. "The imagination, intoxicated with prohibitions," Williams wrote, "rises to drunken heights to destroy the world." See Williams, *I,* 90–91. In 1914 Pound helped to organize a theatrically apocalyptic British avant-garde movement called "vorticism." Advertisements for the vorticist magazine BLAST trumpeted "THE END OF THE CHRISTIAN ERA."

7. Marsden's role as an editor of literary modernists is discussed in Jane Lidderdale and Mary Nicholson, *Dear Miss Weaver* (London: Faber and Faber, 1970); and in Bonnie Kime Scott, *Joyce and Feminism* (Bloomington: Indiana University Press, 1984). Mike Weaver is among the first literary critics to have offered a serious reading of Marsden's own essays. Weaver discusses Marsden's intellectual significance to William Carlos Williams in *AB.* More recent treatments of Marsden's intellectual significance to modernists including James Joyce and Ezra Pound can be found in Ronald Bush, "Excavating the Ideological Faultlines of Modernism: Editing Ezra Pound's *Cantos,*" in *Representing Modernist Texts,* ed. George Bornstein (Ann Arbor: University of Michigan Press, 1991), 67–98; in Clarke, *Dora Marsden and Early Modernism;* in Levenson, *GM;* in Rabaté, "JE"; in Sherry, *RM;* and in von Hallberg, "LI," 66–68.

8. Anarchist thought has been apportioned and traced along various lines.

As mentioned above, a number of turn-of-the-century anarchists distinguished theoretical or "philosophical" varieties of "individualist" anarchism from more "practical" forms that turned on galvanizing collective aims. (Among those who derided "philosophical" anarchists, "practicality" was often a measure of compatibility with progressive and efficacious socialist movements.) Insofar as anarchism may have contributed more as a vehicle for modern "antifoundationalist" thought than as a vehicle for actual social and political change, its most meaningful "ideological faultline" can be said to lie in the distinction between "ethical" and "individualist" branches of historical anarchism. These categories distinguish those anarchists who envisioned the call to action as a step toward a utopian end from those who viewed it more strictly as a means to an end that must in principle remain undefined. The French mutualist Proudhon, for example, was far less disposed toward socialism than was the popular turn-of-the-century anarchist Prince Kropotkin; but as Marsden recognized, Proudhon's appeals to the "ethics" of unimpeded transactions between producers and consumers reflected yearnings toward a utopian collectivity that distinguished Proudhon from his fellow "philosophical anarchist" Stirner. For useful discussions of factions among historical anarchists, see Paul Avrich, *Anarchist Portraits* (Princeton, N.J.: Princeton University Press, 1988); Caroline Cahm, *Kropotkin and the Rise of Revolutionary Anarchism 1872–1886* (Cambridge: Cambridge University Press, 1989); Coon, "CA"; Finlay, *SCEO;* Thomas, *KMA;* David Weir, *Anarchy and Culture: The Aesthetic Politics of Modernism* (Amherst: University of Massachusetts Press, 1997).

9. For discussions of Marx's critique of Stirner, see David Leopold, introduction to Max Stirner, *The Ego and Its Own* (Cambridge: Cambridge University Press, 1995), xi–xxxiii. See also Rabaté, "JE," 49–52; and Jean-Michel Rabaté, *The Ghosts of Modernity* (Gainesville: University Press of Florida, 1996), 223–27. See also Jacques Derrida, *Specters of Marx* (New York: Routledge, 1994), 121–22.

10. Dora Marsden's leaders in the *Freewoman,* the *New Freewoman,* and the *Egoist* bespeak the appeal of Stirner to those modern intellectuals who feared the absorption of radical initiatives by the liberal state. See also Paul Eltzbacher, *Anarchism,* trans. Steven T. Byington (New York: Benj. R. Tucker; London: A. C. Fifield, 1908). See also Walker, "I," xii–xviii.

11. Joyce's complaints about the strictures of literary realism extend to his provocative remarks regarding conventional forms of punctuation. As early as *Dubliners,* Joyce had resisted using quotation marks to designate passages of dialogue. He believed that these "perverted commas" enforced a customary distinction between knowing narrative voices and the more limited voices of characters "contained" within the narrative. *RW,* 14–15. Joyce's comments regarding the "unreality" of such a distinction can be found in a letter to his publisher, Grant Richards, quoted in Richard Ellmann's biography of the writer. See Ellmann, *JJ,* 364. See also Joyce's letter to Valery Larbaud, quoted in Mac-

Cabe, *RW*, 117. William Carlos Williams echoed Joyce's call for the banishment of quotation marks from works of fiction. In a manifesto published in 1940, on the back cover of *First Act*, a reissue of his first two novels, Williams discussed his own refusal to use quotation marks in his early fiction.

12. In *Ulysses* an incidental character inadvertently collapses this divide by misspelling the word "word" as "world." See Joyce, *U*, 63.

13. See Pound, *ABCR*, 52. See also Williams, *SE*, 283.

14. In his *General Idea of the Revolution in the Nineteenth Century*, Proudhon likened political government to a machine that would be overcome by the stronger entity of the "economic organism." For Proudhon this societal organism was powerful because, lacking political impediments to innately ethical transactions between people, it was based on the principle of "reciprocity." Proudhon called on his contemporaries "to dissolve, submerge, and cause to disappear the political or governmental system in the economic system, by reducing, simplifying, decentralizing and suppressing, one after another, all the wheels of this great machine, which is called the Government or the State." Proudhon, *GI*, 240, 171, 173. Tucker placed great stock in Proudhon's notion that the social organism was more powerful than any state. He viewed it as the crowning idea in "that most wonderful of the wonderful books of Proudhon." *IB*, 37.

15. "Underconsumptionist" economists like Kitson believed that shortages and crises could be averted by gearing currency and credit not toward the interests of producers and financiers but rather toward the consumptive needs of consumers. In England and America in the late nineteenth and early twentieth centuries, these "heretical" economists often traveled in anarchist circles. The name of the loosely knit movement is misleading. "Underconsumption" is the condition to be remedied by making currency and credit more available to those who need it.

Kitson quoted the visionary Proudhon—"I will not cease to pursue the truth through the ruins and rubbish"—in the epigraph to his first economic treatise, *A Scientific Solution of the Money Question* (1894). Nearly two decades later, in the pages of Marsden's *Freewoman*, Kitson counted Proudhon "one of the greatest minds in the economic world." By Kitson's reading, Proudhon had shown that "the fundamental cause of misery and industrial slavery was the legalized monopoly of money and credit." See Kitson, "MCI," 256.

16. See Pound, "SA," 161. See also Pound to Dora Marsden, n.d. (ca. September 1913), Dora Marsden Collection, box 1, folder 23, Princeton University Libraries. See also Clarke, *DM*, 110–11.

17. For Pound's discussion of Proudhon's influence on contemporary economic radicals, see Pound, *SP*, 440. Pound hinted at his own awareness of the importance of Kitson's and Marsden's early writings on economics in his essay "Obstructivity," *Apple (of Beauty and Discord)* 1, no. 3 (1920): 168. See chapter 2.

18. Marsden's critique of the gold standard in 1912 displays her early indebtedness to Proudhon. See Marsden, "WRD," 164–65. By the time she launched the *New Freewoman* in June 1913, however, Marsden had begun to recoil from the communitarian bent of Proudhon's thought and from its attendant appeals to ethics and morality. For example, in her *Freewoman* essay "Why Revolt Drags," Marsden had agreed with Proudhon that "property" was a pernicious political instrument ("WRD," 164); but in the *New Freewoman* she began to criticize the overly moralistic nature of Proudhon's injunction that "property is theft." For Marsden, theft was a more vital means of empowerment than was the moralistic banishment of property. Dora Marsden, "The Lean Kind," *New Freewoman* 1, no. 1 (15 June 1913): 1–2. Marsden issued her most stinging criticism of Proudhon, likening his idea of a "Social Contract" society to "a scheme for building a block of flats as high as St. Paul's with lily-stalks for materials," in dialogue with Proudhon's American advocate, Benjamin Tucker. See Dora Marsden, "Views and Comments," *New Freewoman* 1, no. 9 (15 October 1913), 165. See also Benjamin Tucker, "Lego et Penso," *New Freewoman* 1, no. 11 (15 November 1913): 217–18.

19. Benjamin Tucker embraced Proudhon's critique of "interest, rent, and profit" and placed it at the center of his own individualist anarchist doctrine. *IB*, 9.

20. Of Proudhon, Marsden wrote, "When he is looking at things as they exist, he is a strong searchlight; when he is trying to woo his readers to his solutions, he uses methods of cajolery which are positively repellent." Stirner, by contrast, possessed a colder and more penetrating eye, one that allowed him "to completely [see] through and [portray] the whole sham" of "representative government." Dora Marsden, "Views and Comments," *New Freewoman* 1, no. 11 (15 November 1913): 205.

21. "Anarchism," as Tucker explained it, was "*the doctrine that all affairs of men should be managed by individuals or voluntary associations, and that the State should be abolished.*" *IB*, 9. Through this little hinge word "*or*," Tucker proposed a grand confluence of two fundamentally contradictory anarchist traditions.

22. See Pound, *SP*, 440. On Pound's self-styling as a "'left-wing fascist,'" see Redman, *EPIF*, 236. For a larger account of the role of anarchism in the development of fascism in Italy, see Sternhell, *BF*.

23. See Ralph Waldo Emerson, *The Complete Works of Ralph Waldo Emerson*, ed. Edward Waldo Emerson (Boston: Houghton Mifflin, 1903–4): 8:65. This remark is quoted and discussed in John Irwin, *American Hieroglyphics: The Symbol of Egyptian Hieroglyphics in the American Renaissance* (New Haven, Conn.: Yale University Press, 1980), 10–14.

24. On Emerson's importance to Pound, see Lentricchia, *MQ*, 29–30. For a discussion of the largely unacknowledged indebtedness to Emerson of a wide range of modern poets, see Richard Poirier, *Poetry and Pragmatism*.

25. Drawing from a shared reservoir of modern anarchist and related pragmatist sources, Zora Neale Hurston would similarly suggest that the static "cheque word" language favored by Americans of European descent was bound to a lack of sexual vitality. "NE," 24–25, 29.

26. See Weaver, *AB*, 111–12; see also Williams, *AWCW*, 340.

27. In 1947 Williams began to weave excerpts from Social Credit pamphlets into his long collage poem. See Williams, *P*, 73, 273.

28. Pitched against the widespread scientific racism that divided "the races of Europe," Williams's brand of nativism was certainly more "forward looking" than brands based on claims of "Nordic supremacy." At the same time, however, Williams's challenge to Anglo-Saxon racialist premises appears to have rested on the assumption that blackness was a true measure of American difference. In this sense the work of the liberal white poet suggests that W. E. B. Du Bois may have been right when he claimed that "the color-line" was "the problem of the Twentieth Century." See Du Bois, *SBF*, 359.

29. Scholars have long depicted James as an essentially apolitical philosopher. In recent years, however, a few have begun to examine the anarchist sympathies that James displayed during his period of involvement with turn-of-the-century anti-imperialist causes. See George Cotkin, *William James, Public Philosopher* (Baltimore: Johns Hopkins University Press, 1990); see also Gerald E. Meyers, *William James: His Life and Thought* (New Haven, Conn.: Yale University Press, 1986); see also Posnock, *CC*. More often, those who "politicize" James have labored to portray him as a social democrat or as a latent socialist. See Lentricchia, "IPM," 220–49; see also James Kloppenberg, *Uncertain Victory: Social Democracy and Progressivism in European and American Thought 1870–1920* (New York: Oxford University Press, 1986); see also James Livingston, *Pragmatism and the Political Economy of Cultural Revolution, 1850–1940* (Chapel Hill: University of North Carolina Press, 1994). Recently, Deborah Coon has set forth evidence that suggests that James's deepest political sympathies lay with anarchism and that anarchist thought was central to his articulation of philosophical pragmatism. See Coon, "CA." See also her " 'One Moment in the World's Salvation': Anarchism and the Radicalization of William James," *Journal of American History* (June 1996): 70–99.

30. James's much-quoted description of "*reality*" as "*still in the making*" can be found in James, *P*, 599. Emerson's notion of a philosophy of "mobility and fluxions" reached James through a little-known late-nineteenth-century writer, Henry B. Brewster. An American who spent most of his childhood and adult life in Europe, Brewster was acquainted with a number of European and American expatriate artists, including the anarchistic dramatist Henrik Ibsen and the American expatriate novelist Henry James, the brother of William James. Henry presented his brother with a copy of Brewster's first book shortly after its publication in 1887, and William read it carefully and enthusiastically at some point

during the late 1890s or the early years of the new century. Among the many passages that James marked in *The Theories of Anarchy and Law* was one that identified "anarchists" as those "whose philosophical device is: 'All things flow.'" Brewster, *The Theories of Anarchy and Law: A Midnight Debate* (London: Williams & Norgate, 1887), 110. Anarchism, Brewster wrote, "attempt[ed] to meet the demand" set forth in Emerson's call for a "philosophy" of "mobility and fluxions" (112). In answer to Brewster's rhetorical question regarding the application of such a philosophy to "everyday questions," James wrote "Pragm" in the margin of his copy of Brewster's book (109). Here, he explicitly associated his emerging philosophy with anarchist thought. James's copy of this book is at the Houghton Library, Harvard University (AC85.J2376.Zz887b). For a thorough discussion of Brewster's book and its importance to James's pragmatist writings, see Coon, "CA," 271–313.

31. Despite his youthful involvement with revolutionary syndicalist politics, Dewey came to criticize anarchist thinkers for failing to account for history and for social mediation. Although he remained generally "sympathetic" to anarchism as a doctrine of "non-coercive" solutions to social problems, he could not abide its appeals to "the natural goodness of man uncorrupted by social arrangements." In 1920, for example, Dewey declared that although Proudhon's efforts to abolish "the state" were "suggestive," they were based on an overly "universal" appeal to innately ethical pathways of exchange. See Neil Coughlan, *Young John Dewey* (Chicago: University of Chicago Press, 1975), 87–112. See also Sidney Hook, *John Dewey: An Intellectual Portrait* (1939; reprint, New York: Prometheus Books, 1995), 163–64. See also Dewey, *RP*, 189. Dewey preferred democracy as a vehicle whose solutions were not natural or immanent but rather generated through ongoing social processes; he believed that a vibrant American democracy could be realized more through educational reform than through a restructuring of political institutions. Dewey's often vexing visions of modern democracy are set forth in Dewey, *ION*; and in *Liberalism and Social Action* (1935).

32. For James's praise of Swift, see James, *P*, 499–500. Swift critiqued philosophical "First Principles" in the opening paragraphs of the book that James discussed in *Pragmatism*. See Swift, *HS*, 3. Dewey may have played a small and inadvertent role in shaping Swift's indictment of contemporary philosophers. As one of the main contributors to J. M. Baldwin's two-volume *Dictionary of Philosophy and Psychology* (1902), Dewey defined "first principles" as a term "used technically to express primary intuitions, truths to which assent must be given without any further reason or ground." Insofar as Dewey had been a close colleague of Swift's at Johns Hopkins University, it seems likely that the philosopher-turned-anarchist had this well-publicized definition in mind when he wrote *Human Submission* in 1905. See John Dewey, "Contributions to *Dictionary of Philosophy and Psychology*," in Boydston, *Middle Works of Dewey*, 2:214.

33. Throughout his life, Swift vacillated between anarchistic and socialistic forms of radicalism. (Benjamin Tucker was among the anarchists who scolded the young labor agitator in *Liberty* for advocating an insufficiently antistatist brand of radicalism.) James's designation of Swift as an "anarchist" reflects as much the latter's theoretical assault on "First Principles" in *Human Submission* as it does the labor activism for which Swift was known. For discussions of Swift's career and his vexed radical affiliations, see Alexander Keyssar, *Out of Work: The First Century of Unemployment in Massachusetts* (Cambridge: Cambridge University Press, 1986), 210–49. See also William O. Reichert, "The Melancholy Political Thought of Morrison I. Swift," *New England Quarterly* 49 (December 1976): 542–58.

34. Swift's early involvement with pragmatists is chronicled in the ledger of this academic society. See the Ferdinand Hamburger, Jr., Archives of Johns Hopkins University, Record Group 15.040, Metaphysical Club. Although a handful of scholars have discussed the historical relationship between anarchism and pragmatism, Swift's relationships with Peirce, Dewey, and other Baltimore-based pragmatists have as yet gone unnoticed.

35. The Johns Hopkins Metaphysical Club took its name from the now famous Harvard circle formed during the preceding decade. As Charles Peirce recalled, the name adopted by the original Boston society "was half-ironic, half-defiant." "Agnosticism then was riding its high horse, and was frowning superbly upon all metaphysics." Peirce, *PWP*, 269.

36. By Peirce's account, it was this earlier group's discussions that prompted his coinage and formulation of "pragmatism" in a pair of *Popular Science Monthly* articles, "The Fixation of Belief" (1878) and "How to Make Our Ideas Clear" (1879). Peirce's prescription for "clearness of apprehension" hinged on his inelegant suggestion that "the whole of our conception of the object" should depend on our taking into account the "practical" "effects" that "we conceive the object of our conception to have." *PWP*, 31. Like James and Dewey, Peirce sought to make belief systems more dynamic by folding living consequences into the calcified antecedent foundations upon which belief systems rested. For Peirce, as for James (and for John Dewey, as well), the admission of "experience" into "knowledge" would collapse the static empiricist divide between the individual and the community. James and Peirce were not entirely in agreement as to what "pragmatism" was, however. When James and the German philosopher Ferdinand Schiller began to win notice for their own uses of the term "pragmatism" around the turn of the century, Peirce, who was by now embittered by the lack of recognition accorded to him, decided to change the name of *his* philosophy from "pragmatism" to "pragmaticism," a term that he hoped would prove "ugly enough to be safe from kidnappers." *PWP*, 254–55. As Deborah Coon has suggested, the primary difference between the "pragmatism" of the scientist Peirce and that of the individualist James can be found in their respective claims

regarding the etymology of the word. "CA," 22. Whereas James traced the term to its Greek roots, meaning "action," Peirce insisted that he had taken *his* term from Kant, and that its true etymology stemmed from the German word *pragmatisch,* which meant "empirical" or "experimental." James, *P,* 506; Peirce, *PWP,* 252–53. Other scholarly discussions of Peirce's and James's respective philosophies support Coon's etymological plotting of the divergent tempers of the founders of pragmatism. See, for example, Lentricchia, "IPM," 245; West, *AEP,* 42–68; and Rorty, *CP,* 161.

37. Highly publicized bombings and assassinations helped to fuel a popular aversion that had xenophobic underpinnings. Around the turn of the century, many Americans associated anarchism with a rapidly growing body of eastern European immigrants. Written fully a decade before his formative exposure to anarchist thought, William James's account of the Haymarket uprising reflects a stock bourgeois preoccupation with the "racial" composition of the rioters. To his brother Henry in 1886, James proclaimed that "the senseless 'anarchist' riot in Chicago," was "the work of a lot of pathological Germans and Poles." "All the Irish names are among the killed and wounded policemen," James noted, whereas "almost every anarchist name is Continental." James, *LWJ,* 1:252.

38. Dewey often expressed similar nominalist sentiments, but he was less resistant to "abstraction" than was James. See Lloyd, *LO,* 19, 292.

39. In *Human Submission,* the American anarchist Swift had echoed not only Stirner's nominalistic appeals to the authority of individual experience, but also Proudhon's critique of franchise, or "party politics." *HS,* 63–64. Around the time of James's reading of Swift, the philosopher began to refer to pragmatism as an explicitly anarchistic philosophy. Repeatedly in lectures delivered in 1905 (at Wellesley and the University of Chicago), James cited Swift's criticism of the "*smugness*" of established modes of philosophy, marshaling Swift's words and deeds to his own assault on the Absolute. See William James, Notebook 18, "Radical Empiricism and Pragmatism 1905," bMS 1092.9 (4512), James Papers, Houghton Library, Harvard University.

40. Writing in 1909 to James Gibbons Huneker, author of *Egoists: A Book of Supermen,* James declared that he was "impatient" to receive Huneker's essays on Nietzsche and Stirner. He also mentioned having "read a life of Stirner a few years ago, by some conscientious German." The biography to which James referred was written, in German, by the anarchist John Mackay. Prior to the 1907 publication of *The Ego and His Own,* Mackay had been a leading promulgator of Stirner's work in English and American anarchist journals including Tucker's *Liberty.* James's reading of Mackay coincided with the widespread introduction of Stirner to the English speaking world. Scott, *UC,* 507.

41. See James, *LWJ,* 2:100. James's bitter complaint against "*every* great institution" was prompted by his outrage at the French government for its stonewalling of the Dreyfus Affair. His accompanying appeal to neither the "individ-

ual" nor the collective, but rather "the free personal relation," marks a turning point in his political and philosophical thought, which roughly coincides with his own firsthand exposure to Proudhon. Proudhon's guiding "mutualist" premise was that corrupting political mechanisms, such as interest and rent, would give way to a truer "organic" society that was based on immediate economic exchanges. Once this happened, the will of the individual "citizen" would become immediate, or "equal," to the will of the decentralized society at large. Proudhon, *GI*, 268–69. Increasingly around the turn of the century, James came to speak of America as a nation weakened chiefly by its overdeveloped political mechanisms. James, *LWJ*, 2:100. At the same time, he began to conceive of "individualism" as bound to the greater cause of "free personal relation." That James's critique of political mechanisms coincided with his embrace of "free personal relation[s]" suggests that both his exceptionalist's vision of an organic American democracy and his conception of the dynamic, *relational* epistemological systems that should support it, were in some measure supported by Proudhon's vision of a society founded upon immediate economic relations between producers and consumers.

42. William James, *Some Problems of Philosophy*, in *William James: Writings 1902–1910*, ed. Bruce Kuklick (New York: Library of America, 1987), 1065–66. See also James, *LWJ*, 1:163–64, 186–88. For an additional discussion of Renouvier's importance to James, see Perry, *TC*, 135, 152–53.

43. See Wahl, *PPEA*, 78–79. For additional discussions of Proudhon's importance to Renouvier, see J. Alexander Gunn, *Modern French Philosophy* (London: T. Fisher Unwin, 1922), 61; and see William Logue, *Charles Renouvier: Philosopher of Liberty* (Baton Rouge: Louisiana State University Press, 1993), 192. James's strong response to Renouvier may have been an outgrowth of his own childhood exposure to the Proudhonian tenets that lay beneath the French philosopher's pluralism. The household in which James was raised had been a gathering spot for many of New England's leading radical intellectuals in the early 1850s. Among its regular "Saturday dinner" guests was the newspaperman Charles A. Dana, who was at that time one of the strongest advocates of Proudhon in America. Perry, *TC*, 15. Dana can hardly be thought to have made an anarchist of the ten-year-old William; but in introducing James's progressive family to the central Proudhonian idea of a decentralized and relational "barter" society, he may have contributed to James's intellectual heritage, and hence to his eventual interest in Renouvier's pluralist philosophy. Whether through Dana, through Renouvier, or through his own later firsthand exposure to anarchism, James did eventually seek to orient his philosophy, if not his politics per se, around those "*Anarch*[ic]," relational varieties of experience that had been masked, not by political institutions, but by backward-looking, static forms of reason.

44. During the 1880s and 1890s, leading up to his own firsthand discovery of Proudhon, James had cultivated relationships with a number of anarchists and

anarchistically inclined "individualists." Among these radical thinkers and activists were William Salter, Thomas Davidson, Wincenty Lutoslawski, and Morrison Swift. In addition to absorbing elements of Proudhon's thought through these and other radical acquaintances, James would have further encountered nineteenth-century "mutualist" conceptions of a barter-based society through the writings of anarchists affiliated with Benjamin Tucker's "Boston Circle." During the 1880s leading Boston papers printed local anarchist tracts that featured ideas drawn from the corpus of the founder of the "ethical" branch of anarchist thought. For a carefully documented study of James's exposure to various strains of anarchism, and for a sensitive account of his changing responses to anarchism in the 1880s, 1890s, and 1900s, see Coon, "CA."

45. Pierre-Joseph Proudhon, *Selected Writings of Pierre-Joseph Proudhon*, ed. Stewart Edwards, trans. Elizabeth Fraser (New York: Anchor Books, 1969), 214. See also Coon, "CA," 50–51.

46. William James to Karl Stumpf, 6 August 1901, bMS Am 1092.9 (3806), James Papers. See also Coon, "CA," 271.

47. In describing his own "mosaic" variety of "radical empiricism," James placed himself among the "descendants" of the British empiricist Hume. James, "WPE," 1160. As Ralph Barton Perry notes, James identified with British empiricists including Locke, Berkeley, Hume, and Mill, and he hoped to use Renouvier's pluralism to "save" this school from the "skepticism, materialism, and determinism" into which it had "fallen." Perry, *TC*, 153. Dewey suggested that James's pragmatism owed a great deal to yet another early British empiricist, Francis Bacon. Dewey, *RP*, 34, 37–38, 92–93.

48. To date, little has been written about the importance of nineteenth-century evolutionary theory to anarchist thought. But many anarchists sought to plumb the antistatist implications of both philosophical and biological writings on evolution. Among them was the Boston-based individualist-anarchist Victor Yarros, whose writings on anarchism and evolution were esteemed by the members of Benjamin Tucker's Boston Anarchists' Club in the 1880s. Coon, "CA," 70–75. Peter Kropotkin is perhaps the best-known example of an anarchist who openly engaged with the writings of Charles Darwin. In his 1902 treatise *Mutual Aid*, Kropotkin argued for cooperation rather than competition as a guiding principle of evolution; that work became one of the most widely read anarchist texts of the twentieth century.

49. James identified himself as a passive supporter of communitarian anarchist causes in 1901, in a letter addressed to the head of the New York Anti-imperialist League, Ernest Howard Crosby: "Isn't the way for lovers of the ideal to found smaller communities which should show a pattern? . . . through small systems, kept pure, lies one of the promising lines of betterment and salvation. Why won't some anarchists get together and try it. I am too ill (and too old!) or I might chip in myself." Scott, *UC*, 266–67.

50. James's distinction between a static, past-oriented philosophy and a dy-

namic, future-oriented one rests here on what Dorothy Ross has described as an "exceptionalist" vision of American history. As an ideology that took root in the late eighteenth century, exceptionalism holds that, because of its republican government and its unparalleled economic opportunities, America is unburdened by the history and the destiny of its European "parent." This vision of an immanent national destiny fostered an analogous conception of the individual in a democratic society, bringing the latter into alignment with Proudhon's belief in the immanence of the identity of the "citizen" within the "state" modeled on the mandates of the "economic organism." Proudhon, *GI*, 268–69. In the same way that America's future stood outside of the syntax of history, in other words, the American individual stood outside the syntax of the democratic political structures that contained him or her. American individuals were not represented by the democratic society of which they partook. Rather, they were mystically and immediately embodied through it. The particular mechanisms through which James sought to devise a pluralistic American philosophy, however, suggest that his conception of democracy was modeled not only on the Jeffersonian right to property—which Frank Lentricchia sees expressed in the fundamental entitlement to 'self' in James's writings—but also on the "principle" of "reciprocity" that drove Proudhon's relation-based "economic organism." Lentricchia, "IPM," 230; Proudhon, *GI*, 171, 173.

51. The pun on "species" and "specie" would have been a meaningful one for many modern intellectuals. Proudhon formulated his notion of an "economic organism"—or a society that dispensed with "gold" as "the last idol of the Absolute"—before Darwin published his *Origin of Species* (1859). After Darwin, however, many of those intellectuals who sought to banish gold coinage as a form of "commodity money" came to associate the gold standard with outmoded creationist conceptions of the universe. Pound and Arthur Kitson, for example, both intimated that the pernicious "gold fetish" could only appeal to crude and unenlightened minds; and William Carlos Williams blamed a regressive literary "gold" standard for the backward and out-of-touch quality of much contemporary art. One might even speculate that William James's immersion in evolutionary theory served to bolster his own unorthodox economic opinions. James was hardly preoccupied with economic theory; but he did alienate some of his more high-minded liberal friends by supporting William Jennings Bryan's fluid "gold-and-silver" currency standard during the 1900 presidential campaign. On James's support of silverite monetary policies, see Coon, "CA," 141–42.

52. Misunderstanding this point, a range of intellectuals from Bertrand Russell to Frankfurt School critics have mistakenly dismissed pragmatism as a philosophy modeled on the laws of the capitalist market. For a sampling of recent discussions of the twentieth-century reception of pragmatism, see Morris Dickstein, ed., *The Revival of Pragmatism: New Essays on Social Thought, Law, and Culture* (Durham, N.C.: Duke University Press, 1998).

53. James's annotated copies of Darwin's and Reid's works are preserved in

the James Papers at Harvard's Houghton Library. The philosopher's interest in the contingent pathways of genetic succession can be gathered from the notes that he made in the flyleaves and margins of these books. For more comprehensive accounts of Darwin's importance to James, see Paul Jerome Croce, *Science and Religion in the Era of William James* (Chapel Hill: University of North Carolina Press, 1995), 1:87–148. See also Robert J. Richards, *Darwin and the Emergence of Evolutionary Theories of Mind and Behavior* (Chicago: University of Chicago Press, 1987), 409–50. See also Philip P. Weiner, *Evolution and the Founders of Pragmatism* (Cambridge, Mass.: Harvard University Press, 1949).

54. Providing a particularized account of our "actual experience of the way [the] world develops," James's "pluralistic" corrective to reigning rationalist and empiricist tempers would decentralize systems of knowledge not only through a recovery of individual autonomy but also through a recovery of the "free personal relation[s]" that supported the very identity of the individual. James, *ML,* 310; James, *LWJ,* 2:100. In his "anarchist" phase, James used the analogy of a grafted tree to try to account for this relational—and processual—conception of individual identity. Through this metaphor he sought to reconcile the Proudhonian and Darwinist sources of his conception of "pragmatism" as a "radical empiricist" and "pluralistic" assault on the "Absolute." "Small systems the truer systems," James noted in an outline for a lecture on pluralism (ca. 1903–4). "*Graft*-theory. . . . It means *Anarchy* in the good sense. . . . It means *individualism.* . . . that the smaller & more intimate is the truer." James, *ML,* 311. In the lectures that he delivered toward the end of 1906, and in the book, *Pragmatism,* that he published in April 1907, James reiterated his idea that "new truths" might "graft" themselves onto an "ancient body" of old ones (*P,* 512–13); this notion of grafting became central to his ongoing effort "to destroy the notion of . . . [an] Absolute of any sort." James to Karl Stumpf, 6 August 1901, James Papers.

55. According to the Russian formalist critic Roman Jakobson, literary discourse is driven by two competing metalingual operations. These are the substitutional procedures of metaphor and the more wayward contiguous procedures of metonymy. (As examples of metaphor, Jakobson lists synonyms that link the word "hut" to "hovel" and "palace"; and as examples of metonymy, he cites surrounding features and attributes including "thatch litter" and "poverty.") Although Jakobson associated symbolist poetry with metaphor, he also suggested that distinctly modern visual art forms like cubism—which transforms its object "into a set of synecdoches"—were marked by metonymy. Jakobson and Halle, *FL,* 90–92. Literary modernists including Gertrude Stein, Marianne Moore, and William Carlos Williams based their aesthetics on their various understandings of the conceptual affinities between cubism (and also the collage arts that eventually sprang from Picasso's and Braque's cubist portraits) and pragmatism and Darwin's writings.

56. Stein's was by no means a simple "absorption" of James's teachings. As

Lisa Ruddick argues, although Stein initially "defined herself against William James," her thinking eventually "swerved away from James and toward Freud, whose idea of the unconscious confirmed the value of what was happening in her artistic process." See Lisa Ruddick, *Reading Gertrude Stein: Body, Text, Gnosis* (Ithaca, N.Y.: Cornell University Press, 1990), 1–2.

57. Gertrude Stein, *Tender Buttons,* in *Selected Writings of Gertrude Stein,* ed. Carl Van Vechten (New York: Vintage Books, 1990), 461.

58. On the importance of anarchism to Picasso's art, see Patricia Leighten, *Re-ordering the Universe: Picasso and Anarchism, 1897–1914* (Princeton, N.J.: Princeton University Press, 1989). See also Temma Kaplan, *Red City, Blue Period: Social Movements in Picasso's Barcelona* (Berkeley: University of California Press, 1992).

59. Gertrude Stein, "The Gradual Making of the Making of Americans," in *Selected Writings of Gertrude Stein,* ed. Carl Van Vechten (New York: Random House, 1990), 257–58.

60. That Moore claims no writerly authority for these dazzling drifts of expression is made clear by the notes that she appended to her quotational collage poems. Many of Moore's quotes are made up, and even those that are legitimate are eclectic: they are chosen for little more than their texture. It is in the act of decentralizing both syntactic and allusive chains of command, then, that Moore translated James's appeal to grammatical decentralization to the newer collage-bound realm of intertextuality. She devised a method that subordinated both grammatical and textual authority to an accretive accentuation of the color and texture of her idiosyncratic materials.

61. Unlike a large number of leading American writers and critics (including T. S. Eliot, Wallace Stevens, Gertrude Stein, Alain Locke, and W. E. B. Du Bois), Moore did not study under the pragmatist philosophers who taught at Harvard around the turn of the century. She did read James's work enthusiastically at Bryn Mawr, however. There, her favorite teacher was Theodore de Laguna, who published on the subject of pragmatism and evolutionary theory. See Theodore de Laguna and Grace Andrus de Laguna, *Dogmatism and Evolution: Studies in Modern Philosophy* (New York: Macmillan, 1910), 117–34. On Moore's close ties to modern visual arts and artists, see Leavell, *VA.* See also Willis, *VV.*

62. Max Nordau and Otto Weininger were among the best known of the many turn-of-the-century pseudoscientists who decried the hereditary weakening of modern Europeans. See Nordau, *Degeneration* (1895; 2d ed., Lincoln: University of Nebraska Press, 1993). See also Weininger, *SC.* On the status of theories of degeneration in modern European and American culture, see Mosse, *NS,* 145–46; see also Nicholls, *M,* 152–53; see also T. J. Jackson Lears, *No Place of Grace: Antimodernism and the Transformation of American Culture, 1880–1920* (1983; reprint, Chicago: University of Chicago Press, 1994), 49, 112.

63. Pound conceived fascism as a uniquely fluid and improvisational politi-

cal movement, one that was not based on precedent. As he wrote in *JM*, "*The fascist revolution is infinitely more* INTERESTING *than the Russian revolution because it is not a revolution according to a preconceived type*" (24). This processual conception of the state was in fact an integral component of fascist ideology. As the Italian philosopher Camillo Pellizi expressed it in 1924, the new fascist state would be "not a fixed reality but a dynamic process." Pellizi, *Problemi e realta del fascismo* (Florence: Vallecche, 1924), 21; trans. and quoted in Sternhell, *BF*, 231.

64. In taking "necessity" and "contingency" as his analytical axioms, the deconstructionist Paul de Man extended Jakobson's rather static terms *metaphor* and *metonymy* into the realm of sequence and causality. De Man, *BI*, 274. See also de Man, *AR*, 3–15, 63.

65. See Pound, "NS," 68. See also Joyce, "PA," 85. For a discussion of the confused class identifications of a range of European modernists, see Raymond Williams, *The Politics of Modernism* (London: Verso, 1989), 54.

66. See Sherry, *RM*, 53–54. See also Harriet Shaw Weaver and Dora Marsden, "Views and Comments," *Egoist* 3, no. 3 (1 March 1916): 33–35.

67. Walter Benn Michaels notes that at the turn of the century, "Progressive" Americans began to take "the difference between white and black . . . as the essential organizing principle of the citizenry, against the difference between rich and poor." Anglophile writers like Henry James suffered, in Michaels's estimation, because they were "insufficiently alert . . . to the role that racial difference could be made to play in the constitution of American identity." Michaels, *OA*, 140.

68. The pragmatist and Zionist Horace Kallen coined the phrase "cultural pluralism" in 1924. "The American people," Kallen argued, "are a mosaic of peoples, of different bloods and of different origins, engaged in rather different economic fields and varied in background as well as in blood." Kallen, *CD*, 58. As Werner Sollors has noted, Kallen's ideas and rhetoric gained new currency among American humanities scholars who called for the establishment of a "multiethnic" American "mosaic" in the 1970s and 1980s. See Sollors, "CPP," 251.

69. In *OA*, Michaels discusses the modern notion of "cultural pluralism" broadly, and he considers its significance to Williams and to other American writers of the 1920s.

70. As Walter Michaels and Werner Sollors have both noted, many modern liberal advocates of cultural pluralism harbored racist assumptions. See Michaels, *OA*, 64–65. See also Sollors, "CPP," 250–79. Michaels argues, rather provocatively, that cultural pluralism actually intensified racial essentialism. In its "denial of [racial] hierarchy," it "made possible the escape from the common scale and the emergence of an unmeasurable and hence incomparable racial essence." Michaels, *OA*, 66.

71. See West, *AEP*; Hutchinson, *HR*; and Posnock, *CC*.

72. On the importance of anarchist theory to Marcel Duchamp and other avant-garde visual artists, see Allan Antliff, "Anarchy, Politics, and Dada," in *Making Mischief: Dada Invades New York,* ed. Francis M. Naumann and Beth Venn (New York: Whitney Museum of American Art, 1996), 209–13. See also Francis Naumann, *New York Dada 1915–23* (New York: Harry H. Abrams, 1994). Williams's hot-and-cold relationship to pragmatism, and to John Dewey in particular, can be traced back to Williams's manifestos in *Contact,* his avant-garde journal of the early 1920s. See William Carlos Williams, *Contact* 2 (January 1921): n.p., ed. William Carlos Williams and Robert McAlmon.

73. See Dewey, "AL," 685. Dewey criticized "Americanization" agencies for forcing newly arrived immigrants to learn "a language strangely known as English"; and although his critique of the measure of "Anglosaxondom" is certainly implicit in this comment, the word itself does not appear in "Americanism and Localism." Dewey used this word in an earlier letter to Horace Kallen, who coined the term "cultural pluralism."

74. For a powerful account of the complexities surrounding Williams's claims regarding "the American idiom," see Michael North, *The Dialect of Modernism: Race, Language & Twentieth-Century Literature* (New York: Oxford University Press, 1994), 150–62.

75. See also Rorty, *CP,* 80–89; and Lloyd, *LO,* 23, 44. For additional studies of the importance to Dewey of both the idealist and the historicist Hegel, see Richard Rorty, "Dewey between Hegel and Darwin," in *Modernist Impulses in the Human Sciences 1870–1930,* ed. Dorothy Ross (Baltimore: Johns Hopkins University Press, 1994), 54–68; and see Kloppenberg, *Uncertain Victory.*

76. Dewey had criticized the alienating metaphysical stance that he called "the spectator conception of knowledge" before *Experience and Nature.* Dewey, *RP,* 112.

77. See John Dewey, *Experience and Nature* (Chicago: Open Court, 1925), 261–62.

78. For Dewey's own implicit and explicit remarks on the importance of James's pluralism to contemporary social issues, see his "Philosophy and Democracy" (1919), in Boydston, *Middle Works of Dewey,* 11:53. See also his "Principle of Nationality" (1917), in *Middle Works of Dewey,* 10:288.

79. See John Dewey to Horace Kallen, 31 March 1915, Horace M. Kallen Papers, American Jewish Archives, Hebrew Union College, Cincinnati. Westbrook quotes and discusses this letter in *JD,* 213–14. In an essay published a year after the letter to Kallen quoted in the text, Dewey invoked the image of the mosaic, stating that an "authentic America" should be "a juxtaposition of alien elements" rather than "an amalgam." See his "Universal Service as Education" (1916), in Boydston, *Middle Works of Dewey,* 8:185.

80. For accounts of Kallen's coinage of the phrase "cultural pluralism," see

John Higham, *Send These to Me: Jews and Other Immigrants in Urban America* (New York: Atheneum, 1975), 206. See also Schmidt, *HK,* 27–28. See also Sollors, "CPP," 264–79.

81. Kallen discussed the importance of James's pluralism to his social theory in a series of interviews conducted in 1972 and 1973. See Sarah L. Schmidt, "Horace Kallen and the Americanization of Zionism," Ph.D. diss., University of Maryland, 1973, 34, quoted in Sollors, "CPP," 265. See also Schmidt, *HK,* 23–24, 165. See also Kallen, *CD,* 43.

82. Kallen's anarchist sympathies stemmed from his involvement with Boston radicals around the turn of the century. As late as 1933, Kallen claimed a preference for Kropotkin's ideas over those of Karl Marx. See Horace Kallen, *Individualism: An American Way of Life* (New York: Liveright Publishing Corp., 1933), 9–10.

83. That Kallen's thought was forged out of the alliance between pluralism and anarchism is suggested by his recollection of the signal emblem that James concocted in 1904, at the very outset of his pluralist-anarchist phase. In his 1914 study of James's and Bergson's philosophies, Kallen praised particularly his teacher's distinctive "mosaic" conception of "Reality." See Horace Kallen, *William James and Henri Bergson: A Study in Contrasting Theories of Life* (Chicago: University of Chicago Press, 1914), 161–62. Later, in 1924, when Kallen set forth his own vision of a cultural pluralist society, he described it as a "mosaic of peoples, of different bloods and of different origins." Kallen, *CD,* 58. Kallen's own cultural mosaic was "metaphorical" and "immediate" in the Proudhonian anarchist fashion, but it lacked the Darwinist emphasis on process that James had preserved.

84. Horace M. Kallen, "Democracy versus the Melting Pot: A Study of American Nationality" (1915), in *Theories of Ethnicity: A Classical Reader,* ed. Werner Sollors (New York: New York University Press, 1996), 92. Kallen slightly modified this claim when he republished his essay in 1924. Kallen, *CD,* 124.

85. Williams referred to dadaism as "a small, sweet forget-me-not" in *Contact* 5 (June 1923): n.p., ed. Williams and McAlmon.

86. Dewey is reported to have stated, "The falsity of anarchy is in not recognizing what a complex and continual interaction it requires to bring the individual to a consciousness of the whole and of his identity or interest with it." "John Dewey, Political Philosophy Lectures, 1893," transcribed by Charles Horton Cooley, Charles Horton Cooley Papers, University of Michigan. Dewey's remark is quoted and discussed in Ross, *SS,* 168.

87. Stein, "Gradual Making," 257–58.

88. Dewey's essay was written around 1911–12. See also Boas, *MPM,* 205–6.

89. Though Boas disagreed with Darwin's stance on racial hierarchy, he viewed the evolutionist's conception of the "instability of species" as a cornerstone of cultural anthropology. See Boas, *RLC,* 243. Moore agreed with both

Darwin and Boas that life-forms were unstable in generation and that history was driven at least in part by "accidents." Darwin influenced Moore directly (she read his work carefully and repeatedly); Boas affected her poetic subjects and practices indirectly, through the pervasive influence of the modern discipline that he founded.

90. James's politics were "provincial" not because they were "isolationist" but rather because they refused to admit of domestic concerns that might have compromised the integrity of the national body. In his desire to preserve this integrity, James paid little attention to class conflict within America, and he failed to recognize Du Bois's writings on the centrality of racial divisions in *The Souls of Black Folk*. In George Santayana's view, James's impassioned resistance to turn-of-the-century imperialist ventures reflected an "innocent" faith in the "illusory" foundations of the republic. See George Santayana, *The Middle Span* (New York: Charles Scribner's Sons, 1945), 2:169.

91. Mainstream scholars have only recently begun to recognize the broad historical significance of exchanges between African American and European American intellectuals. In many cases, however, these exchanges were one-sided, conditioned by racial and class biases. William James, for example, does not appear to have realized the significance of Du Bois's work to his own discussions of "individual consciousness." As James wrote to his brother Henry in 1903: "I am sending you a decidedly moving book by a mulatto ex-student of mine, Du Bois, professor of history at Atlanta (Georgia) negro College. Read Chapters VII to XI for local color, etc." Henry James, *LWJ*, 2:196. That the pragmatist should have gleaned no more than "local color, etc." from the book that set forth the powerful notion of African American "double-consciousness" testifies both to James's racism and to his unwillingness to embrace any ideology that threatened the integrity of the category of the "American." The first instance that I have found in which a white pragmatist acknowledges Du Bois's theory of "double-consciousness" occurs after World War II. In a 1947 preface written for a planned collection of Claude McKay's poems, John Dewey praised in particular those writings in which "the sense of being a black man in a white man's world . . . comes to its full expression." Dewey to Henry Cowl, October 1947, box 2, folder 2, Claude McKay Correspondence, James Weldon Johnson Memorial Collection, Beinecke Rare Book and Manuscript Library, Yale University.

92. Dorothy Ross argues that American social scientists of the early twentieth century oriented their conceptual systems around distinctly modern appeals to "process." In Ross's view, this emphasis on "process" both reflected and perpetuated a kind of "anti-historicism," in which modern political struggles were contained within the millennial flux of "nature." Ross, *SS*, 387–88. See also Dorothy Ross, "Modernist Social Science in the Land of the New / Old," in Ross, *Modernist Impulses in the Human Sciences*, 188–89. Insofar as this distancing exceptionalist impulse can be said to have conditioned even Boas's progressive concep-

tions of environmentally conditioned identity, it provides a further framework for understanding how "culture" came to be viewed as an orthodox American measure.

93. In Boas's essay "The Measurement of Differences between Variable Quantities," for example, "the Negro" follows "the baboon" in serving as a reference point for the measuring of "racial" differences. Between them, they demonstrate that "race" is contingent on the point of reference selected by the measurer. Significantly, when Boas used "the Negro" as a reference point, he did so in order to challenge the arbitrary physiological markers used by race scientists to distinguish between two allegedly different types of white Europeans. Boas, *RLC*, 184–85.

94. Boas called for racial intermixture in *MPM*, 251–78. For Boas, racial assimilation was not a biologically salubrious practice but rather a means of eradicating the socially conditioned "instinct" toward racial classification and hierarchy. Boas, *AML*, 78–79. In suggesting that the best hope for a just American society lay in the erasure of all markers of difference, Boas implied that democracy could not by nature be an inclusive institution.

95. Hurston's Jamesian assessment of folk culture as a phenomenon that was "*still* in the making" comes from a letter that she wrote to Langston Hughes. Hurston to Hughes, Maitland, Fla., 12 April 1928, box 76, Langston Hughes Collection, James Weldon Johnson Memorial Collection, Beinecke Rare Book and Manuscript Library, Yale University. Displaying a different opinion, and probably a slightly different definition of "the folk," the writer elsewhere dismissed "folk expression" as antiquated and cliché-bound. Zora Neale Hurston, "Are We Citizens," n.d. (ca. 1940–45), typescript fragment, box 1, Hurston Collection, Beinecke Rare Book and Manuscript Library, Yale University.

96. In her autobiography Hurston claimed to have "no need of either class or race prejudice," saying that she preferred the "gift of individualism" to the "solace of easy generalization." Hurston, *DT*, 782. Hurston's subtle criticism of the modern category of "culture" as a measure of identity can be found in Hurston, *EWG*, 226–27. See chapter 6.

97. On Eliot's early study of philosophy, see Levenson, *GM*, 176–86.

98. In *No Place of Grace*, T. J. Jackson Lears argues that turn-of-the-century American culture was marked by a series of reactive, medieval longings. This larger "antimodernist" climate may have softened even ostensibly liberal American intellectuals toward the Proudhonian call for a return to local communities and to direct forms of economic exchange.

Chapter Two. Imagism and the Gold Standard

1. Dora Marsden to Harriet Shaw Weaver, 12 January 1913, Harriet Shaw Weaver Papers, Additional Manuscripts, no. 57354, British Museum, London.

2. Lidderdale and Nicholson, *Dear Miss Weaver,* 47–48.

3. Dora Marsden, "Notice to the Readers of 'The Freewoman,'" *Freewoman* 2, no. 42 (5 September 1912): 311.

4. Jane Marcus, ed., *The Young Rebecca: Writings of Rebecca West 1911–1917* (New York: Viking, 1982), 60–63. According to the poet Pound, who had joined the staff of the *New Freewoman* in 1913, West had quit her post as assistant editor of Marsden's journal because she could not abide its new nexus of "political creeds." West's later criticism of Marsden's economic views suggests that it may have been Marsden's emerging interest in "the economic problem" that prompted West to leave. Ira B. Nadel, ed., *The Letters of Ezra Pound to Alice Corbin Henderson* (Austin: University of Texas Press, 1993), 62–63.

5. For a discussion of Orage's interest in radical economic thought before World War I, see Finlay, *SCEO,* 77. Some modern intellectuals, like Donisthorpe, embraced underconsumptionist economics as a vehicle for the construction of anarchist societies. Others, like Kitson and Meulen, aligned themselves with the "philosophy" of "Individualism" and "Anarchism" but were more committed to radical economic reform than to antistatist objectives. In this they vacillated between liberal and anarchist sympathies. Meulen, *BSP,* 16. See also Benjamin Tucker, *Liberty* 314 (1 June 1895): 4, ed. Benjamin Tucker. Kitson believed that his own economic theories were anarchistic because they were based in part on the writings of the anarchist Pierre Proudhon. But Tucker, the editor of *Liberty,* a leading forum for British and American anarchists around the turn of the century, found Kitson's theories of value to be more compatible with the statist objectives of "State Socialism" than with "Anarchism." See Benjamin Tucker, *Liberty* 323 (7 September 1895): 5, ed. Benjamin Tucker.

6. In a letter written to Kitson in the early 1930s, Pound revealed that he had been familiar with the economist's 1912 *New Age* essays. Pound to Kitson, n.d. (ca. December 1933), Rapallo, Ezra Pound Papers, box 27, folder 1156, Beinecke Rare Book and Manuscript Library, Yale University.

7. Pound's apt summary of the aims of the early pragmatists can be found in Pound, *GK,* 188.

8. Pound met with a range of radical political leaders, along with writers and visual artists associated with the burgeoning British avant-garde movement, in Hulme's Frith Street salon. The British painter Christopher Nevinson remembers that in 1913 Hulme's weekly meetings were attended by "journalists, writers, poets, painters, politicians of all sorts, from Conservatives to New Age Socialists, Fabians, Irish yaps, American bums, and Labour leaders such as Cook and Larkin." Christopher R. W. Nevinson, *Paint and Prejudice* (New York: Harcourt, Brace, & Co., 1938), 85. A. J. Cook and Jim Larkin were leaders of prewar Welsh and Irish syndicalist movements. Cook was the editor of an anarchist paper called "The Worker's Bomb," a journal that contributed to the name and the combative tone of the British "Vorticist" magazine, *BLAST.* David Kadlec,

"Pound, BLAST, and Syndicalism," *ELH* 60 (1993): 1019–20. For an excellent overall discussion of Pound's involvement with artistic and political radicalism in London, see Wallace Martin, *The New Age under Orage* (New York: Barnes & Noble, 1967), 5, 43–44, 121.

9. Pound to Kitson, n.d. (ca. December 1933), Rapallo, Pound Papers, box 27, folder 1156.

10. Ibid.

11. See D. D. Paige, ed., *The Letters of Ezra Pound 1907–1941* (New York: Harcourt, Brace, & Co., 1950), 33. Pound's public assessment of Marsden was never generous, and he grew increasingly vindictive in his remarks after 1916. During that year, Pound's backer, John Quinn, had offered to subsidize the floundering *Egoist* with Pound at its helm. Marsden, who was at that time contributing to the journal but no longer editing it, angered Pound by using her influence to block the attempt. Marsden's refusal to defer to Pound, coupled with her abandonment after 1914 of political commentaries in favor of abstruse philosophical essays, may have motivated Pound's harsh assessment of her as an "ignorant" woman whose philosophical "slosh" marred "the forehead of every [*Egoist*] number." Such comments have long discouraged scholars from taking Marsden seriously as a force in the development of modernism. Nadel, *Letters of Pound to Henderson*, 138, 211. See also Timothy Materer, ed., *The Selected Letters of Ezra Pound to John Quinn, 1915–1924* (Durham, N.C.: Duke University Press, 1991), 60, 71, 96. William Carlos Williams, by contrast, never hid his admiration for Marsden. See Williams, *I*, 97. See also Hugh Witemeyer, ed., *Pound/Williams: Selected Letters of Ezra Pound and William Carlos Williams* (New York: New Directions, 1996), 231.

12. In the opening paragraph of his 1913 essay "The Serious Artist," Pound wrote: "It is curious that one should be asked to rewrite Sidney's 'Defence of Poesy' in the year of grace 1913. . . . In England now . . . we are asked if the arts are moral. We are asked to define the relation of the arts to economics, we are asked what position the arts are to hold in the ideal republic." Pound, "SA," 161. Here, Pound was framing his modern *ars poetica* as a response to a series of broadly public questions. Privately, however, he credited Marsden specifically with asking him the "questions" that prompted his essay. See Pound to Marsden, n.d. (ca. September 1913), Marsden Collection, box 1, folder 23. See also Clark, *DM*, 110–11.

13. Pound to Marsden, n.d. (circa summer 1913), Marsden Collection, box 1, folder 23. See also Clarke, *DM*, 107.

14. Pound coined the "ideogrammic method" as a name for the textual collage style that he used in *The Cantos*. Although he experimented with the sharp juxtaposition of phrases and images in early poems like "In a Station of the Metro" (1913), he did not begin to fully apply this method until the Malatesta Cantos of the early 1920s. In an essay fragment written in the late 1920s or early 1930s, Pound commented, "The patient reader can, I think, find the root of the

ideogrammic method in the notes first published in the *Egoist* under the title *The Serious Artist.*" Pound, *MA,* 118, 162. In this comment Pound misremembered the name of the 1913 journal in which the essay appeared. Nonetheless, his remark suggests that the essay prompted by Marsden's injunction that the poet consider "the relation of the arts to economics" was a pivotal one for the methodology that Pound later explicitly associated with underconsumptionist economic theory. Pound's comment to Marsden *"You done it. You axed me questions"* comes from a 1913 letter that Pound wrote to Marsden. Pound to Marsden, n.d. (ca. September 1913), Marsden Collection, box 1, folder 23. Bruce Clarke is the first scholar to have recognized the significance of this letter to Pound's relationship with Marsden. Clarke, *DM,* 110, 236 n. 31. In addition to Clarke, Ronald Bush and Robert von Hallberg have done much to advance our understanding of Marsden's value to literary modernism.

15. By early 1914 Pound was likening artistic rebellion to class war, issuing bellicose warnings like the following: "The artist has been at peace with his oppressors for long enough. He has dabbled in democracy and now he is done with that folly." Antidemocratic sentiment was a distinguishing feature of modern anarchist rhetoric. Anarchists commonly appealed to "direct action" over democratic political reform. Pound, "NS," 68. Vincent Sherry explains that by the time of this essay, Pound had come to embrace "perceptually immediate" visual art forms as antidotes to "the very debility of democracy—the generalization of identity—that Marsden [had] also located." Sherry, *RM,* 48.

16. On the prewar syndicalist challenge to Britain's liberal government, see George Dangerfield, *The Strange Death of Liberal England, 1910–1914* (1935; reprint, New York: Perigree, 1980), 315. See also Bob Holton, *British Syndicalism: 1900–1914* (London: Pluto, 1976), 133, 176–77.

17. In "Status Rerum," Pound claimed to share a greater affinity with the novelist Ford Madox Hueffer (Ford Madox Ford) than with the poet William Butler Yeats. Ford "believes in an exact rendering of things." Yeats, on the contrary, "has been subjective; believes in the glamour and associations which hang near the words. 'Works of art beget works of art.' He has much in common with the French symbolists." Pound, "SR," 125. In his illuminating account of the aesthetic genesis of imagism, Michael Levenson notes that Pound's praise for the "exact rendering[s]" of the "Impressionist" writer Ford turns on a defining modernist "confusion," one that merges "*realism*" with "*self expression.*" "Ford's Impressionism," Levenson suggests, "is a *subjectivity in which the subject has disappeared.*" Levenson, *GM,* 106, 115, 119.

18. Marsden not only foregrounded "the economic problem" as a way out of "the sex problem"; she also drew from Stirner in resisting the parliamentary aims of suffrage, as well as the strategic appeals to essential "womanly" identities that were sounded in 1913 by the militant wing of the British suffrage movement. See Tickner, *SW,* 223. Through Stirner, Marsden soon came to adapt contempo-

rary complaints against the "symbol" in poetry to a critique of the suffragettes' devotion to "Causes." See von Hallberg, "LI," 66–68. See also Weaver, *AB*, 27.

19. Dora Marsden, "Views and Comments," *New Freewoman* 1, no. 1 (15 June 1913): 3.

20. Hugh Kenner's clear, if overly formalistic, account of Pound's absorption of Douglas in 1919–20 has set the pattern for two generations of Pound scholars. See Kenner, *PE*, 316–17. Richard Sieburth delivers a lucid and compelling post-structuralist account of the economics of Pound's imagist poetry, but he follows Kenner in historicizing the poet's absorption of economics through Douglas. Sieburth, "PWT," 142–72. The literature on Pound and economics is extensive and varied. In historical matters, however, it has remained remarkably orthodox. Leading studies of Pound's economics and politics include books by Casillo, *GD*; Paul Morrison, *The Poetics of Fascism: Ezra Pound, T. S. Eliot, Paul de Man* (New York: Oxford University Press, 1996); Peter Nicholls, *Ezra Pound: Politics, Economics, and Writing* (Atlantic Highlands, N.J.: Humanities Press, 1984); Jean-Michel Rabaté, *Language, Sexuality and Ideology in Ezra Pound's* Cantos (Albany: State University of New York Press: 1986); Redman, *EPIF;* Leon Surette, *A Light from Eleusis* (Oxford: Oxford University Press, 1979).

21. Pound likened his reading of Douglas to a glimpse at Dante's paradise in Canto 38, which was written in 1933. Pound, *C*, 190. "Underworld" is Keynes's designation, not Pound's. Keynes was referring to Douglas's lack of acceptance by an orthodoxy. See John Maynard Keynes, *The General Theory of Employment, Interest, and Money* (1936), in *The Collected Writings of John Maynard Keynes* (London: Macmillan, 1973), 7:32. Orage's overblown characterization of Douglas as "the Einstein of economics" is recounted by Humphrey Carpenter in his biography of Pound. See Carpenter, *A Serious Character: The Life of Ezra Pound* (New York: Delta, 1988), 357.

22. In the obituary to A. R. Orage that Pound wrote for the *New English Weekly*, Pound stated emphatically: "The actual battle with ignorance, in the acute phase wherein I shared, began with Douglas's [1919] arrival [at Orage's office on] Cursitor Street. The earlier Guild Socialism, and all other political or social theory had lain outside my view. (This statement is neither boast nor apology.) I take it I was present at some of the earliest talks between the two leaders." Pound, *SP*, 437.

23. Kitson to Pound, 5 December 1993, London, Pound Papers, box 27, folder 1156.

24. Pound to Kitson, n.d. (ca. December 1933), Rapallo, Pound Papers, box 27, folder 1156.

25. Pound, "Obstructivity," 168.

26. Pound wrote little of the Great War as it was occurring. Afterward, however, it became the focal point of his diatribes against usury. "Hugh Selwyn Mauberley" (1919–20) contained some of Pound's earliest declamations against

the war; as Hugh Kenner has noted, it was also the first of Pound's poems to contain the word "usury." Kenner, *PE,* 317. Pound believed that World War I had been manufactured by munitions makers and financiers who created shortages that forced nations to resort to violence in order to expand their markets. The war may have been especially painful for Pound because he himself did not serve in it. A number of his friends and associates did serve, however. Among them was the brilliant young sculptor Henri Gaudier-Brzeska, of whom Pound was especially fond. Gaudier-Brzeska was killed in action. In Daniel Tiffany's view, the trauma of World War I, and Gaudier-Brzeska's death in particular, were decisive factors not only in Pound's embrace of economic theory but also in his aesthetic development as a whole. See *Radio Corpse: Imagism and the Crypt-aesthetic of Ezra Pound* (Cambridge, Mass.: Harvard University Press, 1995), 48–49. On Pound's desire for clarity in currency and language, see Pound, *GK,* 31. See also Maud Ellmann, "The Imaginary Jew: T. S. Eliot and Ezra Pound," in *Between "Race" and Culture: Representations of "the Jew" in English and American Literature,* ed. Bryan Cheyette (Stanford, Calif.: Stanford University Press, 1996), 97–99; Bob Perelman, *The Trouble with Genius: Reading Pound, Joyce, Stein, and Zukofsky* (Berkeley: University of California Press, 1994), 38–39; Rabaté, *Language, Sexuality and Ideology,* 217–23.

27. Pound to Kitson, n.d. (ca. December 1933), Rapallo, Pound Papers, box 27, folder 1156.

28. Envisioning a Flaubertian " 'prose tradition' of poetry," Pound commented: "The presentative method is equity. It is powerless to make the noble seem ignoble. It fights for a sane valuation." Pound, "AP," 662.

29. Keynes, *Employment, Interest, and Money,* 7:32.

30. Robert Heilbroner and William Milberg, *The Crisis of Vision in Modern Economic Thought* (Cambridge: Cambridge University Press, 1995), 31–35. See also Anna J. Schwartz, introduction to *A Retrospective on the Classical Gold Standard, 1821–1931,* ed. Michael D. Bordo and Anna J. Schwartz (Chicago: University of Chicago Press, 1984), 14. See also Surette, "EPBR," 444.

31. Keynes called for state intervention as a necessary counter to depression in *The Collected Writings of John Maynard Keynes,* vol. 21, *Activities 1931–1939: World Crises and Policies in Britain and America,* ed. Donald Moggridge (London: Macmillan and Cambridge University Press/New York: St. Martin's Press; for the Royal Economics Society, 1982), 60. His refutation of Say's Law can be found in *The General Theory of Employment, Interest, and Money* (London: Macmillan, 1936), 18. See also Robert Skidelsky, *Keynes* (Oxford: Oxford University Press, 1996), 71, 78, 82. See also Surette, *Light from Eleusis,* 83.

32. See Finlay, *SCEO,* 18–22. See also Watner, "EI," 69–75.

33. For a useful discussion of Marx's and Proudhon's respective economic views, see Thomas, *KMA,* 182–83.

34. For a related discussion of the relationship between monetary theories

and theories of values, see Skidelsky, *Keynes*, 49–54. For an application of these terms to Pound's later Douglasite economic beliefs, see Surette, *Light from Eleusis*, 87–88.

35. As Michael Levenson has shown, although Pound's 1913 criticism of Ford's early work marks a break between imagism and postsymbolism, it does not mark a break between imagism and Ford's literary impressionism. Pound remained allied to Ford, at least until 1914, as a writer whose "uncivic" realism dissolved the tension between subjective and objective relation. Levenson, *GM*, 119–20. Peter Nicholls places the imagist struggle against postsymbolism within a larger literary and intellectual context. Nicholls, *M*, 169–72.

36. Herbert Schneidau labels imagism a "disciplinary" aesthetic. Schneidau, *EP*, 3–37. Michael Levenson discusses Schneidau's phrase in *GM*, 111. Hugh Kenner describes imagist criteria as a prescription for "a technical hygiene." Kenner, *PE*, 178.

37. See Kitson, "GF," 94. See also Arthur Kitson, "The Cause of Financial Panics," *Freewoman* 2, no. 39 (15 August 1912): 246–47.

38. Pound later recalled that imagism had to be abandoned because it was overly "STATIONARY." Pound, *ABCR*, 52.

39. MacCabe, *RW*, 160–62.

40. Pound identified himself as a "syndicalist" in a pseudonymously authored *Egoist* essay. See Pound, "S," 254.

41. For a discussion of the vexed class identifications of a range of European modernists, see Williams, *Politics of Modernism*, 54.

42. Pound expressed his wish to found a decentralized guild of artists in "On the Imbecility of the Rich," *Egoist* 1, no. 20 (15 October 1914): 389–90. During the modern period, guilds were favored by both reactionary neomedievalists and revolutionary syndicalists, but Pound intimated in this essay that his own sympathies lay with the latter: "An anarchist paper in America—'The Revolutionary Almanack,'" Pound wrote, "seems to be the only paper in that country which keeps abreast of continental thought." In the context of Pound's essay, this comment displays not only the poet's familiarity with the Boston anarchist Benjamin Tucker but also his glimmering awareness of the relationship between guilds and the self-governing ethical societies championed by the French anarchist Proudhon. (The circuitous route from anarchist to fascist thought is well accounted for by Zeev Sternhell in *The Birth of Fascist Ideology*.) Pound's anti-Semitic radio broadcasts during World War II are discussed in Carpenter, *Serious Character*, 616–17.

43. Andrew Parker and Richard Sieburth are among the best of the poststructuralist readers who have portrayed imagism in this way. See Andrew Parker, "Ezra Pound and the 'Economy' of Anti-Semitism," *Boundary* 2 (fall–winter 1982–83): 116, 120 n. See Sieburth, "PWT," 149.

44. Donald Davie was among the first to suggest that "the development from

imagism in poetry to fascism in politics is clear and unbroken." *Purity of Diction in English Verse* (1952; reprint, New York: Schocken, 1967), 99. Robert von Hallberg takes issue with Davie in "LI," 64. As a critic, the poet Davie was primarily a formalist, but his view of imagism as a protofascistic aesthetic has nevertheless been embraced by many of Pound's poststructuralist readers.

45. For Kitson, the belief that clean currency might be an instrument for restoring ethical value to transactions was rooted in Proudhon's writings. But this belief is also anticipated in the writings of the Victorian art critic John Ruskin, whose ideas regarding the organic relationship of art to politics and economics had reached Pound through A. R. Orage during the early teens. Michael Coyle, "A Profounder Didacticism: Ruskin, Orage, and Pound's Recreation of Social Credit," *Paideuma* 17 (1988): 19–20, 22–23. Ruskin's sweeping accounts of the falling-off of modern from medieval societies led him to stray from the sphere of art history—so much so that he has been said to merit a place in economic history as a forerunner of modern underconsumptionist economic heresy. Finlay, *SCEO*, 26. Underconsumption had arisen as a formal economic doctrine in 1887 with O. E. Wesslau's analysis of Scotland's and England's respective localized and centralized credit systems. Meulen, *BSP*, 5–6; Finlay, *SCEO*, 18. The expansive economic treatises that Ruskin began publishing in 1860, however, contain ethical and analytical traces sympathetic to the more formal underconsumptionist challenges posed by Kitson's *Scientific Solution to the Money Question.* Finlay, *SCEO*, 18–29. In *Unto This Last,* Ruskin advocated an indexing of real, consumable wealth—or production "for the Mouth"—over the "mildewing" nominal wealth of surplus production "for the Ground"; and in *Munera Pulveris* he shifted his assessment of value to a related critique of money, disparaging gold-backed currency as "opaque, . . . half currency and half commodity." Ruskin, *UTL,* 219. See also Ruskin, *MP,* 81.

Kitson's own writings combined left-wing and right-wing antistatism with a liberal progressivism by promoting a mechanistic dismantling of state impediments to the innate social goodness of free trade. Liberal underconsumptionists tended to focus on the benefits of unrestricted credit to producers who would reap an expanded market. Increased consumption would intensify production and strengthen competition to the benefit of society at large. Finlay, *SCEO,* 40–41. Anarchist underconsumptionists saw free money as a boon to consumers who could share in the bounty of industrial production; and the more militant among them relished open credit as a corrosive to capitalist monopolies. Watner, "EI," 69–73. Reactionary underconsumptionist tendencies can be found in the writings of Ruskin, who decried artistic decline in an economy that replaced "the old aristocratic virtue of magnanimity" with "the bourgeois virtue of thrift." Surette, "EPBR," 439. What links these varieties of economic heresy is an ethical emphasis on "real" wealth over its nominal reflection in surplus. The health of society is indexed by transactions, not stockpiles. An apt currency is one that circulates freely. Underconsumptionists all believe with the founding anarchist Proudhon that society will find its way to health, given a currency that does not inhibit its own circulation.

46. See Dora Marsden, "Views and Comments," *New Freewoman* 1, no. 9 (15 October 1913): 165.

47. That Proudhon, Kitson, and Pound each espoused anti-Semitic beliefs should be more than a little bit troubling to students of historical anarchism. Pound's own anti-Semitism is undeniable and unforgivable, and it is in no way diminished or clouded by his intermittent identification with left anarchist politics or by his conception of Mussolini as a "left-wing" fascist. Kitson, who viewed himself as a modern disciple of Proudhon, layered some of his *New Age* and *Freewoman* essays with anti-Semitic overtones; he eventually became so deeply anti-Semitic that by the time he shared a correspondence with Pound in the 1930s, he was speaking favorably of Adolf Hitler's efforts to rid Europe of Jews. Kitson, "MCI," 256. See also Kitson to Homer Pound, 10 June 1936, Pound Papers, box 27, folder 1156. Such a network of anarchist and anti-Semitic thought might tempt us to posit an essential connection between anarchist appeals to "immediacy" and the nascent and often well-disguised nationalist impulses that gripped so many European intellectuals before the war. The notion that an emancipatory social order might be founded on the actions of the "true" individual or, in Proudhon's case, on the exchanges of a "true" community of producers, does seem to have often entailed the construction of an outsider who shores the perimeters of "truth." One of the problems with the agrarian utopias that underlie forms of anarchism and fascism is that they can end up "naturalizing" the exclusion and the persecution of those who have been historically prohibited from owning land. Despite the anti-Semitic beliefs held by many of those who embraced radical anarchist economic theories, critics in the humanities need to be careful in making essentializing theoretical claims, such as those that link all appeals to "immediacy"—a feature that is shared by anarchism and fascism—with anti-Semitism. Such work is valuable insofar as it has sensitized us to the dangers inherent in certain historical lines of thought; but it has also made critics complacent by diminishing their sense of the range of shapes and forms that anti-Semitism has taken in making its inroads into the twentieth century.

48. Leon Poliakov, *The History of Anti-Semitism,* trans. Miriam Kochan (New York: Vanguard Press, 1975), 3:458–72. See also Gilman, *DR,* 177, 296 n. See also Anne Fremantle, *This Little Band of Prophets: The British Fabians* (New York: Mentor, 1959), 204.

49. Mike Weaver was the earliest critic to notice the significance to the arts of Marsden's reading of Stirner. Although many critics have built upon Weaver's pioneering work, Marsden's treatment of "the economic problem" has not yet been discussed.

50. Marsden, "VC," 3. See also von Hallberg, "LI," 67.

51. In her editorial response to Pound, Marsden singled out the word "interest" and then proceeded to tease out its economic overtones. Several paragraphs later, she described the word-bound artist as a corrupt "accountant," one whose abstract productions were "hatched wholly in his own imagination." The scientist, by contrast, was a "carpenter"—a producer of true, material goods. Criticizing artistic treatments of "the mishaps of love," Marsden then invoked Shakespeare's well-known usurer, Shylock, whose loan to Antonio was secured by a pound of flesh. Love lost, she suggested, was "not a losss [*sic*] of interest, but a loss of soul-substance," a "mutilation" that was as "definite and tangible" as a human "hand" severed by a "fallen" "drop-trap." Having so doctored the word that she highlighted at the beginning of her essay, Marsden then restored it to a less metaphorical usage. Describing prose as an unrefined form of poetry, she dismissed it as merely " 'interesting' ": "that is, it holds the attention as does any useful uncompleted process." Here, as in the first occurrence of the word in her essay, Marsden drew attention to the word by placing it in quotation marks. Marsden, "AF," 181–83.

52. Arthur Kitson, "Usury: The Prime Cause of Want and Unemployment," *Freewoman* 2, no. 41 (29 August 1912): 291.

53. Pound's money-blood metaphor appears in "Toward an Orthographic Economy," *Rassegna Monetaria* 9–10 (September–October 1937). Tim Redman translates and discusses this passage in *EPIF,* 139.

54. Hugh Kenner is one of many critics who have noted the conceptual affinities between modern literary aesthetics and modern philosophy and physics. Kenner, *PE,* 153, 154. Richard Sieburth and Jean-Joseph Goux have both noted the affinities between Keynesian economics and structuralist linguistics. See Sieburth, "PWT," 157–58. See also Jean-Joseph Goux, *Symbolic Economies: After Marx and Freud,* trans. Jennifer Curtis Gage (Ithaca, N.Y.: Cornell University Press, 1990), 113.

55. Walter Benn Michaels, *The Gold Standard and the Logic of Naturalism* (Berkeley: University of California Press, 1987), 169.

56. Marjorie Perloff, *The Futurist Moment: Avant-Garde, Avant Guerre, and the Language of Rupture* (Chicago: University of Chicago Press, 1986), xviii. Perloff's account of the relationship between futurism and Pound's poetry broke new ground in the mid-1980s. Since then a number of important studies have appeared, including Lawrence Rainey, "The Creation of the Avant-Garde: F. T. Marinetti and Ezra Pound," *Modernism/Modernity* 1, no. 3 (1994): 195–219; and Sherry, *RM,* 11–16.

57. See also Pound, *MA,* 88. In 1948 William Carlos Williams lodged a variant of Pound's complaint against imagism, one that was vaguely informed by relativity theory. In "The Poem as a Field of Action," he suggested that "imagism was not structural: that was the reason for its disappearance." Williams, *SE,* 283.

58. In an essay published in the *Freewoman* in 1912, Kitson described his ideal

currency in terms similar to those that Pound would use to describe his own "volitionist" currency in the 1930s. "Like blood in the human body," Kitson wrote, "[money] must circulate freely and unhindered to keep trade in a healthy condition." "Cause of Financial Panics," 247. This metaphor was widespread among those radical economists who followed Pierre Proudhon—as Pound had begun to do in the 1930s. Proudhon himself had described gold as a medium that prevented money and credit from circulating. "Royalty will subsist," Proudhon wrote, "as long as we will not have abolished it in its most material and most abstract form—the royalty of gold. Gold is the talisman which congeals life in society, which binds circulation, kills labor and credit, and makes slavery mutual. We must destroy the royalty of gold; we must republicanize specie, by making every product of labor ready money." Proudhon, *Solution of the Social Problem*, 60.

59. For a general account of Fenollosa's intellectual heritage, see Van Wyck Brooks, *Fenollosa and His Circle* (New York: E. P. Dutton, 1962), 2, 61, 63.

60. See also Pound, "NS," 68.

61. As an anarchist, Proudhon distinguished the natural "economic organism," wherein exchanges between producers and consumers were local and unimpeded, from the "political mechanism" that served the pernicious institutions of rent, interest, and profit. "Beneath the governmental machinery," Proudhon wrote, "in the shadow of political institutions, out of the sight of statesmen and priests, society is producing its own organism, slowly and silently; and constructing a new order, the expression of its vitality and autonomy, and the denial of the old politics, as well as of the old religion." As a natural instrument of revolution, this social organism would "dissolve, submerge, and cause to disappear the political or governmental system . . . by reducing, simplifying, decentralizing and suppressing, one after another, all the wheels of this great machine, which is called the Government or the State." Proudhon, *GI*, 243, 173. See also Ridley, *RS*, 26. See also Finlay, *SCEO*, 24.

62. Leon Surette reads and discusses this same passage in *Light from Eleusis*, 101–2.

63. In *Qu'est-ce que la propriété?* (1840), Proudhon fashioned "anarchy" as a means of recovering an innately healthy social order. In so doing, he identified himself as both "an anarchist" and "a firm friend of order." "As man seeks justice in equality," Proudhon wrote, "so society seeks order in anarchy." Proudhon, *What Is Property?*, 2:260, 264. See also Ridley, *RS*, 26.

64. Arthur Kitson, *Industrial Depression* (London: T. Fisher Unwin, 1905), 4–23.

65. Pound's resistance to "theory" was of a piece with his resistance to self-referential postsymbolist poems. See Pound, "SA," 163; see also Schneidau, *EP*, 15–16. On the Italian futurists' contemporaneous critique of symbolist and postsymbolist language, see Filippo Tommaso Marinetti, "Destruction of Syntax—

Imagination without Strings—Words-in-Freedom," in *Futurist Manifestos,* ed. Umbro Apollonio (New York: Viking Press, 1973), 99. See also Perloff, *Futurist Moment,* 174.

66. During his "vorticist" phase, in 1914, Pound described the "image" as "a radiant node or cluster . . . through which, and into which, ideas are constantly rushing." Pound, *GB,* 91–92. Eliot alluded to the similarity between Pound's "vorticism" and Bergson's and James's philosophies in a letter dated 2 February 1915. Eliot, *LTSE,* 86–87. See James, "WPE," 1180–81.

67. At the time he wrote this letter, Eliot was studying with Bertrand Russell, who was an outspoken critic of William James's variety of pragmatism. Michael Levenson recounts Eliot's early assimilation of Bergson, F. H. Bradley, and William James. Levenson, *GM,* 176–86. Discussing the sympathies between Bergson's philosophy and futurist aesthetics, Vincent Sherry views the British avant-garde's resistance to Bergson as fundamental to the differences between vorticism and futurism. Sherry, *RM,* 11–16, 37–42.

68. For James's account of "experience" as a grafted tree, see the 1903–4 lecture notes reproduced in James, *ML,* 310–11. In these lecture notes, James likened his "*graft*-theory" to "*Anarchy* in the good sense." *ML,* 311.

69. Santayana and Dewey were both cautious in their correspondence with Pound; but of the two, it was Santayana who provided the better conduit between Pound's poetic economy and pragmatist philosophy. Santayana shared with the poet not only his situation as a cosmopolitan expatriate in Italy, but also a literary bent and an idealistic temper. Pound was drawn to the nominalistic preference for "things" over "concepts" that Santayana shared with his pragmatist colleagues; but he was also aware of the differences between Santayana and his more empirically disposed colleagues. Ezra Pound, "Review of George Santayana's Letters" (ca. 1959), Pound Papers, box 135. As an unabashed "idealist," Santayana was more forthcoming than either James or Dewey in his efforts to preserve within American philosophy some vestige of the edenic imperatives that lay at the root of Proudhon's conception of a revolutionary "economic organism." This desire surfaced in Santayana's writings on religion, and in his comments on fascism as well.

Santayana did not share Pound's support for either Proudhon or Mussolini. Nevertheless, he expressed a chilly appreciation for the *idea* of fascism as a politics that sought to cultivate "the generative order of society." Cory, *LGS,* 405. This belief in "the generative order of society" was central to Pound's economic views and to his own understanding of pragmatist philosophy. In *Guide to Kulchur* (1938), Pound had invoked the pragmatist "sanction" that "ideas are true only insofar as they lead to action"; and he proposed to materialize its "PROOF" through a freely circulating "volitional" currency (discussed later in this chapter). He was appealing to the Proudhonian notion of a generative, circulating form of currency powerful enough to displace "gold," which Proudhon had called the "last idol of the Absolute." Quoted in Tucker, *IB*, 260. By the 1930s, Pound had come to view not only Proudhon as a champion of the bounty of nature, but Mussolini and Thomas Jefferson as well. The notes that Pound made in the margins of Santayana's books, moreover, suggest that the poet was searching Santayana's writings for evidence of the pragmatist's belief in this very generative principle (see further discussion in this chapter).

70. Dewey was more committed than Santayana to the idea that "knowledge" was rooted in ongoing social processes. This commitment prohibited Dewey from indulging in anything so vague as a mythical appeal to the innately "generative order of society." In place of such a mystical order, however, Dewey did cling to an exceptionalist's confidence in the generative power of American "democracy." Ross, *SS*, 162–69; Lloyd, *LO*, 297–98. And this conception of democracy was in some places tinged not only with the rhetoric of antistatism but also with that of underconsumptionist appeals to the ethical imperative of economic consumption. Westbrook, *JD*, 452–58. In 1930, for example, Dewey suggested that "a cooperatively shared control of industry" would foster "the recognition of final use or consumption as the criterion of valuation, decision and direction." "When the point of view of consumption is supreme in industry," he concluded, "then human values will control economic values." Dewey, *ION*, 5:105. Despite the underconsumptionist shadings of Dewey's vision of an ethical capitalist economy, and despite the overall "millennial" flavor of his confidence in American democracy and democratic processes, however, his commitment to the possibility of a socially bound, processual order rather than an immediate "generative order" was finally incompatible with Pound's vision of a paradisal poetic economy.

In light of Dewey's eccentric vision of democracy and of a cooperative, consumption-driven economy, it is not surprising that Pound should have tried to enlist his aid in propagating "volitionist" economics. Given Pound's emerging anti-Semitic and fascist viewpoints, though, it is not surprising that Dewey's correspondence with him should have been short-lived and awkward. In the handful of letters that he exchanged with the poet between 1934 and 1935, Dewey voiced his concern for the "implications" of the nominalistic economic treatises that Pound placed before him. And he appears not to have been assuaged by Pound's assurances that there was nothing intrinsically anti-Semitic about his underconsumptionist diatribes against interest and usury. To Dewey, Pound had dismissed as "peripheric" the anti-Semitic sentiments expressed by radical economists ranging from Proudhon to Kitson to Pound himself. The "anti=jews," Pound insisted, had strayed from "the essential evil which is USURY." Pound to Dewey, Pound Papers, MSS 43, box 13. Dewey appears to have wisely understood this comment as not a disavowal of racism but rather a tacit approval of it, one that brushes aside the historical reality of anti-Semitic persecution. Shortly after Pound invited Dewey to write a preface for a proposed Yale University Press volume of "New Economic" writings, Dewey ended their correspondence.

71. James's assertion that "relations" are "as real as the terms united by them" comes from an essay (entitled "The Thing and Its Relations") appended to his book *A Pluralistic Universe*. First published as an article in 1905, this essay may well have been a source for Ernest Fenollosa, whose lecture notes titled "The Chinese Written Character as a Medium for Poetry" were compiled between 1905 and 1908.

72. Leland B. Yeager, "The Image of the Gold Standard," in Bordo and Schwartz, *Retrospective on the Gold Standard*, 662–64.

73. Perelman, *Trouble with Genius*, 46, 217.

74. Ibid., 14. Pound envisioned an artist's guild in "Imbecility of the Rich," 389.

75. Santayana's defense of fascism can be found in Cory, *LGS*, 404–5. Pound's notes for a review of this 1955 book can be found at the Beinecke Library. See Pound Papers, MSS 43, ser. 4, box 135, folders 5816–94.

76. Massimo Bacigalupo's much-quoted phrase first appeared in *The Forméd Trace: The Later Poetry of Ezra Pound* (New York: Columbia University Press, 1980), x. Casillo quotes Bacigalupo in *GD*, 328.

77. Ruskin proposed this lyrical alternative to the gold standard in *Munera Pulveris*. *ML*, 85. In *Unto This Last* he insisted that life itself was the only real form of wealth. *UTL*, 222. Pierre Proudhon had called for a removal of the gold standard in his *General Idea of the Revolution in the Nineteenth Century*. He wrote: "Upon what does the money market rest? Upon the scarcity of money. If the quantity of gold and silver were increased ten times, twenty times, the value of these metals would be ten times, twenty times less; in consequence, the rate of interest ten times, twenty times lower. It would end by our esteeming gold and silver no more than iron and copper: they would no longer be lent at interest. The scarcity of money is therefore essential to its function." Proudhon, *GI*, 189.

78. Ezra Pound, "The Order of the Brothers Minor," *New Freewoman* 1, no. 9 (15 October 1913): 176.

Chapter Three. Syphilis and James Joyce's *Ulysses*

1. See also Walkowitz, *PVS*, 254.

2. Vincent Cheng discusses Celtic Revivalist appeals to Irish "purity" in *JRE*, 49–51. In Jim Larkin's radical paper, the *Irish Worker*, an unidentified writer complained that "in Ireland we have been deluged by boastings of the purity of our women and the inviolable honour of our men." "Ourselves and the Purity! Campaign: The Conspiracy of Silence," *Irish Worker* 3, no. 62 (1914), n.p., ed. Jim Larkin.

3. Cheryl Herr discusses the British censorship of Irish nationalist literature in *Joyce's Anatomy of Culture* (Urbana: University of Illinois Press, 1986), 54. In an essay that was suppressed from the *Irish Nationalist* in 1900, Maud Gonne wrote of Queen Victoria's visit that year to Ireland: "Taking the Shamrock in her

withered hand she dares to ask Ireland for soldiers—for soldiers to protect the exterminators of their race! And the reply of Ireland comes sadly but proudly, not through the lips of the miserable little politicians who are touched by the English canker but through the lips of the Irish people: 'Queen, return to your own land.'" Ward, *WIN*, 12. In a lecture delivered in 1907, Joyce also remarked on Queen Victoria's visit to Ireland in 1900; he, however, criticized the racialist premises of Irish nationalist accounts like Maud Gonne's. Recounting the tensions that had surrounded Queen Victoria's somber reception in Dublin, Joyce suggested that it was "historical" factors more than "racial" ones that had made the English temperament so different from the Irish. "[Irish] civilization is a vast fabric," he commented. "In such a fabric, it is useless to look for a thread that may have remained pure and virgin without having undergone the influence of a neighboring thread." Joyce, *CW*, 165–66.

4. Gogarty's remark about the leprous British Army is taken from the first of his three "Ugly England" articles. First published in *Sinn Féin* on 15 September 1906, the final paragraph of the article is reproduced in a footnote in Richard Ellmann's edition of Joyce's letters. Joyce, *LJJ*2, 165.

5. Sydney Gifford Czira recalls Maud Gonne's written entreaties to "Irish girls" "not to associate with the 'enemies of their country'" in an excerpt from her autobiography, *The Years Flew By* (Dublin: Gifford and Craven, 1974), 48. Gifford Czira's recollection is reprinted in Ward, *WIN*, 24. Joyce alluded to Gonne's O'Connell Street handbills in *Ulysses*. *U*, 5.70. See also Gifford and Seidman, *UA*, 86.

6. Kevin C. Kearns, *Dublin Tenement Life: An Oral History* (Dublin: Gill & Macmillan, 1994), 86.

7. Joyce's brother Stanislaus rued the young artist's lapsing Catholicism and his flourishing "libertinism" in 1904. According to Stanislaus, Joyce spoke much during that year of "the syphilis contagion in Europe. . . . The drift of his talk seems to be that the contagion is congenital and incurable and responsible for all manias, and being so, that it is useless to try to avoid it." Joyce, *DSJ*, 50–52. In 1906 Joyce commented in a letter to Stanislaus that syphilis was particularly widespread in Ireland and that this "contagion" had nothing to do with "the judgment of God." By Joyce's reckoning, it was a matter of "venereal ill-luck." *LJJ*2, 170–71. Throughout his life, Joyce enjoyed styling himself a "sinner." Upon the death of his father, for example, he wrote to his editor and patron, Harriet Shaw Weaver: "I was very fond of him always, being a sinner myself, and even liked his faults." James Joyce, *Letters of James Joyce*, vol. 1, ed. Stuart Gilbert (New York: Viking, 1957), 312. "Sinner" or not, Joyce did suffer from a range of lifelong afflictions. The cause of his afflictions, which included failing vision and nerves, has long been a subject of controversy. In his highly influential biography of Joyce, Richard Ellmann gingerly noted that in March 1904 Joyce wrote to his friend Oliver Gogarty requesting "the name of a physician who would cure a

minor ailment contracted during a visit to Nighttown." Ellmann, *JJ*, 156. The Joyce critic and medical doctor J. B. Lyons concurred with Ellmann that Joyce had contracted only a mild case of gonorrhea from the prostitutes in Dublin's red-light district. Lyons thus lent his particular brand of authority to the long-standing effort to quell rumors regarding Joyce's alleged syphilitic condition. Lyons, *TS*, 21–39. (Not only was Nighttown suspected as a source for Joyce's disease; there were also rumors that Joyce's father had been a carrier who had passed the congenital disease on to his son.) Recently, Kathleen Ferris has re-kindled scholarly discussion of Joyce's medical history. Ferris has assembled a new round of archival and textual evidence, including previously "overlooked" portions of Joyce's and Gogarty's 1904 letters. By subjecting these materials to careful medical-historical scrutiny, she makes a strong case for syphilis as the disease that Joyce contracted in 1904. Ferris, *BD*, 25–33.

8. These divided responses to *Ulysses* are drawn from a list of critical excerpts compiled by Joyce's editor, Harriet Shaw Weaver. Harriet Shaw Weaver, ed., Miscellaneous *Egoist* Papers, Weaver Papers, no. 57355.

9. "Interior monologue" and "free indirect discourse" are among the names that critics have given to the modern narrative techniques that facilitate such a merging of narrator with characters.

10. Italo Svevo also noted *Ulysses'* playful narrative "portals" in a 1927 lecture on Joyce's writings. See Italo Svevo, *James Joyce: A Lecture Delivered in Milan*, trans. Stanislaus Joyce (New York: New Directions, 1950), n.p.

11. Derek Attridge argues that in the "Sirens" episode of *Ulysses*, these "bodily displacements and substitutions are enacted in the displacements and substitutions of language." Through this enactment, the "episode insists that neither language . . . nor the body . . . can be seen as merely secondary or subservient to . . . a controlling principle, whether that principle is called 'meaning' or 'the self.'" "Joyce's Lipspeech: Syntax and the Subject in 'Sirens,'" in *James Joyce: The Centennial Symposium*, ed. Morris Beja, Phillip Herring, Maurice Harmon, and David Norris (Urbana: University of Illinois Press, 1986), 64–65. See also Sherry, *JJU*, 82.

12. Joyce made this comment about feminist revolution during a discussion with Arthur Power. Power, *CJJ*, 35.

13. In his 1904 essay "A Portrait of the Artist," Joyce spoke of the artist as an agent who should cure "the general paralysis" of bourgeois society. "PA," 85. For discussions of this early essay, see Seamus Deane, "Masked with Matthew Arnold's Face: Joyce and Liberalism," *Canadian Journal of Irish Studies* 12 (June 1986): 18; see also Fairhall, *QH*, 52; Richard Ellmann writes that despite the fact that Joyce listed 1914 as *Portrait*'s year of completion, the final sections of the novel appear not to have been completed until 1915. Ellmann, *JJ*, 365. The years 1914–15 were clearly critical ones for Joyce in his development as a writer. One of Joyce's closest friends, the Italian novelist Italo Svevo, recalled that although

Ulysses had not yet been written, it had been largely "conceived" by 1915, when Joyce left Trieste for Zurich. (As late as 1921, Svevo aided in the writing of *Ulysses* by delivering old notes that Joyce had left behind in Trieste.) See Svevo, *Joyce Lecture in Milan*, n.p.

14. In his biography of the writer, Ellmann cites a portion of a 1914 letter in which Joyce defended the unorthodox punctuation that he developed in *Dubliners*. Writing to his publisher, Grant Richards, Joyce complained that the conventional placement of quotation marks around spoken words in a text "give[s] an impression of unreality" to a narrative. Ellmann, *JJ*, 364. Joyce preferred a less isolating method of indicating a text within a text: he placed a dash at the beginning of a quoted passage, leaving the end of the passage somewhat permeable. This seemingly small stylistic quirk was central to Joyce's evolving understanding of language and the modern novel. More than a decade later, Joyce made a comment to Valery Larbaud that deepened the implications of his 1914 remark to Richards. While translating *Ulysses* from English to French, Larbaud had asked Joyce, in 1928, whether he should place quotation marks around quoted passages in the novel. Joyce answered, "The fewer quotation marks the better." Even without them, he wrote, it should be clear in *Ulysses* "that [Stephen Dedalus's] mind is full like everyone else's of borrowed words." Joyce's letter to Larbaud of 4 June 1923 is quoted by Colin MacCabe, *RW*, 117.

15. As Richard Ellmann notes, "Joyce's first interior monologue was inserted at the end of *A Portrait of the Artist*, where however he makes it seem less extraordinary by having Stephen write it in a journal . . . Having gone so far, Joyce in *Ulysses* boldly eliminated the journal, and let thoughts hop, step, jump, and glide without the self-consciousness of a journal to account for their agitation." Ellmann, *JJ*, 368–69. In Stephen's second-to-last journal entry, he writes, "Welcome, O life! I go to encounter for the millionth time the reality of experience and to forge in the smithy of my soul the uncreated conscience of my race." Joyce, *PA*, 299. Insofar as Stephen finds himself exiled from the Irish Revivalist movement in *Portrait*, the young artist's desire to "forge . . . the uncreated conscience of [his] race" is necessarily somewhat vexed. In light of Joyce's own youthful writings, the "race" that Stephen seeks to invigorate in *Portrait* is not so much bound by national bloodlines as by the class-based parameters of the bourgeois "masses" that Joyce had referred to in his 1904 essay "A Portrait of the Artist." There Joyce had called for the artist to speak to those who were "not as yet in the wombs of humanity but surely engenderable there." To those "multitudes" the artist would "give the word: Man and Woman, out of you comes the nation that is to come, the lightning of your masses in travail; the competitive order is employed against itself, the aristocracies are supplanted; and amid the general paralysis of an insane society, the confederate will issues in action." "PA," 85. The paralyzed "nation" envisioned by the young revolutionist who fashions this "Portrait" is not a colony of England but a middle-class order stricken by

bourgeois prohibitions. For the antimoralist Joyce, it was neither somatic nor genetic contamination, but rather the very prohibitions that surrounded them that engendered "the general paralysis of an insane society." In Joyce's 1904 "Portrait," the bourgeois middle-class "mass" awaits its charge from the "confederate will" that was associated not only with the lower classes through international socialistic and syndicalist upheaval but also with the omnipotent cosmopolitanism of the aristocratic "race" of vanguard artists who will "supplant," but not erase, the older aristocracy. Joyce's 1904 confusion of proletariat and elitely aristocratic imperatives resembles that of other early modern intellectuals, including the American anarchist Benjamin Tucker, who celebrated a modern artistic vanguard when he conflated "Egoism in Philosophy, Anarchism in Politics, Iconoclasm in Art" in his 1906 *Unique Catalogue of Advanced Literature: The Literature That Makes for Egoism in Philosophy, Anarchism in Politics, Iconoclasm in Art* (New York, 1906).

16. Dora Marsden, the anarchist and feminist who edited the *Egoist,* set forth this conception of the new woman's identity in an *Egoist* essay published in early 1914. Marsden, "CW," 46. That Marsden and Joyce both spoke of identity as fluid in 1914–15 does not in and of itself constitute proof of direct influence. Rather, the affinity between Joyce's "sea" and Marsden's "stream" provides a focal point for a larger set of connections: Marsden's writings reached Joyce at a critical moment, enabling him to express the thematic concerns of his later novel *Ulysses* through experiments in literary form. When Stephen's conception of the artist as "a vital sea" is restored to its position between the failed novel *Stephen Hero* that preceded *A Portrait of the Artist* and the wildly successful experiment that followed it, it marks an updating, through Marsden, of the nineteenth-century anarchist sympathies that Joyce had originally absorbed through Ibsen. The manuscript "Stephen Hero" was Joyce's first attempt at a novel. Written between 1901 and 1906 and not published until 1944, "Stephen Hero" can be viewed as a preliminary draft of *A Portrait of the Artist as a Young Man.* In it Joyce began to explore the rudiments of the aesthetic theory that Stephen elaborated more fully in *Portrait.* In a passage that anticipates the later Stephen's conception of the artist as "a vital sea," for example, Joyce's early "hero" proclaimed, "[The poet] alone is capable of absorbing in himself the life that surrounds him and of flinging it abroad again amid planetary music." Joyce associated "impersonality" with the aquiline aloofness of Ibsen, who had been an early follower of Marsden's teacher, the German anarchist Max Stirner: "It was the very spirit of Ibsen himself that was discerned moving behind the impersonal manner of the artist." (Elsewhere, in a passage that Joyce struck from "Stephen Hero," his protagonist had spoken of "Ibsen with his profound self-approval, Ibsen with his haughty disillusioned courage, Ibsen with his minute and willful energy.") James Joyce, *Stephen Hero* (New York: New Directions, 1944), 80, 41. In light of Joyce's early association, through Ibsen, of artistic "impersonality" with Stirnerian self-

regard, Joyce's later appeal to the artist as a "vital sea" does seem to mark Marsden's ascension over Ibsen as the modern bearer of Stirnerian egoist doctrine.

17. See, for example, Marsden, "VC," 5. See also Marsden, "CW," 45–46.

18. See James Joyce to Harriet Shaw Weaver, 12 July 1915, Weaver Papers, Additional Manuscripts, no. 57345. See also Joyce to Weaver, 5 March 1915, Weaver Papers, Additional Manuscripts, no. 57345. Not only was Weaver mailing issues of the 1914 *Egoist* to Joyce, but Joyce was also using his scarce funds to purchase additional issues from booksellers. The 16 February 1914 issue of the *Egoist*, for example, appears on one of Joyce's bookstore receipts from that year. Ellmann, *JJ*, 788.

19. Rabaté's essay marks a recent resurgence of scholarly interest in Marsden's potential significance to Joyce's writing. See also David Kadlec, "Joyce's 'Penelope' and Woman Suffrage," *Works and Days* 20 (fall 1992): 43–63. Although Joyce never met Marsden, he clearly counted her among his supporters. During the war years, Marsden had been forceful in her public and private advocacy of Joyce against his British censors. See Harriet Shaw Weaver and Dora Marsden, "Views and Comments," *Egoist* 3, no. 3 (1 March 1916): 33–35. See also Marsden to Weaver, February 1916, Weaver Papers, Additional Manuscripts, no. 57354. See also Garner, *BBS*, 142. In his biography, Richard Ellmann makes little of Marsden's editorial dealings with Joyce. More detailed treatments of Marsden and Joyce's professional relationship can be found in Lidderdale and Nicholson, *Dear Miss Weaver*; and in Scott, *Joyce and Feminism*.

20. Rabaté notes that Joyce alludes to Marsden's journal, the *New Freewoman*, in the following passage from *Finnegans Wake*: "Of I be leib in the immoralities? O, you mean the strangle for love and sowiveall of the prettiest? Yep, we open hap coseries in the home. And once upon a week I improve on myself I'm so keen on that New Free Woman with novel inside. I'm always as tickled as can be over Man in a Surplus by the Lady who Pays the Rates." *Finnegans Wake* (New York: Viking Press, 1939), 145.25–31. By Rabaté's reading, this passage holds Marsden's 1913 journal at an ironic distance, one "directed at the mixture of neo-Darwinism and feminism" in the *New Freewoman*. Rabaté concludes that this irony demonstrates Joyce's greater sympathy for the politics of Marsden's later journal, the *Egoist*. Joyce's references to "the strangle for love" and "the sowiveall of the prettiest" are typically parodic, but they cannot be accurately directed toward the *New Freewoman*, whose broadly radical contributors often (but not always) agreed with Marsden that "the sex-problem" could only be solved by addressing "the economic problem." Dora Marsden, "Notice to the Readers," 311. In addition, the *New Freewoman* was not the journal "with novel inside." That journal was the *Egoist* of 1914. In *Finnegans Wake*, then, Joyce appears to have conflated rather than distinguished two journals—the *New Freewoman* and the *Egoist*—that were more conceptually continuous than their names might suggest. What this passage does reflect, however, is that, together with the 1914

Egoist, the back issues of the 1913 *New Freewoman* that Ezra Pound had mailed to Joyce in 1914 had made a lasting impression on the novelist and that in the jokey manner that was characteristic of all of *Wake's* imaginings, Joyce conceived of these journals as a matrix for his groundbreaking work. On Joyce's receipt of back issues of the *New Freewoman* from Pound, see Pound, *PJ,* 17–19.

21. See Gifford and Seidman, U*A,* 251–52; see also Ellmann, *JJ,* 428–29. That this passage pays tribute to Joyce's supporters is borne out by the fact that the "Scylla and Charybdis" episode was completed between late 1918 and early 1919, shortly after *A Portrait of the Artist,* which was first published in book form in December 1916, had begun to gain for its author some measure of success.

22. When Stephen asks for help in both "believing" and "unbelieving," Rabaté notes, he echoes Marsden's discussion of "the value of doubt and the need to resist any authoritative injunction to believe." "JE," 46–47. In her *Egoist* essay, Marsden had complained of

> the voices of authority [that] echo . . . the cry of "Believe, believe." They mean, "Leave decision, leave it, leave it to us," in effect asserting that knowledge is a spurious form, a degraded type of the ideal which is lack-of-knowledge. . . . The sacred is indeed the first weapon of defence against the prying questions of intelligence. . . . Very naturally, therefore, all that one believes is by acquiescence of belief made sacred. "My beliefs are sacred"; they would be no doubt, were the decision left with the believers, but the believer, as the history of belief shows, is encompassed about with enemies: both from within and from without, he is hard pressed. . . . Spontaneously bursts from him the cry: "I believe, help thou my unbelief. I have abandoned the quest: do thou (namely, sluggishness, comfort, whatnot) smother this itch I have to return to pry and poke." ("Authority: Conscience and the Offences," *Egoist* 1, no. 15 [1 August 1914]: 283)

In their respective passages, Marsden and Joyce both quote from Mark 9:24, wherein a distraught father answers Christ's injunction to him—"If thou canst believe, all things are possible to him that believeth"—with the following appeal: "Lord, I believe; help thou mine unbelief." Whether or not Joyce was deliberately quoting Marsden's quotation of the Bible, he was clearly binding her 1914 *Egoist* essay to the "Egomen" of "Scylla and Charybdis." That Joyce would do so several years after the publication of Marsden's essay suggests that the novelist read his British editor's essays with great care and that he read them during a critical period in the development of *Ulysses.*

23. Although Marsden's writings on disease and identity were clearly important to Joyce, they should not be viewed as a missing "key" to *Ulysses.* Joyce's sources were many. The novelist himself, for example, claimed a literary genesis for his signal narrative techniques, tracing their origins to a little-known French novelist, Edouard Dujardin. What a further historical contextualization of *Ulys-*

ses suggests is that such narrative techniques as "interior monologue" and "free indirect discourse" became meaningful to Joyce in part because they were bound to concurrent feminist and anarchist discussions of language and identity.

24. Pankhurst herself acknowledges that in the months before the beginning of World War I, she became an autocratic leader of the movement. Pankhurst, *HWV,* 216. For discussions of the political tactics of such prewar suffragette initiatives as the WSPU's Moral Crusade, see Holton, *FD,* 47. See also Tickner, *SW,* 224.

25. For a discussion of the vexed class affiliations of the suffragette movement, see Sylvia Pankhurst, *The Suffragette Movement: An Intimate Account of Persons and Ideals* (1931; reprint, London: Virago, 1977), 523. See also Tickner, *SW,* 224. See also Holton, *FD,* 47. Bob Holton writes of the rising syndicalist violence in England and Ireland before the war in *British Syndicalism,* 123, 133.

26. Pankhurst's sensationalistic estimates can be found in *GS,* 10, 69. Though her claims were clearly distorted, Pankhurst did draw attention to a serious threat to public health in modern England and Ireland. Judith Walkowitz writes that according to a study released by the Royal Commission on Venereal Diseases in 1916, syphilis carriers were estimated to make up at least 10 percent of Britain's urban population. The percentage of those carrying less serious diseases such as gonorrhea was thought to be much higher. Walkowitz, *PVS,* 50, 270–71 n. 9. For a discussion of the syphilis contagion in modern Dublin, see Murphy, *WSI,* 59.

27. Cliona Murphy discusses the Irish embrace of the British suffragettes' morality campaign. *Suffrage Movement and Irish Society,* 59. Sheila Rowbotham discusses the reaction against this very campaign by radical British women who supported the "new morality." According to Rowbotham, "the new morality was so completely at variance with the standard of the time that it necessarily was restricted to a minority even within the left." As a rule, Rowbotham suggests, these New Moralists were anarchists. (Rebecca West is one of many exceptions to this rule.) Rowbotham, *HH,* 101–2. See also Tickner, *SW,* 223.

28. Marsden labeled her former editorial associate Rebecca West a "humanist" in a 1914 letter to Harriet Shaw Weaver. Since Marsden was a firm believer in Max Stirner's antihumanist doctrines, this designation was a put-down, which marked West as a socialistic feminist rather than an anarchistic one. Marsden to Weaver, 7 July 1914, Weaver Papers, Additional Manuscripts, no. 57354. Despite her "humanism," West was also a New Moralist. She allied her celebration of sexuality with that of the controversial British sexologist Havelock Ellis. "When I feel more charitable," West wrote,

> I think of the words of Havelock Ellis, the great psychologist who has
> thought more deeply on these things than any other man of science: "The
> man who is run over in crossing the street, the family poisoned by unwhole-
> some food, the mother who catches the disease of the child she is nursing, all

these suffer as the involuntary result of the voluntary act of gratifying some fundamental human instinct—the instinct of activity, the instinct of nutrition, the instinct of affection. The instinct of sex is as fundamental as any of these, and the involuntary evils which may follow the voluntary act of gratifying it stand on exactly the same level. This is the essential fact, a human being in following the human instinct implanted within him has stumbled and fallen." (Rebecca West, "Lynch Law: The Tragedy of Ignorance," *Clarion* 1141 [October 17, 1913]: 7)

West sided with Marsden in her critique of Pankhurst's Moral Crusade. See West, "MU," 5. See also Marsden, "CW," 46.

29. Marsden was quoting page 98 of *The Great Scourge.* "CW," 46.

30. On the rise of anarchist sympathies among modern European intellectuals who lacked confidence in representative forms of government, see David Leopold, introduction to Stirner, *Ego and Its Own,* xi. See also Garner, *SSWL,* 74; MacCabe, *RW,* 160–61. Quite apart from his importance to Marsden, Stirner also had an enormous impact on other modern anarchists, including Benjamin Tucker, who eventually published Steven Byington's translation of *Der Einzige und sein Eigentum* (1907). (It was Tucker himself who chose the English title of Stirner's awkwardly named book.) During the decade preceding the English translation of *The Ego and His Own,* John Henry Mackay's biography of Stirner, portions of which were translated and published in radical individualist journals, stimulated interest in the German anarchist, as did the rather polemical writings of James Walker. Publishing under the pseudonym "Tak Kak," Walker spread the gospel of Stirner's egoism in Tucker's New York–based anarchist journal, *Liberty,* and in a number of other turn-of-the-century "individualist" journals, including London's *Eagle and the Serpent: A Journal of Egoistic Philosophy and Sociology.* Marsden's *Egoist,* then, was in fact a late addition to an extensive tradition of late-nineteenth- and early-twentieth-century radical individualist journals. In the late 1890s these journals included not only *Liberty* and the *Eagle and the Serpent,* but also British and American journals ranging from *Egoism* and *I* to later numbers of the *Adult.* Distributors of individualist literature ranged from London and Belfast to Denver and San Francisco.

It is not known whether Joyce became acquainted with Stirner and Nietzsche through radical individualist journals before the *New Freewoman* and the *Egoist,* but Nietzsche's writings enjoyed a considerable popularity in Dublin at the turn of the century. Davison, *CJI,* 112–13. And among radical individualists, many of whom came to embrace anti-imperialist nationalist positions, Stirner was never far from Nietzsche. For a discussion of the relationship between radical individualism and early modern nationalist movements, see Rabaté, "JE," 55–56. Rabaté's discussion of what he calls "egoist nationalism" is borne out not only by the Stirnerian overtones of the name *Sinn Féin* (Ourselves Alone) but also by the fact that after 1902 the *Eagle and the Serpent* changed its name to the *Nationalist.* Rabaté is right to suggest that *Sinn Féin* contains an individualist anarchist appeal to direct "economic solutions for Ireland rather than a hitherto sterile parliamentary agitation," but he overstates Joyce's endorsement of Arthur Griffith's nationalist movement between 1906 and 1908. Rabaté, "JE," 55.

31. Dominic Manganiello, *Joyce's Politics* (London: Routledge & Kegan Paul, 1980), 72, 77–79. For an additional account of Joyce's extensive interest in anarchist political theory, see Richard Ellmann, *The Consciousness of Joyce* (New York: Oxford University Press, 1977), 82–83.

32. Georges Borach, who was one of Joyce's language students in Zurich while Joyce was writing *Ulysses,* testifies to his teacher's antistatist sympathies. According to Borach, Joyce declared in 1919: "As an artist I am against every state. Of course I must recognize it, since indeed in all my dealings I come into contact with its institutions. The state is concentric, man is eccentric. Thence arises an eternal struggle. The monk, the bachelor, and the anarchist are in the same category. Naturally I can't approve of the act of the revolutionary who tosses a bomb in a theater to destroy the king and his children. On the other hand, have those states behaved any better which drowned the world in a blood-bath?" Borach, "CJJ," 326. In *Anarchism* (which was a book that Joyce owned), Paul Eltzbacher quoted extensively from *The Ego and His Own.* By Eltzbacher's account, Stirner's work amounted to "a scientific teaching" regarding the fundamentally flawed nature of the liberal state (95). The anarchist James Walker, whose work was supported and published largely by Tucker, summed up Stirner's work in terms that account for its appeal to modern intellectuals who were disenchanted with linguistic and political systems of representation: "In Stirner we have the philosophical foundation for political liberty." Walker, "I," xiv.

33. Bruce Clarke has challenged the long-held assumption that Marsden's "feminist" journal, the *New Freewoman,* was fashioned into the *Egoist,* a more broadly "individualistic" forum, by the "men of letters"—Pound, Allen Upward, Huntly Carter, Reginald W. Kauffmann, Richard Aldington—who wrested control of the forum from Marsden. As Clarke has shown, Marsden was a formidable intellectual presence who fully commanded the tenor of her journal: she impressed Pound, for example, with her broadly individualistic ideology well before the *New Freewoman* changed its name. Influential aesthetic treatises like the one that Pound set forth in "The Serious Artist" (1913) were fashioned in direct response to Marsden's intellectual and ideological challenges to the poet. Clarke, *DM,* 129–30. See also Pound to Marsden, n.d. (ca. July 1913), Pound/Marsden Letters, RP 3387 (iv), British Museum, London.

34. Stirner's critique of liberal ideology also entailed challenges to leading currents of mid-nineteenth-century European radical thought. Stirner's assault on the "ethical anarchism" of the French "mutualist" Pierre Proudhon, for example, was bound to his attack on the "left-Hegelianism" of the German

philosopher Ludwig Feuerbach. (Proudhon's conception of an innately ethical "economic organism" lay at the root of Pound's economic theories and his compositional collage method in *The Cantos*, and Feuerbach's writings on humanist ideology were instrumental in Karl Marx's early formulation of dialectical materialism.) Marx and Engels devoted several hundred pages of *The German Ideology* to a refutation of *The Ego and His Own*, a gesture that indicates that "Saint Max's" critique of Feuerbach had carried force in mid-nineteenth-century radical intellectual circles in Germany. See Leopold, introduction to Stirner, *Ego and Its Own*, xi–xxxiii. See also Rabaté, "JE," 49–52; and Rabaté, *Ghosts of Modernity*, 223–27. See also Derrida, *Specters of Marx*, 121–22.

35. Robert von Hallberg quotes and discusses this passage in "LI," 66.

36. Some modern anarchists, such as Benjamin Tucker and James Walker, insisted that Stirner's "individual" provided a complement to Proudhon's conception of the "association." Others, including Marsden, found Proudhon's doctrines to be incompatible with Stirner's.

37. In a 1916 *Egoist* essay, Weaver and Marsden protested the censorship by British printers of Joyce's *Portrait of the Artist*, arguing that the very moralistic social forces that had led to the suppression of women had also led to the suppression of Joyce's first novel. Harriet Shaw Weaver and Dora Marsden, "Views and Comments," *Egoist* 3, no. 3 (1 March 1916): 33–35. Although Weaver helped to supply details for this essay, the overall argument was Marsden's. See Marsden to Weaver, February 1916, Weaver Papers, Additional Manuscripts, no. 57354. See also Garner, *BBS*, 142.

38. See Ewa Ziarek, "The Female Body, Technology, and Memory in 'Penelope,'" in *Molly Blooms: A Polylogue on 'Penelope' and Cultural Studies*, ed. Richard Pearce (Madison: University of Wisconsin Press, 1994), 276–77.

39. In the controversial *Freewoman* leader on "Bondwomen" that earned her an international reputation as an anarcho-feminist spokesperson, Marsden condemned the vote and the marriage contract as a pair of enervating mechanisms. Dora Marsden, "Bondwomen," *Freewoman* 1, no. 1 (23 November 1911): 1–2. As an "eccentric" artist, Joyce identified with nonviolent forms of anarchism. Borach, "CJJ," 326. As Colin MacCabe notes, Joyce's "hatred of the institution of marriage was paralleled by his dislike for parliamentary democracy." *RW*, 160. See also Fairhall, *QH*, 52.

40. Judith Walkowitz notes that in their campaigns against the mandatory screening of "suspicious women" for venereal diseases, Victorian feminists often drew upon essentializing conceptions of women. Finding a vivid example of such essentialism in a passage excerpted from a book published in Boston in the 1880s, Walkowitz writes that "repealers [of the Contagious Diseases Acts] accepted the prevailing view of the uterus as the site of female mysteries: 'God has implanted in women an instinct which impels them as strongly as possible to conceal the organs of generation from the sight and touch of men. He has

enabled them to give effect to this instinct by framing their bodies in such a manner as to completely shelter those organs, and to bring their whole muscular strength to bear on their defense in case of attack.'" *PVS*, 129–30, 292 n. 60. Marsden loathed such reactive depictions of women. She called for each woman to claim her strength independently, through her own hands, even if theft was the only available means of empowerment. (As an anarchist, Marsden believed that the only real form of power was economic. Political power was a phantom; it weakened those who sought it by fostering dependence on the state.) See Marsden, "Bondwomen," 2; and Marsden, "CW," 45–46. See also MacCabe, *RW*, 160–62.

41. Dora Marsden, "The Heart of the Question," *New Freewoman* 1, no. 4 (1 August 1913): 61, 62.

42. Stirner wrote that "the fixed idea may also be perceived as 'maxim,' 'principle,' 'standpoint,' and the like. Archimedes, to move the earth, asked for a standpoint *outside* it. Men sought continually for this standpoint, and every one seized upon it as well as he was able. This foreign standpoint is the *world of mind*, of ideas, thoughts, concepts, essences, etc.; it is *heaven*." Stirner, *EO*, 80. In *A Genealogy of Morals*, which was widely read by British, Irish, and American individualists around the turn of the century, Nietzsche offered a variant of Stirner's critique of the entwined imperatives of moralism and idealism: "Let there be no deception in this point: what constitutes the most pertinent characteristic of modern souls and modern books is not 'falsehood,' but the incarnate *innocence* in moralistic mendaciousness. . . . I have no doubt as to the only *use* which posterity will make of modern books, of *all* modern things. . . . It can only be the use as emetics and this because of their moral dulcification and falseness, their inmost feminism which delights in calling itself idealism." Nietzsche, *AGM*, 10:191.

43. This account of Nietzsche's "ascetic ideal" is Michel Harr's. See Harr, "NML," 23.

44. For discussions of the complex relationship between feminists and eugenicists in modern England, see Rowbotham, *HH*, 105–6; and Tickner, *SW*, 222.

45. Helene Stöcker and Dora Marsden argued this point in a manifesto that they collaborated on in 1912, "IMW." Bessie Drysdale also celebrated the vigorous love-child. Drysdale, "BM," 6. And although the German "psycho-biologist" Otto Weininger was anything but a feminist, he too helped to circulate the notion that the children of unions governed by powerful mutual attraction tended to be more vigorous than the children of unions that had been determined by social or economic criteria. Weininger, *SC*, 43–44.

46. Rebecca West was among those New Moralist feminists who took note of the social significance of emerging treatments for syphilis. In her own scathing review of *The Great Scourge*, West suggested that one of the dangers of modern suffragette appeals to womanly restraint was that they fostered an outmoded

sense of shame and secrecy. In West's judgment, it was "criminal" to discourage sufferers from seeking the new forms of treatment that were available. West, "MU," 5. See also Garner, *SSWL*, 67.

47. For accounts of the discovery of Salvarsan and its use and reception in Germany and England, see Louise Creighton, *The Social Disease and How to Fight It: A Rejoinder* (London: Longmans, Green & Co., 1914), 49–50; see also William Bynum, "SHP," 5; see also Walkowitz, *PVS*, 254. On the emergence in Germany of the Motherhood Protection and Sexual Reform League, which advocated state support for single mothers, see Bessie Drysdale, "International Notes," *Freewoman* 1, no. 4 (14 December 1911): 79.

48. Paul Weindling discusses Stöcker's synthesis of Darwin and Nietzsche. *HR*, 154. Marsden's careful editing of the manuscript that Stöcker submitted to the *Freewoman* amounts almost to an act of collaboration. Her attention reflects not only an editor's concern for grammar and stylistic clarity but also her recognition of the value of Stöcker's contribution to the *Freewoman*'s anarchist platforms. This contribution lay in Stöcker's suggestions that "race poison" might be combated not by the suppression but by the elevation of individual sexual initiative. Stöcker and Marsden, "IMW." Stöcker's fully edited manuscript was published as Helene Stöcker, "Interpellation. To Men and Women of All Civilized Countries," *Freewoman* 2, no. 35 (18 July 1912): 174.

49. Following Stirner's critique of abstraction, Marsden argued that "Race" and "Woman" were merely "Empty concepts." As such, they performed "the old trick" of "subjugating the real to the unreal." "*A* woman" is a real thing, Marsden suggested. As such, she should not subordinate her wants to those of a "faked-up authority" like "the community, the State, the Race." Marsden, "VC," 5. See also Marsden, "Views and Comments," *New Freewoman* 1, no. 2 (1 July 1913): 24. Although Marsden appreciated Stöcker's appeal to the imperative of women's sexual initiative, as an anarchist she could not abide by the reformist ends to which this imperative was put. In the *Freewoman* she criticized the initiatives of the Motherhood Protection and Reform League. Calls for "the State endowment of motherhood," she argued, "repudiat[ed] the human responsibilities of women [and so] slam[med] the door in the face of freedom." Marsden, "Woman: Endowed or Free?" *Freewoman* 1, no. 15 (29 February 1912): 281.

50. Ferris draws these passages from manuscripts listed as VI. B.19, p. 172, and V. A.2, p.3, in the Poetry/Rare Books Collection, University Libraries, State University at New York, Buffalo. She quotes them in *BD*, 55.

51. When the nationalistic Citizen of "Cyclops" dismisses English "civilization" as "syphilisation," he echoes the racialist and moralist sentiments behind Arthur Griffith's and Maud Gonne's propaganda regarding "leprous" English soldiers in India and Ireland. The Citizen's pun on "civilization" sounds typically Joycean, but the word "syphilisation" was not coined in *Ulysses*. Nor was it native to Ireland per se. At the turn of the century, when urbanization was widely

associated with post-Darwinian fears of "degeneration," it was a commonplace that civilization was synonymous with contagious diseases. The American anarchist Morrison Swift, whose critique of modern American idealist philosophers struck a chord for William James in 1905–6, was among those who speculated on the origins of the pun. Swift, *HS*, 27.

52. For discussions of the place of syphilis in European racial stereotypes, see Cheng, *JRE*, 208–15; and Gilman, *PHI*, 81.

53. Joyce to Weaver, 7 October 1921, Weaver Papers, Additional Manuscripts, no. 57345.

54. Always wary of divisive forms of punctuation, Joyce referred to quotation marks as "perverted commas" in a letter to Harriet Shaw Weaver written 11 July 1924, quoted in MacCabe, *RW*, 14. Joyce described "Penelope" as the "clou" of *Ulysses* in a 1921 letter to Frank Budgen, quoted in Ellmann, *JJ*, 516.

55. In a letter to Frank Budgen, Joyce wrote that Molly is "sane full amoral fertilisable untrustworthy engaging limited prudent indifferent Weib. 'Ich bin das Fleisch das stets bejaht!' " Budgen, *MU*, 272.

56. This description of *Ulysses* as an X-ray of consciousness can be found in the critical excerpts that Harriet Shaw Weaver compiled shortly after the novel's publication. Harriet Shaw Weaver, ed., Miscellaneous *Egoist* Papers, Weaver Papers, no. 57355.

57. For a discussion of the status of the term *individualism* in modern British and American intellectual and literary circles, see von Hallberg, "LI," 66–67. As an early-twentieth-century popularizer of Stirner's and Nietzsche's nineteenth-century writings, James Huneker linked the two as the prophet and the poet of this very tendency. *E*, 352. See also Clarke, *DM*, 20.

58. In his index of turn-of-the-century writings about Stirner, Benjamin Tucker suggests that Nietzsche's "sudden fame" was instrumental to the European and American rediscovery of the founder of philosophical anarchism. Benjamin R. Tucker, "Publisher's Preface," in Stirner, *EO*, viii. Neil Davison writes that "translations of Nietzsche had . . . gained followings in London, New York, and Dublin by 1899, and the Irish capital was at the forefront of this enthusiasm." *CJI*, 112–13.

59. Stanislaus Joyce, *My Brother's Keeper* (New York: Viking Press, 1958), 160.

60. Marsden's essay "Bondwomen" testifies to her thorough engagement with Nietzsche (1–2). Bruce Clarke views Marsden's construction of the autonomous "freewoman" as "a feminist retort to Nietzsche's [masculine] Übermensch." *DM*, 63. In his 1904 essay "A Portrait of the Artist," Joyce endows the artist with an electrifying Nietzschean will. Neil Davison argues that "one should in the end not consider Joyce himself 'a Nietzschean' in the sense that the title implies taking the principal theories—Eternal Recurrence, The Death of God, and the *Übermensch*—as a center of one's philosophical belief." Nevertheless, "Joyce's rejection of Christian morality, his commitment to sexual freedom,

righteous individualism, and the amorality of art place him squarely in the Nietzschean camp." Davison, *CJI*, 114.

61. On the British suffragettes' responses to Marsden's writings, see Garner, *SSWL*, 64; Garner, *BBS*, 142. Marsden wrote appreciatively of Joyce's assaults on morality in Harriet Shaw Weaver and Dora Marsden, "Views and Comments," *Egoist* 3, no. 3 (1 March 1916): 35. Nietzsche's account of the destructive legacy of the ascetic ideal can be found in *AGM*, 106–7, 200–201.

62. Mandatory speculum examinations were among the most controversial of the provisions of the Contagious Diseases Acts that were passed in England beginning in the 1860s. Under these acts, any "suspicious women" who were found in the area of British military garrisons could be detained for medical examination and treatment. See Bynum, "SHP," 8. See also Walkowitz, *PVS*, 255–56.

63. Judith Walkowitz describes the Victorian speculum as a kind of "steel penis." *PVS*, 146, 295 n. 36. As Walkowitz notes, "the official response to [modern] feminist activities—in particular the forced feeding of militant suffragists in prison—carried the same perverse overtones of sexual violence and outrage as had the speculum examination in the 1870s and 1880s." *PVS*, 255–56.

64. Nietzsche discussed the significance of grammar to philosophy in *Beyond Good and Evil*, trans. R. J. Hollingdale (Harmondsworth, Eng.: Penguin, 1973), 20. See also Sarah Kofman, *Nietzsche and Metaphor*, trans. Duncan Large (Stanford, Calif.: Stanford University Press, 1993), 119.

65. Otto Weininger viewed modern "degeneration" as a widespread loss of masculine traits such as the capacity to discern and to act. In its "softness" of character, Weininger suggested, the contemporary public was both essentially feminine and essentially Jewish. *SC*, 73. For a broad discussion of Weininger's significance to literary modernism, see Nicholls, *M*, 152–53.

66. Elsewhere, Nietzsche wrote: "Linguistic means . . . are useless for expressing 'becoming'; it accords with our inevitable need to preserve ourselves to posit a crude world of stability, of 'things,' etc. We may venture to speak of atoms and monads in a relative sense; and it is certain that the smallest world is the most durable— There is no will: there are treaty drafts of will that are constantly increasing or losing their power." Friedrich Nietzsche, *The Will to Power*, trans. Walter Kaufmann and R. J. Hollingdale (1967; reprint, New York: Vintage, 1968), 380–81. Michel Harr discusses this passage, offering "fulgurations of the will" as a translation for Nietzsche's "*Willens-Punktationen*." "NML," 10. Walter Kaufmann and R. J. Hollingdale admit to being uncertain about their own translation of Nietzsche's phrase as "treaty drafts of will." They suggest that "perhaps the point is that the will is not a single entity but more like a constantly shifting federation or alliance of drives." Nietzsche, *Will to Power*, 381.

67. See Pankhurst, *GS*, 66. Discussing Pankhurst's writings on venereal disease, Rebecca West took particular issue with Pankhurst's reference to blindfolded women. "MU," 5. Judith Walkowitz notes that the designation "of women

as 'the Sex,' as sexual objects to be bought and sold by men" had a long history in England, extending back to "pre-Victorian" times. *PVS*, 128, 291 n. 53. See also Keith Thomas, "The Double Standard," *Journal of the History of Ideas* 20 (1959): 213.

68. Weininger supposed that men and women were essentially different in character. Emphasizing sexuality in particular, he traced these differences to anatomical and physiological roots. For discussions of Weininger's popularity among modern European intellectuals, see Mosse, *NS*, 145–46; Davison, *CJI*, 138–46; and Nicholls, *M*, 152.

69. The historical feminist sources of Joyce's unauthorized fiction finally place modern literature in dialogue not with poststructuralist conceptions of *écriture féminine* or even with progressive historical feminist assessments of the politics of modernism, but rather with more contemporary antihumanist challenges to identity politics, challenges that stir controversy by resisting the literal directives of progress. Although antihumanist feminists like Butler do not draw directly from anarchists or from anarcho-feminists like Marsden, they appeal through French poststructuralists to Nietzschean premises that were historically allied to modern anarchist critiques of identity.

70. Joyce's own account of the distortion of the Irish by English interpreters can be found in his 1907 essay "Ireland at the Bar." Joyce, *CW*, 198. See also Cheng, *JRE*, 152–53.

Chapter Four. William Carlos Williams, Prohibition, and Immigration

1. Williams, *SE*, 28. See also William Carlos Williams, *Contact* 1, no. 2 (May 1932): 110, ed. William Carlos Williams.

2. Williams's fellow poet Ezra Pound was among the many modern artists and intellectuals for whom temperance advocates like Rep. Andrew J. Volstead and William Jennings Bryan embodied the worst of America's puritanical spirit. Pound, *LE*, 391. In the 1920s the anti-immigrationist author Lothrop Stoddard was one of the leading voices to speak out against the dangers of immigrant "hordes." See Stoddard, *RT*, 160.

3. Williams viewed prohibition as a symbol of all that was wrong with a country that neglected and suppressed its most innovative artists. For Williams's complaint regarding his wealthy country's unwillingness to support its artists, see Williams, *EK*, 120. In James Joyce's novel about the flight to continental Europe of a young Irish novelist, Stephen Dedalus is disturbed by a vision of his Irish nationalist friend, Davin, caught in an incestuous embrace with his sister. *PA*, 268–69.

4. See the Nation Press, "The Week," *Nation*, 25 January 1919, 109.

5. See Sean Dennis Cashman, *Prohibition: The Lie of the Land* (New York: Macmillan, 1981), 21. See also Sinclair, *EE*, 20.

6. On European immigrants as drunkards, see Alphonso Alva Hopkins, *Profit and Loss in Man* (New York: Funk & Wagnalls Co., 1908), 234. Hopkins's reference to "Besodden Europe" is quoted in Sinclair, *EE*, 19. On immigrants as godless rabble-rousers, see Crafts, *WD*, 17. Twenty years before this rhetoric reached its pitch in America during the second decade of the century, the American anarchist Benjamin Tucker spoke out against the association of immigrants with alcohol. Tucker portrayed both economic protectionism and prohibition as diseases engendered by the innately defensive and insular body of the modern state: "The pretense that the foreign merchant who sells goods to American citizens or the individual who offers his I O U are invaders is as flimsy as the prohibitionist's pretense that the rumseller and the drunkard are invaders." Tucker, *IB*, 117–18.

7. See Dr. Alfred C. Reed, "Immigration and the Public Health," *The Popular Science Monthly*, October 1913, 325.

8. Anti-Saloon League of America, *Proceedings of the Sixteenth National Convention* (Westerville, Ohio: American Issue Publishing Co., 1915), 74.

9. For accounts of American immigration and the National Origins Act, see Higham, *PAN*, 300–330; see also Cravens, *TE*, 177–78; Haller, *HA*, 155–57; Zinn, *PH*, 373.

10. Williams made this statement in the 1920 prologue to *Kora in Hell: Improvisations. I*, 17.

11. For Williams's protests against modern America's prohibitions, see *EK*, 96. For his appeals to "locality" and "contact," see *SE*, 28.

12. The American painter Marsden Hartley sounded this call in his book *Adventures in the Arts* (1921; reprint, New York: Hacker Art Books, 1972), 60. Williams referred to Hartley's book in his own writings of the early 1920s. On Hartley's significance to Williams, see Dijkstra, *CSW*, 130–31.

13. William Carlos Williams, *Contact* 1 (December 1920): 10, ed. Williams and McAlmon.

14. Williams's suggestion that alcohol cracks open the calcified shell of the artist's personality comes from a journal entry that is quoted in Mariani, *NWN*, 265. Williams's most vivid embodiment of an artistic shattering of words can be found in *The Great American Novel* (1923). *I*, 160.

15. In a chapter titled "The Waste Land" in his autobiography, Williams wrote: "These were the years just before the great catastrophe to our letters—the appearance of T. S. Eliot's *The Waste Land*. There was heat in us, a core and a drive that was gathering headway upon the theme of a rediscovery of a primary impetus, the elementary principle of all art, in the local conditions. Our work staggered to a halt for a moment under the blast of Eliot's genius which gave the poem back to the academics. We did not know how to answer him." *AWCW*, 146.

16. Mike Weaver quotes Williams's comments to Riordan. *AB*, 45–46.

17. I draw this phrase from the writings of the modern assimilationist Mary

Antin. See *They Who Knock at Our Gates* (Boston: Houghton Mifflin, 1914), 54–55.

18. The early-nineteenth-century French zoologist Lamarck argued that changes to the body of an organism were passed directly on to subsequent generations. George Stocking writes that many modern advocates of immigrant assimilation held to an antiquated Lamarckian belief that the children of immigrants would become more genetically Americanized as their parents assimilated themselves to a distinctly American environment. *RCE,* 245. Dewey's essay "Americanism and Localism" responded directly to an earlier *Dial* essay in which James Oppenheim had set forth a Lamarckian conception of the American idiom. In his essay "Poetry—Our First National Art," Oppenheim had written: "But where to find [an expression more native to ourselves]? We have no folk, no soil song or literature: we have only our American speech, the resultant of new environment, mixture of races and new experience. This American speech is decidedly different in flavour and construction from English speech. It is not Colonial, but native, that is, environmental." "Poetry—Our First National Art," *Dial* 68, no. 2 (February 1920): 240.

19. See Reed, "Immigration and Public Health," 317, 325. See also Burton Peter Thom, M.D., "Syphilis and Degeneration," *Journal of Nervous and Mental Disease* 53 (January–June 1921): 8–9, 16–17.

20. William James associated his anarchistic and pluralistic "*graft*-theory" with idiomatic assaults on the idea of " 'the' mother-tongue." James, *ML,* 310–11; James, *P,* 592.

21. Joseph Riddel offers this deconstructionist assessment of T. S. Eliot's poetry in *The Inverted Bell: Modernism and the Counterpoetics of William Carlos Williams* (Baton Rouge: Louisiana State University Press, 1974), 215.

22. For discussions of Williams's relationship with Marsden, see Weaver, *AB,* 23; Clarke, *DM,* 173–217.

23. In her 1914 *Egoist* editorial "The Chastity of Women," Marsden argued that promiscuous or "vicious" persons are merely those who translate their appetites into actions. By taking action, they put their impulses "to the test of experience and for the time being destroy [them]." "Pure" persons, on the other hand, "suppress" their impulses and thereby "turn [them] inward." In so doing, they cultivate their appetites "into an atmosphere and a permanent obsession." By this line of reasoning, the "chaste" person resembles "the drugtaker and the drunkard." He or she lives in a world of shadows that is also visited by political reformists—those devotees of "Causes" who trade initiative and direct action for the deathly pleasures of an "atmosphere." Marsden, "CW," 45.

24. Dorothy Ross discusses John Dewey's commitment to the idea of an "ongoing democratic process" in *SS,* 168. As one of the earliest American advocates of "cultural pluralism," Dewey envisioned an "American nationalism" based on a different sort of "unity" from that of "the separate states of Europe."

America's "unity" would be "created by drawing out and composing into a harmonious whole the best, the most characteristic which each contributing race and people has to offer." Dewey, "Principle of Nationality," 288–89; Westbrook, *JD*, 212–14. William James's writings on philosophical pluralism were an important source for the conceptions of cultural pluralism that Horace Kallen and Dewey came to embrace during World War I. Sollors, "CPP," 250–79.

25. Dewey echoed both Peirce and James in describing pragmatism as a philosophy based upon "consequent" phenomena. See Dewey, *PC*, 24. Although not published in book form until 1931, Dewey's assessment of pragmatism is based on an essay that he published in the early 1920s. See Dewey, "DPA," 411–30. For a discussion of Dewey's postwar embrace of William James, see Lloyd, *LO*, 298–99. For Dewey, the situation of America's immigrants helped to stitch the forward-looking imperatives of pragmatism into history. See Dewey, "AL," 684–88.

26. Williams's much-repeated remark about a poetic idiom based on "the speech of Polish mothers" is quoted in Kenner, *PE*, 127–28, 401–2. By misquoting Williams, Kenner has lent his own stamp to one of the best-known axioms of modern American poetry. In his autobiography Williams wrote: "At City College, New York, at a luncheon speaking engagement, I was defending our right as Americans to our own language, saying that English . . . does not primarily concern us. 'But this language of yours,' said one of the instructors, himself an obvious Britisher, 'where does it come from?' 'From the mouths of Polish mothers,' I replied." *AWCW*, 311. Williams's interest in immigrant idioms dates back to the 1920s. In *In the American Grain* (1925), Williams wrote: "A while ago, just here, I heard a Polish woman saying to her daughter: 'You bust your coat with your fifty sweaters.'" For Williams, this comment was marked by an "immediacy," a "sense of design," and "a delicious sincerity." It was not part of "a scheme, nor a system of procedure," but was a "careless truth" spoken "straight out of the ground." *IAG*, 206. Williams's remark about a poetry christened with "champagne and semen" is quoted in Mariani, *NWN*, 229.

27. John Dewey to Horace Kallen, 31 March 1915, Horace M. Kallen Papers, American Jewish Archives, Hebrew Union College, Cincinnati. Dewey's letter to Kallen on the subject of "cultural pluralism" is quoted and discussed in Westbrook, *JD*, 213–14.

28. Richard Rorty argues that Dewey's efforts to restore metaphysics to local social conditions and uses ultimately rested upon their own universalizing or naturalizing foundations. Rorty, *CP*, 73–74. Dewey's nationalistic leanings and his related attempts to affiliate pragmatism with modern physics, are discussed in more detail later in this chapter.

29. Stoddard's remark is quoted and discussed in Michaels, "AM," 40.

30. In his essay on the origins of cultural pluralism, Sollors discusses the importance of this early-twentieth-century notion to late-twentieth-century dis-

cussions of the American literary canon. "CPP," 250–58. Sollors notes that in the 1970s and 1980s discussions of canonical reform were driven by appeals to a multiethnic American cultural "mosaic"; but he does not trace the historical genesis of this enduring American metaphor (257). In William James's writings, the metaphor of a "mosaic philosophy" marked an open historical convergence of philosophical pluralism and anarchist thought. James, "WPE," 1180–81; James, *ML*, 310–11. James's writings and lectures of 1904–8 were laced with implicit and explicit references to the "anarchistic" nature of his new philosophy; and Horace Kallen acknowledged that it was this phase of James's thought that prompted his later "cultural pluralist" conception of an American "mosaic of peoples." Kallen, *CD*, 58.

31. Sollors notes that though Kallen did not use the term *cultural pluralism* in print until 1924, he had begun to use it in conversation long before. "CPP," 263. James spoke of his desire to mount a pluralistic assault on the notion of an "Absolute" in a letter written in 1901. See James to Karl Stumpf, 6 August 1901, James Papers. See also Coon, "CA," 271. James's vaguely militant account of his philosophical objectives soon gave way, in his 1906–7 lectures on pragmatism, to an open association of philosophical with anarchist critiques of foundations. James, *P*, 498–500, 600.

32. James was an appreciative reader of a variety of anarchists including Max Stirner, but his association of "*Anarchy* in the good sense" with the "small systems" of a decentralized society testifies to the influence of a more socially inclined anarchist tradition rooted in the writings of Pierre Proudhon. See Scott, *UC*, 507. See also Coon, "CA," 50–51. In lecture notes made during 1903–4, James likened "pluralism" to something that he called "*graft*-theory," which he in turn likened to "*Anarchy* in the good sense." *ML*, 310–11. In these notes, and in essays on pluralism published during that same period, James suggested that the pluralistic "universe" bore the structure of a grafted tree, or a mosaic. "WPE," 1180–81. James himself did not bother to tease out the racial implications of the metaphysical speculations that he identified with anarchism, but his writings on pluralism provided conceptual models that enabled later American intellectuals to supplant the overarching syntax of racial hierarchy with the bartered material of immediate "difference."

33. As an anarchist who resisted the idea of democratic and even socialistic forms of governance from above, Proudhon believed that all mechanistic "political institutions" would be dissolved through the emergence of the more relation-based "economic organism." *GI*, 240–43.

34. James's graft and mosaic served as apt metaphors for an "individual's" pluralistic "experience" of the world because they foregrounded the immediacy of the conjunctions—the *and*s and the *if*s—between moments isolated within the stream, or continuum, of that person's consciousness. In foregrounding these conjunctions, both models diminished the importance of the antecedent material that joins together the "tissue" that composes them. In the graft, James

found an entity that muted the identitarian significance of its antecedent parent stock; in the mosaic he found one that neutralized the extrinsic "bedding" that holds its constituent pieces in place. Although James remained vaguely committed to democratic processes, his celebration of "small systems" suggests that he appreciated the antistatist implications of his metaphors for pluralism. James, *ML*, 311.

35. According to Proudhon, the innately ethical "economic organism" would displace all "political" impediments to free association. Once the governmentally enforced institutions of rent, interest, and property were removed, the will of the individual "citizen" would simply become "equal" to the will of the society. Proudhon, *GI*, 268–69. In the late nineteenth century, the American anarchist Benjamin Tucker helped to spread Proudhon's gospel by suggesting that in a "headless" anarchist society, the "individual" was not only continuous with, but also integral to, the very "voluntary association[s]" that determined the true pathways of exchange. Tucker, *IB*, 9. Coupled with the French anarchist's identification of "interest" as an impediment to an ethical society, Proudhon's appeal to immediacy between the individual and the ideal state would eventually lead the fascist poet Ezra Pound to praise him as a champion of ethical theories of currency. *SP*, 440. Dorothy Ross provides a thorough historical account of the idea that America "occupies an exceptional place in history" because of its "republican government and economic opportunity." *SS*, xiv. For discussions of Dewey's belief that " 'America is too new to afford a foundation for an a priori philosophy,' " see Lloyd, *LO*, 297–99; Ross, *SS*, 162–71.

36. Michaels and Sollors both caution that the liberals who formulated "cultural pluralism" were prone to racist attitudes themselves. Michaels, *OA*, 64–65; Sollors, "CPP," 269–73.

37. For Michaels, America's historical pluralist moment "represent[ed] a theoretical intensification rather than a diminution of racism." *OA*, 65. With its "denial of hierarchy," cultural pluralism "made possible the escape from the common scale and the emergence of an unmeasurable and hence incomparable racial essence" (66). Michaels's claim that pluralism is more "essentially" racist than scientific racialism is a contemporary provocation that has generated its own set of responses; but his account of the emergence of "culture" in the 1920s as a kind of "immediate" bedding, one that displaced the hierarchical "syntax" of race, is an important one for understanding the anarchist and pragmatist genesis of modern literature and culture.

38. Calvin Coolidge, *America's Need for Education* (Boston, 1925), 56. Coolidge's comment is quoted and discussed in Michaels, *OA*, 3.

39. Williams declares Poe to have been a uniquely "American" writer. *IAG*, 226. He discusses Poe as an "original" writer who lets "composition *show*" and is therefore "abstract" (229–30). Michaels quotes and discusses these passages in *OA*, 83.

40. Joseph Riddel spoke to a generation of poststructuralist readers of Wil-

liams by suggesting that in Williams's poetry "the local" is not to be found in history but rather in the "centerless center" of language. *Inverted Bell*, 13.

41. Among the most innovative of Williams's recent readers, Michaels and Lisa Steinman both have trouble accounting for the contradictory impulses that drive Williams's early aesthetics. In portraying Williams as a writer committed to the materiality of his medium, Michaels says little of the clarity that distinguishes much of Williams's early writing. Steinman does take notice of the representational tension in Williams's early writing; and she describes it as an outgrowth of his uncritical embrace of two distinct aspects of science in modern America. In his imagist emphasis on a poetic fidelity to the object, Steinman writes, Williams was allied to technological sciences, embracing the skyscraper aesthetic that seemed to place American design and building at the forefront of an international modernism. At the same time, Williams identified his art with the work of more process-based theoreticians such as modern physicists. This latter identification coincided with the rise of Einstein's popularity in America, a phenomenon that "seemed to offer proof [to Williams] that Americans could admire and find a place for creative intelligence, the results of which were not measured commercially." Steinman, *MA*, 101. As Steinman notes: "Most writers did not confront the tensions implicit in their descriptions of poems as alternately objects and process; many were probably not aware that they generally looked to technology for their vocabulary and analogies when describing poems as objects and to the new physics when describing poems as actions or processes" (57). She suggests that it was not until the 1930s and 1940s, after Williams had begun to gradually absorb the theories of Einstein and of Alfred North Whitehead, that the "mature" poet came to see that there was "no discrepancy between a celebration of process and [a more empirical] attention to structure" (108–9). (Whitehead was the philosopher and popularizer for whom reality was constructed as a flow of events.)

Steinman is wise to abjure an overly hasty reconciliation of the divided sympathies that seem to characterize Williams's earlier writings. But the anarchist and pragmatist contexts of Williams's early poetry are themselves rife with conceptual contradictions. As James's pluralist metaphors illustrate, anarchism and pragmatism seek to merge substance with process and the one with the many. In light of these appeals, the sharp "contradictions" that characterize Williams's early aesthetics may constitute something other than divided sympathies.

42. See Marianne Moore, "Things Others Never Notice," *Poetry* 44 (1934): 104.

43. Wallace Stevens, "William Carlos Williams," in *William Carlos Williams: A Collection of Critical Essays*, ed. J. Hillis Miller (Englewood Cliffs, N.J.: Prentice-Hall, 1966), 65.

44. William Carlos Williams, *Contact* 3 (spring 1921): 15, ed. Williams and McAlmon. Williams's remark alluded to Marcel Duchamp's cagey assessment in

1917 of the condition of the arts in America: "The only works of art America has given are her plumbing and her bridges." Duchamp was sincere in his enjoyment of the fruits of American design and engineering, but his words were intended to sting. Here, Duchamp was speaking to the organizing committee of the New York Independents Exhibition. This ostensibly progressive committee had recently barred the iconoclastic expatriate from exhibiting one of his recent pieces, a porcelain urinal signed "R. Mutt." See Marcel Duchamp, "The Richard Mutt Case," *Blind Man* 2 (May 1917): 5. See also Steinman, *MA,* 79.

45. For many contemporary readers, such a processual conception of identity will seem politically evasive. It undermines the gender- or race- or class-based alliances that seem necessary to solidarity and coalitional action. From a historical Marxist standpoint, or from the standpoint of a modern African American intellectual like W. E. B. Du Bois, who wrote of "the problem of the Twentieth Century" as not a philosophical or aesthetic matter but rather as the tangible historical problem of "the color-line," Williams's notions of idiom and identity appear haughty and remote. Du Bois, *SBF,* 359. By placing Williams and other European American modern writers in the context of African American intellectual history, a growing number of academic critics have come to recognize that Williams's conception of the American idiom was racially circumscribed, as were the pragmatist appeals to American pluralism that spurred Williams to try to imagine a uniquely American form of poetic measure.

46. Proudhon believed that antecedent political structures would be overthrown by an "economic organism" that was structured according to the dictates of "*Reciprocity.*" This "new principle" called for "*direct communication between producers and consumers*" as a revolutionary force that would "dissolve, submerge, and cause to disappear the political or governmental system in the economic system, by reducing, simplifying, decentralizing and suppressing, one after another, all the wheels of this great machine, which is called the Government or the State." Proudhon, *GI,* 90–91, 173.

47. As a philosopher who was committed to a variety of liberal reform programs, Dewey was more concerned than James was to ground "knowledge" in ongoing social processes. For this reason he was less willing than his individualistic predecessor to embrace anarchism as a viable political strategy. In lectures delivered at the University of Michigan in early 1893, for example, Dewey distanced himself from the anarchistic appeals for immediacy that informed much of the radical political and economic thought of the "Gilded Age": "The falsity of anarchy," he claimed, "is in not recognizing what a complex and continual interaction it requires to bring the individual to a consciousness of the whole and of his identity or interest with it." "Dewey Political Philosophy Lectures." See also Ross, *SS,* 168. By Dorothy Ross's reading, Dewey rejected the anarchist call for the immediate reconstruction of a golden-age village economy in favor of a more sophisticated conception of an "ongoing democratic experience," one that

allowed for the necessity of gradual progress and political mediation (168). In the process, however, he clung to a Hegelian belief that such a "democratic experience" would "turn individual self-interest into the interest of the whole" (169). Ross suggests that for Dewey this appeal to immediacy between the one and the many rested on a "millennial vision of American history" (166). According to this "exceptionalist" vision of America's unique destiny, the needs of the individual would ultimately be reconciled with those of the republic.

Despite his strong disavowal of anarchist appeals to immediacy, and despite his reservations regarding both James's and Kallen's brands of "pluralism," Dewey did maintain a tentative affinity for certain anarchist premises, and he did draw from James's "mosaic" critique of unifying causes and antecedents. See Dewey, *Experience and Nature*, 261–62. These affinities led to some inconsistencies in Dewey's thought. He displayed his sympathy for anarchist models of decentralization in his youthful attraction to syndicalism and in his later "liberal" vision of "a cooperatively shared control of industry," a vision that would foster "the recognition of final use or consumption as the criterion of valuation, decision and direction." Dewey, *ION*, 105. It was a commitment to a larger "modernist" interest in decentralized and relation-bound models, then, that encouraged Dewey to draw from James's pluralist models; this commitment ultimately encouraged Williams to draw from Dewey in adapting anarchistically driven aesthetics of immediacy to more "progressive" American interests.

48. William Carlos Williams, *Contact* 1 (December 1920): 1, ed. Williams and McAlmon.

49. Filtered as they were through Dewey's assault on overly Anglicized standards of Americanness, Proudhonian anarchist tenets supported the revulsion toward bookish literary culture that Williams expressed in his early *Contact* manifestos. Later in his career Williams came to restore the pragmatist tenets that supported his idea of an indigenous American poetry to the very anarchistic economic premises with which William James had initially allied them. Williams embraced Silvio Gesell's idea of a freely circulating monetary currency in the late 1940s. Weaver, *AB*, 111–12; Williams, *AWCW*, 340. Here, he followed Pound in absorbing Proudhonian conceptions of an innately ethical "economic organism" in the form of economic theory. Pound, *SP*, 440. It was during the 1940s, moreover, that Williams came to speak out against poetry that was fashioned out of overly literary "gold." Williams, *W*, 9. In its place, he called for an "intrinsically" American poetry made from a more useful material. Williams referred to this material as the "Babbitt metal" of American "speech" (9, 8). In formulating his conception of the American poem as a "machine made of words" (8), then, Williams folded Dewey's complaint against the measure of "Anglosaxondom" back into the more explicitly economic cast of the anarchist thought with which it had been circuitously allied. He restored William James's vaguely "anarchistic" complaint against the idea of " 'the' mother-tongue" to Proudhon's sharper

complaint against the gold standard as the "last idol of the Absolute." (Proudhon's comment about the gold standard is quoted in Tucker, *IB*, 260.)

50. Williams, *Contact* 1 (December 1920): 1, ed. Williams and McAlmon.

51. James's and Williams's and Dewey's conceptions of "Americanness" are sadly ignorant of Du Bois's conception of the "color-line." And although this ignorance pervades and gravely weakens their public positions, their political stances nevertheless do have some redeeming qualities. Through Dewey's writings, the divide between "static" and "mobile" varieties of identity, as well as calcified and vibrant forms of measure, was linked to a particular historical body of Americans. And putting aside the very important question of whether America's various immigrant populations would have wanted the sort of mass advocacy granted to them by Dewey and Williams, the very act of such advocacy constituted a bold and constructive political stance during what was by all measures a particularly reactionary moment in American history.

52. William Carlos Williams, *Contact* 2 (January 1921): n.p.

53. William Carlos Williams, *Selected Letters*, ed. John C. Thirlwall (New York: New Directions, 1957), 49.

54. In devising his conception of a poetic measure that was wedded to the American idiom, Williams drew from Dewey's essay particularly and from pragmatist conceptions of a "pluralistic universe" more generally. Nevertheless, the poet was not an adherent of "pragmatism" per se. In his autobiography, Williams recalled his "chance" "discovery" of Dewey's axiom "the locality is the only universal" as a turning point in his poetic development. *AWCW*, 391. But Dewey's axiom was important to Williams because it had a local, rather than a universal, significance. Although he was appreciative of Dewey's ideas, Williams was skeptical of Dewey as an academic figure. For example, in *The Embodiment of Knowledge*, a collection of unpublished writings from the late 1920s, Williams allied himself with Dewey's calls for the reform of American schools. Like Dewey, he criticized those educational methods that divorced knowledge from actual experience. But he distinguished his own brand of reform from Dewey's. Faulting Dewey for seeking to base his reforms on such academic disciplines as psychology, sociology, and philosophy, Williams suggested that the philosopher "might do worse" than to follow in the poet's own footsteps. Meaningful correctives, Williams intimated, would somehow emanate from the less systematized and hence more "partial and tentative" material of poetry. Echoing a then popular trope that fashioned the modern physicist as a new kind of poet, Williams went on to cite Einstein as an example of an academic who had restored "incompleteness," and hence a living measure of contingency, to an otherwise insular discipline. Of Dewey's educational philosophy, Williams concluded, "It is the poetic conception (see Einstein's reported statement—among others) of the universe that is the correct one." *EK*, 7.

55. Stephen Cushman, *William Carlos Williams and the Meanings of Measure*

(New Haven, Conn.: Yale University Press, 1985), 19. See also Hollander, *VR,* 110–11.

56. Cushman, *Williams and the Meanings of Measure,* 21–22.

57. Hollander's definition of enjambment can be found in "The Metrical Emblem," *Essays on the Language of Literature,* ed. Seymour Chatman and Samuel R. Levin (Boston: Houghton Mifflin, 1967), 119. Cushman discusses Hollander's definition in *Williams and the Meanings of Measure,* 31.

58. See Moore, "Things Others Never Notice," 103. Kenner's colorful description of Williams's flat Jersey speech can be found in "A Note on *The Great American Novel,*" in Miller, *Williams Critical Essays,* 91.

59. In suggesting that static varieties of knowledge are encased within "an immune monastic impeccability," Dewey was partaking of a widespread metaphor that, for many modern intellectuals, was directed against the sterility of fixed standards and traditions. In the spirit of Nietzsche and the individualist anarchist Max Stirner, the British editor Dora Marsden had associated disease with static Victorian conceptions of woman and womanliness. And on the American side, William James spoke of philosophy itself in terms of disease. Of his own "unholy" desire to set down "the Universe's hash in one more book" before he died, James wrote: "I am convinced that the desire to formulate truths is a virulent disease." James's use of the disease metaphor is double-edged. Through it he jabs self-deprecatingly at his own ambitions as a philosopher: "Childish idiot—as if formulas about the Universe could unruffle its majesty, and as if the common-sense world and its duties were not eternally the really real!" Henry James, *LWJ,* 2:199. At the same time, however, James uses the metaphor of infection to praise the vibrant fertility of his work. In portraying himself as a seasoned seeker who has yet to set down the "truths" that he seeks to "formulate," James asks his reader to distinguish between the vibrant act of formulating truths, which is healthful and American, and the more deathly act of possessing static formulas, which is sickly and European. Dewey would make a similar distinction in 1916, writing that "the situation in which thinking occurs is always a doubtful one" and that "*Acquiring* is always secondary, and instrumental to the act of *inquiring.*" See Dewey's *Democracy and Education: An Introduction to the Philosophy of Education* (1916; reprint, New York: Macmillan, 1920), 173. See also Steinman, *MA,* 89–90. Through this distinction between inquiry and acquisition, James, like Dewey and Williams, views "infection" as a sign of vitality rather than morbidity.

60. Dewey is quoting William James from his 1907 book, *Pragmatism:* "The import of the difference between pragmatism and rationalism," wrote James, "is now in sight throughout its whole extent. The essential contrast is that *for rationalism reality is ready-made and complete from all eternity, while for pragmatism it is still in the making, and awaits part of its complexion from the future.* On the one side the universe is absolutely secure, on the other it is still pursuing its

adventures." James, *P*, 599. James's distinction between a ready-made world and a universe that was "still in the making" came to circulate widely among early-twentieth-century American intellectuals. In a 1928 letter to Langston Hughes, Zora Neale Hurston used James's phrase to describe the improvisatory nature of Negro folk culture. Hurston to Hughes, 12 April 1928, Hughes Collection.

61. See West, *AEP*, 80. See also Zinn, *PH*, 373.

62. Bertrand Russell, *A History of Western Philosophy* (New York: Simon and Schuster, 1945), 832.

63. As Lisa Steinman notes, modern physicists were not as united in their theories as they were thought to have been by American poets and by the American public at large. Einstein, for example, came to criticize the "unnaturalness" of quantum mechanics and Heisenberg's uncertainty principle. Williams, like most nonphysicists, was oblivious to many of the finer points of the emerging field in part because he absorbed the ideas of modern physicists indirectly. His initial exposure to Einstein probably came from the newspapers, which had begun to publicize the theory of relativity in 1919–20. By 1921 the press was describing Einstein as a "Poet in Science." Steinman, *MA*, 103. Steinman suggests that "Williams's early images of Einstein and of motion draw mostly on the common misconceptions about the relationship between Einsteinian physics and Bergsonian philosophy" (100). Later on, in the 1920s, he turned to "popularizers" including Bertrand Russell, Alfred North Whitehead, and Charles Steinmetz (66–67, 100). See also Weaver, *AB*, 47–52, 65–66.

64. Williams quoted Dewey in William Carlos Williams, *Contact* 2 (January 1921), n.p., ed. Williams and McAlmon. The particular phrase that he quoted is from Dewey, "AL," 687. Williams memorialized his "discovery" of Dewey's phrase in letters written in the 1930s and then again in his autobiography. *AWCW*, 391.

65. Williams delivered a shorthand account of Einstein's displacement of the nominalistic stasis of imagism, writing in 1948 that "imagism was not structural: that was the reason for its disappearance." *SE*, 283. In this retrospective assessment, the poet explicitly linked relativity theory to his own echo of Pound's retrospective criticism of imagism. In *The ABC of Reading*, Pound had described "the defect of earlier imagist propaganda" as a matter of reference. Imagism was weakened by its attention to only "the STATIONARY image." Pound, *ABCR*, 52. In "The Poem as a Field of Action" (1948), however, Williams suggested that Einstein had dictated an altogether new structure for poetry, one that had dispensed with such static imagist premises as its archaic appeal to "free verse." Lisa Steinman discusses Williams's relation of modern physics to imagist poetics. Steinman, *MA*, 69.

66. Williams later elaborated this connection between poetry, relativity, and astronomy in a passage from *Paterson* that speaks to Ezra Pound's Canto 45. In his well-known incantation against monetary interest, Pound blamed usury for

the degradation of the arts and crafts. "With usura," Pound intoned, the Renaissance painter's "line grows thick." In place of usury, Williams blamed a lack of "invention," or scientific vision, for the ossification of poetry. Without "a new mind" by which

> the stars are new measured, according
> to their relative positions, the
> [poetic] line will not change . . .
>
> .   .   .   .
>
> [but the old line will] go on
> repeating itself with recurring
> deadliness[.]
> (Williams, *P*, 50)

Elsewhere in *Paterson*, however, Williams followed Pound in associating the corrosion of language and poetry with the hoarding of money (73, 273).

67. In her richly contextualized reading of Williams's encomium to Einstein, Lisa Steinman writes that "the poem's style reinforces our sense of motion and fluidity." Steinman, *MA*, 103. In making this assessment, Steinman does not distinguish between this rather haltingly apportioned free-verse poem and the more sinuous stanzas that characterize the better poems, such as "Queen-Anne's-Lace," that Williams wrote during the years immediately preceding his formal breakthrough in *Spring and All* (103). In its formulaic lineation, and in its intermittent bursts of bombast and levity, "St. Francis Einstein of the Daffodils" does have a breezy, tossed off quality, but it is not one that can be characterized as "fluid." And Williams likely knew that this was not one of his better efforts. Steinman notes that in the issue of *Contact* in which the poem first appeared, Williams decided to mockingly present the poem as a "sample" for commercial consumption, which readers could purchase for a minimum price of fifty dollars; and she suggests that he may have done so to express his "uneasiness with Einstein's popularity." But Williams may also have been uncomfortable with the quality of his tribute to Einstein.

68. By Steinman's reading, the poem's presentation as a commodity for sale to the public expresses an "irony" regarding the popular reception of Einstein. Moreover, Einstein's arrival "at the time in fashion" and his efforts to procure "freedom/for the daffodils" evince a flippant tone that seems pitched at the sudden popular status bestowed upon the scientist by the press. Steinman, *MA*, 103–4. Nevertheless, the accumulation in the poem of images pertaining to immigration and Zionism indicate that Williams was also aware of Einstein as a political figure and that as an outspoken Zionist, Einstein had been welcomed in New York not only by fawning publicists but also by a constituency that faced more pressing issues than those dictated by the "fashion" of commerce. Restored to the context of the outspoken Zionist's first visit to America, Williams's con-

cern for the serious political overtones of Einstein's arrival keep pace with his "ironic" condemnation of Einstein's celebrity status.

69. Einstein's comments are reprinted in *Ideas and Opinions. IO,* 5. Dewey's discussion of American isolationism can be found in "Our National Dilemma," *New Republic* (24 March 1920): 118.

70. William Carlos Williams, *Contact* 5 (June 1923): n.p.

Chapter Five. Marianne Moore and Eugenics

1. Some of the tools used to gauge the mental soundness of immigrants at Ellis Island can be seen in an archival photo in Alan M. Kraut, *The Huddled Masses: The Immigrant in American Society, 1880–1921* (Arlington Heights, Ill.: Harlan Davidson, Inc., 1982), n.p.

2. Moore discussed her own poems-in-process, likening words on the page to clustering chromosomes, in an interview with Donald Hall published in "The Art of Poetry: Marianne Moore," in *Writers at Work: The Paris Review Interviews,* 2d ser., reprinted in Charles Tomlinson, ed., *Marianne Moore: A Collection of Critical Essays* (Englewood Cliffs, N.J.: Prentice-Hall, 1969), 34.

3. Quoted in Willis, *VV,* 16.

4. T. S. Eliot, "Marianne Moore," *Dial* 75, no. 12 (December 1923): 594–97; reprinted in Tomlinson, *Marianne Moore,* 48–49.

5. Willis discusses the importance of seventeenth-century English prose stylists for the young poet. *VV,* 6. Marie Borroff reads Moore's syntax and prosody against the "promotional prose" of modern feature articles and magazine advertisements in *Language and the Poet: Verbal Artistry in Frost, Stevens, and Moore* (Chicago: University of Chicago Press, 1979), 80. After T. S. Eliot's *Dial* review, William Carlos Williams praised Moore for her dynamic rendering of judiciously selected materials in a review of his own. Williams, "MM," 54. Eliot's and Williams's appraisals of Moore's early poetry are discussed in Molesworth, *LL,* 204–5, 206–7.

6. Of the many contemporary critics who read Moore's poetry through post-structuralist theoretical frameworks, Cristanne Miller does the best justice to Moore's historical social and political engagements. Miller uses feminist theory to facilitate a nuanced recovery of Moore's second-wave, "communitarian" feminist milieu; and she uses postcolonialist and African American literary theory to place Moore in a more indirect dialogue with historical discussions of race and identity. See Cristanne Miller, *Marianne Moore: Questions of Authority* (Cambridge, Mass.: Harvard University Press, 1995), 128–66. See also Cristanne Miller, "Marianne Moore's Black Maternal Hero: A Study in Characterization," *American Literary History* 1, no. 4 (1989): 786–815.

7. Cofer did not use the quoted phrase, but he echoed its humanistic sentiments throughout his paper on immigrant screening. I have borrowed this

memorable phrase from the modern assimilationist Mary Antin. *They Who Knock,* 54–55.

8. For an account of the demographic impact of immigrants and immigrant families on America's largest cities during the early twentieth century, see John D. Buenker and Edward R. Kantowicz, *Historical Dictionary of the Progressive Era, 1890–1920* (Westport, N.Y.: Greenwood Press, 1988), 145.

9. See Daniel J. Kevles, *In the Name of Eugenics: Genetics and the Uses of Human Heredity* (Berkeley: University of California Press, 1985), 80–84; see also Higham, *PAN,* 156; and Cravens, *TE,* 83–84, 227–32.

10. See also Maldwyn Allen Jones, *American Immigration* (1960; 2d ed., Chicago: University of Chicago Press, 1992), 236–37.

11. Van Wyck Brooks described the arts in America as "weak and sickly" in "The Literary Life," in *Civilization in the United States,* ed. Harold E. Stearns (New York: Harcourt Brace & Co., 1922), 182; Brooks identified commercialism and immigration as impediments to American artistic development in "The Splinter of Ice," *Seven Arts* (January 1917): 273.

12. See Randolph Bourne, "The Puritan's Will to Power," *Seven Arts* (April 1917): 631–32.

13. See Dewey, "AL," 684–88. Marsden Hartley advocated "a freshly evolved" localism in modern American art in *Adventures in the Arts,* 60. T. S. Eliot denigrated the Ku Klux Klan as a popular "middle class" American phenomenon in his 1923 *Dial* essay "Marianne Moore," 50. This estimate of Ku Klux Klan membership in the early twenties appears in Jones, *American Immigration,* 236. Other historians have suggested that up to five million Americans belonged to the Klan during this period.

14. Williams, *SE,* 28; Williams, *I,* 151; Williams, *IAG,* 33–34.

15. Discussions of metonymy in Moore's writing can also be found in Bonnie Costello, *Marianne Moore: Imaginary Possessions* (Cambridge, Mass.: Harvard University Press, 1981), 135. Linda Leavell relates Moore's metonymic tendencies to forms and practices in the modern visual arts, including the "straight photography" of Alfred Stieglitz and Paul Strand. *VA.*

16. See also Darwin, *VAP,* 1:318, 10, 102. Moore praised Darwin's scientific writings for their directness and their "pressure of business" in a 1927 *Dial* column reprinted in Willis, *CPMM,* 178.

17. John Dewey, *Essays in Experimental Logic* (Chicago: University of Chicago Press, 1916), 304; quoted in Moore, 1250/2.

18. De Laguna's particular interest in philosophy and evolutionary theory is documented in de Laguna and de Laguna, *Dogmatism and Evolution,* 117–34.

19. Richard Poirier discusses the Emersonian roots of James's writings on language in *Poetry and Pragmatism,* 122, 134–37.

20. Linda Leavell provides a thorough discussion of Moore's use of collage and other visual arts techniques in *VA.*

21. See Donald Davie, *Articulate Energy: An Inquiry into the Syntax of English*

Poetry (1955; reprint, St. Claire Shores, Mich.: Scholarly Press, Inc., 1971), 147–60. See also Dijkstra, *CSW*, 64–65. See also Elizabeth Arnold, "Mina Loy and the Avant-Garde," Ph.D. diss., University of Chicago, 1990, 93–109.

22. Yvor Winters used this metaphor to describe the density of Loy's verse in "Mina Loy," *Dial* 80, no. 6 (1926): 496.

23. De Laguna and de Laguna, *Dogmatism and Evolution*, 117–34.

24. Hamilton Cravens discusses the importance of cytological study to theories of natural selection during the first decade of the twentieth century. *TE*, 39–45.

25. See Marianne Moore, Biology Lecture Notes (1908), notebook 1251/24 (VII 05 04), Rosenbach Archive, Rosenbach Library and Museum, Philadelphia. For an account of Darwin's development of a "blending" theory of heredity, see Eiseley, *DC*, 217.

26. See Gregor Mendel, *Experiments in Plant Hybridization* (1965; reprint, Cambridge, Mass.: Harvard University Press, 1973), 3.

27. Charles Davenport, "Animal Morphology in its Relation to Other Sciences," *Science*, n.s., 20 (1904): 698; quoted in Cravens, *TE*, 15.

28. Ward and Hall's call for immigration restriction is quoted in Jones, *American Immigration*, 222.

29. For a thorough listing and discussion of Burbank's hybrids, see Dreyer, *GTG*, 102. An extensive index of the compound words that appear in Moore's poems can be found in *A Concordance to the Poems of Marianne Moore*, ed. Gary Lane (New York: Haskell House, 1972), 459–94.

30. Haller identifies Burbank's unique neo-Lamarckian endorsement of eugenics. *HA*, 62–63. Dreyer writes that Burbank regarded *Variation* as Darwin's truest and most useful work. *GTG*, 33. See also Burbank, *THP*, 82, 66, 40.

31. Moore quoted in *LL*, 32.

32. Marianne Moore, Reading Diary 1924–1930, notebook 1250/5 (VII 02 01), Rosenbach Archive.

33. See also Troy Duster, *Backdoor to Eugenics* (New York: Routledge, 1990), 18.

34. Costello, *Marianne Moore*, 199–200.

35. Alphonse de Candolle, *Origin of Cultivated Plants* (New York: D. Appleton & Co., 1892), 226–27.

36. See Laurence Stapleton, *Marianne Moore: The Poet's Advance* (Princeton, N.J.: Princeton University Press, 1978), 80.

37. See de Candolle, *Origin of Cultivated Plants*, 222–25.

38. See Stapleton, *Marianne Moore*, 80.

Chapter Six. Zora Neale Hurston and "The Races of Europe"

1. Reviewing *Their Eyes Were Watching God* in 1938, Alain Locke branded Hurston's novel a species of "folklore fiction." Locke praised Hurston's "gift for poetic phrase, for rare dialect, and folk humor," but he complained that these

very qualities kept Hurston "flashing on the surface of her community and her characters and from diving down deep either to the inner psychology of characterization or to sharp analysis of the social background." Alain Locke, "Jingo, Counter-Jingo, and Us," *Opportunity* 16 (January 1938): 10.

2. Hurston discussed the African American folk practice of "playing the dozens" in her autobiography, *Dust Tracks on a Road:* "The bookless may have difficulty in reading a paragraph in a newspaper, but when they get down to 'playing the dozens' they have no equal in America, and, I'd risk a sizeable bet, in the whole world. Starting off in [the] first by calling you a seven-sided son-of-a-bitch, and pausing to name the sides, they proceed to 'specify' until the tip-top branch of your family tree has been 'given a reading.' " *DT*, 720. See also Gates, "ST," 182.

3. Stefan Kühl, *The Nazi Connection: Eugenics, American Racism, and German National Socialism* (New York: Oxford University Press, 1994), 42–44.

4. See, for example, Anne Douglas, *Terrible Honesty: Mongrel Manhattan in the 1920s* (New York: Farrar, Straus, & Giroux, 1995). In *Our America* Walter Michaels differs from Douglas in viewing "culture" as committed to the very racist tenets that it sought to supplant. Michaels, *OA*. In *Color & Culture* Ross Posnock charts a theoretically and historically informed middle course between Douglas's and Michaels's positions with respect to "culture." Posnock, *CC*.

5. Quoting William James's 1907 book, *Pragmatism,* John Dewey described pragmatism as a philosophy attuned to the contingent movements of a "still plastic" "universe," one that was "still," in "[William] James' words," " 'in the making,' 'in the process of becoming.' " Dewey, *PC*, 25. See also James, *P*, 599. For a thorough discussion of the historical interchanges between pragmatist philosophers and cultural anthropologists, see Hutchinson, *HR*, 62–93.

6. As early as 1934, for example, Franz Boas had argued that the rise of fascism in Germany was following the deterministic contours of "a false philosophy of race." See his "Aryans and Non-Aryans," *American Mercury* 32, no. 125 (May 1934): 221. See also Hill, *SR*, 5.

7. *The Races of Europe* was the title of an 1899 anti-immigration tract by an American economist named William Ripley. Ripley's book was popular among readers who had begun to distinguish the "new immigration" from eastern and southern European countries from the "old immigration" from northern Europe. Ripley argued that European "Alpines" and "Mediterraneans" were biologically inferior to their northern neighbors. By emigrating to America, these inferior subspecies were weakening the nation's "Nordic" genetic legacy. See Stocking, *RCE*, 58–62. See also Higham, *PAN*, 154.

8. In his study of the historical development of cultural anthropology, George Stocking writes that although Boas himself was not "a relativist in a consistent sense," the school of anthropology that he founded was nonetheless bound to a pervasive "cultural relativism," defined by its resistance to the idea of a "single

standard of cultural evaluation." *RCE*, 228. Walter Michaels labels Boas "a universalist," noting that Boas himself had claimed in *Anthropology and Modern Life* to seek the " 'psychological and social data [that would be] valid for all mankind' and 'basal for all culture.' " Michaels, *OA*, 173 n. 199; Boas, *AML*, 207.

9. Although he disagreed with the evolutionist on the subject of racial hierarchy, Boas believed that "Darwin's views of the instability of species" were central to "anthropology" as a discipline with "distinct beginnings" in the life sciences. *RLC*, 243. In *Anthropology and Modern Life*, Boas evinced a pragmatist grasp of the broader implications of the Darwinian conception of "the instability of species": "Even a hasty consideration of the history of man shows that accidents . . . are the rule in every society." *AML*, 210–11. The anthropologist echoed here not only William James's suggestion that history hinged on "internal molecular accidents" (*WB*, 223) but also John Dewey's claim in *Essays in Experimental Logic* that "the barest glance at human history shows that mistakes have been the rule" (425). As a philosopher, Alain Locke was steeped in the writings of pragmatists including William James, Josiah Royce, John Dewey, and George Santayana; he too appears to have recognized the significance of Darwin's notion of "the instability of species" to Boas's conception of "culture." In a lecture typescript, "Race Contacts and Inter-Racial Relations," Locke wrote: "We know how relentlessly Professor Boas has hunted down the subtle assumptions of biological and psychological group capacities, reducing them to factors of environmental control and indeterminate variability." Alain Locke, "Race Contacts and Inter-Racial Relations," n.d., lecture typescript, box 164-125, folder 5, Alain Locke Papers, Moorland-Spingarn Research Center, Howard University. For a well-documented account of the reciprocal exchanges between modern African American intellectuals, pragmatists, and advocates of "culture" and "cultural pluralism," see Hutchinson, *HR*, 78–93.

10. In *The Souls of Black Folk*, W. E. B. Du Bois tried to ground American philosophy in history by declaring "the problem of the Twentieth Century [to be] the problem of the color-line." *SBF*, 359. Hurston was at times less than entranced by Du Bois's rather abstract intellectual efforts. In a 1931 letter to her patroness, Charlotte Mason, she included Du Bois among those African American " 'leaders' " who fought "inky battles" on behalf of "kappa key" "intellectuals" while neglecting to seek "benefits for the humble." "Oh so little to improve the lot of the man in the street," she lamented. "Nobody is going to waste time and golden syllables telling the bottom black what to do to help himself." Hurston to Mason, New York City, 10 October 1931, box 164-199, folder 7, Locke Papers.

11. Karla F. C. Holloway portrays Hurston as a writer who actively resisted the ideas and influence of Boas, her "paternal white overseer." *The Character of the Word: The Texts of Zora Neale Hurston* (Westport, Conn.: Greenwood Press, 1987), 2, 116. George Hutchinson, on the other hand, insists that Hurston's view

of Boas was "unambiguously positive—a bright student's view of an admired teacher." *HR*, 70, 463–64 n. 36. Bemoaning the "displacement" of class issues and urban migration from Hurston's conception of Negro folk culture, Hazel Carby compares Hurston unfavorably to Richard Wright, who displays what Carby deems a more "modernist" understanding of the constructedness of discourses. Wright is not a folk writer, but as he traffics in a politically efficacious species of indeterminacy, his "modern" narratives provide a measure for the failings of Hurston's folklore fiction. By Carby's reading, Wright's "modernism" managed "to explode the discursive category of the Negro as . . . the product of a society structured in dominance through concepts of race," whereas the more conservative Hurston violated the spirit of indeterminacy that was native to culture, using the folk "to reclaim an aesthetically purified concept of blackness." Hazel Carby, "The Politics of Fiction, Anthropology and the Folk: Zora Neale Hurston," in *New Essays on* Their Eyes Were Watching God, ed. Michael Awkward (Cambridge: Cambridge University Press, 1990), 79. In resisting the assumption that modernism turns on the explosion of such deterministic categories as "the Negro," Walter Michaels differs from Carby (and indeed from the majority of Hurston's recent readers). For Michaels, it is Hurston's "commitment to the politics of Negro identity that makes her the real modernist." *OA*, 168 n. 163.

12. See Michael Awkward, *Inspiriting Influences: Tradition, Revision, and Afro-American Women's Novels* (New York: Columbia University Press, 1989), 56. See also Henry Louis Gates, Jr., afterword to Zora Neale Hurston, *Jonah's Gourd Vine* (1934; reprint, New York: Harper & Row, 1990), 214–15.

13. Hale, "BA," 446–47.

14. See also Jacques Derrida, *Dissemination* (1972), trans. Barbara Johnson (London: Athlone Press, 1982), 93.

15. See Gayatri Chakravorty Spivak, *In Other Worlds: Essays in Cultural Politics* (New York: Methuen, 1987), 209.

16. The later conservative political affiliations that have so dogged Hurston's reputation, including her support of Robert Taft's Republican presidential candidacy in 1951, were not rooted in a desire to thwart social change. They stemmed rather from her disillusionment with the empty self-referentiality of social programs that were rooted in the "easy generalization[s]" of class- or race-based alliances. In the spirit of Stirnerian anarchists like the British feminist Dora Marsden (whom Hurston appears not to have known), Hurston linked her resistance to such generalizations to her "individualism," which she defined negatively as her lack of a "herd instinct." See Hurston, *DT,* 782, 794.

17. Hurston's work as a folklorist led her to conceive of "Negro expression" as an inventive set of practices that were rooted in "drama." During the late 1920s, as she gathered folk songs and stories in the rural South, she used a pragmatist lexicon to speak of "Negro folk-lore" as a vibrant modern phenomenon. To Langston Hughes, she described its body of songs, stories, and folk-rhymes as

not a static legacy but a font of "gorgeous possibilities," which was to be valued not because it was ancestrally bound but because it was "*still* in the making." Hurston to Hughes, Eatonville, Fla., 8 March 1928, box 76, Hughes Collection. See also Hurston to Hughes, Maitland, Fla., 12 April 1928, box 76, Hughes Collection. The fluid interchange between folk materials and the written productions of Harlem Renaissance artists may have contributed to Hurston's conception of the improvisatory nature of African American speech and speaking practices. As Hurston traveled among workers in sawmills and phosphate mines and turpentine camps, for example, she used Hughes's second book of poetry, *Fine Clothes to the Jew* (1927), as an ice-breaker among subjects who were suspicious of her as a Barnard-trained outsider. According to Hurston, these workers would improvise on-the-spot variations to Hughes's verses, which had themselves been based on blues lyrics that the urban poet had adapted from W. C. Handy and from singers in Harlem cabarets. Hurston to Hughes, Magazine, Ala., 10 July 1928, box 76, Hughes Collection. The verses of some of the work songs that Hurston later recorded bear a strong resemblance to certain stanzas in Hughes's 1927 blues poems. The open question as to whether or not these verses were in fact "indigenous" to her rural southern subjects was exactly Hurston's point when she wrote that folklore was "*still* in the making." In the act of recording it, she was helping to make it.

18. Alain Locke, "Jingo, Counter-Jingo, and Us," 10. See also Richard Wright, "Between Laughter and Tears," *New Masses* 25 (5 October 1937): 22–25.

19. Hurston's use of the modern narrative as a theater for the dynamic enactment of identity can, with some justification, be described as "hieroglyphic." Hurston herself used this word to describe the dynamic and visually immediate qualities of spoken forms of rural southern "Negro expression." As a cultural anthropologist, she had worked throughout the late 1920s and the early 1930s to discern the "laws" that governed black vernacular practices; and by the time she wrote *Their Eyes Were Watching God* in 1936, she had found that she could express some of these laws through modern narrative practices. In "Characteristics of Negro Expression," a 1934 essay based on her five-year study of rural southern folklore, Hurston suggested that African American speech and speaking practices were bound by a universal love of "drama." Rooted in the local performative venues through which identity was "acted out daily" "by strolling players," this love of drama had crept into the very semantic material of the Negro's folkish locutions. In her essay Hurston suggested that black vernacular speech was characterized by a desire not just to statically embody abstract concepts but to actively dramatize them. Because dramatic "action is prior to speech," Hurston reasoned, the Negro had found it "easier to illustrate" ideas through word pictures "than to explain" them through words. (This desire to illustrate dramatic action culminated in the sort of "primitive" compound words that flavored the dialect of folk characters like Lige, Sam, and Walter; it

also played a role in Hurston's distinctive use of free indirect discourse.) It was in "Characteristics" that Hurston placed a metaphorical "hieroglyph" at the root of what was essentially an oral medium. She claimed there that "the white man thinks in a written language and the Negro thinks in hieroglyphs." Thinking visually, in "hieroglyphs," the Negro trafficked in "double words"—formulations like "chop-axe," "suck-bottle," and "kill-dead"—that were allied to the dynamic processes of "barter." By contrast, abstract white "cheque words" masked the vitality of these processes. "NE," 24, 25. See also Hurston to Hughes, Magazine, Ala., 10 July 1928, box 76, Hughes Collection.

20. John Dewey, "Events and Meanings," in *Character and Events,* ed. Joseph Ratner (New York: Henry Holt, 1929), 125–29. See also John Patrick Diggins, *The Promise of Pragmatism: Modernism and the Crisis of Knowledge and Authority* (Chicago: University of Chicago Press, 1994), 4. Richard Poirier suggests that James too would have disliked the "Draconian" deployment of antilinear narrative in *Ulysses.* See his *Poetry and Pragmatism,* 43.

21. Josiah Royce, *Race Questions, Provincialism, and Other American Problems* (New York: Macmillan, 1908), 29–30.

22. Boas's article entitled "Race Problems in America" was published in the journal *Science* in 1909, one year after the publication of Royce's book. Boas assimilated Royce's work through contacts like John Dewey, who came to Columbia in 1904 and who began to influence Boas's work by 1910. Boas and Dewey cotaught a seminar at Columbia in 1914–15. (For a discussion of Boas's relation to pragmatist philosophers, see Hutchinson, *HR,* 66, 88, 468 n. 35.) In the bibliography that he appended to his manuscript notes for his book *The Negro,* Du Bois listed Royce's "RACE QUESTIONS" as one of his own sources for the study of the "Negro race" in America. Du Bois, typescript for *The Negro,* box 2, folder 52, Du Bois Collection, James Weldon Johnson Memorial Collection, Beinecke Rare Book and Manuscript Library, Yale University. Alain Locke, too, was a reader of Royce. As a student at Harvard during the first decade of the twentieth century, Locke immersed himself in the writings of pragmatist philosophers, William James particularly. Locke had planned to do his graduate work under Royce at Harvard, but Royce died while Locke was overseas, at Oxford, about to return to Harvard to begin work on his Ph.D. As an undergraduate, Locke had studied under Horace Kallen, who was at that time working as an assistant to James and Santayana. See Hutchinson, *HR,* 39–42, 81–82, 84–86.

23. Du Bois did not entirely dismiss William James's advocacy of the indeterminate and contingent nature of "the pluralistic universe." In 1944, in fact, Du Bois recalled that James had prompted him at an early date to "measure the element of Chance in human conduct." W. E. B. Du Bois, "My Evolving Program for Negro Freedom," in *What the Negro Wants,* ed. Rayford Logan (Chapel Hill: University of North Carolina Press, 1944), 58, quoted in Posnock, *CC,* 35. Ross

Posnock suggests that there may even be a vague political basis for Du Bois's and James's shared enjoyment of chance and contingency. Noting that Du Bois and James both celebrated the idea of "anarchy" in their writings, he suggests that both intellectuals cultivated "anarchic, aesthetic impulses." *CC,* 34–35, 149. In James's case, if not in Du Bois's, however, these "impulses" ran deeper than Posnock allows: they can be traced to an extensive network of nineteenth- and twentieth-century anarchist traditions that shaped the pragmatist's pluralistic vision of a "mosaic philosophy." Du Bois, for his part, was no more committed to anarchism than he was to James's pragmatism. Despite his Jamesian training, and despite his occasional references to "the spirit" of "anarchy," Du Bois was finally a socially and historically bound thinker, one who avoided abstract appeals to "process" and mystifying claims to "immediacy."

24. In *Their Eyes Were Watching God,* Janie struggles to participate in rural southern speaking traditions, but she is also betrayed by the "cocked and loaded" "tongues" of the womenfolk in Eatonville and the menfolk in the Florida " 'Glades." Hurston's strongest condemnation of "folk expression" can be found in an unpublished, undated essay fragment entitled "Are We Citizens." Here she associates folk expression not with vitality but with the sort of regressive piety that is embodied by Janie's grandmother in the novel: "While certain cosmic things have been going on in the nation and the world, we have been . . . shut in a banquet hall gorging ourselves on a feast of phrases. . . . These folk expressions . . . have come down to us from the Reconstruction. But a lot of years have gone down the back slope of time since Reconstruction. Is it not possible for us to lose our way in a tangle of Reconstruction concepts and phrases . . . ?" Hurston, "Are We Citizens."

25. Hurston, "Their Eyes Were Watching God," holograph manuscript, box 2, folder 27, Hurston Collection. See also Hurston, *EWG,* 200.

26. James quoted in Zamir, *DV,* 36.

27. See also Zamir, *DV,* 14, 85.

28. See Ralph Waldo Emerson, "Nature," in *Ralph Waldo Emerson: Essays and Poems,* ed. Joel Porte, Harold Bloom, and Paul Kane (1983; reprint, New York: Library of America, 1996), 7, 11. See also Zamir, *DV,* 15.

29. In Hurston's first novel, *Jonah's Gourd Vine* (1934), a rural southern black speaker criticizes Du Bois as an effete intellectual: "DuBois? Who is dat? . . . Whut did dis DuBois ever do? He writes up books and papers, huhn? . . . Writing! Man Ah thought you wuz talkin' 'bout uh man whut had done sumpin. Ah thought maybe he wuz de man dat could make side-meat taste lak ham." Hurston, *Jonah's Gourd Vine,* in Cheryl A. Wall, ed., *Zora Neale Hurston: Novels and Stories* (New York: Library of America, 1995), 125–26.

30. Much of Hughes's early poetry had revolved around Du Bois's conception of two Negro souls. "The Negro" who "speaks" in Hughes's well-known poem "The Negro Speaks of Rivers," for example, is at once a collective racial

subject and a self-alienated lyric speaker—an "I"—who views himself at a remove through the measuring eyes of white readers. Thematic and formalist renderings of double-consciousness can be found in the writings of a range of modern African American artists. James Weldon Johnson, the formidable "Lord Jim" to Hurston, for example, had drawn freely from *The Souls of Black Folk* in formulating his notion of the "dual personality" in *The Autobiography of an Ex-Colored Man* (1912). Hurston's use of Du Bois's notion is more complicated than Hughes's or Johnson's in part because so many of her novels and stories were set in segregated communities like the "pure Negro" Florida township in which she herself was raised. *DT,* 561. Hurston acknowledged that Eatonville was a world apart from post-Reconstruction "Georgia, Alabama and West Florida." But still the "transmitted memory" of Jim Crow had "crawl[ed]" into "the skin[s] of the young people" who grew up there. Hurston, "Dust Tracks on a Road," holograph manuscript, box 1, folder 9, Hurston Collection. As one whose own skin had absorbed an awareness of the historical dimensions of color in America, Hurston's conception of African American expression, and her sense of how such expression might be adapted to a modern narrative, was indebted to a version of the Du Boisian notion of "the color-line." Hurston's version, however, was more heavily conditioned than Hughes's or Johnson's.

31. In pitting the visual and dynamic immediacy of "primitive" word pictures against the abstract remove of "more civilized" "cheque words," Hurston drifts into an uneasy alignment with a range of canonical European American writers. Her appeals to the directness of the American Negro "hieroglyph" can themselves be traced back to Emerson, who had celebrated "Nature" as the American poet's "hieroglyphic"; and they can be coupled with the contemporaneous writings of Ezra Pound, whose ideogrammic method of poetic composition turned on a belief that pure money and pure language might be linked as curative systems of reference. Emerson, *Complete Works,* 8:65. Pound's work was not altogether unknown to Hurston. His essay "A Note on Leo Frobenius," for example, had appeared in Nancy Cunard's *Negro,* the 1934 anthology in which Hurston's "Characteristics" appeared. In this essay the poet had brazenly chastised Harlem's "Afro-American intelligentzia" [*sic*] for their indifference to the German anthropologist's studies of African drum languages. Drum languages were important to Pound not only as an aesthetic complement to the Chinese ideograms that provided a natural gold standard for his relational method of composition, but also because they appeared to be culturally and economically allied to classical Chinese writings. As living instances of a language untainted by the abstractions of a usurious *Hochkulturen,* Pound believed, they should have telegraphed to Harlem's intellectuals their "true charter of nobility." See Pound, "A Note on Leo Frobenius," in Nancy Cunard, *Negro: An Anthology* (1934; abridged by Hugh Ford, 1970; reprint, New York: Continuum, 1996), 393. See also Pound, *MA,* 149.

In "Characteristics of Negro Expression," Hurston may or may not have had the author of *The ABC of Economics* (1933) in mind when she extended her metaphor of Negro word pictures into the modern Poundian realm of language and money. Here, she placed her analogy in the didactic rhetorical frame of the radical economists that Pound had first absorbed during the teens and then flatly imitated in his writings of the thirties. "Let us make a parallel," Hurston began, in the voice of the "money scientists" who lent a mechanistic thrust to Pound's evolving aesthetic program. "Language is like money. In primitive communities actual goods . . . are bartered for what one wants. This finally evolves into coin, the coin being not real wealth but a symbol of wealth. Still later even coin is abandoned for legal tender, and still later for cheques." "NE," 24. Hurston's metaphorical association of "primitive" languages with direct barter transactions took a distinctly Poundian turn when she extended her language-money metaphor into a condemnation of overcivilized literary stylists. Fashioning an analogy that the underconsumptionist poet had explored in his own writings of the 1930s and eventually set forth explicitly in his *Guide to Kulchur* (1938), Hurston described John Milton's elevated diction in *Paradise Lost*, which shunned concretely local Germanic cognates in favor of Greek and Latinate abstractions, as a "cheque word" language, one that was associated with a collapse of "natural" monetary practices. "NE," 24. However Pound factors or fares in these opening passages of her essay, Hurston's sly *ars poetica* points to one of the central distinctions between her understanding of the significance of language to identity and the understanding held by many of her European American modernist peers. Despite her characteristic appeals to the modern interval between "civilized" cheque words and purer barter forms, Hurston differed from European American champions of "primitive" languages. Unlike Pound, and unlike T. S. Eliot (who had summoned not the visual but the onomatopoetic immediacy of Sanskritic thunder-words in *The Waste Land* [1922]), Hurston was not primarily concerned to marshal a set of "true" cultural productions against a set of more derivative, or tainted, ones. Mediating "Negro expression" through the ephemeral measure of local performance, Hurston muffled the claims of modernists who appealed to "primitive" directness in order to stage their own capacity to decipher timeless truths.

32. Locke's interest in the social and even the racial consequences of relativity theory can be traced to his acquaintance with an African American philosopher named Albert Dunham. Dunham, who was then completing his doctorate at the University of Chicago, had begun teaching at Howard University in 1930. (He was known to many as the husband of Katherine Dunham, the African American dancer and choreographer who supported Hurston's theatrical stagings of folk materials in Chicago in 1934 and who collected folk dances in Jamaica and Haiti in 1936, only months before Hurston began her own anthropological studies in those countries. *DT,* 808.) Although Dunham's dissertation drew extensively from pragmatists, including James, Royce, Dewey, Santayana, and

Charles Peirce, it was most particularly indebted to the writings of Alfred North Whitehead. In notes written around 1930, Locke associated Dunham's writings with Einstein's theory of relativity; he described his new colleague's philosophy generally as "a constructive effort in the metaphysics of relativity." Alain Locke, notes, box 164-142, folder 10, Locke Papers. See also Albert Millard Dunham, "The Concept of Tension in Philosophy," Ph.D. diss., University of Chicago, 1933.

33. See also Williams and McAlmon, eds., *Contact* 2 (January 1921): n.p.

34. Alain Locke, "Race Contacts and Inter-Racial Relations." This typescript is undated, but Locke's remark that America was at that time "spending itself" in an "orgy" of "reactionary" racialist treatises, books like "Lothrop Stoddard's 'The Rising Tide of Color'" (1920), suggests that it was written in the 1920s.

35. In a telegraph sent to "the dean of Negro writers and scholars" in 1951, Hughes testified that "Dark Water [*sic*]" had "greatly influenced" him in his youth. Hughes to Du Bois, box 52, Hughes Collection.

36. W. E. B. Du Bois, typescript carbon of "Darkwater," ca. 1918, box 1, folder 22, W. E. B. Du Bois Collection.

37. Ibid.

38. See Gayatri Chakravorty Spivak, "Can the Subaltern Speak?" 271–313. See also Frantz Fanon, *The Wretched of the Earth,* trans. Constance Farrington (New York: Grove Weidenfeld, 1968), 163.

39. The characterization of Du Bois as an "old school" "thinker" was Hurston's. Though she eventually came to criticize Du Bois for his insensitivity to the needs of the rural "bottom black," she had also praised the integrity of his urban reforms against the self-promoting excesses of newer black nationalist leaders like Marcus Garvey. "Marcus Garvey," Hurston wrote, "was much in advance of the old school of thinkers. There have been some whisperings concerning W. E. B. Du Bois on account of his efforts to lower the violent mortality rate among his people, and advance their interests generally, but he never learned how to keep the people's money, and so missed true greatness." Hurston, "The Emperor Effaces Himself," n.d., typescript, box 1, folder 15, Hurston Collection.

40. In a 1931 letter to Charlotte Mason, Hurston complained that "our so-called leaders are a degenerate and self-seeking lot. The poor Negro, the real one in the furrows and cane-brakes are the least of his thoughts. A few paltry dollars and some white person's tea table is his goal. Alain is different but all the others are awful. He is not popular with them either and I can see why. You must hang with the gang or be shot in the back." Hurston to Mason, New York, 10 October 1931, box 164-199, folder 7, Locke Papers.

41. In attempting to enlist Locke's aid in a new arts journal, *Fire!* Hurston referred to Du Bois's NAACP organ, *Crisis,* and Charles S. Johnson's *Opportunity,* which was the literary journal of the Urban League. "Don't you think too that it is not good that there should be only two outlets for Negro fire? Your work

in Philosophy is less confining than either of the others, why can't our triangle—Locke—Hughes—Hurston do something with you at the apex?" Hurston to Locke, New York, 11 October 1927, box 164-38, folder 28, Locke Papers.

42. In June of 1928, Locke wrote to Hurston: "I read your *How It Feels To Be Colored Me* with great pride and interest until I realized that maybe you had opened up too soon. I had that feeling because I had myself several times made the same mistake. The only hope is in the absolute blindness of the Caucasian mind. To the things that are really revolutionary in Negro thought and feeling they are blind." Locke to Hurston, 2 June 1928, box 164-38, folder 28, Locke Papers. In her answer to Locke's letter, Hurston recalled having recently proclaimed that "white people could not be trusted to collect the lore of others." She was referring to a remark that she had let slip to Charlotte Mason. Mason, who was white, had been momentarily offended. Hurston to Locke, Magazine, Ala., 14 June 1928, box 164-38, folder 28, Locke Papers.

43. In the Alain Locke Papers at Howard University's Moorland-Spingarn Research Center, a series of letters exchanged between Charlotte Mason, Alain Locke, and Zora Neale Hurston suggest that the three went to great lengths to prevent the white ethnographer Paul Radin from interviewing Cudjo Lewis, an elderly Alabama farmer who was believed to be the last African-born slave living in North America. Lewis was well known in African American intellectual and artistic circles. Hurston had already published a largely plagiarized essay about him in Carter Woodson's *Journal of Negro History*, and Lewis's African stories had been recorded by the African American folklorist Arthur Huff Fauset and printed in Locke's 1925 anthology, *The New Negro*. Robert Hemenway, *Zora Neale Hurston: A Literary Biography* (Urbana: University of Illinois Press, 1977), 96–101. See also Hill, *SR,* 61–72. Mason, Locke, and Hurston were alarmed when Lewis began to draw the attention of Radin, a white cultural anthropologist who was affiliated with Boas's circle. Most of the surviving correspondence regarding Radin and Cudjo Lewis is in the form of letters exchanged between Mason and Locke in 1928; but Hurston herself had been involved in this racist and apparently anti-Semitic effort to block Radin's access to Lewis. Considered together with Hurston's caginess toward Boas regarding her anthropological fieldwork, this correspondence suggests that Hurston's relationships with the white anthropologists whom she is said to have unequivocally "admired" may have been complicated by racial as well as professional and financial considerations. And if Hurston did harbor an antagonism toward Boas and Radin, it may also have been conditioned by the same sort of anti-Semitic sentiments expressed by Mason and Locke in their 1928 letters. In 1931, for example, Hurston complained to Mason that African American artists and intellectuals were stealing her ideas. According to Hurston, they had taken "their ethics from the tin-pan alley Jew, who in turn despises them not only for being petty crooks, but lacking in originality in even that." See boxes 164-38, 164-68, 164-199, Locke Papers.

44. The typescript of "Barracoon" can be found in box 164-186, folder 2, Locke Papers.

45. "Pink-toes" was sometimes used as an epithet for Communists (whose methods Hurston despised); but in *Dust Tracks* it clearly stands for "the Anglo-Saxon" who thinks "that everybody else owes him something just for being blonde." *DT,* 793.

46. Alain Locke, "The New Negro," in *The New Negro,* ed. Alain Locke (1925; New York: Atheneum, 1992), 7.

47. Hurston, in fact, credited Johnson with "gathering and publishing" the initial body of material that would later spark "the so-called Negro Renaissance." "Later on," Hurston wrote, "the best of this material was collected in a book called *The New Negro* and edited by Dr. Alain Locke." In a reckoning that came after Hurston's falling out with Locke, that anthologist, who is often credited as a founder of the Harlem Renaissance, is portrayed as a late-comer, a follower of Johnson. *DT,* 682.

48. In calling for the division of the foundational "unit" that was shouldered by "Negroes in America," Johnson may have laid a groundwork for the later work of progressive white cultural anthropologists like Melville Herskovits. A protégé of Franz Boas, Herskovits echoed Johnson's suggestion that "Negroes in America" should be thought of not as one body, but "many." See Herskovits, *AAN,* 2.

49. See Hutchinson, *HR,* 446–47; and Posnock, *CC,* 57, 188. See also North, *Dialect of Modernism;* Aldon Nielsen, *Reading Race: White American Poets and the Racial Discourse in the Twentieth Century* (Athens: University of Georgia Press, 1988).

50. Aldon Neilsen reads T. S. Eliot's deployment of "an African American allusion" in *The Waste Land*—"O O O O that Shakespeherian Rag"—as a similar instance of "resignifying minstrelsy in which whites dress up their language in blackface to represent their own representation of blackness to themselves." See his *Writing between the Lines: Race and Intertextuality* (Athens: University of Georgia Press, 1994), 124–25, 7. Representations of this sort by European American writers helped white pluralists to set the limits within which to construct varieties of Americanness that were neither black nor European. See Michaels, *OA,* 145 n. 22.

51. "Shoot it Jimmy!" is from the 1923 prose-poetry compilation *Spring and All,* in which Williams began to experiment with heavily enjambed idiom poems. Enjambment was at this time becoming central to Williams's conception of an improvisational form of measure, one that was somehow indigenously "American."

52. In *Dust Tracks on a Road,* Hurston wrote of the inadequacy of such categories as "race" and "class." She thus sounded nominalistic anarchist premises similar to those that had been expressed a generation earlier by the British

anarcho-feminist Dora Marsden. In the pages of the *New Freewoman* (1913) and the *Egoist* (1914), "Individualist" journals read by modernists including Ezra Pound and James Joyce, Marsden had attacked the emptiness of seductive categories like "Woman" and "Race." Here Marsden followed Stirner in preferring *privatim* assessments of identity to the liberal's *generatim* assessments. Von Hallberg, "LI," 66. Hurston displayed a similar nominalistic suspicion of classification: "I found that I had no need of either class or race prejudice. . . . The solace of easy generalization was taken from me, but I received the richer gift of individualism." *DT,* 782.

53. In a study based on data gathered in 1923–26, to which Hurston contributed by measuring the skulls of African Americans in Harlem, Melville Herskovits outlined two factors that militated against the use of the "Negro" as a biologistic category. The first was the historical intermixture of Americans of African descent with Native Americans and European Americans. The second was drawn from the example of the diverse "races of Europe":

> The use of the word "Negro" to describe him is without justification from a biological point of view. It is this very fact of mixture, particularly the amount of mixture represented in the American Negro population and various portions of it, that has constituted a stumbling-block in the study of this group from other than sociological and economic points of view. And to all this there is added another difficulty, not generally recognized, that not only is there considerable variation in the traits of Europeans who compose the ancestry on the White side, but that there are as great differences between the various types of African Negroes who were brought to this country, and who became the forefathers of the present colored population. (Herskovits, *AAN,* 2)

Herskovits's claim would be echoed by W. E. B. Du Bois in 1940: "It is easy to see that a scientific definition of race is impossible." Du Bois, *Dusk of Dawn: An Essay toward an Autobiography of a Race Concept* (1940; reprint, New York: Harcourt, Brace & Co., 1975), 137; quoted in Anthony Appiah, "The Uncompleted Argument: Du Bois and the Illusion of Race," in *"Race," Writing, and Difference,* ed. Henry Louis Gates, Jr. (Chicago: University of Chicago Press, 1986), 32.

54. Wright, "Between Laughter and Tears," 25. Sterling Brown, "Luck Is a Fortune," *Nation* 166 (16 October 1937): 409–10.

55. See Mary Helen Washington, foreword to *Their Eyes Were Watching God* (New York: Harper & Row, 1990), xi–xii.

56. Like a number of Hurston's critics, Gates makes a hedging and fleeting claim that *Their Eyes* "makes impressive use" of "the metaphor of double-consciousness as the prerequisite to becoming a speaking subject." "ST," 192. In dialogue with Barbara Johnson, he notes that Janie's coming into being turns on

her cultivation of an "inside" self in the face of limits imposed on her public expression. Janie was raised in the house of the white family that employed her grandmother, and she spent her early years unaware that her skin marked her as different from the other children in the house. At the age of six, she looked at a photograph of the family and found a "dark little girl" that she could not initially recognize as herself. As an orphan named "Alphabet"—"so many people had done named me different names"—raised in a white family, Janie's upbringing seems tailored to engender what Du Bois identified as the Negro's "peculiar sensation" of "double-consciousness, this sense of always looking at oneself through the eyes of others, of measuring one's soul by the tape of a world that looks on in amused contempt and pity." Hurston, *EWG*, 181–82; Du Bois, *SBF*, 364. Janie's encounters with the very measuring tape that Langston Hughes had come to bemoan in "The Negro Artist and the Racial Mountain" are ubiquitous in the novel, and it is because of the holds of white standards on her grandmother and on the first two men that she marries that she comes to cultivate an inner self that she holds apart from the world. Living in largely segregated communities, however, Janie's contact with the white world is increasingly mediated by black men like the skulking Logan Killicks and the self-trumpeting Mayor Starks. For this reason her experience of "two souls, two thoughts, two unreconciled strivings" in the novel comes to be increasingly conditioned by gender. And if Alphabet's childhood assumption of "different names" was associated at first with her race, this same destabilization of identity becomes a gendered phenomenon as Janie's surnames begin to leap-frog from "Crawford" to "Killicks" to "Starks" to "Woods." By invoking gender as a divide that conditions Du Bois's sensation of "double-consciousness," Hurston frees the historical mechanism from its overly literal dependence on those "authenticating" categories of identity with which it is conventionally associated. She thereby enables it to retain its conceptual and political force and function while freeing it from the dependence on the overly static identitarian tendencies that she wishes to examine. For a discussion of gender in *Their Eyes Were Watching God,* see Barbara Johnson, "Metaphor, Metonymy, and Voice in *Their Eyes Were Watching God,*" in *Black Literature and Literary Theory,* ed. Henry Louis Gates, Jr. (Methuen: New York, 1984), 205–19. See also Cynthia Bond, "Language, Speech, and Difference in *Their Eyes Were Watching God,*" in *Zora Neale Hurston: Critical Perspectives Past and Present,* ed. Henry Louis Gates, Jr., and K. A. Appiah (New York: Amistad Press, 1993), 204–17.

57. Of her childhood in the all-black town of Eatonville, Hurston wrote: "Nothing had ever happened in our vicinity to create [racial] tension. But people had memories and told tales of what happened back there in Georgia, and Alabama and West Florida that made the skin of the young people crawl with transmitted memory." Zora Neale Hurston, holograph manuscript of "Dust Tracks on a Road," box 1, folder 9, Hurston Collection. In her introduction to

Mules and Men, Hurston suggested that whereas "the Indian resists [the] curiosity [of 'the white person'] by a stony silence," "the Negro offers a feather-bed resistance. That is, we let the probe in, but it never comes out. It gets smothered under a lot of laughter and pleasantries." Hurston, *Mules and Men* (1935), in *Zora Neale Hurston: Folklore, Memoirs, and Other Writings,* ed. Cheryl A. Wall (New York: Library of America, 1995), 10.

58. In Gates's view, Hurston's signal achievement lay in her recognition that because it was structurally linked to "traditional modes of Afro-American rhetorical play," the modern technique of "free indirect discourse" could serve to represent "Janie's . . . quest to become a speaking black subject." "ST," 175, 165.

59. While Hurston was completing the manuscript of *Dust Tracks,* she published a profile of an African American Florida cattleman in the *Saturday Evening Post.* The magazine's editors inserted the word "Negro" under her by-line for the essay. Cheryl A. Wall, "Chronology," in Wall, *Hurston Novels and Stories,* 1025–26.

60. Hurston, "Dust Tracks on a Road," holograph manuscript, box 1, folder 9, Hurston Collection.

61. Zora Neale Hurston, "How It Feels to Be Colored Me" (1928), in *Hurston Folklore, Memoirs, and Other Writings,* 828.

62. In a chapter that her publishers removed from *Dust Tracks on a Road,* Hurston identified herself as a "poor" "Negro" who was sympathetic to the radical aims of the "Communist Party." But she criticized Communism as an ideologically based form of radicalism that was weak on two fronts. It appealed to the "herd instinct" and so stifled individual action; and it ultimately fostered a reinscription of the very class lines that it sought to abolish. "The people who founded this country, and the immigrants who came later, came here to get away from class distinctions," Hurston wrote. "I am all for the idea of free vertical movement, nothing horizontal." *DT,* 793–94.

ACKNOWLEDGMENTS

First thanks go to Robert von Hallberg, always my teacher. Bill Brown and Elizabeth Helsinger, also at the University of Chicago, pushed me to deepen this project in its early stages. Colleagues here at Georgetown—Leona Fisher, Pam Fox, George O'Brien, and Michael Ragussis—were generous and supportive as I labored to finish. My Georgetown students have challenged me in ways that have bettered this book; and from among them I gained two invaluable research assistants, Jason Decker and Matt Hofer. Friends near and far have shared ideas and encouragement: I'm especially grateful to Jessica Burstein, Bruce Clarke, Michael Molasky, Mark Morrisson, Paul Peppis, Kenneth Reinhard, and Eric Shutt. For helping me to balance this book's interdisciplinary commitments, I thank my editor, Robert Brugger, and my two readers, Brian Lloyd and Dorothy Ross. The Mellon Foundation and Georgetown University provided fellowships that made it easier for me to research and write. In my research, I was aided by librarians at the British Museum, and at the Rosenbach Museum in Philadelphia, and at special collections at Harvard University, at Howard University, at Johns Hopkins, at Princeton, at the University of Chicago, and at Yale. For food and table, and for all the warmth that surrounds it, I thank my in-laws, Saul and Gerda Bernstein, and especially my father, Charles Kadlec. My wife, Carolyn, continues to teach me about writing, and about other, more valuable forms of exchange. My thanks to her are lighter, and therefore weightier, than the words on this page.

INDEX

Aldington, Richard, 12, 55, 102, 280n.33
Anderson, Pearl, 154
Antin, Mary, 128, 156, 287–88n.17, 299–300n.7
Antliff, Allan, 255n.72
Appiah, Anthony, 313n.53
Arnold, Elizabeth, 301n.21
Asquith, Herbert Henry, 99
Attridge, Derek, 273n.11
Avrich, Paul, 242n.8
Awkward, Michael, 304n.12

Bacigalupo, Massimo, 271n.76
Bacon, Francis, 250n.47
Baker, Houston, 186–87, 203, 207
Bateson, William, 170
Bell, Alexander Graham, 173
Benda, Julien, 35
Benét, William Rose, 176
Bergson, Henri, 15, 80, 256n.83, 269nn.66, 67, 297n.63
Berkeley, George, 250n.47
Boas, Franz, 36, 172, 257–58n.92; *Anthropology and Modern Life*, 37, 187–88, 258n.94, 302–3n.8; "Aryans and Non-Aryans," 186, 302n.6; and Darwin, 187, 256–57n.89, 303n.9; and Dewey, 37, 45–46, 49, 187, 256n.88, 303n.9,

306n.22; and Herskovits, 209–10, 312n.48; and Hurston, 48–52, 186–88, 195, 201–2, 204–5, 209–10, 221, 224, 303–4n.11, 311n.43; and W. James, 187, 303n.9; and Locke, 303n.9, 311n.43; "The Measurement of Differences," 49–50, 204–5, 258n.93; *Mind of Primitive Man*, 37, 46, 258n.94; and Moore, 46–48, 256–57n.89; *Race, Language and Culture*, 256–57n.89, 303n.9; "Race Problems in America," 306n.22; and Royce, 192, 306n.22; and Williams, 205–7
Bond, Cynthia, 314n.58
Borach, Georges, 280n.32, 281n.39
Bordo, Michael D., 263n.30
Bornstein, George, 241n.7
Borroff, Marie, 299n.5
Bourne, Randolph, 134, 158, 300n.12
Bradley, F. H., 269n.67
Braque, Georges, 32, 207, 252n.55
Brewster, Henry B., 245–46n.30
Brooks, Van Wyck, 157–58, 268n.59, 300n.11
Brown, Sterling, 211, 313n.54
Bryan, William Jennings, 123, 251n.51, 286n.2
Budgen, Frank, 119, 284nn.54, 55
Buenker, John D., 300n.8

Burbank, Luther, 170, 173, 175–78, 183, 301nn.29, 30; *The Training of the Human Plant*, 176–77, 301n.30
Burke, Kenneth, 139
Bush, Ronald, 241n.7, 261n.14
Butler, Judith, 6, 118, 286n.69; *Gender Trouble*, 6, 118
Byington, Steven, 242n.10, 279n.30
Bynum, William, 283n.47, 285n.62

Cahm, Caroline, 242n.8
Carby, Hazel, 304n.11
Carpenter, Humphrey, 262n.21, 264n.42
Carter, Huntly, 280n.33
Cashman, Sean Dennis, 286n.5
Casillo, Robert, 85, 88, 262n.20, 271n.76
Cheng, Vincent, 271n.2, 284n.52, 286n.70
Cheyette, Bryan, 263n.26
Clark, Ronald, 125, 146, 148
Clarke, Bruce, 239n.5, 241n.7, 243n.16, 260nn.12, 13, 261n.14, 280n.33, 284nn.57, 60, 288n.22
Cofer, Leland E., 152, 156–57, 299n.7
Cook, A.J., 259n.8
Cooley, Charles Horton, 256n.86
Coolidge, Calvin, 128, 135, 157, 171–72
Coon, Deborah, 24, 242n.8, 245n.29, 246n.30, 247n.36, 248n.36, 250nn.44, 45, 46, 48, 251n.51, 290nn.32, 34
Cory, Daniel, 269n.69, 271n.75
Costello, Bonnie, 179, 300n.15, 301n.34
Cotkin, George, 245n.29
Coughlan, Neil, 246n.31
Coyle, Michael, 265n.45
Crafts, Wilbur F., 124, 287n.6
Cravens, Hamilton, 133, 157, 170, 172, 178, 181, 287n.9, 300n.9, 301nn.24, 27
Creighton, Louise, 283n.47
Croce, Paul Jerome, 252n.53
Crosby, Ernest Howard, 250n.49
Cunard, Nancy, *Negro*, 308n.31
Cushman, Steven, 140–41, 143, 295–96n.55, 296nn.56, 57
Czira, Sydney Gifford, 272n.5

Dana, Charles A., 249n.43
Dangerfield, George, 261n.16
Darwin, Charles, 173, 250n.48; and Boas, 187, 256–57n.89, 303n.9; and Dewey, 42–43, 169–71, 187, 303n.9; and Hurston, 192; and W. James, 26–29, 168–71, 191–93, 195, 251–52n.53, 252n.54, 303n.9; and Lamarck, 171; and Locke, 303n.9; and Moore, 46–47, 161–63, 165–66, 168, 170–71, 175, 180–82, 256–57n.89, 300n.16; *The Origin of Species*, 169, 171, 251n.51; and Stöcker, 106, 283n.48; *Variation of Animals and Plants Under Domestication*, 28, 161–63, 166, 170–71, 176, 180–81, 300n.16, 301n.30
Davenport, Charles, 173, 177–78, 301n.27
Davidson, Thomas, 250n.44
Davie, Donald, 264–65n.44, 300–301n.21
Davison, Neil, 115, 279n.30, 284n.58, 284–85n.60, 286n.68
de Candolle, Alphonse, 179–81, 301nn.35, 37; *Origin of Cultivated Plants*, 180
de Laguna, Grace Andrus, 253n.61, 300n.18, 301n.23
de Laguna, Theodore, 47, 166, 168, 253n.61, 300n.18, 301n.23
de Man, Paul, 159–60, 254n.64
Deane, Seamus, 273n.13
Derrida, Jacques, 188, 242n.9, 281n.34, 304n.14
Dewey, John, 22, 24, 37, 49, 53, 81–82, 126, 133–35, 137, 148, 155, 158, 180, 182–83, 198, 256n.86, 257n.91, 269n.69, 289n.28, 300n.13, 309n.32; "Americanism and Localism," 40, 130, 132, 138–39, 144–46, 149–50, 161, 163, 198, 288n.18; and Boas, 45–46, 303n.9, 306n.22; and Darwin, 42–43, 169–71, 187, 303n.9; "Darwin's Influence upon Philosophy," 169–70, 195; *Democracy and Education*, 166, 296n.59; and Du

Bois, 295n.51; *Essays in Experimental Logic*, 166, 300n.17, 303n.9; *Experience and Nature*, 41–42, 294n.47; *German Philosophy and Politics*, 240n.2; and Hegel, 41, 146–47, 294n.47; *Individualism, Old and New*, 246n.31, 270n.70, 294n.47; and W. James, 41–42, 144–46, 250n.47, 288–89n.24, 289n.25, 293–94n.47, 296nn.59, 60, 302n.5; and Joyce, 191; and Kallen, 42–43, 255n.73, 289n.27, 294n.47; and Moore, 165–66, 168–70; "Our National Dilemma," 299n.69; *Philosophy and Civilization*, 144–45, 289n.25, 296n.60, 302n.5; "Philosophy and Democracy," 41–42, 255n.78; and Pound, 270n.70; "Principle of Nationality," 41–42, 255n.78, 288–89n.24; on Proudhon, 246n.31; *Reconstruction in Philosophy*, 45–46, 246n.31, 255n.76; "Some Connexions of Science and Philosophy," 46; and Swift, 23, 246n.32, 247n.34; "Universal Service as Education," 42, 255n.79; and Williams, 40–45, 130–32, 136, 143–44, 150, 255n.72, 295n.54, 297n.64
Dickstein, Morris, 251n.52
Diggins, John Patrick, 306n.20
Dijkstra, Bram, 125, 287n.12, 301n.21
Donisthorpe, Winthrope, 55, 259n.5
Doolittle, Hilda, 129
Dos Passos, John, *U.S.A.*, 175
Douglas, Anne, 302n.4
Douglas, Major C. H., 56, 60–62, 79–80, 87, 262nn.20, 22; *Economic Democracy*, 61
Dowson, Ernest, 65
Dreyer, Peter, 170, 175–76, 301nn.29, 30
Drysdale, Bessie, 106, 282n.45, 283n.47
Du Bois, W. E. B., 4, 7, 38, 253n.61; *Crisis*, 310n.41; *Darkwater*, 199–200, 207; *Dusk of Dawn*, 313n.53; and Herskovits, 313n.53; and Hughes, 194, 199–200, 307–8n.30; and Hurston, 192, 196–201, 207–8, 220–21, 303n.10,

307n.29, 310n.39; and W. James, 49–50, 192, 194–95, 257nn.90, 91, 295n.51, 306–7n.23; and C. Johnson, 204, 207; and J. W. Johnson, 194, 307–8n.30; and Locke, 199–201; "My Evolving Program for Negro Freedom," 306–7n.23; "The Negro," 306n.22; and Royce, 192, 306n.22; *The Souls of Black Folk*, 188, 192, 194–97, 204, 207, 220–21, 245n.28, 257nn.90, 91, 293n.45, 303n.10, 307–8n.30, 313–14n.56; and Williams, 207, 245n.28, 293n.45, 295n.51
Duchamp, Marcel, 255n.72, 292–93n.44
Dujardin, Edouard, 277n.23
Dunham, Albert: and Einstein, 309–10n.32; and Locke, 309–10n.32; and Whitehead, 309–10n.32
Dunham, Katherine, 309–10n.32
Duster, Troy, 301n.33

Eastman, Max, 9
Eddington, Arthur, 146–48
Einstein, Albert, 122–23, 125–26, 136–37, 297nn.63, 65, 298nn.67, 68; and Dewey, 145–47, 198; *Ideas and Opinions*, 122, 145–46, 149, 299n.69; and Locke, 198, 309–10n.32; and Williams, 145–49, 198, 292n.41, 295n.54
Eiseley, Loren, 171, 301n.25
Eliot, Charles, 175
Eliot, T. S., 4, 38, 83, 126, 130, 253n.61; and Bergson, 80; "Burbank with a Baedeker," 175; and W. James, 52–53, 80–81; "Marianne Moore," 300n.13; and Moore, 154; and Pound, 52–53, 80–81; and Santayana, 80; *The Waste Land*, 29, 127, 129, 287n.15, 309n.31, 312n.50; and Williams, 287n.15
Ellis, Havelock, 278–79n.28
Ellmann, Maud, 263n.26
Ellmann, Richard, 93, 242n.11, 272n.4, 273nn.7, 13, 274nn.14, 15, 276nn.18, 19, 277n.21, 280n.31, 284n.54

Eltzbacher, Paul, 101, 242n.10, 280n.32
Emerson, Ralph Waldo: and Brewster, 245–46n.30; and Hurston, 194, 308–9n.31; and W. James, 22, 35, 166–67, 193–94, 245–46n.30; and Pound, 19, 244n.24
Engels, Friedrich, 13, 281n.34

Fairhall, James, 273n.13, 281n.39
Fanon, Frantz, 310n.38
Faulkner, William, *The Sound and the Fury*, 190
Fauset, Arthur Huff, 311n.43
Fenollosa, Ernest: *The Chinese Written Character as a Medium for Poetry*, 56, 77–79; and W. James, 271n.71; and Pound, 56, 77–81
Ferris, Kathleen, 93, 107, 273n.7, 283n.50
Feuerbach, Ludwig, 13; and Marx, 280–81n.34; and Stirner, 280–81n.34
Finlay, John, 88, 242n.8, 259n.5, 263n.32, 265n.45, 268n.61
Ford, Ford Madox, 65–66, 261n.17, 264n.35
Ford, Henry, 175
Frank, Waldo, 125
Fremantle, Anne, 266n.48
Freud, Sigmund, 253n.56
Frobenius, Leo, 308n.31
Frost, Robert, 38, 83

Galton, Sir Francis, 173
Garner, Les, 276n.19, 279n.30, 281n.37, 283n.46, 285n.61
Garvey, Marcus, 310n.39
Gates, Jr., Henry Louis, 51, 189–90, 215, 302n.2, 304n.12, 313–14n.56, 315n.58; and Hurston, 189–90; *The Signifying Monkey*, 214
Gaudier-Brzeska, Henri, 263n.26
Gesell, Silvio, 20, 56, 62, 82, 87, 137, 294n.49
Gifford, Don, 272n.5, 277n.21
Gilbert, Stuart, 272n.7

Gilman, Sander, 90, 108, 266n.48, 284n.52
Goddard, Henry H., 128
Gogarty, Oliver, 91, 94, 113, 272–73n.7; "Ugly England," 91, 272n.4
Gonne, Maud, 91, 271–72n.3, 272n.5, 283n.51
Gourmont, Rémy de, 35, 61–62
Goux, Jean-Joseph, 267n.54
Grant, Madison, 162, 172–74; *The Passing of the Great Race*, 157
Gray, John, 65
Griffith, Arthur, 280n.30, 283n.51
Gris, Juan, 38
Gunn, J. Alexander, 249n.43

Hale, Dorothy, 188, 190, 304n.13
Hall, Donald, 153, 299n.2
Hall, G. Stanley, 23
Hall, Prescott, 173–74, 301n.28
Haller, Mark H., 125, 129, 133, 157, 173, 177–78, 181, 287n.9, 301n.30
Handy, W. C., 305n.17
Harr, Michel, 118, 282n.43, 285n.66
Hartley, Marsden, 125, 287n.12, 300n.13
Hegel, G. W. F., 77, 146, 255n.75
Heilbroner, Robert, 263n.30
Heisenberg, Werner, 297n.63
Hemenway, Robert, 311n.43
Herr, Cheryl, 271n.3
Herskovits, Melville: *Anthropometry of the American Negro*, 312n.48, 313n.53; and Boas, 312n.48; and Du Bois, 313n.53; and Hurston, 210, 313n.53
Higham, John, 128, 157, 174, 178, 256n.80, 287n.9, 300n.9, 302n.7
Hill, Lynda Marion, 207, 302n.6
Hitler, Adolph, 266n.47
Hoffman, Abbie, 10
Hollander, John, 140–43, 296nn.56, 57
Hollingdale, R. J., 285n.66
Holloway, Karla, 303n.11
Holton, Bob, 261n.16, 278n.25
Holton, Sandra, 277n.25

James, William (*continued*)
167, 192–93; and Proudhon, 24–26, 29, 32–33, 81–83, 134–35, 137, 249n.41, 249–50n.44, 252n.54, 290n.32; and Renouvier, 25, 249n.43; *Some Problems of Philosophy*, 249n.42; and Stirner, 24, 248n.40, 290n.32; "The Stream of Thought," 30–31, 167, 191; and Swift, 23–24, 247n.33, 248n.39, 284n.51; "The Thing and Its Relations," 271n.71; *The Varieties of Religious Experience*, 193; *The Will to Believe*, 168, 170, 172, 191; and Williams, 130, 292n.41, 294–95n.49; "A World of Pure Experience," 22, 33, 80, 290nn.30, 32

Jefferson, Thomas, 20, 22, 270n.69

Johnson, Barbara, 313–14n.56

Johnson, Charles S., 183, 202–4, 312n.48; *Ebony and Topaz*, 203–4, 207; 312n.47; and Hurston, 194, 207, 308n.30; and Locke, 202–3, 312n.47; *Opportunity*, 310n.41

Johnson, Georgia Douglas, 199

Johnson, James Weldon, 194, 308n.30; *The Autobiography of an Ex-Colored Man*, 308n.30; and Du Bois, 194, 308n.30

Jones, Maldwyn Allen, 300nn.10, 13, 301n.28

Joyce, James, 2, 9, 35, 67–68, 123, 127, 132, 150, 155, 214–15, 224–25, 313n.52; and Bergson, 15; and Ibsen, 275–76n.16; and Marsden, 12, 15, 98–99, 103, 120–21, 131, 275–76n.16, 276–77n.20, 277nn.22, 23, 279–80n.30, 281n.37, 285n.61; and Nietzsche, 15, 17, 52, 100, 113–14, 117–18, 120–21, 279n.30, 284–85n.60; and Pound, 67, 92, 101, 103, 277n.20; and Stirner, 15–17, 52, 100–101, 103, 105, 113–17, 121, 275–76n.16, 279n.30, 280n.32; and Weaver, 97–98, 276n.18, 281n.37, 284nn.53, 54; *Dubliners*, 92, 98, 113, 274n.14; *Finnegans Wake*, 276–77n.20; "Ireland at the Bar," 119, 286n.70; "A Portrait of the Artist," 127, 254n.65, 273n.13, 274–75n.15, 284n.60; *A Portrait of the Artist as a Young Man*, 14, 96–98, 215, 223, 273n.13, 274n.15, 275n.16, 277n.21, 281n.37, 286n.3; *Stephen Hero*, 275n.16; *Ulysses*, 1, 4, 7–8, 15–16, 34, 52, 92–99, 103–15, 119–21, 183–84, 190–91, 200, 221, 243n.12, 272n.5, 273nn.8, 9, 274nn.13, 15, 275n.16, 277n.21, 277–78n.23, 283n.51, 284nn.56, 64

Joyce, Stanislaus, 92, 113, 272n.7, 273n.10, 284n.59

Kallen, Horace, 36–37, 239n.2, 254n.68, 256n.82, 290n.31; and Dewey, 42–43, 255n.73, 289n.27, 294n.47; and W. James, 42–43, 134, 256n.83, 289n.24, 290n.30, 294n.47; and Kropotkin, 42; and Locke, 42, 306n.22; and Proudhon, 42, 256n.83

Kant, Immanuel, 248n.36

Kantowicz, Edward R., 300n.8

Kaplan Temma, 253n.58

Kauffmann, Reginald, 280n.33

Kaufmann, Walter, 285n.66

Kearns Kevin, 272n.6

Kenner, Hugh, 65, 142–43, 262n.20, 262–63n.26, 264n.36, 267n.54, 289n.26

Kevles, Daniel, 300n.9

Keynes, John M., 63, 67, 74, 76, 83, 263n.31, 267n.54; *The General Theory of Employment, Interest, and Money*, 63, 262n.21, 263n.31

Keyssar, Alexander, 247n.33

Kitson, Arthur, 251n.51; "The Cause of Financial Panics," 66, 77, 268n.58; and Douglas, 60–62; "The Gold Fetish," 56, 57, 65, 66, 70; and Marsden, 17, 54–55, 58–59, 64–67, 71–74; "Money, Capital, and Interest," 64, 243n.15, 266n.47; and Pound, 17, 55–82, 85,

87–89; and Proudhon, 17, 56–57, 64, 71, 81, 243n.15, 259n.5, 265–66n.45, 266n.47, 267n.58; *A Scientific Solution to the Money Question*, 243n.15, 265n.45; and Tucker, 17; "Usury: The Prime Cause of Want and Unemployment," 73

Kloppenberg, James, 245n.29, 255n.75

Kofman, Sarah, 285n.64

Kraut, Alan, 299n.1

Kropotkin, Peter, 42, 242n.8, 256n.82; *Mutual Aid*, 250n.48

Kühl, Stefan, 302n.3

Kuklick, Bruce, 249n.42

Lamarck, Jean-Baptiste de, 128, 162, 171, 288n.18

Lane, Gary, 301n.29

Larbaud, Valery, 242n.11, 274n.14

Larkin Jim, 259n.8, 271n.2

Lears, T. J. Jackson, 253n.62, 258n.98

Leavell, Linda, 253n.61, 300nn.15, 20

LeBon, Gustav, 35

Leighton, Patricia, 253n.58

Lentricchia, Frank, 38, 83, 239n.5, 244n.24, 245n.29, 248n.36, 251n.50

Leopold, David, 242n.9, 279n.30, 281n.34

Levenson, Michael, 239n.5, 241n.7, 258n.97, 261n.17, 264nn.35, 36, 269n.67

Lewis, Cudjo, 201–2, 311n.43

Lewis, Wyndham, 35

Lidderdale, Jane, 241n.7, 259n.2, 276n.19

Lippmann, Walter, 240n.4

Livingston, James, 245n.29

Lloyd, Brian, 146, 240n.1, 248n.38, 255n.75, 270n.70, 289n.25, 291n.35

Locke, Alain, 4, 38, 134, 224, 253n.61; and Boas, 201–2, 303n.9, 311n.43; and Darwin, 303n.9; and Du Bois, 199–201, 207; and Dunham, 309–10n.32; and Einstein, 198–99, 309–10n.32; and Hurston, 50, 190, 199, 201–2, 207, 301–2n.1, 310n.40, 310–11n.41,

311nn 42, 43, 312n.47; and W. James, 42, 303n.9, 306n.22; "Jingo, Counter-Jingo, and Us," 190, 301–2n.1; and C. Johnson, 202–3, 312n.47; and Kallen, 42, 306n.22; and C. Lewis, 201–2, 311n.43; and Mason, 311n.43; *The New Negro*, 201–3, 207, 311n.43, 312n.47; "Race Contacts and Inter-Racial Relations," 199, 303n.9; and Royce, 303n.9, 306n.22.

Locke, John, 250n.47

Logue, William, 249n.43

Longfellow, Henry Wadsworth, 38

Lowell, Amy, 58

Lowell, James Russell, 38

Loy, Mina, 167, 301n.22

Lutoslawski, Wincenty, 250n.44

Lyons, J. B., 90, 273n.7

MacCabe, Colin, 14, 93, 242–43n.11, 264n.39, 274n.14, 279n.30, 281n.39, 282n.40, 284n.54

Mackay, John, 248n.40, 279n.30

Manganiello, Dominic, 101

Marcus, Jane, 259n.4

Mariani, Paul, 287n.14, 289n.26

Marinetti, F. T., 76, 183, 268–69n.65

Marsden, Dora, 35, 44, 304n.16; "The Art of the Future," 72–73, 267n.51; "Authority: Conscience and the Offenses," 98, 277n.22; "Bond-women," 104–5, 281n.39, 281–82n.40, 284n.60; "The Chastity of Women," 97–101, 114, 119, 275n.16, 276n.17, 279n.29, 281–82n.40, 288n.23; *Egoist*, 12, 54, 58–59, 68, 97–98, 131–32, 276–77n.20, 279n.30, 280n.33, 313n.52; *Freewoman*, 12, 54–55, 71, 73; "The Heart of the Question," 105, 282n.41; and Joyce, 14–17, 97–121, 276n.19, 277nn.22, 23, 281n.37, 285n.61, 313n.52; and Kitson, 17, 54–60, 71–74; "The Lean Kind," 18, 244n.18; *New Freewoman*, 12, 18, 57–60, 68, 72, 80–

Nicholson, Mary, 241n.7, 259n.2, 276n.19

Nielsen, Aldon, 312nn.49, 50

Nietzsche, Friedrich, 6, 296n.59; *Beyond Good and Evil*, 285n.64; *A Genealogy of Morals*, 115–16, 282n.42, 285n.61; and W. James, 248n.40; and Joyce, 15, 17, 52, 94, 98, 100, 107, 113–15, 117–18, 120–21, 279n.30, 284–85n.60; and Marsden, 105–6, 114–15, 118–21, 284–85n.60; and Stirner, 113, 115–16, 282n.42; and Stöcker, 283n.48; *Will to Power*, 285n.66

Nordau, Max, 253n.62

North, Michael, 255n.74, 312n.49

Oppenheim, James: 150; "Poetry-Our First National Art," 288n.18

Orage, A. R., 18, 55, 57–58, 60, 81, 87, 259n.5, 262n.21, 262n.22

Paige, D. D., 260n.11

Pankhurst, Christabel, 98–99, 109; *The Great Scourge and How to End It*, 98–100, 104–5, 117–19, 278n.26, 279n.30, 282n.46, 285n.67; *Unshackled*, 99

Pankhurst, Emmeline, 72, 99

Pankhurst, Sylvia, 278n.25

Parker, Andrew, 264n.43

Pearson, Karl, 173

Peirce, Charles, 23–24, 26, 168, 247nn.34, 35, 289n.25, 310n.32; "The Fixation of Belief," 247n.36; "How to Make Our Ideas Clear," 82, 247n.36

Pellizi, Camillo, 254n.63

Perelman, Bob, 83–84, 263n.26

Perloff, Marjorie, 76, 267n.56, 269n.65

Perry, Ralph Barton, 249n.42, 250n.47

Picasso, Pablo, 31–32, 208, 252n.55, 253n.58

Poe, Edgar Allan, 128, 135, 291n.39

Poirier, Richard, 239n.5, 244n.24, 300n.19, 306n.20

Poliakov, Leon, 266n.48

Posnock, Ross, 38, 239n.5, 245n.29, 302n.4, 306–7n.23, 312n.49

Pound, Ezra, 1, 4, 6, 9, 14, 29–30, 34, 44, 94, 101–2, 132, 137, 150, 166, 208, 223–25, 241n.6, 251n.51, 286n.2; and Dewey, 81–82, 269n.69, 270n.70, 297–98n.66; and Douglas, 56, 60–63, 76, 87, 264n.34; and Emerson, 19, 244n.24; Fenollosa, 56, 77–81; and Gourmont, 35, 61; and Hurston, 208; and Joyce, 67, 98, 100, 103, 276–77n.20; and W. James, 52–53, 80–83; and Kitson, 17–18, 55–64, 73–78, 82, 85, 87–89, 243n.17, 259n.6, 270n.70; and Marsden, 12–13, 17–18, 54–73, 77, 80, 87, 241n.7, 243n.17, 260nn.11, 12, 267n.51, 280n.33; and Moore, 182; and Proudhon, 16–19, 56–57, 67, 81–83, 103, 120, 243n.17, 269n.69, 281n.34, 291n.35, 294n.49; and Ruskin, 19, 70, 79; and Santayana, 81, 85–87, 269–70n.69, 271n.75; and Stirner, 12–13, 15–18, 55–73; and Williams, 18–21, 136; *ABC of Reading*, 67, 76, 297n.65, 309n.31; *The Cantos*, 2, 8, 18–21, 56, 60, 67, 77, 85–87, 92–93, 155, 181, 183, 260n.14, 281n.34, 297–98n.66; *Cathay*, 136; "Cavalcanti," 175; *Gaudier-Brzeska: A Memoir*, 52–53, 80, 269n.66; *Guide to Kulchur*, 4, 57, 81–82, 263n.26, 269n.69, 309n.31; "Hugh Selwyn Mauberley," 262–63n.26; "In a Station of the Metro," 260n.14; "In the Wounds," 18, 57, 81, 243n.17; *Jefferson and/or Mussolini*, 6, 20, 254n.63; "The New Sculpture," 59, 77, 254n.65, 261n.15, 268n.60; "A Note on Leo Frobenius," 308n.31; "Obstructivity," 61–62, 243n.17; "On the Imbecility of the Rich," 68, 84, 264n.42, 271n.74; "Pragmatic Aesthetics," 81; "Review of George Santayana's Letters," 269n.69; "The Serious Artist," 59, 69–70, 72, 88, 243n.16,

Scott, Frederick J. Down, 248n.40, 250n.49, 290n.32
Seidman, Robert, 272n.5, 277n.21
Sherry, Vincent, 35, 93, 109, 254n.66, 261n.15, 267n.56, 269n.67, 273n.11
Sieburth, Richard, 262n.20, 264n.43, 267n.54
Sinclair, Andrew, 124, 286n.5, 287n.6
Skidelsky, Robert, 263n.31, 263–64n.34
Sollors, Werner, 133–34, 254nn.68, 70, 256nn.80, 81, 84, 289n.24, 289–90n.30, 290n.31, 291n.36
Spencer, Herbert, 168
Spivak, Gayatri, 5, 188, 200, 304n.15, 310n.38
Stapleton, Laurence, 182, 301n.36
Stein, Gertrude, 4, 30–31, 38, 44, 83, 155, 252n.55; and Freud, 252–53n.56; "The Gradual Making of the Making of Americans," 44, 253n.59; and W. James, 30–31; *Tender Buttons*, 30–31
Steinman, Lisa, 148–49, 292n.41, 293n.44, 296n.59, 297nn.63, 65, 298nn.67, 68
Steinmetz, Charles, 198, 297n.63
Stepto, Robert, 211
Sternhell, Zeev, 70–71, 244n.22, 254n.63, 264n.42
Stevens, Wallace, 38, 83, 253n.61; on Williams, 136
Stieglitz, Alfred, 300n.15
Stirner, Max: *The Ego and His Own*, 12–13, 101–3, 105, 116, 209, 240n.5, 242n.9, 248n.40, 279n.30, 280n.32, 282n.42; and Feuerbach, 280–81n.34; and Hurston, 209, 304n.16; and Ibsen, 245n.30, 275–76n.16; and W. James, 24, 248n.40, 290n.32; and Joyce, 15–17, 52, 94, 100–101, 103, 105, 107, 113–17, 121, 275–76n.16, 279n.30, 280n.32; and Marsden, 8, 12–14, 17–18, 54–55, 60, 72, 98, 101–5, 117–19, 121, 131–32, 242n.10, 244n.20, 261–62n.18,

266n.49, 281n.36, 283n.49, 296n.59, 313n.52; and Marx, 13, 242n.9, 281n.34; and Nietzsche, 113, 115–16, 282n.42, 284nn.57, 58; and Pound, 12–13, 15–18, 55–73; and Tucker, 11–12, 240–41n.5; and Williams, 13, 18, 131–32, 134, 137, 150–51
Stöcker, Helene, 106, 109, 114, 283n.48; and Darwin, 283n.48; "Interpellation," 106, 283n.48; and Marsden, 106, 282n.45, 283n.49; and Nietzsche, 283n.48
Stocking, George, 157, 172, 173, 178, 288n.18, 302n.7, 302–3n.8
Stoddard, Lothrop, 133, 286n.2, 289n.29, 310n.34; *The Rising Tide of Color*, 133, 310n.34
Strand, Paul, 300n.15
Sunday, Billy, 123
Surette, Leon, 79, 262n.20, 263nn.30, 31, 264n.34, 265n.45, 268n.62
Svevo, Italo, 273n.10, 273–74n.13
Swift, Morrison, 23–24, 246n.32, 250n.44, 284n.51; and Dewey, 23, 246n.32, 247n.34; *Human Submission*, 23, 246n.32, 247n.33, 248n.39, 284n.51; and W. James, 23, 246n.32, 284n.51; and Proudhon, 248n.39; and Stirner, 248n.39
Symons, Arthur, 65, 113

Thirlwall, John C., 295n.53
Thom, Burton, 288n.19
Thomas, Keith, 286n.67
Thomas, Paul, 242n.8, 263n.33
Tickner, Lisa, 261n.18, 278n.24, 282n.44
Tiffany, Daniel, 263n.26
Tomlinson, Charles, 299nn.2, 4
Tucker, Benjamin, 11, 19, 101, 250n.44, 264n.42, 287n.6; *Instead of a Book*, 11, 269–70n.69, 294–95n.49; and Kitson, 259n.5; "Lego et Penso," 244n.18; *Liberty*, 10–11, 241n.5, 259n.5; and Marsden, 12–13, 244n.18, 281n.36; and

139, 287n.10; *Paterson*, 18, 20–21, 181, 297–98n.66; "The Rose is Obsolete," 40; "Shoot it Jimmy!", 206, 312n.51; *Sour Grapes*, 141; *Spring and All*, 13, 16, 38–40, 127–30, 139–44, 158, 206, 241n.6, 298n.67, 312n.51; "St. Francis Einstein of the Daffodils," 147–49, 198, 298n.67, 298–99n.68; *The Wedge*, 2, 36, 40, 44, 138, 239n.1, 294–95n.49

Willis, Patricia, 153, 253n.61, 299nn.3, 5, 300n.16

Winters, Yvor, 301n.22

Witemeyer, Hugh, 260n.11

Woodson, Carter, *Journal of Negro History*, 311n.43

Wright, Richard, 190, 211, 303–4n.11

Yarros, Victor, 250n.48

Yeager, Leland B., 271n.72

Yeats, William Butler, 60, 65–66, 73, 113, 261n.17

Yerkes, Robert, 157, 173

Zamir, Shamoon, 188, 307nn.26, 27, 28

Ziarek, Ewa, 104, 281n.38

Zinn, Howard, 287n.9, 297n.61

Related Books in the Series

*Consciousness in New England: From Puritanism and
Ideas to Psychoanalysis and Semiotic*
James Hoopes

*A Consuming Faith: The Social Gospel and Modern
American Culture*
Susan Curtis

*Sublime Thoughts / Penny Wisdom: Situating Emerson
and Thoreau in the American Market*
Richard F. Teichgraeber III

*Left Out: Pragmatism, Exceptionalism, and the Poverty
of American Marxism, 1890–1922*
Brian Lloyd

*Darwinism and the Linguistic Image: Language, Race,
and Natural Theology in the Nineteenth Century*
Stephen G. Alter